# The Designer's Guide to
# PRESENTING
# NUMBERS,
# FIGURES, AND
# CHARTS

# The Designer's Guide to
# PRESENTING NUMBERS, FIGURES, AND CHARTS

## BY SALLY BIGWOOD AND MELISSA SPORE

**ALLWORTH PRESS**
NEW YORK

Allworth Press books may be purchased in bulk at special discounts for sales promotion, corporate gifts, fund-raising, or educational purposes. Special editions can also be created to specifications. For details, contact the Special Sales Department, Allworth Press, 307 West 36th Street, 11th Floor, New York, NY 10018 or info@skyhorsepublishing.com.

17 16 15 14 13          5 4 3 2 1

Published by Allworth Press, an imprint of Skyhorse Publishing, Inc.
307 West 36th Street, 11th Floor, New York, NY 10018.

Allworth Press® is a registered trademark of Skyhorse Publishing, Inc.®, a Delaware corporation.

www.allworth.com

Cover and interior design by Mary Belibasakis
Page composition/typography by Susan Ramundo

Library of Congress Cataloging-in-Publication Data is available on file.

ISBN: 978-1-62153-266-8

Printed in the United States of America

*This book is dedicated to Sophia and Ulysses.*

# Table of Contents

Acknowledgments                                                                    ix

1. Introduction                                                                     1

2. Handling Numbers                                                                 7

3. Using Tables                                                                    25

4. Introduction to Charts                                                          37

5. Basic Charts                                                                    53

6. Technical and Specialist Charts and Data Visualization        69

7. Table or Chart?                                                                 83

8. Working with Numbers                                                            87

9. Nonnumerical Charts and Information Graphics                     95

10. Numbers and Page Design                                                      107

Glossary                                                                          115

Exercises and Answers                                                             121

Index                                                                             133

# Acknowledgments

MANY PEOPLE HAVE helped in the course of writing this book. It could not have been written without the work of Myra Chapman, A. S. C. Ehrenberg, and Edward R. Tufte. We are grateful to Professor David Targett for his data analysis trick discussed in Chapter 8. The National Center for Education Statistics provided much of the raw data used in the book, although the names of school districts have been fictionalized. We would like to thank Christine Johnstone, Jessica Lawler, Perry Millar, Brian Parkinson, Sue Oldfield, James Guilliford, and David Wheelwright.

# Chapter 1

# Introduction

NUMBERS ARE EXCITING. They tell a story. The trick is to know what story to tell and to tell it clearly.

This book is not about how to use a spreadsheet, choose the most appropriate statistical technique, or manage software. It is not about how to make numbers more "interesting." Instead, it gives advice on the simple steps necessary to transform raw data into readable, relevant information. It is about how to communicate numbers to other people.

Simple guidelines for presenting figures, tables, and graphs have been established over the past forty years, but few people are aware of them. This book draws together these principles and explains the straightforward steps needed to make your tables and charts meaningful.

## A COMMUNICATION SKILL

There are a number of reasons why presenting numerical information is a key communication skill for the twenty-first century:

- Numbers are persuasive. Numbers provide sound evidence for many decisions in life, from buying a car to government investment in education or the military.
- User-friendly tables, charts, and numbers shorten meetings, save time, and make a good impression. In the same way that most people appreciate well-written, concise reports, they also appreciate clear, succinct numerical information.

▲ Poor presentation leads to poor decision making. We will never know the amount of time or money lost through misunderstanding or misinterpreting badly presented figures.

▲ Most tables and charts require only basic arithmetic to be understood. This means that well-designed tables and charts can communicate nearly all numerical information to the public.

Many highly numerate specialists—accountants, engineers, and economists—sometimes present numbers poorly. Like other people, it would be helpful for them to learn the easy steps to communicating data to their audience. The skill is easily learned and is a practical and valuable tool that will help you both understand data and communicate it to others.

**The *Challenger* tragedy**. The 1986 explosion of the *Challenger* space shuttle, in which seven astronauts died, is the most famous example of poor numerical communication. The evening before takeoff, engineers recommended NASA cancel the launch because unexpected cold weather could damage certain components of the shuttle. Their hastily composed numerical charts focused on selective information (the effect of decreasing warm weather) and omitted equivalent data (cold temperatures). NASA found the argument unconvincing, and the rocket was launched, exploding after seventy-three seconds. A full explanation of the graphs and decisions is found in Edward R. Tufte's book *Visual Explanations*.

## IMPROVING STANDARDS

There are simple steps you can take to help improve readability standards in numbers, charts, and graphs. We suggest you:

▲ Appreciate that numbers, like words, can be communicated well or badly. Given a choice, most of us would prefer to communicate well.

- ▲ Learn and use the simple principles explained in this book.

- ▲ Try to see tables and charts from the audience's point of view. Will they understand the numbers from the way you have shown them? Will they be persuaded by your use of figures?

- ▲ Object when you see confusing tables and charts. Play a part in trying to improve standards. If you cannot decipher a table or chart, presume that other people cannot either. Let the editor or author know. Explain that the problem may be with the presentation, not your mathematics.

- ▲ Recommend your workplace or organization adopt standards around the presentation of numbers, tables, and charts.

## BUT IS IT ART?

There is an ongoing and often heated debate between those who prioritize the aesthetic potential of numerical presentation and those who emphasize the role of display in efficient communication of information. Some argue that clever, innovative design makes data more interesting and inviting. Others, like Professor Edward Tufte, argue that if your numbers are dull, you should find some exciting numbers, not decorate the ones you've got.

Ultimately it depends on what your purpose is. If you are working for a client, what is his or her preference? A few magazines and websites, for instance, will desire an entertaining, eye-catching display that readers have to puzzle through. More commonly, and at the other end of the spectrum, company executives will not thank a designer for an artistic interpretation of quarterly sales figures.

Business information, public relations, and web page design provide opportunities to practice another form of art. Can you make the complex look simple? As graphic designer Paul Rand said, "The big art of design is to make complicated things simple." Like world-class plastic surgeons and the best stand-up comics, keep in mind this Latin phrase: "Ars est celare artem." That is, "The art is to conceal the art."

# THE CHAPTERS

The chapters in this book are set out as follows:

Chapter 2, "Handling Numbers," lays out principles for presenting numerical information. These ideas are basic for good communication. The chapter also includes a guide to rounding numbers.

Chapter 3, "Using Tables," makes detailed recommendations for table construction and discusses reference and demonstration tables.

Chapter 4, "Introduction to Charts," explains the purposes of numerical charts, discusses the drawbacks of "chart junk," and provides guidance on chart design.

Chapter 5, "Basic Charts," examines the three most common numerical charts: bar, line, and pie. It describes the advantages and disadvantages of each type and how to design them for communication.

Chapter 6, "Technical and Specialist Charts and Data Visualization," defines a wide selection of old and new types of charts. It explains which are best at communicating and which are capable of analyzing only. It also offers a definition of data visualization.

Chapter 7, "Table or Chart?" sets out criteria for choosing between tables and charts for your data.

Chapter 8, "Working with Numbers," offers practical advice on working with numbers, including the two stages, making figures cogent, presenting figures on PowerPoint, and analyzing figures quickly.

Chapter 9, "Nonnumerical Charts and Information Graphics," defines terms, points out what often goes wrong, and offers several examples.

Chapter 10, "Numbers and Page Design," gives general guidance on numbers and page layout, the use of color, and presenting in different technologies.

## Using This Book

We do not anticipate people to read this book from cover to cover. It is much more like a cookbook you can dip into when you wish. We suggest, however, that you begin by reading chapter 2 on plain figures and chapter 4 on introducing charts. These two chapters will give you a good grounding in using numbers to communicate.

## Want to Know More?

Read "The Crystal Goblet," by Beatrice Ward—a few paragraphs written in 1932 and as powerful now as they were then; widely available on the Internet.

# Chapter 2

# Handling Numbers

MANY PEOPLE FIND numbers a trial. One reason for this is that numbers are frequently presented in a haphazard and muddled fashion with no apparent order or organization, with a dearth of visual clues, and with little context or explanation.

No wonder the straightforward task of making sense of numbers is discouraging as well as demanding.

Numbers (or figures—the words are interchangeable) are most valuable and memorable when relevant data is selected and presented in a way that emphasizes what is significant. Setting out figures in a succinct and unambiguous manner helps the readers understand the numbers.

The guiding principle of data presentation is: data should always be presented for the convenience of the reader.

Beyond that, there are six useful principles on presenting numbers, and five of them are explained in this chapter. These rules were set out by Professor A. S. C. Ehrenberg at the London Business School in the 1970s. They can help you organize numbers, set them out coherently, focus on what is important, and communicate them to your audience. They bring out the patterns and exceptions in the numbers. By following these simple rules, numerical lists and tables become coherent, interesting, and memorable.

The six rules of plain figures are:

- ▲ Put figures in an order.
- ▲ Add focus.
- ▲ Keep comparisons close.

- ▲ Round figures for clarity.
- ▲ Provide a written summary.
- ▲ Use layout to guide the eyes.

Information on layout appears in chapter 3. The other rules of plain figures are discussed below.

Of course, there will be times when it will not be the designer's job to reorder, round, or add focus to numbers or draft a written summary. Nonetheless, an understanding of the rules will help you make sound decisions when designing numerical information.

## PUT FIGURES IN AN ORDER

List numbers in a logical order; most often this will be largest to smallest.

Size order helps the reader make comparisons and see patterns and exceptions in the data. Patterns are likely to tell us something important, for example, "Sales rose consistently." Exceptions reveal key questions, for example, "Why did sales rise everywhere but in Chicago?"

Putting numbers in size order allows readers to make comparisons quickly.

Largest to smallest is often preferable to the other way around. Usually the greater the number, the more important an item is. For example, $1,000,000,000 is usually more important than $1,000.

Further, most people find it easier to subtract

   878
  -152

than to subtract

   152
  -878

**Example 2.1: Order figures numerically.** The use of alphabetical order, on the left, is unhelpful compared with size order, on the right. In the list to the right the population of New York stands out against other large cities. You can easily see, for instance, that Houston is the fourth largest city in population terms. Size order allows readers to see the relative standing of each item.

Resident population (millions) of the eight most populous cities in the United States, 2011

✓

| Chicago, IL | 2.7 | New York, NY | 8.2 |
| Dallas, TX | 1.2 | Los Angeles, CA | 3.8 |
| Houston, TX | 2.0 | Chicago, IL | 2.7 |
| Los Angeles, CA | 3.8 | Houston, TX | 2.0 |
| New York, NY | 8.2 | Philadelphia, PA | 1.5 |
| Philadelphia, PA | 1.5 | Phoenix, AZ | 1.4 |
| Phoenix, AZ | 1.4 | San Antonio, TX | 1.3 |
| San Antonio, TX | 1.3 | Dallas, TX | 1.2 |

Source: United States Census Bureau, Annual Estimates, July 2011.

## Multiple Comparisons

Ordering by size places numbers into a pattern (highest to lowest) that helps the reader quickly grasp the relationship between numbers.

**Example 2.2: Ordering for decision making.** In the first table below, alphabetical order produces a random array of numbers. In the second table, both rows and columns are in size order (according to overall totals). Looking at this table, many readers will quickly recognize the pattern and be able to use the ordered data efficiently.

Sales, 2013 (alphabetical order)

|  | East | North | South | West |
| --- | --- | --- | --- | --- |
| Blue | 750 | 710 | 720 | 720 |
| Green | 600 | 600 | 680 | 850 |
| Orange | 890 | 850 | 870 | 870 |
| Red | 300 | 230 | 240 | 240 |
| Yellow | 480 | 420 | 500 | 420 |

✓ Sales, 2013 (size order)

|         | West | East | South | North |
|---------|------|------|-------|-------|
| Orange  | 870  | 890  | 870   | 850   |
| Blue    | 720  | 750  | 720   | 710   |
| Green   | 850  | 600  | 680   | 600   |
| Yellow  | 420  | 480  | 500   | 420   |
| Red     | 240  | 300  | 240   | 230   |

With size order, most readers can easily spot several points: Orange outsells all other products by far, while sales in the North are lower than the other regions. Furthermore, sales of Green in the West are exceptionally high—both for the West and for Green.

This exception is difficult to find in the first table. Often it is the exceptions that are the most interesting and important part of the whole data set; they are what readers want and need to see.

## Not Always Size Order

▲ Size order is not always logical or suitable. In long tables and reference tables, alphabetical order may be more useful. For stocks and shares and in other instances, chronological order is most appropriate. Consider how readers may use the information and organize the data so that the arrangement serves their purpose.

▲ In a series of tables, order should be consistent. For example, in a series of fifty tables setting out detailed unemployment statistics for each US state, a consistent order would be logical and convenient.

## ADD FOCUS

You can help readers understand numbers by listing averages, totals, and percentages.

▲ Averages provide a row or column summary. They help to bring out the patterns and exceptions in the data. Totals give readers the big picture.

- Percentages give an idea of proportion.
- Choose among averages, totals, or percentages. Presenting all three, or even two of the three, will clutter a table and obscure the overall message.

**Example 2.3: Averages give focus.** In this table, notice the averages column. It makes patterns and exceptions easy to spot. Glancing down this column, you see an apparent year-by-year increase. Also, an exception becomes obvious, that is, 2010 was an exceptionally good year for sales.

Averages columns are rarely seen in tables, but they can be a practical, efficient way of pointing readers to exceptions in the data.

✓   Sales 2008–2013 (thousands)

|      | West | North | South | East | Average |
|------|------|-------|-------|------|---------|
| 2008 | 170  | 179   | 183   | 188  | 180     |
| 2009 | 175  | 181   | 185   | 191  | 183     |
| 2010 | 189  | 194   | 199   | 199  | 195     |
| 2011 | 181  | 185   | 188   | 194  | 187     |
| 2012 | 192  | 194   | 191   | 195  | 193     |
| 2013 | 193  | 194   | 194   | 195  | 194     |

Also, please note the gap or space between the main columns and that of the average. This visual clue helps readers distinguish the different type of data being presented.

## Totals

Totals show the aggregate, whereas averages show a summary. Though common, totals are not always necessary. Include totals when you think your audience will need them, for instance, in budgets.

**Example 2.4: Totals help give the big picture.** Totals can complete a table and give it focus.

Budget for ABC charity, 2013  ($)

| | |
|---|---|
| Salaries, payroll taxes, and benefits | 637,322 |
| Printing and publications | 235,000 |
| Special events | 79,500 |
| Supplies | 28,500 |
| Professional fees and insurance | 10,385 |
| Miscellaneous | 3,485 |
| Total | 994,192 |

## Percentages

Percentages are rarely as helpful as averages, but do show proportions.

**Example 2.5: Percentages show proportions.** Showing percentages can be helpful to readers.

Total numbers involved in sporting activities and proportion, by sport

| | Total (thousands) | % |
|---|---|---|
| Walking | 560 | 28 |
| Swimming | 440 | 22 |
| Bicycle Riding | 380 | 19 |
| Jogging | 300 | 15 |
| Yoga | 260 | 13 |
| Bowling | 60 | 3 |
| Total | 2,000 | 100 |

# KEEP COMPARISONS CLOSE

Numbers to be compared should be physically close to one another. Proximity helps readers compare the numbers.

"Keep comparisons close" is a general principle, but can be specifically applied to how numbers are set out. Numbers in columns are physically closer to one another than figures in rows. Numbers in rows are necessarily separated by blank space. Numbers in columns are easy to add, subtract, and compare. We seldom encounter numbers horizontally, so the unfamiliar layout adds to the difficulty. When designing a table, put numbers to be compared in columns, not rows.

**Example 2.6: Compare numbers in columns.** The first list below is organized in a long row and demands reading across blank space. The second list is a single-spaced column, and the numbers are stacked physically close to each other, nearly touching. The figures in the second display are easier to add, subtract, and compare.

Population of five counties, 2013 (thousands)

| Greenville | Franklin | Springfield | Clinton | Jackson |
|---|---|---|---|---|
| 438 | 243 | 222 | 204 | 181 |

✓

|  | (thousands) |
|---|---|
| Greenville | 438 |
| Franklin | 243 |
| Springfield | 222 |
| Clinton | 204 |
| Jackson | 181 |

## Compared with What?

You can only keep comparisons close if you know which items to compare. Which comparisons will be most beneficial to your readers? What are they interested in?

**Example 2.7: Selecting comparisons.** The table below shows exports of apples and pears over several years. The first presentation emphasises comparison between apples and pears. The revised table is more convenient for most readers; it compares like—with like, that is, apples against apples and pears against pears. It is easier to compare numbers going down a column rather than across a row.

Tonnes of fruit exported  2010–2013

|        | 2010   | 2011   | 2012   | 2013   |
|--------|--------|--------|--------|--------|
| Apples | 54,000 | 53,000 | 58,000 | 62,000 |
| Pears  | 4,300  | 4,400  | 4,600  | 4,800  |

✓

|      | Apples | Pears |
|------|--------|-------|
| 2010 | 54,000 | 4,300 |
| 2011 | 53,000 | 4,400 |
| 2012 | 58,000 | 4,600 |
| 2013 | 62,000 | 4,800 |

## Compare Like with Like

As with apples and pears, you can only compare numbers that are alike. Figures come in various forms—miles and kilometers; dollars, yen, and pounds sterling; miles per hour and feet per second. Take the opportunity to transform the numbers into comparable information.

**Example 2.8: Compare like with like.** The list on the left mixes two different measures—4 oz. and 1 oz. Many readers would conclude from it that liver sausage has fewer calories than ham, which is not the case.

|                      |          |   |                  ✓  | ✓                |
|----------------------|----------|---|----------------------|------------------|
| Chilled meats        | Calories |   | Chilled meats        | Calories per 4 oz. |
| Beef (4 oz)          | 225      |   | Salami               | 500              |
| Chicken (4 oz)       | 153      |   | Liver sausage        | 300              |
| Ham (4 oz)           | 109      |   | Beef                 | 225              |
| Liver sausage (1 oz) | 75       |   | Chicken              | 153              |
| Salami (1 oz)        | 125      |   | Ham                  | 109              |

The revised version, on the right, uses a single, common scale that makes the numbers comparative. It takes a little more effort to calculate items on the same basis, but people will not be mislead or confused by your figures. As Mies van der Rohe said, "Don't try to be original. Try to be good."

## Organize Tables so the Numbers Can Be Conveniently Compared

The "keep comparisons close" rule also applies to the way in which information may be presented, as the example below illustrates.

**Example 2.9: Show percentages so they can be compared.** In the first table, comparable items are not close to one another, that is, the number of males is not close to the number of females. The numbers and percentages intersect, making it impossible for the eye to scan across a row and make comparisons with ease.

Favorite vegetable

|  | Male | | Female | |
|---|---|---|---|---|
|  | No. | % | No. | % |
| Corn | 430 | 43 | 444 | 35 |
| Carrots | 383 | 39 | 134 | 11 |
| Broccoli | 67 | 7 | 392 | 31 |
| Other | 111 | 11 | 291 | 23 |
| Total | 991 | 100 | 1,261 | 100 |

If readers need both the numbers and the proportions, give them two simple tables comparing like with like.

✓

|  | Numbers of respondents | | Percentage of respondents | |
|---|---|---|---|---|
|  | Males | Females | Males | Females |
| Corn | 430 | 444 | 43 | 35 |
| Carrots | 383 | 134 | 39 | 11 |
| Broccoli | 67 | 392 | 7 | 31 |
| Other | 111 | 291 | 11 | 23 |
| Total | 991 | 1,261 | 100 | 100 |

# ROUND FIGURES FOR CLARITY

Rounding is a simple technique that improves communication dramatically. It makes numbers look simpler. It assists comparison of numbers and makes them easier to remember.

Rounding numbers is the single most helpful step you can take if you want people to understand, compare, and recall figures later.

## *Memory and Mental Arithmetic*

Take a number like 249,687. Most people can remember it only until they are interrupted, but they can remember the rounded version (250,000) even after interruptions. Detailed numbers are difficult to recall because of limitations in our short-term memory. Rounded numbers are memorable.

Most people can perform mental arithmetic with numbers of two digits, but not with more detailed figures. For instance, try to compare 723 with 238 without pen and paper. When they are rounded to 720 and 240, it is easy to see that the first is about three times larger than the second. Rounding makes mental arithmetic easier.

**Example 2.10: Rounded numbers look simpler.**
Consider this short table:

Pencils sold  (thousands)

|      | North | South | Total |
|------|-------|-------|-------|
| 2010 | 256.8 | 73.3  | 330.1 |
| 2011 | 359.3 | 79.4  | 438.7 |
| 2012 | 447.8 | 83.9  | 531.7 |
| 2013 | 498.8 | 98.8  | 597.6 |

Can we remember any of the numbers if we look away? What can we say about total sales without looking back at the table?

Understanding a set of numbers involves comparing them. This is not easy with the above table. Mentally comparing the total pencils sold in 2010 and 2013 is taxing for most adults (597.6 minus

330.1 equals 267.5). Most of us, consciously or unconsciously, round numbers first.

| | North | South | Total |
|---|---|---|---|
| 2010 | 260 | 73 | 330 |
| 2011 | 360 | 79 | 440 |
| 2012 | 450 | 84 | 530 |
| 2013 | 500 | 99 | 600 |

*Numbers have been rounded, so columns may not total.*

When we present the same data rounded, readers find it much easier to make comparisons and remember the numbers.

Using the rounded figures, we can quickly see that total pencil sales nearly doubled between 2010 and 2013. We can also see that in the North almost twice as many pencils were sold in 2013 as in 2010 (500,000 versus 260,000). Further, it is clear that in the South the difference in sales was much less dramatic.

Most people will be able to recall these patterns later: sales in 2013 were twice those of 2010, except in the South.

## Making Decisions

Most decisions in business, government, and elsewhere are made on rounded figures; details of more than two digits rarely influence a decision. If you are buying a car, do you think to yourself, "I have $11,224.16"? Or do you think, "I have $11,000"? We round all the time to simplify and compare.

## Accuracy

Some people resist rounded numbers, arguing that they are not accurate. "Accurate" figures often do not exist. The only figures available may be estimates or numbers captured at a certain time. For instance, the population of the United States was estimated at 313,875,741 on July 4, 2012, by the United States Census Bureau U.S. and World Population Clocks. But every day people are born and die, come and go. The actual number is not known, changes every minute, and does not matter: The rounded number (310,000,000) serves almost all purposes.

## Misleading

Beware of spurious accuracy, for instance, a customer service department reporting that last quarter 98.3857 percent of telephone calls were answered within ten seconds. This is misleading because some readers may believe that the records are accurate to four decimal places, which is unlikely to be so.

Such precision is usually shown because those responsible believe that reducing the decimal places may affect decision making. It will not. The rounded figure of 98 percent (or 98.4 percent in particular circumstances) will improve decision making because it allows managers to concentrate on the big problems and not be bogged down by false precision.

## Who Cannot Round?

Of course, bookkeepers, precision engineers, and pharmacists cannot round their work. They need to account for every penny, every millimeter, and every dose. But most of us are not bookkeepers, engineers, or pharmacists, but even these professionals can round when figures are for the purpose of general management and public communication.

Other instances in which you cannot round include:

- data intended for audit trails or other control checks
- data for foreign exchange transactions
- reference tables (where raw data is essential)
- in the middle of calculations

### Variable Rounding to Two Effective Digits

At school, you were probably taught fixed rounding; all figures are converted to tens, hundreds, or thousands. An alternative method, called "variable rounding," is statistically valid, simple to calculate, and more practical for everyday use. With variable rounding, you round to two (occasionally three) effective digits, regardless of the size of the number.

Variable rounding has the advantage over fixed rounding that it maintains all figures, and no number, no matter how small, is reduced to zero.

| A | B | C |
|---|---|---|
| Original | Fixed rounding to thousands | Variable rounding to two effective digits |
| 28,732 | 29,000 | 29,000 |
| 4,116 | 4,000 | 4,100 |
| 267 | 0 | 270 |
| 42 | 0 | 42 |

**Example 2.11: Fixed and variable rounding.** Fixed rounding (column B) reduces some items to zero. In variable rounding (column C) all the numbers are rounded to two digits.

## Exceptions

When figures in a series are numerically close, you need more than two digits. Showing only two digits is too approximate and camouflages distinctions in the numbers. Take, for example, the series 857, 865, 877, and 889. Rounding to two digits would give us 860, 870, 880, and 890, and an effective loss of precision. When figures are numerically close, use three digits.

**Example 2.12: When more than two effective digits are needed.** Look again at the reported 98.3857 percent of telephone calls answered within ten seconds (mentioned on page 18). Use the figures for the previous quarter (or perhaps for the same quarter the year before) as comparators, and then round so that the difference between the two results is discernible to the reader.

Telephone calls answered within ten seconds

| | Original number | Rounded to ✓ | Original number | Rounded to ✓ | Original number | Rounded to ✓ |
|---|---|---|---|---|---|---|
| Quarter 2 | 95.8395 | 96 | 98.1385 | 98.1 | 98.2867 | 98.29 |
| Quarter 3 | 98.3857 | 98 | 98.3857 | 98.4 | 98.2573 | 98.26 |

Once again, you present the data for the convenience of the reader and leave out unnecessary detail.

**Rounding totals.** You need to round totals independently from other numbers. Do this by adding up the original numbers and noting the total. Then round each individual number, including the total.

Without independent rounding, errors are likely to creep in. Do not round the figures, add them up, and then round the resultant total. That is rounding twice, and the answer is likely to be inaccurate.

## ROUNDING TOTALS

Expenditure (thousands)

|            | Original   | Rounded    |
|------------|------------|------------|
| Michigan   | 8,488,723  | 8,500,000  |
| Wisconsin  | 6,308,452  | 6,300,000  |
| Minnesota  | 640,891    | 640,000    |
| Iowa       | 481,438    | 480,000    |
| Total      | 15,919,504 | 16,000,000 |

*Columns may not equal totals due to rounding.*

The total in the second column has been rounded "independently," and as frequently happens, this figure does not equal the sum of the rounded numbers above (which comes to 15,920,000). Readers will sometimes notice the disparity, so a short explanation is helpful. Add a line at the end to your table saying, something such as

*Figures have been rounded independently, so columns may not equal totals.*

Or

*Numbers are rounded for greater clarity. Columns may not equal totals. Exact numbers are available.*

Another alternative is to omit the total and add a sentence at the bottom of the numbers stating,

*The total expenditure was approximately $16 million for the period.*

## PROVIDE A WRITTEN SUMMARY

Numbers, tables, and charts that appear in reports (including sales statements, annual reports, and progress reports) should be accompanied by a written summary. Summaries allow the author to explain why the data is worthy of attention. They are a second opportunity to get the message across to the reader. Use them to emphasise conclusions, trends, anomalies, and patterns.

### *Tips*

- ▲ Tables and charts should be accompanied by an explanation. If you do not tell the readers what the numbers mean, many of them will never know.

- ▲ Writing "Table X shows that there has been little change over the last five years" is more helpful to readers than merely stating "Please see Table X for the outcomes."

- ▲ Summarize the overall patterns in the table as well as important exceptions. There is no need to mention all the numbers.

**Example 2.13: Written summary.** The table from example 2.2 is represented below with totals added. It contains twenty-nine numbers. Readers will need direction to work out the meaning and important features. The summary we give is written for a general audience.

✓    Table A. Sales, 2013  $ (thousands)

|        | West  | East  | South | North | Total |
|--------|-------|-------|-------|-------|-------|
| Orange | 870   | 890   | 870   | 850   | 3,480 |
| Blue   | 720   | 750   | 720   | 710   | 2,900 |
| Green  | 850   | 600   | 680   | 600   | 2,730 |
| Yellow | 420   | 480   | 500   | 420   | 1,820 |
| Red    | 240   | 300   | 240   | 230   | 1,010 |
| Total  | 3,100 | 3,020 | 3,010 | 2,810 |       |

*Sales (Table A) are closely spread across the four territories, although sales in the West are highest. Sales of Orange are twice as high as sales of Yellow and roughly three times those of Red. Sales of Green are exceptionally high in the West.*

This direct statement explains both what the table does (shows sales across the divisions) and what the specific figures mean. By citing the table reference number (or letter), you ensure that readers consult the correct table.

## SUMMARY

This chapter begins by explaining the guiding principle of data presentation: data should always be presented for the convenience of the reader. The chapter goes on to explain five of the six rules of plain figures. The rules help to organize and set out numbers so they can be understood quickly and communicated effectively. For many people, the rules take the stress out of numbers.

The rules are:

1. Put figures in an order. Size order is often appropriate and helps readers see the relationship between numbers.

2. Add focus. Averages give a point for comparison, helping readers to discern patterns and exceptions in the data. Totals give the big picture. Percentages, though less critical, are useful for establishing proportion.

3. Keep comparisons close. Physical proximity helps comparisons. Figures in columns are easier to compare than those in rows. In order to use this principle, you must choose what numbers should be compared and ensure the items are comparable.

4. Round numbers to improve communication. Rounding is an easy measure that simplifies numbers.

5. Provide a summary in the text. Help your reader understand the data and connect it to your overall argument or point.

These guidelines are easily incorporated into almost anyone's work. By following them, you can improve your presentation of numbers and hence help your audience to understand your point. Some will even be grateful for the clear display.

## WANT TO KNOW MORE?

Ehrenberg, A. S. C. "The Problem of Numeracy." *The American Statistician* 35, no. 2 (May 1981): 67–71 (available on the Internet free of charge).

Tufte, Edward R. *The Visual Display of Quantitative Information.* Cheshire, CT: The Graphics Press, 2001.

Wainer, Howard. "How to Display Data Badly." *The American Statistician* 38, no. 2 (May 1984): 137–147 (available on the Internet free of charge).

# Chapter 3

# Using Tables

TABLES LIST NUMBERS in a systematic fashion. They order, supplement, simplify, explain, and condense written material. As with all data presentation, tables should be designed for the convenience of the reader.

Thoughtful organization and visual clues enhance understanding of tables. Ill-considered layout and over engineering are common and misdirect readers as to what is important; such affectations reduce readability.

You can use tables to:

- ▲ show a multitude of figures (in some case hundreds)
- ▲ list precise numbers
- ▲ extract numbers easily
- ▲ identify patterns and exceptions in the data
- ▲ present data with more than one unit (e.g., both the number of students at several schools and the ratio of students to teachers)
- ▲ show a wide range of figures (e.g., the population of every town in Nebraska)

---

**Tables: What Often Goes Wrong?**

- ▲ Inadequate and obscure wording
- ▲ Failure to distinguish between a reference table and a demonstration table
- ▲ Too much data in a demonstration table
- ▲ Confusing layout

---

# COMPONENTS OF A TABLE

Below we set out the different components of a table.

**Example 3.1: Components of a table.**

| County | Student/ teacher ratio | Number of | |
|---|---|---|---|
| | | students/ thousands | Classroom teachers (FTE*) |
| Springfield | 14.4 | 2 | 140 |
| Fairview | 15.3 | 20 | 1,300 |
| Franklin | 15.6 | 12 | 750 |
| Salem | 18.1 | 60 | 3,300 |
| Clinton | 19.3 | 77 | 4,000 |
| Greenville | 19.7 | 170 | 8,700 |
| Total / average | 16.5 | 341 | 18,190 |

Table 3.1  Numbers of schools, students, teachers, and student:teacher ratio, 20012/13 for the six districts

* FTE = full time equivalent
Source: Education Department

Labels: Number and table title; Column spanner; Column headings; Table spanner; Row headings; Footnotes and sources

# SUCCESSFUL TABLES

Successful tables communicate their purpose with ease. They are designed for efficient comprehension and easy application. They contain the minimum of numbers to serve their purpose.

When you are designing tables, keep in mind these three principles:

▲ simplicity of layout

▲ clarity of wording

▲ attention to page design (discussed in chapter 10)

You also need to know which type of table you are designing, which is explained below.

# TWO TYPES OF TABLES

There are two types of tables: reference and demonstration. Understanding the difference between the two will help you make appropriate design choices.

## Reference Tables

Reference tables (also called look-up tables) are used for specific information, such as train schedules, sports scores, stock market listings, budget books, most business spreadsheets, etc. Their purpose is to be exact when people need the information.

Reference tables by nature contain large amounts of data; some show hundreds of numbers. They are readable because they are designed thoughtfully with a minimum amount of clutter.

## Tips for Reference Tables

▲ Use raw numbers. Numbers are not rounded in reference tables. You do not want to miss the 1:37 train because the time was rounded to 1:40.

▲ Place reference tables in appendixes of reports. These tables rarely appear in a report itself.

▲ Present numbers in the simplest format, for example, column headings should say "millions" rather than each number having seven place digits.

▲ Insert blank spaces. In longer tables add a blank row every four or five lines. This helps the reader identify rows and hold his or her place.

**Example 3.2: A U.S. Census Bureau reference table.** The bureau produces hundreds of such tables each year.

## Table 233. Educational Attainment by State: 1990 to 2009

[In percent. 1990 and 2000 as of April. 2009 represents annual averages for calendar year. For persons 25 years old and over. Based on the 1990 and 2000 Census of Population and the 2009 American Community Survey, which includes the household population and the population living in institutions, college dormitories, and other group quarters. See text, Section 1 and Appendix III. For margin of error data, see source]

| State | 1990 | | | 2000 | | | 2009 | | |
|---|---|---|---|---|---|---|---|---|---|
| | High school graduate or more | Bachelor's degree or more | Advanced degree or more | High school graduate or more | Bachelor's degree or more | Advanced degree or more | High school graduate or more | Bachelor's degree or more | Advanced degree or more |
| **United States** | **75.2** | **20.3** | **7.2** | **80.4** | **24.4** | **8.9** | **85.3** | **27.9** | **10.3** |
| Alabama | 66.9 | 15.7 | 5.5 | 75.3 | 19.0 | 6.9 | 82.1 | 22.0 | 7.7 |
| Alaska | 86.6 | 23.0 | 8.0 | 88.3 | 24.7 | 8.6 | 91.4 | 26.6 | 9.0 |
| Arizona | 78.7 | 20.3 | 7.0 | 81.0 | 23.5 | 8.4 | 84.2 | 25.6 | 9.3 |
| Arkansas | 66.3 | 13.3 | 4.5 | 75.3 | 16.7 | 5.7 | 82.4 | 18.9 | 6.1 |
| California | 76.2 | 23.4 | 8.1 | 76.8 | 26.6 | 9.5 | 80.6 | 29.9 | 10.7 |
| Colorado | 84.4 | 27.0 | 9.0 | 86.9 | 32.7 | 11.1 | 89.3 | 35.9 | 12.7 |
| Connecticut | 79.2 | 27.2 | 11.0 | 84.0 | 31.4 | 13.3 | 88.6 | 35.6 | 15.5 |
| Delaware | 77.5 | 21.4 | 7.7 | 82.6 | 25.0 | 9.4 | 87.4 | 28.7 | 11.4 |
| District of Columbia | 73.1 | 33.3 | 17.2 | 77.8 | 39.1 | 21.0 | 87.1 | 48.5 | 28.0 |
| Florida | 74.4 | 18.3 | 6.3 | 79.9 | 22.3 | 8.1 | 85.3 | 25.3 | 9.0 |
| Georgia | 70.9 | 19.3 | 6.4 | 78.6 | 24.3 | 8.3 | 83.9 | 27.5 | 9.9 |
| Hawaii | 80.1 | 22.9 | 7.1 | 84.6 | 26.2 | 8.4 | 90.4 | 29.6 | 9.9 |
| Idaho | 79.7 | 17.7 | 5.3 | 84.7 | 21.7 | 6.8 | 88.4 | 23.9 | 7.5 |
| Illinois | 76.2 | 21.0 | 7.5 | 81.4 | 26.1 | 9.5 | 86.4 | 30.6 | 11.7 |
| Indiana | 75.6 | 15.6 | 6.4 | 82.1 | 19.4 | 7.2 | 86.6 | 22.5 | 8.1 |
| Iowa | 80.1 | 16.9 | 5.2 | 86.1 | 21.2 | 6.5 | 90.5 | 25.1 | 7.4 |
| Kansas | 81.3 | 21.1 | 7.0 | 86.0 | 25.8 | 8.7 | 89.7 | 29.5 | 10.2 |
| Kentucky | 64.6 | 13.6 | 5.5 | 74.1 | 17.1 | 6.9 | 81.7 | 21.0 | 8.5 |
| Louisiana | 68.3 | 16.1 | 5.6 | 74.8 | 18.7 | 6.5 | 82.2 | 21.4 | 6.9 |
| Maine | 78.8 | 18.8 | 6.1 | 85.4 | 22.9 | 7.9 | 90.2 | 26.9 | 9.6 |
| Maryland | 78.4 | 26.5 | 10.9 | 83.8 | 31.4 | 13.4 | 88.2 | 35.7 | 16.0 |
| Massachusetts | 80.0 | 27.2 | 10.6 | 84.8 | 33.2 | 13.7 | 89.0 | 38.2 | 16.4 |
| Michigan | 76.8 | 17.4 | 6.4 | 83.4 | 21.8 | 8.1 | 87.9 | 24.6 | 9.4 |
| Minnesota | 82.4 | 21.8 | 6.3 | 87.9 | 27.4 | 8.3 | 91.5 | 31.5 | 10.3 |
| Mississippi | 64.3 | 14.7 | 5.1 | 72.9 | 16.9 | 5.8 | 80.4 | 19.6 | 7.1 |
| Missouri | 73.9 | 17.8 | 6.1 | 81.3 | 21.6 | 7.6 | 86.8 | 25.2 | 9.5 |
| Montana | 81.0 | 19.8 | 5.7 | 87.2 | 24.4 | 7.2 | 90.8 | 27.4 | 8.3 |
| Nebraska | 81.8 | 18.9 | 5.9 | 86.6 | 23.7 | 7.3 | 89.8 | 27.4 | 8.8 |
| Nevada | 78.8 | 15.3 | 5.2 | 80.7 | 18.2 | 6.1 | 83.9 | 21.8 | 7.6 |
| New Hampshire | 82.2 | 24.4 | 7.9 | 87.4 | 28.7 | 10.0 | 91.3 | 32.0 | 11.2 |
| New Jersey | 76.7 | 24.9 | 8.8 | 82.1 | 29.8 | 11.0 | 87.4 | 34.5 | 12.9 |
| New Mexico | 75.1 | 20.4 | 8.3 | 78.9 | 23.5 | 9.8 | 82.8 | 25.3 | 10.4 |
| New York | 74.8 | 23.1 | 9.9 | 79.1 | 27.4 | 11.8 | 84.7 | 32.4 | 14.0 |
| North Carolina | 70.0 | 17.4 | 5.4 | 78.1 | 22.5 | 7.2 | 84.3 | 26.5 | 8.8 |
| North Dakota | 76.7 | 18.1 | 4.5 | 83.9 | 22.0 | 5.5 | 90.1 | 25.8 | 6.7 |
| Ohio | 75.7 | 17.0 | 5.9 | 83.0 | 21.1 | 7.4 | 87.6 | 24.1 | 8.8 |
| Oklahoma | 74.6 | 17.8 | 6.0 | 80.6 | 20.3 | 6.8 | 85.6 | 22.7 | 7.4 |
| Oregon | 81.5 | 20.6 | 7.0 | 85.1 | 25.1 | 8.7 | 89.1 | 29.2 | 10.4 |
| Pennsylvania | 74.7 | 17.9 | 6.6 | 81.9 | 22.4 | 8.4 | 87.9 | 26.4 | 10.2 |
| Rhode Island | 72.0 | 21.3 | 7.8 | 78.0 | 25.6 | 9.7 | 84.7 | 30.5 | 11.7 |
| South Carolina | 68.3 | 16.6 | 5.4 | 76.3 | 20.4 | 6.9 | 83.6 | 24.3 | 8.4 |
| South Dakota | 77.1 | 17.2 | 4.9 | 84.6 | 21.5 | 6.0 | 89.9 | 25.1 | 7.3 |
| Tennessee | 67.1 | 16.0 | 5.4 | 75.9 | 19.6 | 6.8 | 83.1 | 23.0 | 7.9 |
| Texas | 72.1 | 20.3 | 6.5 | 75.7 | 23.2 | 7.6 | 79.9 | 25.5 | 8.5 |
| Utah | 85.1 | 22.3 | 6.8 | 87.7 | 26.1 | 8.3 | 90.4 | 28.5 | 9.1 |
| Vermont | 80.8 | 24.3 | 8.9 | 86.4 | 29.4 | 11.1 | 91.0 | 33.1 | 13.3 |
| Virginia | 75.2 | 24.5 | 9.1 | 81.5 | 29.5 | 11.6 | 86.6 | 34.0 | 14.1 |
| Washington | 83.8 | 22.9 | 7.0 | 87.1 | 27.7 | 9.3 | 89.7 | 31.0 | 11.1 |
| West Virginia | 66.0 | 12.3 | 4.8 | 75.2 | 14.8 | 5.9 | 82.8 | 17.3 | 6.7 |
| Wisconsin | 78.6 | 17.7 | 5.6 | 85.1 | 22.4 | 7.2 | 89.8 | 25.7 | 8.4 |
| Wyoming | 83.0 | 18.8 | 5.7 | 87.9 | 21.9 | 7.0 | 91.8 | 23.8 | 7.9 |

Source: U.S. Census Bureau, 1990 Census of Population, CPH-L-96; 2000 Census of Population, P37. "Sex by Educational Attainment for the Population 25 Years and Over"; 2009 American Community Survey, R1501, "Percent of Persons 25 Years and Over Who Have Completed High School (Includes Equivalency)," R1502, "Percent of Persons 25 Years and Over Who Have Completed a Bachelor's Degree," and R1503, "Percent of Persons 25 Years and Over Who H(ave Completed an Advanced Degree," <http://factfinder.census.gov/>, accessed February 2011.

## Demonstration Tables

Demonstration tables make a point or an argument in a concise way. They are short and to the point. Typically, demonstration tables are made up from data selected from one or more reference tables.

**Example 3.3: Demonstration table.** Below is a demonstration table showing the maintenance costs of various roller coasters. It has been organized to reveal a pattern, that is, the older the roller coaster the higher the maintenance costs. By ordering the data this way, an exception in the sequence—the disproportionately high cost of Fairview's maintenance—is obvious.

✓ Table 3.3. Age and maintenance costs, roller coasters, 2012–2013, Champagne Roller Coasters Inc.

| Location of roller coaster | Age of roller coaster (years) | Maintenance costs ($) | | |
|---|---|---|---|---|
| | | Wheel nuts | Ball bearings | Total |
| Springfield | 87 | 2,400 | 700 | 3,100 |
| Mawavi | 66 | 1,400 | 520 | 1,920 |
| Fairview | 65 | 1,700 | 900 | 2,600 |
| Clinton | 41 | 650 | 450 | 1100 |
| Salem Town | 17 | 100 | 80 | 180 |

Often, several succinct demonstration tables will successfully communicate better than a single complex table. Too much data confuses and intimidates the audience, who are counting on you for information, not volume.

## Tips for Demonstration Tables

▲ Keep the table as concise as possible so the reader can focus on the issues at hand.

▲ Set up your demonstration table according to a logical and obvious pattern. Ensure that exceptions are apparent. (Often exceptions in the data are the most interesting part of the table. They are what your readers want and need to see.)

- ▲ Point out both patterns and exceptions in any written or oral summary.

## SIMPLICITY OF LAYOUT

A simple and uncluttered table communicates numbers more successfully than a "busy" or decorated one. Poor layout, rather than difficult material, accounts for most confusion with tables.

### *Gridlines*

Gridlines clutter tables without adding information. Vertical lines stop the eyes scanning across a row of figures to make comparisons. Even before you put numbers in the grid, it is crowded with lines.

Grids were once necessary for creating handwritten tables, such as in ledger books. Computer software, especially spreadsheet programs, make these obsolete. Consider this figure:

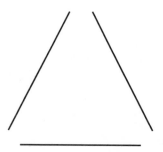

These lines are recognizable as a triangle even though the drawing is incomplete. Similarly, the human eye does not need grid lines to follow the layout of a table. Edward Tufte coined the term "the dreaded grid" to describe lines that create muddle and introduce ugliness into tables without adding information.

**Example 3.4: The dreaded grid.** Gridlines dominate the first table on the next page. The vertical lines stop the eye scanning across the rows. The horizontal lines interrupt numeric comparisons and make mental calculations more difficult.

Table A. Staffing at three depots, 2010–2012

|         | Springfield | Greenville | Auburn | Total |
|---------|------------:|-----------:|-------:|------:|
| 2010    | 73          | 54         | 27     | 154   |
| 2011    | 78          | 55         | 29     | 162   |
| 2012    | 81          | 48         | 31     | 160   |
| Average | 77          | 52         | 29     |       |

In Table B, space rather than lines helps the reader understand the relationships. Notice that space is used to delineate totals and averages.

✓    Table B. Staffing at three depots, 2010–2012

|         | Springfield | Greenville | Auburn | Total |
|---------|------------:|-----------:|-------:|------:|
| 2010    | 73          | 54         | 27     | 154   |
| 2011    | 78          | 55         | 29     | 162   |
| 2012    | 81          | 48         | 31     | 160   |
| Average | 77          | 52         | 29     |       |

## Other Layout Tips

- ▲ Avoid bold and shading. Readers need to see the numbers, not the decoration.
- ▲ Align numbers and column headings to the right. This allows the natural shape of numbers to communicate. Watch out for spreadsheets that tend to align headings to the left and numbers to the right. This invites confusion.
- ▲ Vary the width of columns as logic and space demands.
- ▲ Single-spaced tables keep figures close to one another. In long tables, a blank line inserted every four or five lines helps readers keep their place.

**Example 3.5: Use layout to guide the eyes.** In table C below, shading and bold distract the viewer from focusing on the content. The % and $ signs are repeated needlessly. The rows are wide-spaced, and the columns are of standardized length, although the length of the wording varies greatly. The table is pointlessly elongated and offers no clues as to how to read the information.

Table D uses space rather than ink to promote readability. It is single spaced, and column width varies with the size of the content. Shading and bold are avoided. Numbers are aligned to the right, and the $ and % signs are integrated into the column headings.

**Table C. Key operational and financial data from joint venues**

| Year ending December 31 | Wholesale items | Market share | Total net sales and revenue | Net income |
|---|---|---|---|---|
| 2010 | 1,600 | 13.6% | $31,000 | $3,300 |
| 2011 | 1,400 | 12.8% | $26,000 | $3,100 |
| 2012 | 900 | 13.3% | $21,000 | $1,400 |
| Average per year | 1,300 | 13.2% | $26,000 | $2,600 |

✓   Table D. Key operational and financial data from joint venues

| Year ending December 31 | Wholesale items | Market share (%) | Total net sales and revenue ($) | Net income ($) |
|---|---|---|---|---|
| 2010 | 1,600 | 13.6 | 31,000 | 3,300 |
| 2011 | 1,400 | 12.8 | 26,000 | 3,100 |
| 2012 | 900 | 13.3 | 21,000 | 1,400 |
| Average per year | 1,300 | 13.2 | 26,000 | 2,600 |

# CLARITY OF WORDING

Incomplete and obscure wording can make an otherwise useful table incomprehensible. Titles, column and row headings, and other text (e.g., a source or footnote) should have a specific purpose. If the wording is insufficient or confusing, many people will ignore your table altogether.

Tables should be self-explanatory. Someone coming across a table in a report or on a web page should be able to understand it from the title and labels alone.

## *Table Titles*

Titles should be definitive and comprehensive, giving all the necessary information. Readers need to know:

> What: customers, elementary schools, TV programs, home electronics, etc.
>
> Where: Chicago, South Korea, St. Elmo's Community Center, Dr. Abdul's clinic, etc.
>
> When: 2013, 1945–1975, May and June, third quarter, etc.
>
> Units: acres, thousands, barrels of oil, percentages, ounces of fat, dollars, etc.

The order in which title information appears is not important as long as it states what, where, when, and units. It is helpful to give tables a reference number or letter. This allows you to reference tables in your summary, reducing the chances of confusion.

**Example 3.6: Examples of comprehensive table titles.**

| Number | Subject | Detail | Location | Dates or period | Units |
|---|---|---|---|---|---|
| Table 9.2 | Unemployment | Males and females | Chicago, IL | 2nd quarter, 2012 | % of workforce |
| No. A | Trauma center patients | Type of patient (in-patient, adult, etc.) | Shreveport, LA | 2012 | Thousands |
| Fig. 5B | Pizza | Type of pizza (Hawaiian, veggie, pepperoni, etc). | US | May 2012 | Calories per slice |

## *Labeling Columns and Headings*

Labels need to be coherent. Here are some best-practice ideas:

▲ Avoid abbreviations unless they are well known, for instance, YMCA, USAF, SUV. Unfamiliar abbreviations confuse and exasperate people. For instance, does "GM" refer to General Motors, grams, genetically modified, geometric mean, grand master, or gross margin?

▲ Eliminate footnotes, which are disruptive. Try to include all necessary information in your headings. If you must use footnotes, marking them with asterisks is preferable. Some readers confuse footnote numbers with the contents of the table.

▲ Include sources on tables. This not only helps the reader, but is also beneficial when you want to check the information in eighteen months' time.

▲ Use upper and lower case text rather than ALL CAPS. The words are easier to read. People tend to read by the shape of words, and capital letters have less shape. Furthermore, ALL CAPS can indicate emphasis, like in shouting.

▲ Ensure the text is large enough to read. There is some evidence that tables are easier to read if slightly smaller than the surrounding text. Be aware of your audience, however. If your document is for the public, then twelve-point type is recommended. Many people over fifty years of age find smaller size print difficult to read.

## SUMMARY

Tables are an excellent device for displaying large quantities of figures. Reference tables use exact numbers to list specific data. Demonstration tables present selected figures to make a point, showing a trend.

Tables benefit from adherence to the rules of plain figures.

Successful tables communicate with ease. Patterns and exceptions stand out, at least once you have explained them in your summary. The most readable tables organize content for the readers' convenience through a simple layout and clarity of wording.

Tables need comprehensive titles and succinct headings. The layout should be simple, with white space replacing gridlines, shading, and bold. Tables should only be as wide as they need to be, and column headings and numbers should be aligned to the right. Several short, simple tables are likely to communicate more easily than one complex table.

## WANT TO KNOW MORE?

Few, Stephen. *Show Me the Numbers*. Burlingame, CA: Analytics Press, 2004.

Wainer, Howard. "Improving Tabular Displays." *Journal of Educational and Behavioural Statistics* 22, no. 1 (Spring, 1997): 1–30 (available on the Internet free of charge).

Tufte, Edward R. *The Visual Display of Quantitative Information*. Cheshire, CT: The Graphics Press, 2001.

# Chapter 4

# Introduction to Charts

A NUMERIC CHART (or graph, the more traditional term) is a diagram showing numerical trends and relationships. Charts organize, analyze, and summarize data and often work as communication tools. The best charts—those that communicate with ease—are instantly coherent, tell a single story, and transform raw data into vivid information.

This book covers a range of charts from the common pie chart to specialist analytical charts. Individual types are defined and discussed in the chapters 5 and 6. The terms "chart" and "graph" are used interchangeably.

Charts excel at demonstrating trends, correlations, and other relationships that are difficult to see in tables or to describe in words. Charts are good at showing the big picture and broad sweep of information; conversely, they are less successful at showing detail. If the readers need precise numbers, give them a good table rather than a chart to provide such specifications.

It is rare for a chart to demand anything of a viewer beyond basic arithmetic. Charts that look complex usually do so because of poor design, not abstruse content.

## CHARTS: WHAT OFTEN GOES WRONG?

- using a chart to explain no particular point or points
- gratuitous decoration and overengineering
- using the wrong type of chart (see chapters 5 and 6)
- inadequate or misleading wording

**Example 4.1: Good charts communicate simply.** The best charts—the ones that communicate with ease—are both memorable and simple. The following chart illustrates a simple message—that sales of laptops have overtaken those of PCs. The trends evident in this chart would be more difficult to pick up looking at raw data. Also, there is a pattern or shape that may imprint itself on your memory.

✓ **Chart 4.1**

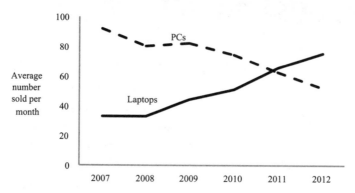

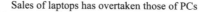

Four features make charts readable:

- ▲ clarity of message
- ▲ simplicity of design
- ▲ clarity of words
- ▲ integrity of intention and action

These features are explained below.

## CLARITY OF MESSAGE

Charts work best (i.e., they communicate without effort) when displaying a specific story, for instance, "Coffee production is up." If your story is muddled, then your chart will be, too.

    Charts are like jokes. If you have to explain them, they have failed.

## Determining the Message

This table contains raw data:

Sales of laptops 2006–2012

| | Models | | | |
|------|--------|--------|--------|--------|
| | A | B | C | D |
| 2006 | 33,000 | 44,000 | 49,000 | 25,000 |
| 2007 | 35,000 | 38,000 | 47,000 | 22,000 |
| 2008 | 40,000 | 40,000 | 42,000 | 21,000 |
| 2009 | 41,000 | 44,000 | 37,000 | 23,000 |
| 2010 | 45,000 | 44,000 | 34,000 | 24,000 |
| 2011 | 47,000 | 41,000 | 30,000 | 24,000 |
| 2012 | 51,000 | 42,000 | 25,000 | 23,000 |

It is possible to stuff all this reference data into a single chart, but the display would not be coherent. Reference data belongs in tables.

To create an intelligible, reader-friendly chart, select data that is relevant and ignore the rest. For instance, from the above table you might wish to emphasise Model A with the message, "Sales of Model A increase steadily." Alternatively, you could compare sales: "Sales of Model A increase as sales for Model C slump." Or you might wish to isolate 2012 sales, directing the reader with, "Model A sales are double the sales for Models C and D."

Once you have decided on what you want to say, you can choose which type of chart to use—say, a line chart or a bar chart.

You can also use the message as the title of the chart.

## The Title

The most helpful titles explain or summarize the point of the chart, for instance, "Sales of laptops increase." It is more common for chart titles to describe the subject, but not suggest the overall significance.

**Example 4.2: Explanatory titles add interest.** See how the title of chart 4.2 B transforms dull survey results into attention-grabbing information.

**Chart 4.2 A**

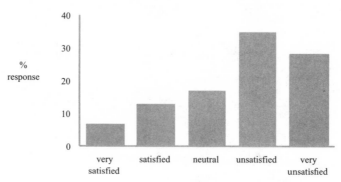

Satisfaction with new recreation center

✓ **Chart 4.2 B**

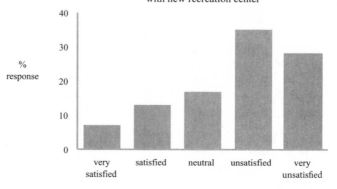

Most users are dissatisfied
with new recreation center

**Example 4.3: Explanatory titles get the point across**. The chart below was drawn up for hospital administrators. A busy manager looking at the first chart might miss the point (that for two consecutive years there was an increase in emergency room visits in December and January). The summarizing title on chart 4.3 B makes the message difficult to miss.

**Chart 4.3 A**

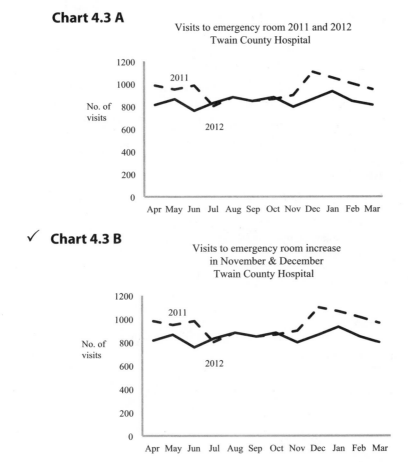

Visits to emergency room 2011 and 2012
Twain County Hospital

✓ **Chart 4.3 B**

Visits to emergency room increase
in November & December
Twain County Hospital

With less common types of charts (say, scatter plots and histograms), an explanatory title reassures readers that they have interpreted the information correctly.

# SIMPLICITY OF DESIGN

Charts rely on straightforward presentation. The sign of a good chart is that the numbers are emphasised, not the decoration.

To achieve design simplicity, choose one of the plainest charts offered by your software. Microsoft *Chart Wizard*, for example, supplies over seventy choices of "standard" charts, but only six or so are useful if you wish to communicate with another living being.

## Chart Junk

Chart junk is decoration that interferes with meaning. Chart junk can be alluring to the novice, but it clouds the message and looks amateurish.

The following examples illustrate how clutter and inappropriate elements interfere with a chart.

Chart junk consists of unnecessary and distracting elements. The most common of these are:

- gridlines
- patterned bars and slices
- shaded backgrounds
- bold
- borders
- inappropriate and confusing colors
- unnecessary numbers and values

Chart junk is any adornment that does not add information. Edward R. Tufte, who coined the term "chart junk," discusses many examples in detail in his books.

**Example: 4.4 Avoiding chart junk.** Chart A on the next page is more useful than those that follow in this chapter because of its direct expression and lack of decoration. Overall, the emphasis is on what the data means (how the bars compare), not on the design. White space rather than formatting is adroitly employed to show the bars to the reader.

### ✓ Chart 4.4 A

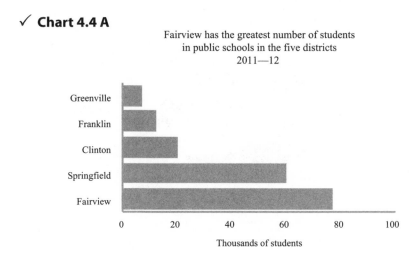

Fairview has the greatest number of students
in public schools in the five districts
2011—12

Prefer plain fills to patterns. Patterned bars (as shown in chart 4.4 B below) overwhelm the display and distract readers from comparing the length of the bars—which is, of course, the point of any bar chart. In chart 4.4 C, background shading is equally unhelpful in that it slyly deflects emphasis away from the bars.

### Chart 4.4 B

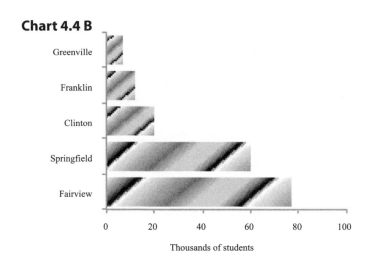

**Chart 4.4 C**

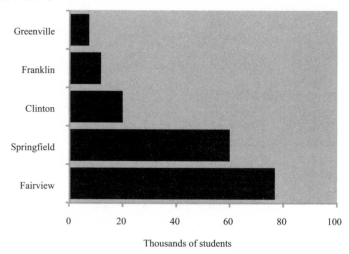

Thousands of students

Pointless borders, as in chart 4.4 D, subtly divert attention from the bars.

**Chart 4.4 D**

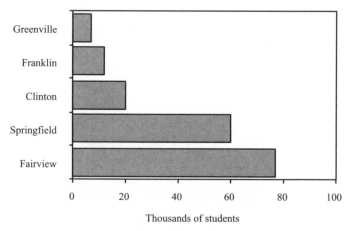

Thousands of students

Dark gridlines overwhelm chart 4.4 E. They prevent viewers from concentrating on the overall picture. Faint gridlines are less intrusive and, in some circumstances, can enhance perception and encourage accurate interpretation. On the other hand, grids frequently add nothing. Remember, charts work best when showing broad trends and relationships, not fine detail.

Tick marks on chart axes (not illustrated) suffer the same disadvantages as gridlines.

**Chart 4.4 E**

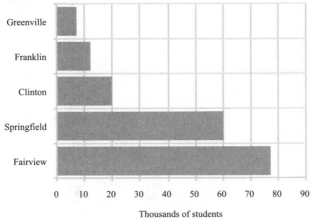

Thousands of students

**Chart 4.4 F**

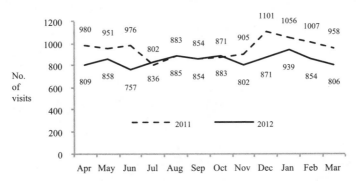

In line chart F (which is the same as the chart in example 4.3), data labels clutter the image so that the point of the chart—that there is an increase in visits to emergency room in December and January—is difficult to detect without careful study.

However, if the chart is to be used for scientific or technical purposes, or if more precise information is essential, the data may be useful to readers. The best solution in these circumstances is to add a data table. Data labels spoil the detection of trends in a chart.

Three-dimensional charts frequently distort data. They make data look more complicated than it is, while the art of communication is to make things look simple.

In chart G, you may guess that the value for Fairview is about 80,000, but it is difficult to make even a crude guess at the numbers for the other four school districts.

**Chart 4.4 G**

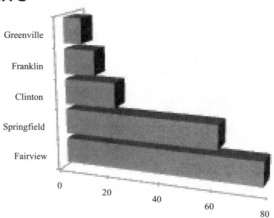

Thousands of students

**Chart 4.4 H**

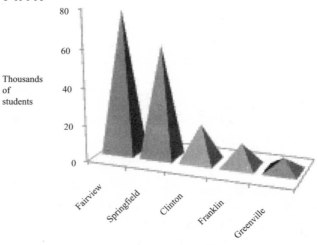

Similarly, odd shapes—as in chart H—will not help readers understand your message or the data. Even readers who take the time to study the chart are unlikely to make sense of it.

## CLARITY OF WORDS

Words that introduce, describe, and summarize help a chart communicate. Pithy wording helps.

### Lucid Labels

Labels play an indispensable role in making charts intelligible. The term "label" covers both the words and the numbers. Advice on labeling specific types of charts is listed under those sections in chapters 5 and 6. Here are some general tips:

- Adopt succinct language. This takes practice, but pays off.
- Use upper and lower case text rather than all capital letters. People read by the shape of words and CAPS have little shape.
- Employ text large enough to read.
- Place text horizontally for legibility. Avoid vertical or angled text, which is more difficult to read.
- Directly label each line, bar, and pie slice. The eye movements involved in flicking from the legend to the chart interrupt memory. Direct labels are more convenient for the reader and reduce the risk of misunderstanding.
- Avoid abbreviations unless they are well known, such as FBI, YMCA, NASA, etc. Even within your own organization or profession, think carefully before using abbreviations.

**Example 4.5: Obscure labels.** This simple line chart is incomprehensible to anyone who is unfamiliar with the term "BRIC." It refers to the economies of Brazil, Russia, India, and China but many, including educated people, would not know this.

**Chart 4.5**

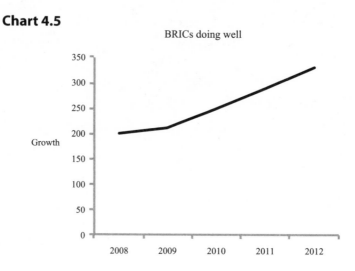

**Example 4.6: Directly label charts and avoid legends.** Directly labeling bars, lines, and slices increases accuracy of interpretation and is more convenient for readers, as the two charts below illustrate.

**Chart 4.6 A**

✓ **Chart 4.6 B**

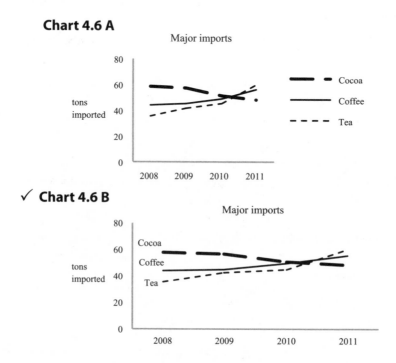

## Include a Summary or Discussion

Charts should be explained or discussed in the surrounding text. Never include an illustration in a report or on a website without referring to it in the text. If the information in the chart does not merit discussion, why include it at all?

A summary can be as short as a sentence or as long as several paragraphs, for instance:

> *Chart 4.6 illustrates that tea and coffee imports have increased over the four years, whereas cocoa import has fallen.*

Notice how the summary starts off by citing the chart number. This ensures that the reader is looking at the correct chart; it looks professional.

## Check, Check, and Recheck

Inadequate or ambiguous wording is one of the most common mistakes in charts. It is important to check your wording and also to get someone else to review it. Then recheck it.

# INTEGRITY OF INTENTION AND ACTION

Many people think charts and statistics lie and mislead. Ill-designed charts leave users feeling disconcerted, excluded, and innumerate. Even well educated readers can feel a lack of confidence in their ability to decipher charts. Some charts may be designed to mislead, but negligence is more frequently the cause of unintelligible charts.

Integrity is as important in graphics as in life. Your charts need not only to be honest, but also to appear to be honest. Accurate, simple, well-labeled charts give confidence to the reader. You can avoid problematic charts by double-checking the data and the presentation.

Below are a few suggestions.

## Name Your Source

Attributing the source for the data gives it authority. It also prevents people from asking you where the numbers came from. In a year, even you may not recall the origin. Adding a list of sources or bibliography is good practice even if the public never sees your work.

## Scale

Choose scale carefully. The unit of comparison and errors may mislead or confuse readers. Scale should accurately represent data and never obscure it. Professionals advise to begin axes at zero or explain why you have not done so. This is to prevent distortion as example 4.7 illustrates.

**Example 4.7: Scale represents data.** Modifying scale can change the message of a chart. The two charts below present the same data. In chart A, the measurement (y-axis) starts at 1,500, and a striking decline is revealed. In chart B, the axis starts at 0, and the trend takes on a different, far less dramatic, shape.

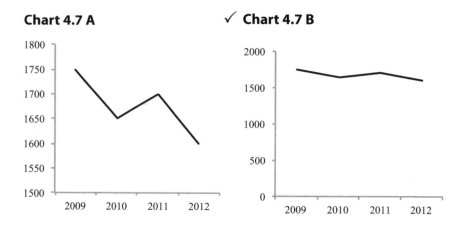

**Chart 4.7 A**                    ✓ **Chart 4.7 B**

Of course, both charts start with 2009 rather than "year one." In displaying time, be sensible and fair. If in 2013 you are considering buying shares in Sears, Roebuck & Co. (founded in 1893), you do not need a 120-year share-value history. Data for the last five or so years would be sufficient.

## Technical Integrity

Charts must be numerically accurate. Your charts may replace numbers with pictures, but the underlying figures demand credibility. If complex relationships and technically sophisticated matters are represented, ensure that they are statistically sound. Such issues are outside the scope of this book, but introductory statistics texts are widely available.

## Maintaining Credibility

To establish and maintain your integrity, ensure that

- scale reflects the numerical information
- titles and labels describe the data
- money is adjusted for inflation (using standardized units)
- a consistent scale is maintained in a series of charts (changing scale can confuse or deceive readers)
- the differences in numbers, not distinctions in design, are emphasised
- you compare like with like

# SUMMARY

Charts are a means of illustrating numeric trends and relationships. They are better at broad points than at fine detail. The best charts enjoy identifiable features. Firstly, they have an unequivocal message. Readers understand their point, which is stated in the title. Your choice of data of the story you wish to tell, makes the difference between a good chart and a bad one.

Successful charts benefit from simple design. The type of chart chosen should be uncomplicated—and never three-dimensional or odd shaped. Chart junk should be deleted—including gridlines, patterned bars, busy backgrounds, shading, and legends.

The best charts enjoy clear and simple labels. Ill-considered wording is a common cause of incomprehensible charts. Labels need to be succinct, horizontal, and large enough to read. Label bars, lines, and slices individually. Avoid abbreviations unless commonly known. A summary discussion should always be included.

Finally, successful charts possess integrity of intention and action. Many people are suspicious of charts and statistics. It is more common to mislead people by accident than by design, but it is better not to mislead at all. Communicate honestly by listing your sources, making scale evident, and ensuring your work is statistically valid and presented in context.

## WANT TO KNOW MORE?

Few, Stephen. *Show Me the Numbers*. Burlingame, CA: Analytics Press, 2004.

Robbins, Naomi B. *Creating More Effective Charts*. Hoboken, NJ: John Wiley & Sons, 2005.

Tufte, Edward R. *The Visual Display of Quantitative Information*. Cheshire, CT: The Graphics Press, 2001.

# Chapter 5

# Basic Charts

OVER THE LAST few hundred years, a variety of numeric charts have developed for the purposes of analyzing data or expressing ideas. All types are successful when correctly employed. This chapter looks at the most popular, common types of numeric charts. Technical and specialist charts are discussed in chapter 6

## Which Chart to Use When?

✓ useful  ✓✓ very useful

| | Parts of a whole | Use for Changes over time | Comparisons |
|---|---|---|---|
| Bar | ✓✓ | ✓ | ✓ |
| Line | | ✓✓ | ✓ |
| Pie | ✓ | | |

## BAR CHARTS

Bar charts represent quantities through bars or columns. Bar charts compare differences between two or more sets of numbers. You can use bar charts to:

- ▲ compare different quantities (e.g., the cost of loans from different banks or the number of students at different colleges)
- ▲ show changes over time (however, line charts are frequently better at this)
- ▲ show parts of a whole, such as divisions of a budget, sales figures from all branches, etc.

Example 5.1: A simple bar chart.

✓ **Chart 5.1**

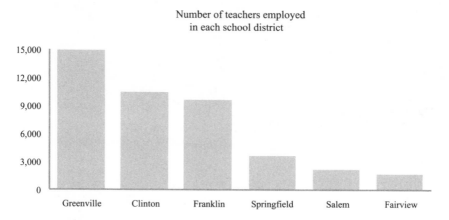

## *Bar or Column?*

Bars may be placed horizontally or vertically, in which case they are called columns. Horizontal bars are easier to label, and more bars can be shown down the side of a chart than across its base.

Some people find it logical to show speed and distance with columns and to show money and other measures associated with "up" and "down" through horizontal bars.

**Example 5.2: A simple horizontal bar chart.** This horizontal bar chart is a version of the bar chart in example 5.1.

✓ **Chart 5.2**

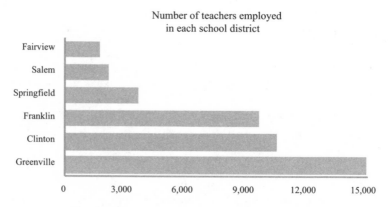

## *Constructing Bar Charts*

Below is some specific advice on designing bar charts.

- ▲ Use bars of equal width and varying lengths. Unequal widths create optical distortions, causing readers to misunderstand the relative values.

- ▲ Order bars by size if logical to do so. Doing so gives the chart an appearance of order and a professional look, and it helps the reader see relationships quickly.

- ▲ Label clearly.

**Example 5.3: Ordering bars by size.** The first chart is arranged alphabetically. The eye must adjust to the variety in bar lengths. Rearranged by size (as in the second chart), relationships are immediately apparent. These charts contain the same data as in example 5.1.

✓ **Chart 5.3 A**

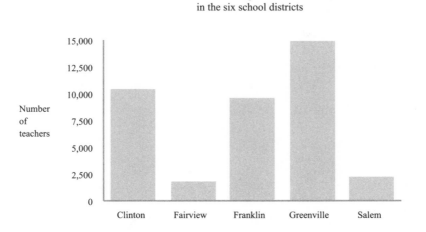

Greenville has the largest number of teachers
in the six school districts

✓ **Chart 5.3 B**

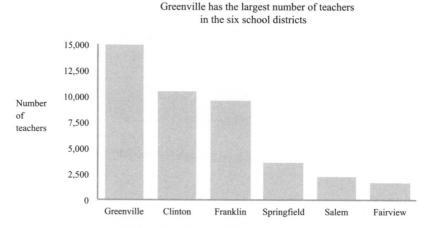

Greenville has the largest number of teachers
in the six school districts

## Bars Representing Parts of a Whole

Bar charts can show parts of a whole, although pie charts are more frequently employed for this purpose. The advantage of a bar chart is that
the reader can assess the lengths of the bars at a glance, but comparing
the size of pie slices is more difficult, as example 5.4 illustrates.

In either case, it is helpful to include the total under the title so the
reader has an idea of overall size.

**Example 5.4: Showing parts of a whole with a bar chart and a pie chart.**

✓ **Chart 5.4 A**

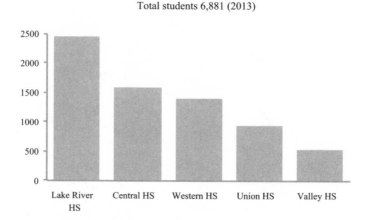

Lake River High School has the largest
number of students
Total students 6,881 (2013)

**Chart 5.4 B**

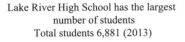

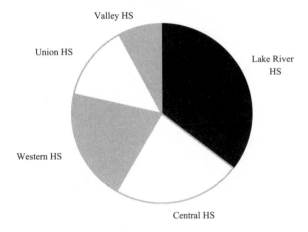

## *Paired Bar Charts*

Paired bars (sometimes called grouped bar charts) compare two or more coupled items. You can use them to contrast males and females, two time periods, levels of car ownership in two states, etc.

Paired bar charts are less than ideal: charts communicate more efficiently when presenting just one message, and these offer at least two ways of seeing the data. Readers may puzzle over what information to compare.

Like component bars and layered line charts (discussed later in this chapter), paired bars can distort information and may be confusing. Keep your message simple and test samples on friends.

The principle, as always, is that information to be compared should be physically close. Comprehensive and comprehensible titles and summaries will help compensate for these problems.

**Example 5.5: Paired bar chart.** It is important to choose the correct primary category for paired bar charts. Below, chart A focuses on the sport and who plays it (males or females). Chart B primarily looks at males and what sport they play, then at females and what sport they play.

## ✓ Chart 5.5 A

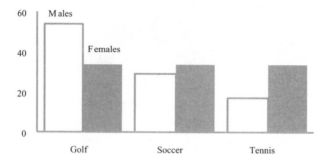

More males than females play golf, but
more females play soccer and tennis
% participants

## ✓ Chart 5.5 B

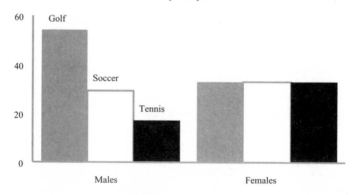

More males play golf than soccer or tennis.
Equal numbers of females play all three sports
% participants

## *Component Bar Charts*

Component (also called sub-divided or stacked) bars consist of two or
more segments. Like paired bar charts, they have subcategories. Like pie
charts, they are used to show parts of the whole. A component bar chart
has parts of a whole stacked on top of one another. A paired bar chart
has parts of a whole plotted side by side.

Component bars rarely justify themselves. They are needlessly
complex, necessarily telling more than one story. Further, they easily

distort the appearance of the data. There is so much information packed into a component bar chart that it is hard for the reader to find meaning.

When the lowest or initial segments of a component bar chart vary in size—as they usually do—the subsequent segments begin at different points. The sizes of the individual segments become difficult to detect and comparisons distorted. Even with a definitive title, the chart is likely to remain a puzzle to the reader.

**Example 5.6: Component bar chart.** In chart A, the varying lengths of the first segment (bronze) means that the sizes of the subsequent segments are difficult to compare. This data may be more effectively presented as a table, or one may combine the three classes of metal and present a simple bar chart as in chart 5.6 B.

**Chart 5.6 A**

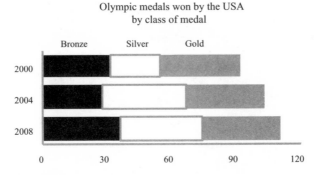

**✓ Chart 5.6 B**

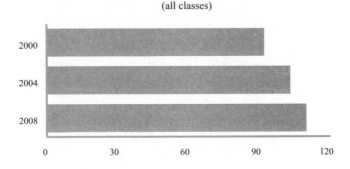

## *Negative Bars*

Bar charts are capable of carrying negative information, such as financial losses and negative percentage changes. With a definitive title, these charts can communicate with ease.

**Example 5.7: Negative bar chart.** Labelling always presents a problem with negative quantities. Popular software manufacturers seem unwilling to help. Listing the bars by size and including an explanatory title assists readers in following the message.

✓ **Chart 5.7**

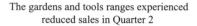

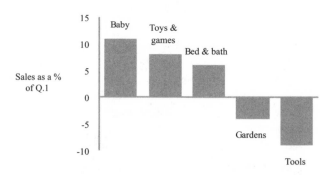

## *Changes Over Time*

Although bar charts can be used to show changes over time, line charts are usually more effective at this.

**Example 5.8: Bar charts over time.** The bar chart below is readable, but only when the data is presented as a line graph do the trends come alive. With the line graph, you can quickly track the changes over the period.

**Chart 5.8**

**Example 5.9: Demonstrating time.** Bar charts are preferable for showing time changes when there are fewer than four data points, as shown in chart B. Line graphs work best when a trend is detectable, that is, four data points or more.

**Chart 5.9 A**

✓ **Chart 5.9 B**

# LINE GRAPHS

Line graphs demonstrate changes in a series, usually over time. Line graphs have a great ability to show trends—the ups and downs in the long-term picture. You can use line graphs to:

- ▲ measure changes over time, such as minutes, months, years, centuries, unemployment or birth rates, sales per month, or crop yields per year
- ▲ measure other continuums or linear expressions, such as temperature or distance
- ▲ show relationship among several figures

Line graphs can be elegant. Also, unlike bar and pie charts, they have the ability to show patterns that are difficult to identify by looking at the numbers in a table.

Understanding line charts is easy if they are kept simple in design and given an explanatory title.

**Example 5.10: A simple line graph.** This graph depicts increases in speed. Although most line graphs demonstrate changes over time, they can also show other linear expressions. Another example would be, for instance, how contamination levels vary with increasing distance from the origin.

✓ **Chart 5.10 A**

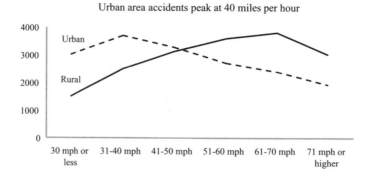

## *Constructing Line Graphs*

Design, labeling, and placement of charts follows the general guidelines discussed in chapter 4. Line graphs especially rely on

- ▲ a limited number of lines
- ▲ direct labelling

Use up to four lines. More lines clutter the chart, cause labeling to be problematic, and make patterns difficult to identify. If you have more than four lines, try combining categories or using a table.

Place labels on lines and avoid legends. This helps to assure accurate interpretation.

**Example 5.11: How many lines?** Chart A below presents no explicit story; it merely presents reference material. By combining categories—as in chart B—a simpler, more coherent chart can be created.

## Chart 5.11 A

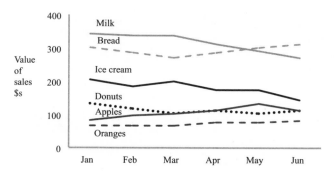

Sales of major food items

## ✓ Chart 5.11 B

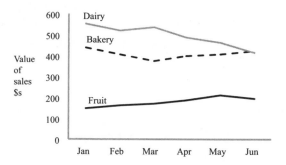

Sales of dairy and fruit fell during May and June

## Too Few Data Points

As discussed in example 5.9, line graphs need four or more data points to show a valid trend.

## Layered Line Graphs

Layered line graphs (sometimes called area line graphs) are often seen in newspapers and textbooks. They share the problems of component bar charts. Because the segments are piled on top of one another, the shape of the upper categories can become distorted. These charts sacrifice comprehension for showmanship.

**Example 5.12: Layered line graph.** This chart layers the data presented in chart B in example 5.11. Nothing is gained by using layers, and only confusion is added.

**Chart 5.12**

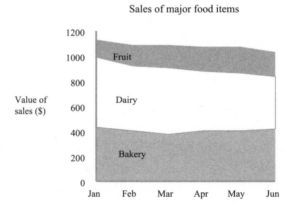

If you use a layered line graph, place the layer with the steepest or sharpest slope at the top and that with the least slope at the bottom. That should reduce some of the distortion. Even following this rule, readers may misinterpret the comparisons.

# PIE CHARTS

Pie charts show parts of a whole in a circle. No points for guessing why it is called a pie chart. You can use pie charts to:

- ▲ show parts of a whole by percentages, such as the breakdown of a budget or the percentage of students at local elementary, middle, and high schools

- ▲ emphasize how components make up the whole

**Example 5.13: Simple pie chart.**

**Chart 5.13**

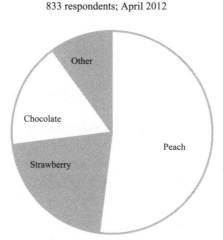

Most customers prefer our peach ice cream
833 respondents; April 2012

## *The Problem with Pies*

Pie charts demand that the viewer compare quantities in a circle, but most of us think linearly. It is easier to compare lengths of bars or columns along a straight line than wedge shapes in a circle. Despite their popularity, pie charts do not communicate well. Specialists in visual literacy, as well as many statisticians, avoid them.

On the positive side, many people seem to like pie charts, so we offer some advice on designing and presenting them. Understanding the disadvantages of the shape will help you use them as effectively as possible.

## *Constructing Pie Charts*

Constructing pie charts is relatively straightforward. Follow the general guidelines set out in chapter 4. To successfully use pie charts, do the following:

- ▲ Arrange the slices in an order, usually largest to smallest, beginning at the twelve o'clock position. This helps readers grasp the relative sizes accurately. Many software programs do not do this automatically; you have to reorder the data to achieve size order.

- ▲ Give some idea of volume or quantity. Add this in the title so the reader will understand the size of the whole.

- ▲ Limit the number of slices. Pies work best with four or fewer slices. More than three crowd the chart and can be difficult to label.

- ▲ Avoid comparing two or more pie charts with one another. Although such displays are common, twin pies compound the problem of comparing information presented in a circle.

Pie charts communicate most successfully when showing a whole divided into four or fewer parts. For clarity, each pie slice needs an individual label, and too many labels hinder comprehension.

**Example 5.14: Limit the number of slices.** The nine slices in chart A make the data almost useless. You could substitute a legend, but the reader would have to flick from a pie slice to the legend and back again. Legends add muddle, not clarity. The revised chart, B, combines categories, and the chart becomes easy to understand. But notice also chart C. It is only trying to tell one story, which is what charts do best. Whereas charts A and B look vague, chart C is decisive. Remember that charts excel at showing the big picture and are less effective at showing detail. Multiple categories reduce the impact of the image.

## Chart 5.14 A

Value of food sold, popular products
Total value $1,263  July 2012

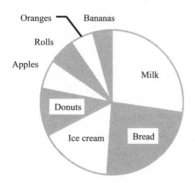

## Chart 5.14 B

Nearly half the value of our popular products comes from dairy
Total value $1,263  July 2012

## ✓ Chart 5.14 C

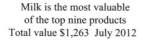

Milk is the most valuable
of the top nine products
Total value $1,263  July 2012

## *Comparing Pie Charts*

Newspapers and advertising often present two or more pie charts side by side for comparison. Try to avoid this. Comparing slices within a single pie chart is difficult enough without expecting the reader to then compare data from another circle.

**Example 5.15: Comparing pie charts.** These two pie charts have been placed side by side with the purpose of easy comparison. However, their differences need to be studied. Splitting the data between two charts makes it more difficult to read and understand. Comparative pie charts are a puzzle for the reader to work out.

### Chart 5.15 A

College majors chosen by females, 2012

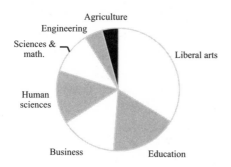

### Chart 5.15 B

College majors chosen by males, 2012

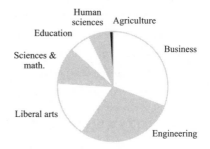

A simple table (page 68) gives more detail and is easier to read. As is often the case, numbers are more vivid than charts.

Choice of college major subject by gender (numbers), 2012

|  | Males | Females | Total |
|---|---|---|---|
| Liberal arts | 300 | 660 | 1,000 |
| Business | 550 | 290 | 840 |
| Engineering | 510 | 93 | 600 |
| Education | 110 | 340 | 460 |
| Sciences and mathematics | 190 | 220 | 410 |
| Human sciences | 19 | 280 | 300 |
| Agriculture | <u>83</u> | <u>110</u> | <u>200</u> |
| Total | 1,800 | 2,000 | 3,800 |

*Figures have been rounded, so columns may not equal totals.*

## SUMMARY

There are three basic types of numeric charts: bar, line, and pie.

Bar charts can be displayed either horizontally or vertically. Bar charts can be used to show parts of a whole, show changes over time, and compare quantities; they can also be used to show negatives clearly. Paired and component bar charts have important disadvantages for both designers and readers.

Line graphs are most frequently used to show changes over time, although they also have other uses. They need to illustrate over four or more data points and communicate most easily when kept to four or fewer lines. There are problems associated with layered line graphs.

Finally, pie charts can be used to show parts of a whole. They remain popular although their circular display presents fundamental comprehension problems to readers. To ease readability, limit the number of pie slices and arrange in size order clockwise from the twelve o'clock position. Two or more comparative pies aside one another present the reader with an unnecessarily complex display to unravel.

## WANT TO KNOW MORE?

Few, Stephen. *Show Me the Numbers.* Burlingame, CA: Analytics Press, 2004.

Tufte, Edward R. *The Visual Display of Quantitative Information.* Cheshire, CT: The Graphics Press, 2001.

# Chapter 6

# Technical and Specialist Charts and Data Visualization

A CHART MAY be called technical or specialist if:

▲ its primary purpose is analyzing and exploring data (e.g., tools to explore multivariate data, that is, data involving two or more variables) or

▲ it has been designed for a specific audience familiar enough with the display to read and interpret it quickly and accurately (e.g., to the trained eye, stock charts instantly indicate changes of commodity prices; to the inexperienced, they require time to decode and interpret)

Some of these, like scatter plots and histograms, were developed long ago. Others, like tree maps, are relatively new and a response to technological change and the growth of data. Still others are variations of old charts (sparklines are a type of line or bar graph) or combinations of classic charts put together to tackle modern problems (executive dashboards).

**Data visualization.** In its broadest sense, data visualization may be defined as the use of images for information. It is a

twenty-first century expression, and a final definition has yet to be settled. Thus, it may cover anything from a simple bar chart to motion charts and parallel coordinates. Data visualization is linked with interactive software and the handling of huge amounts of data yet is not limited to displays with those features.

The term "data visualization" is particularly, but not exclusively, used to encompass

- displays that appear in newspapers and magazines such as the *New York Times* and the UK's *Guardian*, which present data relating to newsworthy issues (e.g., election results, competition among search engines, and the proliferation of nuclear weapons across countries) in a series of charts or tables or a single graphic

- displays where multiple representations of charts (or tables) are used (for instance, business information presented on a dashboard or score card)

- new types of charts designed for specialists analysis of data (for instance, tree maps)

---

All charts add value when appropriately employed. Some specialist charts can successfully be used for both analysis and communication, whereas others are effective only for analysis by statisticians, business analysts, etc. Using the wrong chart, or using a chart wrongly, is likely to lead to wasted time, confusion, and poor decision making. The table below categorizes the charts discussed in this chapter by their functions and effectiveness as a communications tool.

Functions of technical and specialist charts

| | At the discovery stage* | At the presentation stage* it can communicate to: | | |
|---|---|---|---|---|
| | Type of analysis provided | General audience | Specialist audience | Not a communications tool |
| Scatter plot | Multivariate analysis | ✓ | | |
| Bubble chart | Multivariate analysis | ✓ | | |
| Motion chart | Multivariate analysis | ✓ | | |
| Histograms | Frequency distribution | ✓ | | |
| Radar chart | Multivariate analysis | | ✓ | |
| Dashboard | Presentation of management information | | ✓ | |
| Sparkline | Abbreviation of classic charts | | ✓ | |
| Stock chart or candlestick | Presentation of price variations in a market | | ✓ | |
| Superimposed | Comparison of two sets of data | | | ✓ |
| Parallel coordinates | Analysis of categorical data | | | ✓ |
| Tree map | Analysis of hierarchical data | | | ✓ |

* For the difference between the discovery and presentation stages, see chapter 8

**Example 6.1 ✓ : Titles make a difference.** Poor labeling—rather than difficult or specialist content—makes this scatter plot difficult to interpret. Example 6.2 shows the same chart with comprehensible and comprehensive wording that is accessible to the general public.

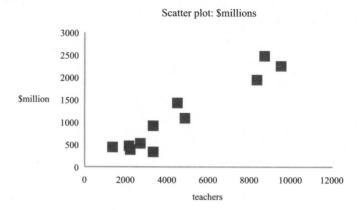

Scatter plot: $millions

Below, different types of specialist and technical charts are defined and explained with emphasis on their use as tools of presentation.

## SCATTER PLOTS

Scatter plots reveal if there is a relationship between variables shown through dots. Like line graphs, scatter plots are plotted on horizontal and vertical axes.

You can use scatter plots to:

- ▴ identify if a correlation between variables exists
- ▴ analyze large amounts of data (scatter plots often show hundreds of data points; they can reveal outliers, that is, deviations from the overall pattern)
- ▴ present sophisticated data analysis to a wide audience

**Example 6.2: Scatter plots.** Below are two scatter plots designed to communicate information to a wide audience. Chart A depicts a positive correlation between the numbers of teachers in a school district and the amount spent on education. You can tell that the correlation is positive because the dots curve upward from bottom left to top right. As could be predicted, districts that spend more on education also tend to have more teachers.

✓ A: Positive correlation

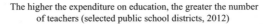

The higher the expenditure on education, the greater the number
of teachers (selected public school districts, 2012)

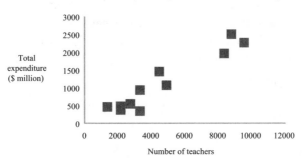

A comprehensive, explanatory title gives viewers confidence that
they have understood the chart.

Chart B shows the same data but also includes an outlier, Rose Hill.
With this you can see that Rose Hill's expenditure on education is high
relative to the number of teachers employed when compared to the other
districts. The summary points to that fact, so you can be sure that viewers
will be able to interpret the chart accurately.

✓ B:  Scatter plot with outlier

Rose Hill's expenditure on education is relatively high for the
number of teachers employed compard with other districts
(selected public school districts, 2012)

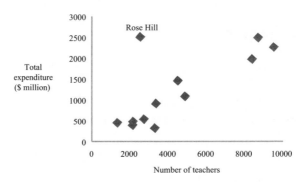

## Bubble Charts

Bubble charts are scatter plots with a third (and sometimes forth) variable, the bubble. They show if there is a correlation between variables.
The bubble size is often used to depict the population of the item in
question, as is the case in example 6.3.

Occasionally, and especially on the Internet, bubbles are shown in several colors with the colors signifying a fourth variable.

**Example 6.3: Bubble chart.** The chart below uses the same data as in example 6.1 A, but the size of bubble varies according to the number of under eighteen year olds in the local population. It is apparent that districts with large populations of children (the biggest bubbles) are likely to spend more on education and to have more teachers.

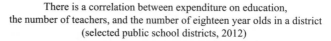

There is a correlation between expenditure on education, the number of teachers, and the number of eighteen year olds in a district (selected public school districts, 2012)

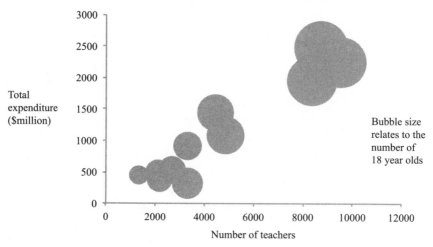

## MOTION CHARTS

Motion charts are animated bubble charts that illustrate even more variables than a multicolored bubble chart.

The most famous motion chart is the product of Hans Rosling, a Swedish public health expert. Examples of his work are viewable on his website, www.gapminder.org/, and on other public sites, such as You Tube.com. They can be stunning (as is Rosling's) and help viewers see changes over time of populations, wealth, and longevity.

## RADAR CHARTS

Radar charts—also called spider graphs or star charts—are circular charts frequently used to display performance measures. Radar charts can be used to analyze multivariate data—each axis will represent a variable.

Radar charts may be useful as a communication tool to an audience familiar enough with the data to have an expectation of the result. For instance, they may be used effectively for weekly management information. In such cases, experienced viewers can glance at the radar and quickly interpret readings as being higher or lower than expected.

Radar graphs are unhelpful in annual reports and other one-off reports where readers are unfamiliar with the content of the chart. In those cases, a simple table, as in example 6.4 B, is more likely to communicate ideas efficiently.

## *Advice*

Keep the chart as simple as possible.

- ▲ Use subtle gridlines or none at all. Grids may be confused with lines of measure.

- ▲ Radar charts provide only a broad understanding of the data. For precise information, use a table (as in example 6.4 B).

- ▲ Use a maximum of six indicators (that is, six star points); more are difficult to interpret.

**Example 6.4: Radar chart and table.** The chart shows five variables related to company performance compared over two quarters and shown on a scale of 0-6, where 0 is poor and 6 the excellent. Chart A may inform frequent users of changes at a glance. For audiences unfamiliar with the data, a well laid out table, as is table B, will communicate more effectively.

A Radar chart

Performance was worse in the 3rd quarter
(4.5 and above meets annual target)

B Table with the same data

Scores for Quarter 2 and 3 4.5 and above

|                      | Q.2 | Q.3 |
| -------------------- | --- | --- |
| Sales                | 4.5 | 4.2 |
| Delivery periods     | 2.8 | 2.7 |
| Payments             | 5.8 | 3.2 |
| Returns              | 4.2 | 3.8 |
| Customer satisfaction| 5.3 | 2.1 |
| Average              | 4.5 | 3.2 |

# HISTOGRAMS

Histograms illustrate the distribution or frequency of items within a range. They look similar to bar charts and communicate by giving the reader a picture of where, within given ranges, the data is dispersed.

Histograms are used to:

- anticipate the likelihood of events based on observations (for instance, most students will score between 70 percent and 89 percent on a test)

- summarize vast amounts of data (for instance, in August most sales were made between 10 a.m. and noon)

- analyze and check information (for instance, that most respondents to a large consumer survey are between thirty and fifty years of age)

Histograms are frequently used to analyze data but, like scatter plots, can also be used as a communication tool.

**Example 6.5✓: A simple histogram.** Notice the style: column bars are used, and there are no gaps between the bars.

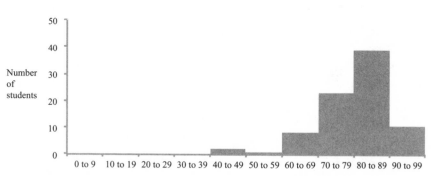

Most students scored between 70 and 89 on the biology test
(84 students; May 2013)

## *Advice for Presenting Histograms*

- The widths of bars should be proportionate to the size they represent. This resizing of individual bars is difficult to achieve on many software programs. In some cases, you can work around this by creating categories of equal size.

- By convention, columns are used rather than horizontal bars.
- By convention, there are no gaps between the columns.
- The minimum number of bars is five and the maximum twenty. No pattern emerges with fewer than five bars, and a chart with more than twenty bars is unwieldy and uninformative.

## Superimposed Graphs

Superimposed graphs compare two sets of data on one graph, each with its own y-axis. Commonly, they are a combination of bar and line graphs, but occasionally two lines with different scales are shown.

A major disadvantage of superimposed graphs is that the two y-axes are easily confused. To an extent, this can be overcome by thoughtful labeling.

Another problem is that both y-axes should ordinarily start at the same point, and that would usually be 0. Different starting points can drastically alter the appearance of the chart and distort any comparison.

**Example 6.6: A superimposed chart.** With two axes, superimposed charts are easily misread. Notice how the y-axes labels identify which data they refer to (bars or lines).

**Chart 6.6**

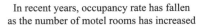

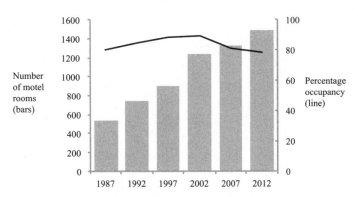

An alternative to a superimposed chart is presenting two graphs close to one another, as shown below. With two graphs, relationships are obvious and labeling unambiguous.

✓

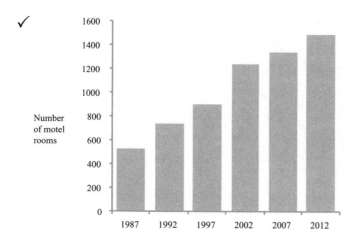

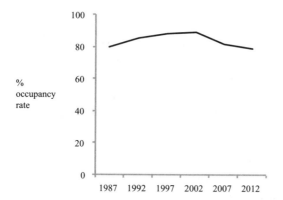

# DASHBOARDS

A dashboard is a single-page display of business information or key performance indicators that can be read at a glance the way a driver uses a vehicle's dashboard.

Dashboards (or executive dashboards) typically show two or more charts or tables and are updated automatically and regularly. They are used to monitor, rather than analyze, what is going on. They are typically a computer application and, in more sophisticated models, users are able to "drill down" for greater detail.

Advice on dashboard design is widely available online and in books. A few important points:

▴ use the rules of plain figures, and design for the convenience of the audience

▲ ensure labels and text are large enough to read

▲ avoid relying on color as the only way to interpret an indicator (color on screens varies; viewers may be color-blind)

▲ provide consistent measures (for instance, show everything in US dollars to two decimal places, thousands of tons of weight, etc.)

Also, the following rules apply if the data will be read from a screen:

▲ Keep to a single page. (No scrolling!)

▲ Avoid design that hides data and forces users to click for detail.

▲ Avoid designs that move from one data set to another at predetermined periods, say every ten seconds. This frustrates users who need more time or less.

**Example 6.7: An executive dashboard.** A large amount of data can be collated and presented conveniently for the target audience of managers.

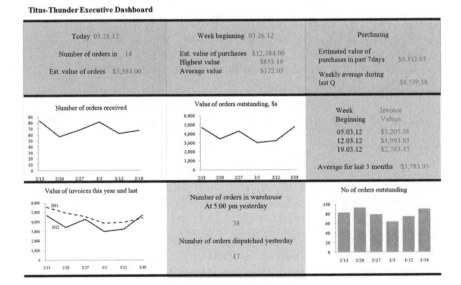

# OTHER SPECIALIST CHARTS

A brief discussion on a few more specialist charts is set out below.

**Parallel coordinates** are used to analyze individual data elements across numerous categories. One application would be exploring data from fifteen thousand individual school districts by categories such as students, teachers, finance, number and type of schools, etc. With parallel coordinates, researchers and analysts are able to detect patterns and exceptions and make informed comparisons. This can lead, for instance, to the spotting of errors in a data collection or informing and refining future research. Parallel coordinates are not a tool for presentation; they are used just for analysis.

**Tree maps** are computer-aided charts used to represent proportional values and hierarchal relationships at the same time. They display dozens of rectangles distinguishable by color and size. Tree maps may be used, for instance, to analyze the consumption of limited resources, such as finance or computer storage.

Two important points:

- ▴ Tree maps are sometimes misused to show simple parts of a whole in a rectangle. The result is an overly complex chart, which is difficult to interpret. A simple table, a bar chart, or a pie chart is easier to read.

- ▴ When designing a tree map, remember to use color sensitively. Around 8 percent of American males are color blind.

**Sparklines** are very small, condensed line charts inserted into lines of text. The size allows sparklines to be embedded in the text like this: ⬚ . They usually present a trend of some sort and are appropriate for data that changes frequently, like stock market quotes. Labels, axes, or coordinates are omitted because sparklines are restricted to audiences who are familiar with the data and trained in using it.

The original use of sparklines was in medical reports and showed, for instances, the changes in a patient's temperature or glucose levels. They are also used to show variations in stock market prices and exchange rates fluctuations.

**Stock charts** (or candlestick charts) are time-series bar charts that represent the changes in stock market prices of a particular product. Stock charts help traders ascertain the current supply and demand for items, with each bar showing four points: opening price, closing price, highest price, and lowest price.

To a trained eye, the design of each bar is immediately informative. For instance, a large "shadow" (stalk or point) below a bar (or candle) is a sign of strength, and a large "shadow" above a bar indicates weakness.

**Example 6.8: A stock chart.** This stock chart presents data for a company, covering five days. When the closing price is lower than the opening, the body (or bar or candle) is dark (or filled); when the closing price is higher, it is white (or not filled).

**Chart 6.8**

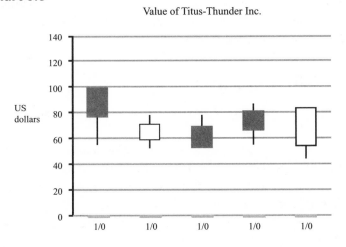

Value of Titus-Thunder Inc.

## SUMMARY

Technical and special charts are those that are designed primarily for the purpose of analyzing data or for a trained audience. Some of these charts can be used to communicate with a general audience, while others are not useful as a communication tool. As always, coherent titles and wording makes technical and specialist charts readable.

Data visualization is a new term and remains imprecisely defined. By some definitions, it covers everything from the humble pie chart to specialist, interactive charts designed.

Scatter plots, bubble charts, and motion charts are used to identify relationships among variables on an x-y axes plot. Radar charts are frequently used to display performance measures and may be useful for an audience familiar with their content.

Histograms look like bar charts, illustrate the distinction between items within a range, and have a number of practical uses.

Superimposed graphs usually display a combination of line and bar charts. They usually involve two scales and because of this are easily misinterpreted.

Dashboards are used to show business or performance data on a single page or screen and typically show several charts as well as other data. There is much advice online and elsewhere about designing readable dashboards, but the rules of plain figures are a sound starting point.

Other types of specialist charts exist, such as parallel coordinates, tree maps, sparklines, and stock charts. Before employing any of these, you should ensure you understand the purpose of the chart and how it can most effectively be used.

## WANT TO KNOW MORE?

Few, Stephen. *Information Dashboard Design*. Sebastopol, CA: O'Reilly Media, 2006.

———. "Data Visualization: Past, Present & Future." *Perceptual Edge*. 10 Jan. 2007 (available on the Internet free of charge).

Harris, Robert L. *Information Graphics: A Comprehensive Illustrated Reference*. New York: Oxford University Press, 1999.

Iliinsky, Noah, and Julie Steele. *Designing Data Visualization*. Sebastopol, CA: O'Reilly Media, 2009.

Tufte, Edward R. *The Visual Display of Quantitative Information*. Cheshire, CT: The Graphics Press, 2001.

Wainer, Howard. "How to Display Data Badly." *The American Statistician* 38, no. 2 (May 1984): 137-147 (available on the Internet free of charge).

Yau, Nathan. *Visualize This*. Indianapolis, IN: Wiley Publishing, 2011.

There are numerous websites about charts and data visualizations. These are among the most useful and relevant:

http://flowingdata.com/ (Nathan Yau's entertaining data visualization website)

www.perceptualedge.com (Stephen Few's website; excellent blog and free downloads about data presentation and visualization)

www.visualisingdata.com (UK website specializing in data visualization)

## Chapter 7

# Table or Chart?

TABLES AND CHARTS may be seen as tools of communication. When correctly employed, the most modest tool will work wonders. Similarly, when expected to perform a job outside its functionality, the most sophisticated device will fail. This chapter explains how to choose between a table or a chart, and the following diagram illustrates the process involved in this choice:

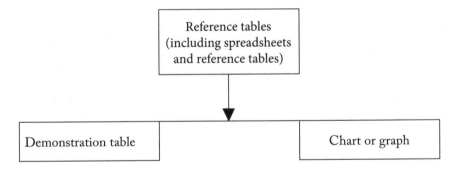

The choice of table or chart should be based on the data and your purpose. Tables and each type of chart possess individual traits that compliment particular uses. When choosing, bear in mind the needs and expectations of the audience.

Although currently unfashionable, tables have much going for them. A well-designed reference table allows convenient lookup of information; a thoughtfully considered demonstration table displays patterns and exceptions that cannot be shown in a chart. On the other hand, a correctly employed chart will reveal relationships that are difficult to see when looking at a reference table.

**Table or chart?** The lists below explain the efficacious use of tables and the more common types of charts.

Table – The default choice. Use for:

- ▲ precise numbers
- ▲ large amounts of numbers (reference material)
- ▲ great range between the smallest and largest numbers (for instance, the numbers 59 and 3,500,000 are perceptible in a table, but on a chart the 59 is likely to be lost)
- ▲ data that includes more than one unit (e.g., thousands of people and percentage of unemployment; a mixture of units cannot be shown easily on any chart)

Chart – Employ only when it will communicate the concept more easily than a table. Use for:

- ▲ trends (as in a line graph)
- ▲ correlation between variables (as in a scatter plot)
- ▲ frequency distribution (as in a histogram)
- ▲ changes across time and distances, and in temperature (as in a line graph).

## Tips

- ▲ Use tables as your default. They are more versatile than charts.
- ▲ Do a quick sketch of your table or chart, and see what it looks like before investing time on your computer.

**Example 7.1: Tables can be the most efficient way to present data.** In the example below, the author wanted to illustrate how much was spent on the four major food categories (fruit, dairy, baked goods, and fish) and also to give detail about the fruit. On a table it is easy to display these two different ideas.

Unfortunately, the only type of chart that is appropriate for this combination of ideas—a composite of two linked pie charts—is taxing even with data labels included.

✓  Cost of food purchased, March 2013 ($)

| Fruit | Apples | 56 |
|---|---|---|
| | Bananas | 35 |
| | Oranges | 22 |
| | | 113 |
| Dairy | | 99 |
| Baked goods | | 73 |
| Fish | | 44 |
| | | 329 |

**Chart 7.1**

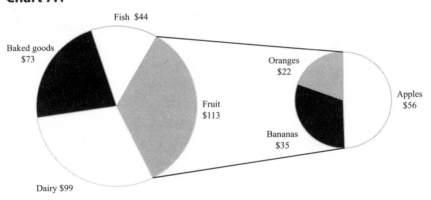

On the other hand, there are times when charts communicate trends and the patterns in data that are hard to see when looking at a table, as example 7.2 illustrates.

**Example 7.2: Use a chart to show trends.** The table and chart below present the same information. The chart shows patterns more vividly than the table. By merely glancing at the chart, you can see that participation in the workforce fell for men and increased steadily for women from 1950 through 2000. After that, participation fell for women as well as men. Detecting those trends in the table (see next page) takes much study.

Participation in the workforce by gender,
% of population aged 18 to 62, 1950—2010, Greenville

|  | Males | Females |
|---|---|---|
| 1950 | 88 | 35 |
| 1960 | 85 | 39 |
| 1970 | 81 | 43 |
| 1980 | 79 | 47 |
| 1990 | 78 | 52 |
| 2000 | 75 | 61 |
| 2010 | 73 | 59 |

✓ **Chart 7.2**

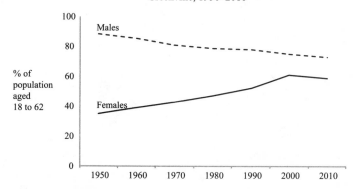

As women's participation in the workforce has increased;
participation by men has fallen.
Greenville, 1950–2010

## SUMMARY

Before choosing between a table and a chart, consider the data and your purpose. Tables often communicate numeric ideas more readily than charts. Charts can usefully reveal trends and patterns that are difficult to see in tables, but use a chart only when you are sure it will communicate more effectively than a table.

### WANT TO KNOW MORE?

Few, Stephen. *Show Me the Numbers*. Burlingame, CA: Analytics Press, 2004.

Tufte, Edward R. *The Visual Display of Quantitative Information*. Cheshire, CT: The Graphics Press, 2001.

Chapter 8

# Working with Numbers

WORKING EFFICIENTLY WITH numbers is a skill largely borne of experience, but this chapter offers a few suggestions and shortcuts that may help. It sets out the two stages of working with numbers, discusses how to make data relevant to an audience, and offers a trick on how to analyze data quickly.

## TWO STAGES

There are two stages in working with figures: discovery and presentation.

### Stage One: Looking to Discover

When first examining a data set, you may wish to play with the numbers and try out different charts or demonstration tables in an effort to identify patterns and exceptions, trends, and relationships. The outcome of this discovery stage should be a clear understanding of what the numbers mean.

## STAGE TWO: TELLING A STORY

Once you have settled on a message or story for your audience and have chosen the optimal method of displaying it, you are at the presentation stage. The display should no longer be a puzzle but a precise, coherent demonstration table or chart designed, as always, for the convenience of the audience.

Knowing the difference between the discovery and presentation stages—and being able to identify what stage you are at—will save time and frustration.

# SELECTING SPECIFIC NUMBERS, TABLES, AND GRAPHS

To make your numeric presentation cogent, present your data with comparisons and show, where appropriate, cause and effect. Moreover, it is vital that your data be timely and accurate.

## *Compare*

When you use numbers, compare. Compare to last year, or to last century, or to Norway, or to your competitors, or to common expectations. Comparisons make numbers relevant.

Look at the two examples below. The first gives some information, but we do not know if the number of accidents is to be expected or if it is unusual. By introducing comparisons—the second example below—the information becomes more relevant and informative.

(a) In 2012, forty-three accidents were reported at the Greenville depot of the Diaz Track & Tool Company.

(b) The Greenville depot reported forty-three accidents in 2012. This was 10 percent less than the previous year and well below the seventy plus accidents reported by the Auburn branch.

## *Illustrate Cause and Effect*

Showing cause and effect makes numbers exciting as well as informative. Reasons and results make up the stories that numbers tell. If you include figures in your work, they must somehow contribute to your overall purpose. This report, from a large retail store, sets out a valid point with obvious logic.

*A second rainy, cold summer has reduced our sales of sunscreen by 12 percent. However, umbrella sales increased by nearly 40 percent.*

Relationships should be established, not coincidental.

## *Be Timely*

Sales figures from sixteen years ago will not persuade anyone, but last quarter's figures might. Sometimes getting timely figures takes extra effort, but it does make your work more persuasive, vital, and pertinent.

## *Be Accurate*

Nothing can kill your credibility quicker than unreliable figures.

Most of us work with secondary data that was gathered from surveys, government publications, newspapers or journals, company reports, or elsewhere. If you are working with other people's numbers, tailor the message to the audience through your selection and presentation.

Remember to credit the source, and do not distort information.

# SIMPLE DATA ANALYSIS

Human beings are inclined to choose numbers to support their own ideas, suspicions, and prejudices. This "number picking" can lead to mistaken, distorted, or misleading impressions. A quick, rough analysis will help you gain a balanced view. Below is a short and simple, if crude, technique to analyze data.

## *Five Steps to Simple Data Analysis*

**Step 1:** Reduce the data. Disregard data not relevant to the issue at hand.

**Step 2:** Represent the data. Use the rules of plain figures. Reorganize, order, and round numbers so the data is easy to read and understand.

**Step 3:** Find patterns. Have a quick look at the data and try to identify patterns in it, for instance:

- ▲ The average expenditures are similar within + or - 20 percent.

- ▲ There was a steady increase until 2010 and a fall since.

Identifying patterns is a simple way of working out overall trends. Often, patterns are obvious, for instance, increases or decreases over time. Look for simple, obvious patterns, and do not overcomplicate your task. If there appears to be no pattern, this alone tells you something.

**Step 4:** Identify exceptions. Having discerned a pattern, check the data for exceptions. Exceptions are often more important than the patterns. For example:

Percentage increase in sales over previous year

| | |
|---|---|
| 2008/09 | 3.9 |
| 2009/10 | 5.8 |
| 2010/11 | 4.1 |
| 2011/12 | 4.5 |
| 2012/13 | 4.9 |

In this list we can see that the percentages in 2009/10 were unusually high.

Beware!

▲ Exceptions may be typographical or recording errors. This happens a lot; it may be the explanation for the exception in the list above.

▲ Exceptions can be too numerous to be helpful. In that case, review the pattern.

**Step 5:** Compare. Compare the patterns and exceptions with other data, for instance, other time periods, geographical areas, manufacturers, products. This will either help you validate the pattern you have devised or cause you to question it.

**A worked example of simple data analysis.**
You are interested in learning more about kindergarten and pre-kindergarten education offered by local school districts. You come across this data set:

| School districts | No. of students | Total population under 18 | No. of schools | Full-time equivalent classroom teachers | Student/ teacher ratio | Total revenue ($ million) | No. of kindergarten and prekindergarten teachers | Librarians/ media specialists |
|---|---|---|---|---|---|---|---|---|
| Ashland | 34,011 | 44,029 | 54 | 1,771.60 | 15.66 | 393 | 119 | 55 |
| Clinton | 60,003 | 64,702 | 78 | 3,317.19 | 18.09 | 779 | 179 | 92 |
| Fairview | 49,407 | 57,262 | 72 | 2,694.64 | 18.34 | 510 | 274 | 79 |
| Franklin | 76,861 | 83,208 | 85 | 3,993.71 | 19.25 | 935 | 277 | 97 |
| Salem | 39,883 | 45,383 | 47 | 2,130.56 | 18.72 | 505 | 124 | 56 |
| Springfield | 20,268 | 31,239 | 33 | 1,321.06 | 15.34 | 424 | 103 | 34 |

Follow the stages of simple data analysis.

1.  Reduce the data. What data is relevant? You could just look
    at the number of teachers in kindergartens and prekinder-
    gartens, but some districts are bound to have more teachers
    than others. If possible, you want to find a "weight" that
    may indicate a pattern of some kind. After examining the
    table, you decide you will keep the following:

    ▲ name of school district

    ▲ number of students (to act as a weight)

    ▲ number of teachers in kindergarten and prekindergarten

2.  Reorganize the data. Round the data, and order it by the
    "weight," that is, the number of students, as shown here:

|  | No. of students (thousands) | No. of kindergarten and prekindergarten teachers |
|---|---|---|
| Franklin | 77 | 280 |
| Clinton | 60 | 180 |
| Fairview | 49 | 270 |
| Salem | 40 | 120 |
| Ashland | 34 | 120 |
| Springfield | 20 | 100 |

*Figures have been rounded.*

3.  Look for a pattern. The pattern is that the greater the num-
    ber of students in a school district, the greater the number
    of kindergarten teachers and prekindergarten teachers.

4.  Look for exceptions. You can see that Fairview has a dispro-
    portionately high number of teachers in kindergarten and pre-
    kindergarten education compared with other school districts.

5.  Compare. Knowing that there are more teachers in kinder-

garten and prekindergarten education in Fairview does not tell you a lot, but it is a start. You may need to look at data for the previous year or try to get other data.

---

## SUMMARY

Understanding discovery and presentation stages of working with numbers will help you clarify your task and save time and frustration. It encourages displays that are germane, content rich, and coherent for readers. Numbers are meaningful when they make comparisons, demonstrate cause and effect, and are timely and accurate. Finally, "simple data analysis" is a rough and ready method to help you identify useful messages in a set of data.

## WANT TO KNOW MORE?

Moon, Jon. *How to make an IMPACT.* Upper Saddle River, NJ: FT Press, 2007.

Most introductory statistics textbooks.

# Chapter 9

# Nonnumerical Charts and Information Graphics

Information graphics is a broad term that encompasses, among others, charts, graphs, tables, and maps. This chapter looks specifically at flow and organizational charts, text tables, and timelines, although the general advice and "what could go wrong" sections apply to all types of information graphics. The function of all of these is to analyze, order, summarize, and structure information primarily for communication purposes.

Unfortunately, many of these devices were developed to analyze what was going on rather than to communicate to others. Consequently, they sometimes suffer from inconsistent and obscure conventions. Readers need strong direction through design, labels, and symbols.

## GENERAL GUIDELINES

- ▲ Rely on the classics. Inventing a successful graphic scheme is almost impossible. Leonardo da Vinci did it. New formats are usually complications of archetypical ones. To quote Professor Tufte, "Don't get it original—get it right."

- ▲ Take time. Think things through. Become aware of the explicit point you are trying to show. That awareness will lead you to make good decisions over how to summarize and structure the information.

- ▲ Ensure titles and labels are concise, comprehensive, and comprehensible.

▲ User test. Show it to coworkers or, even better, members of the public. Ask them to describe what they see and what message they get from it.

# WHAT COULD GO WRONG?

There are four common problems that bedevil nonnumerical charts: ambiguous purpose, indistinct start and end points, vague or inadequate wording, and unnecessary clutter.

## Ambiguous Purpose (Including Hybrid Charts)

As with their numeric cousins, nonnumerical charts are more coherent when they possess a single, unequivocal purpose rather than several purposes or a vague objective.

Hybrids are mergers of charts (e.g., a flow and organizational charts) or modifications of standard charts (e.g., a flowchart customized for finance purposes). Hybrids seldom communicate with ease. Two or three single-purpose charts are more digestible than one confusing display. Be vigilant.

## Indistinct Start Points, Direction Arrows, and End Points

The entry point should always be obvious and either at the top or on the left-hand side of the page. Surprisingly, access to many graphics start in the middle or at the bottom, and this baffles readers at least for a few seconds.

Clarity in the initial step is paramount.

## Vague, Truncated, or Misleading Wording

Inadequate wording will leave readers puzzled and frustrated. Use the title to explain the purpose of the chart and ensure each chart is self-explanatory. Use abbreviations only when you are sure most people will be familiar with them, for instance, FBI or SUV.

Flowcharts and timelines demand precise descriptions when there is little space. It is a difficult balance between explaining a step or point succinctly and providing insufficient information to enlighten readers.

If essential, use call-outs, footnotes, or even a separate document to clarify.

## *Clutter*

Clutter consists of chart junk, unnecessary detail, and superfluous design elements (shapes, colors, meandering arrows, etc.). It hides the information you wish to showcase. It is a barrier to communicating ideas effectively.

The following paragraphs discuss particular types of nonnumerical charts and information graphics.

## FLOWCHARTS

Flowcharts (or process charts) graphically represent movement. They display sequential events, steps in a process, functions, etc., in an organized fashion. Flowcharts are common and used for a variety of purposes, including staff training, troubleshooting instructions, testing the logic or a program or system, and checking performance quality.

Flowcharts are often required because the phenomenon itself is complicated and text explanations are convoluted. Do not underestimate the time it takes to create an excellent flowchart.

**Consider the audience**. Flowcharts originated in engineering and manufacturing. Designed and used by insiders, they can helpfully portray complex relationships when users are familiar with the endeavor. Two points:

- ▲ A large vocabulary of symbols has developed for flowcharts, but symbols only useful to an audience familiar with them. Avoid technical terms and symbols when addressing a general audience.

- ▲ There is evidence that some readers prefer a list with delineated steps to a flowchart, even though it has been proven that a flowchart will save time and improve efficiency. Think about your audience before settling on a design.

## What Could Go Wrong?

In addition to the general points made at the beginning of this chapter, several problems tend to emerge when designing flowcharts.

Firstly, steps may be inadvertently omitted or merged. This is usually because of poor analysis or overfamiliarity with the subject, though deadline pressures also play a part. Isolating each step in a process is crucial. Decide on a level of detail and stick to it; if necessary, create separate charts for other layers.

Further, the complexity of flow-charts can be a major problem. Careful reflection of your overall objectives—of precisely what process you are describing—will improve the quality.

### Design Tips

- Start at the top or left. Never start a flow from the center, right, or lower parts of the chart.

- Keep arrows and directional signs simple. Research suggests that arrowheads (→) are preferred to terminal points (o), and plain arrows (→) are preferable to block arrows (⇨) or triangles (▷).

- Avoid showing values or figures: flowcharts are primarily about movement, not quantity. Numbers may distract rather than inform readers of flow or value.

- Double-check for accuracy. Identifying and correctly placing each step can be tricky. Inaccuracy is a sure way to lose credibility.

**Example 9.1: Flowchart.** This chart is based on an example produced by the Library of Congress and attempts to plot the process of handling requests and responses for information from libraries across the world. The first chart suffers from (1) absence of clear entrance, pathway, or direction, (2) chart junk, and (3) apparent superfluous information. The second example is a simplified, straightforward version of the same journey.

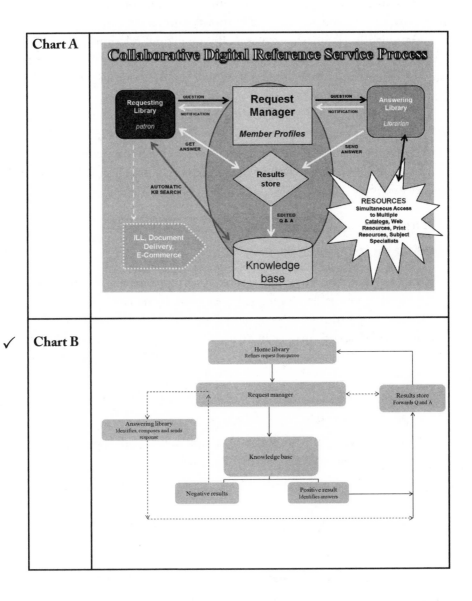

# ORGANIZATIONAL CHARTS

These portray formal relationships within a group, such as a corporation, government department, agency, or other organization. They assume a hierarchy and show direct lines of authority and responsibility.

Organizational charts may specify reporting relationships, individual accountability, functions, or systems, but not all of these in one presentation. Charts may be built around a product, service, geographic centers, teams, or other factors.

If the organization enjoys a strict hierarchy, designing the chart is relatively easy. Frequently, however, organizations get their work done through cross-management, informal arrangements, temporary assignments, nonsubordinate relationships, or indirect reporting. These are harder to depict.

## *Design Tips*

Consider the following when drawing up such charts:

- ▲ **Supervision and reporting.** The classic organizational chart covers both supervision and reporting at once. If the chart is simple enough, a few dotted or weighted lines (straight, never meandering, or with sharp turns) can be used to distinguish relationships. If the chart gets too busy, split it into two. Repetition is preferred to confusion.

- ▲ **Title comprehensively.** Add a date and, if needed, include a discussion sentence or two on the chart.

- ▲ **Avoid arrows.** Define reporting through layout and design. Few connecting lines and arrows should be necessary.

- ▲ **Avoid shading.** Keep borders faint. Let blank space, rather than ink, guide the eyes.

- ▲ **Keep it simple.** As always, avoid clutter and chart junk.

**Example 9.2: An organizational chart**. Below is an example of a straightforward organizational chart for part of a community college.

Note the simple lines and that the chart restricts itself to hierarchical relationships and avoids superfluous information such as telephone numbers, email addresses, etc.

**Organizational chart—community college**

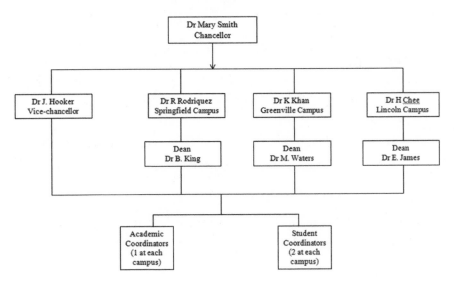

Rivers District Community College
Organizational chart, Spring 2013

# TIMELINES

A timeline is any information graphic organized by time. It clarifies the chronology or sequence of events and conveys a sense of change over time.

Use of timelines extends from historians and journalists to teachers and social policy researchers. Lawyers use them to explain evidence to jurors. They promote logical, sequential thinking and analysis and encourage viewers to see influences and cause and effect. The best timelines demonstrate both the chronology of events and the relationship among incidences.

Simple tables with time as the first column (or top row) are the most readable way of presenting the information.

Timelines should be self-explanatory with informative titles.

**Digital timelines.** Screens limit the amount of information a viewer can take in as compared to paper. Links, multiple views, and zooms may add value to a timeline but may also interfere with the main story. Such add-ons can prevent viewers from making useful comparisons and mental links.

## Design Tips

- Avoid overengineering. Timelines are essentially simple, and so should be their design.
- Use succinct language, and avoid obscure terms and abbreviations.
- Keep to one purpose only. Do not add more or extraneous points.

**Example 9.3: A simple timeline.** A simple, understated design makes the content easier to read and compare.

Timeline of history of the United States of America, 1800–1810

|  | Serving president | Western expansion | Military conflicts and events | Other events |
|---|---|---|---|---|
| 1800 | Washington | Indiana Territory formed by Act of Congress; Federal Government takes control over Connecticut Western Reserve (now northeastern Ohio) | Quasi War, 1798–1800; governor of Virginia, James Monroe, calls in militia to put down a slave revolt lead by Gabriel Prosser | Amnesty granted to Pennsylvania Dutch farmers involved in Fries's Rebellion; census established the population at 5.3 million, including 890,000 slaves |
| 1801 | Jefferson | Creation of Ohio | Quasi War, 1798–1800; First Barbary War begins |  |

| 1802 | Jefferson | | Quasi War ends October; First Barbary War continues | |
| 1803 | Jefferson | Louisiana purchase agreed | First Barbary War continues | Burr-Hamilton duel; Hamilton shot |
| 1804 | Jefferson | Lewis and Clark's expedition begun | First Barbary War continues; Treaty of St. Louis agreed between the Sauks and the Meskwaki tribes | |
| 1805 | Jefferson | Michigan Territory is crated; Lewis and Clark arrive at Pacific Ocean | Battle of Derne in First Barbary War; war ends | Andrew Jackson kills a man in a duel |
| 1806 | Jefferson | Agreement to construct the first American federal highway, the National Road; Zebulon Pike's expedition | | Noah Webster publishes his dictionary |
| 1807 | Jefferson | Pike discovers the Rio Grande | | Robert Fulton's first steamboat; Aaron Burr arrested for treason (later acquitted) |
| 1808 | Jefferson | | Pacific Fur Company set up by John Jacob Astor | Import of slaves is banned |
| 1809 | Madison | Illinois Territory established | | Meriwether Lewis dies |
| 1810 | Madison | Republic of West Florida annexed by US | Pacific Fur Company establishes itself on Columbia River | |

# TEXT BOXES

Text boxes are chunks of text separate from the main body of a document or a web page. They are often made distinguishable by borders or as shaded areas.

Text boxes are as versatile as text itself. They are ideal for checklists and directions. They may be used for

- promoting a particular message
- presenting examples or cases
- showcasing information that might be lost on a page
- including nonessential but interesting information
- breaking up a page of text

## Design Tips

- Use faint lines and borders. Let layout establish sections and divisions.
- Employ bullet points and bold sparingly. Overuse reduces impact.
- Keep to a maximum of about half a page either vertically or horizontally; larger boxes reduce impact.
- Keep shading light to emphasize the text.

**Example 9.4: A short text box explaining the origin of the pie chart.**

### History of the Pie Chart

Although graphs have been around since at least the tenth century, **William Playfair** (1759–1823), a Scottish political economist, was the first person to develop pie charts. They first appear in his book *The Statistical Breviary*, published in 1801.

In the mid-1800s, **Florence Nightingale** famously used pie charts to illustrate the avoidable deaths of soldiers in the Crimean War. By the 1920s, pie charts had entered common usage. However, by the late twentieth century, statisticians and others began to voice criticism of pie charts. They point to the difficulty the brain has in accurately comparing two or more wedge-shaped slices placed in a circle. Despite their broad popularity, pie charts do not always communicate well.

## SUMMARY

This chapter looked at specific examples of nonnumerical charts and information graphics after first outlining the problems that frequently occur in such displays. Flowcharts are common and display steps in a process or sequential events. Organizational charts show relationships within an organization, usually hierarchical. Timelines include any graphic that is organized by time. Text boxes are useful to describe or promote particular examples, cases, or messages in a way that will not be lost on the page. As always, the most useful design device is subtlety and allowing the information to speak for itself.

## WHAT TO KNOW MORE?

Harris, Robert L. *Information Graphics: A Comprehensive Illustrated Reference.* New York, NY: Oxford University Press, 1999.

Schriver, Karen A. *Dynamics in Document Design.* New York, John Wiley & Sons, 1997.

# Chapter 10

# Numbers and Page Design

THE TERM "page design" refers to the visual appearance of a print or web page. Design can make or break a report. The best layout will ensure your page looks professional and promotes easy reading. The worst will confound and mislead, look amateurish, and be difficult to read.

In addition to how to set out tables and charts on the page, this chapter looks at the use of color on pages, showing numbers on PowerPoint, and the challenge of presenting in different technologies.

## NUMERICAL TABLES

Tables look best when either aligned to the left or centered on the page. For best effect, place them at the top or the bottom of a page. The alternative—surrounding a table with text—makes reading both the text and the table more difficult. Whatever placement you choose, stick with it throughout the document. It gives the document a more professional appearance.

Tables that are slightly smaller than the surrounding text look more professional. So if your report is in an eleven-point font, try casting your tables in ten point.

When placing a table on a page, ensure it is

- single-spaced
- only as wide as it needs to be (tables that are artificially stretched across the page make numbers harder to compare)
- placed immediately before or after any summary or explanation about it

- not split across two pages; it needs be seen as a whole (a long reference table may be an exception)

### Checklist for Readable Tables

- Does the table design follow the rules of plain figures?
- Are rows and columns ordered logically?
- Have you reduced the data of demonstration tables as much as possible?
- Are titles and headings legible?

## CHARTS

The location of a chart on the page can add to its success in reaching readers. To achieve the greatest effects, keep the following in mind:

- Place charts at the top or bottom of the page. Avoid the middle, and never surround the chart with text.
- Align charts to the left or center on the page.
- Arrange any chart as close as possible to the text that explains or summarizes it. The best practice is to insert the chart immediately following the relevant paragraph. Charts should not be in an appendix where people can find them only with effort.
- Charts look more professional and carry more authority when they are small, as example 10.1 illustrates.

**Example 10.1: Smaller charts carry more authority.** Notice that the smaller of these two charts (which are the same as in example 4.1) somehow looks more authoritative. Keep your charts small, but be sure that the wording is legible.

✓ **Chart 10.1 A**

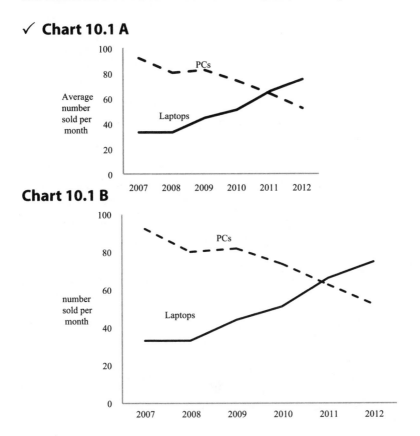

**Chart 10.1 B**

## Software and Charts

Software programs make assumptions about how data is plotted and charts are displayed. Typically, programs spew out legends, shadings, gridlines, colors, values, and other dross. They offer dozens of choices, most of which promote junk at the expense of the communication. See chapter 4 for a full discussion of chart junk.

Country and western singer, Dolly Parton, once famously quipped, "It takes a lot of money to look this cheap." With similar back-to-front logic, it takes a lot of effort to produce a simple chart. You need to become familiar with your software program and get to know chart functions. They allow you to delete borders and grids, change shading and size, and label and reorder bars or pie slices.

It gets easier with experience.

Design tips:

- ▲ Stick to the simplest charts available.
- ▲ Learn how to label bars, lines, and pie slices individually. In some cases—for instance, labeling lines on charts in certain programs—this is more difficult than it should be.
- ▲ Wording should be horizontal and large enough to read.

**Example 10.2: Modifying software charts.** The following two charts show the same data, but the second has been "dejunked." It is free of grids, superfluous shading, borders, etc. The useless legend box has been deleted, and the text is horizontal. Paradoxically, simplicity has to be worked for.

## Chart 10.2 A

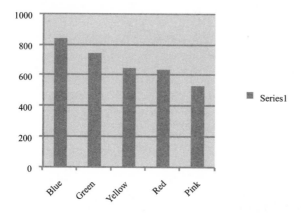

## ✓ Chart 10.2 B

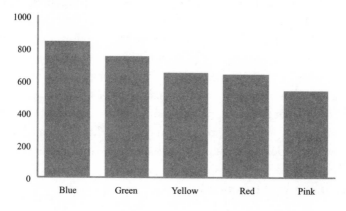

## COLOR

Color is a key identifier throughout our lives. We perceive objects of the same color as similar regardless of shape, size, purpose, and location. Color can animate design; it can also be overused and misused.

When creating charts or other illustrations, color is an important consideration. It has culturally specific meanings—in the West, red indicates danger or passion, but in China red signifies happiness. Colors often vary on different computer monitors. To use color well, you need to think about your audience and its needs.

A few recommendations about color on charts:

- Keep colors unobtrusive and mute. Emphasize the data, not the design.
- Select colors in a logical and consistent manner. People associate items according to color regardless of the designers' intentions. For instance, red and pink items are assumed to be related.
- Sharp images and contrasts can reenforce distinctions. Strong colors against white or light gray will maximize the distinctions.
- Some 5–10 percent of the population suffers from color vision deficiency (color blindness). Distinctions of color—say slices on a pie chart—may be lost to them. Sharp contrasts (e.g., light, dark, light, dark, etc.) will help.

**Using color.** Although color brightens up charts, reports, websites, and presentations, it has limitations. It does not photocopy well, and many people cannot make color distinction. Because of this, color should never be the only way to identify bars, lines, or pie slices or to interpret other features.

## GETTING THE MOST FROM DIFFERENT MEDIA

Every presentation medium—print, computer monitor, and presentation software—carries distinct features. Tables and charts transfer between mediums only with distortion. Ideally, tables and charts should be created for, and usually in, the medium in which they will appear.

## Print

Print has been the standard method of written communication for centuries, and most people work better in print than in other medium.

Here are two tips for using paper to its maximum effect:

▲ Construct tables and charts with photocopying in mind. Many people have no access to a color photocopier, and color costs more. Black-and-white photocopying of colored charts can lose vital information. Keep in mind that people sometimes reduce the size of the page when photocopying, making labels difficult to read.

▲ Documents intended to be distributed as email attachments or through Adobe Acrobat and other such programs may be affected by the recipients' technology. Even page sizes can differ. To guarantee a good standard of presentation, keep graphics simple.

## Computer Screen

Computer screens "hold" less information than paper, so design all tables and charts to be shown on web pages and CDs with this in mind. For instance, the detail in a reference table is easily readable on paper but is much less so on a web page. If possible, include tables on a PDF file so readers can download it.

Clutter is a major problem on web pages. It is off-putting when not confusing. Google's simple elegance contributes to its popularity over competing search engines, such as Excite and Yahoo. Its unfussiness allows users to immediately understand its purpose and how to proceed.

A few suggestions to consider when designing websites and CDs:

▲ Fit tables and charts on a single screen. Scrolling is *not* an acceptable alternative. Viewers need to see a whole table for it to be meaningful. Successful charts rely on their visual punch to communicate. Screens that demand scrolling miss the big picture.

▲ Stick to "web-safe" colors. These are a collection of over 200 colors that should remain consistent across all operating systems.

▲ As with paper, ensure that contrasts are sharp and obvious. Unlike on paper, brilliant colors (white, yellows, violets, and greens) can be contrasted against a dark background on computer screens.

▲ Integrate graphics with text. Links to other pages are acceptable, but repeat the title on each new screen to maintain context.

## NUMBERS AND POWERPOINT

The origins of PowerPoint lay in marketing, so the software is likely to be a useful device for selling soap powder and other consumer goods. It is less successful for scientific, technical, statistical, or financial discourse. Not everything in the world can be explained with bullet points. Some concepts, ideas, and actions are best described in sentences and paragraphs, that is, the same way they have been communicated for hundreds of years.

PowerPoint is a poor tool for statistical or financial presentations because it thrives on the big picture, not detail. Consider transferring the detail of your talk to a written handout. Use slides for illustrations, headlines, and summaries.

Charts project well onto a screen and are coherent, especially after being explained. Unfortunately, the detail in tables overwhelm viewers. Additionally, reader-friendly tables are difficult to design on PowerPoint. A simple alternative is to show table averages or totals on a slide and include full tables in any handout.

**Example 10.3: Limit the amount of text on slides.** The left-hand slide below has eleven "words," and the right has two. Eleven words is not many, but the second slide is eye catching and powerful. Headlines work better on PowerPoint than does detail.

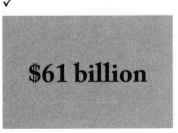

## SUMMARY

Successful page design will make a paper or web page look professional and be readable.

Place both tables and charts thoughtfully on a page and close to any written summary. Ensure tables are single-spaced and narrow; tables should not be stretched over two pages. Keep charts small and plain, and ensure the text is readable. Use color with logic and sensitivity to promote an overall image. Consideration needs to be given to color blindness and the cost of color printing.

When working in print, keep photocopying in mind. Graphics should be simple and designed for convenient and efficient transfer. Design PowerPoint displays with the understanding that this software is not a good medium for numeric information. On computer screens, present tables and charts on a single page, ensure contrasts are obvious and sharp, and integrate graphics with text.

## WHAT TO KNOW MORE?

Schriver, Karen A. *Dynamics in Document Design*. New York: John Wiley & Sons, 1997.

# Glossary

**Average**                In common usage (and in this book), "average" stands for the arithmetic mean calculated by adding up items and dividing the total by the number of items.

**Axis**                   A fixed reference line in graphs. The horizontal line is called the x-axis. The vertical axis is called the y-axis. Plural is axes.

**Bar graph or graph**     A diagram that represents quantities through the length of bars or columns.

**Big data**               An information technology term that refers to the collection of data sets so large and complex that it becomes difficult to process using on-hand database management tools. The term often implies the questionable premise that tradition or conventional ways of presenting and analyzing the data are not capable of dealing with "big data."

**Bubble chart**           A type of scatter plot (see term "Scatter Plot") with a third and sometimes a fourth variable, the bubble. Bubble charts indicate if there is a correlation among the variables.

**Chart**                  A visual representation of data. The term may be used interchangeably with "graph," but unlike graph, chart can also represent nonnumerical data, for example, flowcharts, organizational charts, etc.

**Chart junk**             Unnecessary decoration in graphs.

| | |
|---|---|
| **Circle graph** | A pie chart. |
| **Column graph** | A vertical bar graph. It displays data by comparing the height of bars. |
| **Dashboard (information)** | A single-page display of business information or key performance indicators designed to be read by managers, etc., similar to the way in which a driver uses a vehicle's dashboard. |
| **Data** | Figures, facts, and statistics collected together for reference or analysis. Data must be interpreted (usually through patterns); it is meaningless by itself. Formally, data is plural, the singular is datum. In practice, data has come to be used for both. |
| **Data reduction** | The practice of reducing data from large sets to a controllable or manageable size that is of practical use by decision makers. |
| **Data visualization (dataviz)** | The use of images for information; the use of graphical presentation to represent complex data to improve understanding. This is a new and developing field; a single definition has yet to be universally agreed. |
| **Demonstration tables** | Numeric tables constructed from selected figures to illustrate a particular point, observation, or message. |
| **Digit** | Any of the numerals from 0 to 9, especially when forming part of a number. |
| **Effective digits** | Digits that vary within a series of numbers. |
| **Figure** | A number, especially one that forms part of official statistics or relates to the financial performance of a company. |
| **Graph** | A diagram showing numeric relationships measured along a pair of axes at right angles. |

**Grouped bar**        A graph that presents pairs of bars.

**Histogram**         A graph that illustrates the distribution or frequency of items within a given range.

**Information**        Facts that have been organized into a meaningful form.

**Information graphic**  A broad term that encompasses charts, graphs, numeric tables, maps, etc., that are designed to show the content in ways that are easy to understand.

**Legend**           The wording on a map or diagram explaining the symbols used.

**Linear**           Able to be represented by a straight line on a graph.

**Line graph**        A graph that compares variables through a line or lines.

**Mean (arithmetic mean)**  The average of a set of numbers calculated by adding them together and dividing by the number of items.

**Median**           A quantity lying in the midpoint of a set of ordered numbers. It is calculated by crossing off an equal number of entries from below and above.

**Metric**           A measure established as an example against which others of the same type are compared.

**Mode**            The value that occurs most frequently in a given set of numbers.

**Multivariate data**    Data containing or linking more than one variable.

**Negative correlation**  A relationship between values that plots as a downward slope on a line graph or scatter plot. As one value increases, the other decreases.

**Number**            An arithmetic value, expressed as a word, symbol, or figure, representing a particular quantity and used in counting and making calculations, for showing order in a series, or for identification. Interchangeable with "figure."

**Ordinal**           A number indicating a place in an ordered sequence, for instance, first, second, twelfth, thirty-third, etc.

**Outlier**           A data point on a graph that is exceptionally distant from the mass. Outliers are surprising and may indicate an error or an important exception.

**Percentage**        A rate, number, or amount in each hundred; any proportion or share in relation to the whole.

**Pie chart**         A type of graph in which a circle is divided into sectors that each represents a proportion of the whole.

**Positive correlation**  A relationship between values that plots as an upward slope on a line graph or scatter plot. As one value increases, the other decreases.

**Radar charts**      A circular chart frequently used to display performance measures; radar charts can also be used to analyze multivariate data.

**Ranking**           A position in a scale; ordering of numbers from smallest to largest or largest to smallest.

**Reference table**   A numerical table containing raw data primarily to be used for reference. Examples include baseball league tablets, bus timetables, television program schedules, and government statistical tables.

**Scale**             A standard system for measuring or grading something; a ruler-like measurement for the x- and y-axis of a graph.

**Scatter plot (scattergram, scatter diagram)** — A graph in which data is plotted, but the points are not joined into lines; the pattern of dots reveals any correlation.

**Statistics** — Information obtained by collecting and analyzing numerical data in large quantities.

**Superimposed graph** — A single graph that compares two sets, each with its own y-axis; often it is a combination of a bar and line graph.

**Table** — A set of facts or figures displayed systematically, especially in columns and rows. (See also *reference table*.)

**Typography** — The appearance, composition, and organization of typeset material.

**Variable** — Something that is likely to change. Line graphs and scatter plots, for instance, contain at least two variables—numerical values—that are plotted on the x and y axes.

**X-axis** — The horizontal axis in a graph.

**Y-axis** — The vertical axis in a graph.

## WANT TO KNOW MORE?

Harris, Robert L. *Information Graphics: A Comprehensive Illustrated Reference.* New York: Oxford University Press, 1999.

# Exercises and Answers

The following exercises are designed to test your skill at using the principles and concepts set out in this book.

Suggested answers are listed at the end of this section.

## EXERCISES

### Exercise 1: Patterns and Exceptions

This table shows the percentage of staff who replied "yes" when asked if they were generally satisfied with aspects of their working conditions.

Employee satisfaction, February 2013; percentage of 834 respondents

|  | Hours | Salary | Supervisor | Working conditions | Average |
|---|---|---|---|---|---|
| Clinton | 68 | 75 | 88 | 76 | 77 |
| Fairview | 81 | 73 | 79 | 69 | 76 |
| Franklin | 71 | 78 | 90 | 84 | 81 |
| Salem | 67 | 73 | 87 | 42 | 67 |
| Average | 72 | 75 | 86 | 68 | |

*(a)* Reorder the columns and rows from largest to smallest by average size. What are the main patterns and exceptions in the data?

*(b)* Go back to the original table. Can you now see the patterns and exceptions?

### Exercise 2: Proximity

This table was drawn up to help mangers decide in which of two locations to establish their regional warehouse.

(c) What rule of plain figures does this layout break?

(d) How can the table be improved?

| Springfield | | Greenville |
|---|---|---|
| 395.9 | Land (square miles) | 294.3 |
| 54.43 | Normal daily mean temperature (F) | 59.38 |
| 1,100,843 | Population | 788,374 |
| $103,389 | Median household income (2011) | $83,453 |
| 92.86% | Population who are high school graduates | 80.99% |
| 88.72% | Households with home computers with Internet access | 71.23% |

## Exercise 3: Order

Suggest ways in which this list may be made more reader friendly.

| | Total revenue ($) |
|---|---|
| Auburn | 130 million |
| Clinton | 9.3 million |
| Greenville | 94 million |
| Jackson | 780 million |
| Salem | 38 million |
| Springfield | 2.4 billion |

## Exercise 4: Fixed and Variable Rounding

Round the following numbers:

| Original | Variable rounding to two effective digits | Fixed rounding to thousands |
|---|---|---|
| 764,375 | | |
| 23,694 | | |
| 5,872 | | |
| 438 | | |
| 38 | | |
| 11.3 | | |

## Exercise 5: Rounding to Two Digits

Round the following numbers using variable rounding:

Round to two digits

| | |
|---|---|
| Series 1 | 88,722 |
| | 54,114 |
| | 25,555 |
| | |
| Series 2 | 504 |
| | 496 |
| | 494 |
| | 487 |
| | |
| Series 3 | 9,811 |
| | 622 |
| | 89 |
| | 42.777 |
| | 5.388 |
| | 0.75577 |
| | 0.063844 |

## Exercise 6: Mental Arithmetic

Work out the difference between 437.96 and 661.42 without using a pen, paper, or calculator. Now compare 440 and 660 in your head.

## Exercise 7: Which Chart?

Which type of chart would you use to express these ideas?

1. The value of Titus-Thunder Inc. shares fell month by month during the last two quarters of 2012.

2. Eight percent of the school's budget goes on administration.

3. The greater the number of orders in a month, the higher the expenditure on transport.

4. Sales representatives with thirty-one to forty-two months experience achieve higher levels of sales than any other group.

5. The IT department had the highest staff turnover.

6. There was a sharp increase in the annual sales of hammers between 2012 and 2013.

## Exercise 8: Table or Graph?

You want to understand the changes over the years shown in the table below.

- ▲ What type of graph would be best for your purposes?
- ▲ Roughly plot the graph on a piece of paper.
- ▲ Which is better at explaining the story, table or graph?

| | 1980 | 1985 | 1990 | 1995 | 2000 | 2005 | 2010 |
|---|---|---|---|---|---|---|---|
| % permanent staff with highest qualification | | | | | | | |
| High school diploma or equivalent | 72 | 65 | 55 | 52 | 46 | 41 | 33 |
| Associate degree or better | 23 | 34 | 39 | 45 | 51 | 57 | 66 |

## Exercise 9: Simple Data Analysis

The five steps of simple data analysis are explained in chapter 9. The steps are:

1. reduce the data
2. represent the data according to the rules of plain figures
3. find patterns in the data
4. identify exceptions to the patterns
5. compare with other data

Examine the following reference table with the objective of getting a better understanding of sickness rates at the various branches of the company.

Miscellaneous data about staff and branches, 2012–2013

| | Average turnover per week ($) | No. of staff | Turnover per member of staff ($) | FTE* staff | Salary costs per year ($) | Payroll tax ($) | Training costs (2010) ($) | Days sick per branch | Staff turnover rate |
|---|---|---|---|---|---|---|---|---|---|
| Clinton | 2,680.78 | 5 | 336.16 | 3.80 | 87,400.37 | 21,935 | 988.47 | 27.10 | 15.40 |
| Greenville | 16,384.57 | 22 | 381.12 | 11.40 | 308,523.34 | 77,131 | 2,385 | 49.50 | 13.53 |
| Springfield | 5,574.38 | 12 | 464.53 | 9.40 | 173,375.36 | 43,250 | 2,195.00 | 39.52 | 9.35 |
| Salem | 4,310.18 | 11 | 391.83 | 8.56 | 171,200.48 | 42,730 | 2,250.38 | 46.61 | 15.85 |
| Jackson | 3,583.49 | 8 | 447.94 | 5.40 | 107,485.00 | 26,753 | 2,184 | 38.40 | 11.48 |

* FTE: full-time equivalent staff.

Source: HR

## SUGGESTED ANSWERS

### Exercise 1 Answer

Once you have ranked the data numerically, spotting patterns and exceptions is easier.

Most staff members are reasonably satisfied at work, and those in Franklin are the most satisfied. Staff in Salem are least satisfied and are particularly dissatisfied with working conditions. A disproportionately high percentage of Salem staff are satisfied with their supervisor, a high percentage of Franklin staff enjoy their working conditions, and a high proportion of Fairview staff like the hours.

*Results of employee survey; % of respondents*

|          | Supervisor | Salary | Hours | Working conditions | Average |
|----------|------------|--------|-------|--------------------|---------|
| Franklin | 90         | 78     | 71    | 84                 | 81      |
| Clinton  | 88         | 75     | 68    | 76                 | 77      |
| Fairview | 79         | 73     | 81    | 69                 | 76      |
| Salem    | 87         | 73     | 67    | 42                 | 67      |
| Average  | 86         | 75     | 72    | 68                 |         |

### Exercise 2 Answer

(a) The broken rule is proximity: numbers to be compared should be placed close to one another. Descriptions of the data should go either above the numbers or to the left, but never in-between.

(b) Round numbers for convenient comparison.

(c) The table does not have a title.

Below is a more reader-friendly presentation of the data.

| | Population thousands | Land (square miles) | Normal daily mean temperature (F) | Median household income (2011) ($ thousand) | Population who are high school graduates | Households with home computers with Internet access |
|---|---|---|---|---|---|---|
| Springfield | 1,100 | 400 | 54 | 100 | 93% | 89% |
| Greenville | 790 | 290 | 59 | 84 | 81% | 71% |

Or you could swap it around so the two towns are in columns and the detail is presented in rows.

## Exercise 3 Answer

Below is the reorganized table.

Employ a single unit rather than mixing millions and billions. When converting units, usually opt for the lowest common denominator. In this case, millions is preferable to billions. The problem with billions is that one of the items is relatively low—Clinton's $9.3 million would equal 0.09 billion, a concept difficult for most people to grasp.

Size order is preferable to alphabetical.

| | Total revenue ($ million) |
|---|---|
| Springfield | 2,400.0 |
| Jackson | 780.0 |
| Auburn | 130.0 |
| Greenville | 94.0 |
| Salem | 38.0 |
| Clinton | 9.3 |

## Exercise 4 Answer

| Original | Variable rounding to two effective digits | Fixed rounding to thousands |
|---|---|---|
| 764,375 | 760,000 | 764,000 |
| 23,694 | 24,000 | 24,000 |
| 5,872 | 5,900 | 6,000 |
| 438 | 440 | 0 |
| 38 | 38 | 0 |
| 11.3 | 11 | 0 |

## Exercise 5 Answer

| | | Round to two digits using variable rounding |
|---|---|---|
| Series 1 | 88,722 | 89,000 |
| | 54,114 | 54,000 |
| | 25,555 | 26,000 |
| Series 2 | 504 | *These cannot be rounded under "variable* |
| | 496 | *rounding" because they are too close numeri-* |
| | 494 | *cally. Rounding them would introduce unac-* |
| | 487 | *ceptable rounding errors.* |
| Series 3 | 9,811 | 9,800 |
| | 622 | 620 |
| | 89 | 89 |
| | 42.777 | 43 |
| | 5.388 | 5.4 |
| | 0.75577 | 0.76 |
| | 0.063844 | 0.06 or 0.1* |

* *Some people consider the 0 before the decimal place as relevant; others do not. If you think it is relevant, then the answer is 0.1. If you think it is not, then the answer is 0.06.*

## Exercise 6 Answer

The two amounts differ by 223.46. Was the time and effort involved worthwhile? Would 220 (the rounded calculation) rather than 223.46, be more helpful and convenient for your audience?

## Exercise 7 Answer

1. line
2. pie (or possibly bar)
3. scatter plot
4. histogram (frequency distribution)
5. bar
6. bar (for a line graph you need at least four periods)

## Exercise 8 Answer

In these circumstances, a line graph (chart A) excels both over the original table or over a paired bar chart (chart B). The line graph reveals the trends over the period with effortless ease.

Most readers find it difficult to discern the trend by just looking at the numbers in the table. With the paired bar chart, trends are perceptible only with a struggle.

✓ **Chart 8 A**

Our employees are increasingly better qualified.
(The highest qualification of staff)

## Chart 8 B

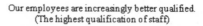

Our employees are increasingly better qualified.
(The highest qualification of staff)

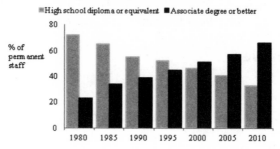

| % permanent staff with highest qualification | 1980 | 1985 | 1990 | 1995 | 2000 | 2005 | 2010 |
|---|---|---|---|---|---|---|---|
| High school diploma or equivalent | 72 | 65 | 55 | 52 | 46 | 41 | 33 |
| Associate degree or better | 23 | 34 | 39 | 45 | 51 | 57 | 66 |

# Exercise 9 Answer

1. Reduce the data. For this exercise, all you need to know is the numbers of staff (or the FTE staff—either will work) and the number of sick days.

2. Represent the data. Round the data and order it by size, as shown below.

3. What is the pattern? The greater the number of staff, the more sick days were taken.

Sick leave in branch by no. of staff

|  | No. of staff | Days sick 2012–2013 |
|---|---|---|
| Greenville | 22 | 50 |
| Springfield | 12 | 40 |
| Salem | 11 | 47 |
| Jackson | 8 | 38 |
| Clinton | 5 | 27 |

Or you might have used FTE staff:

Sick leave at various branches

|  | FTE* staff numbers | Days sick 2012–2013 |
|---|---|---|
| Greenville | 11.0 | 50 |
| Springfield | 9.4 | 40 |
| Salem | 8.6 | 47 |
| Jackson | 5.4 | 38 |
| Clinton | 3.8 | 27 |

*Full-time equivalent staff numbers*

# Index

## A

Accuracy, 17–18
Area line graphs. See Layered line
graphs
Averages, 10–11
Axis, 50, 75, 77

## B

Bar charts, 53–61
changes over time, 60–61
component, 58–59
constructing, 55
designing, 55
negative, 60
paired, 57–58
representing parts of a whole, 56
Bubble charts, 73–74

## C

Candlestick charts. See Stock charts
Chart junk, 42–47
Charts, 37–52
bar. See Bar charts
basic, 53–68
bubble, 73–74
clarity of message, 38–39
color on, 111
and data visualization, 69
design of, 42–47
hybrid, 96
integrity of intention and action,
49–51
location of, 108
motion, 74
nonnumerical, 96–97
numeric, 37
organizational, 100–101
pie. See Pie charts
radar, 74–75
selection of, 83–86
software and, 109–110
specialist. See Specialist charts
title, 39–41
Circle graph. See Pie charts
Clutter, 97, 112
Color
on charts, 111
"web-safe," 112
Columns, 54
Communication skill, 1–2
Component bar charts, 58–59
Computer screens, 112–113
Credibility maintaining, 51

## D

Dashboards, 78–79
Data analysis, simple, 89–93
Data presentation, guiding
principle of, 7
Data visualization, charts and, 69
Demonstration tables, 29–30
Design
bar charts, 55
charts, 42–47
dashboards, 78–79
flowcharts, 98–99
organizational charts, 100–101
web pages, 112–113

Digital timelines, 102
Digits, variable rounding to two
    effective, 18–19

**E**

Ehrenberg, A. S. C., 7
Effective digits, 18–19
Executive dashboards, 78–79

**F**

Figure
    in order, 8–10
    rounding, 16–20
    rules for, 7–8
Flowcharts, 96, 97
    design, 98–99

**G**

Graphics information, 95
Graphs
    layered line, 64
    line. *See* Line graphs
    radar, 74–75
    selecting specific, 88–89
    superimposed, 77–78
Gridlines, 30–31
Grouped bar charts, 57–58

**H**

Histograms, 76–77
Horizontal bars, 54
Hybrid charts, 96

**I**

Information graphics, 95
    guidelines, 95–96
Integrity in graphics
    maintaining, 51
    naming source, 49–51
    scale, 50
    technical, 50–51

**K**

"Keep comparisons close"
    principle, 12–15

**L**

Labels
    columns and headings, 34
    lucid, 47–49
Layered line graphs, 64
Layout, simplicity of, 30–32
Legend, 47, 66
Line graphs, 62
    constructing, 63
    layered, 64
Look-up tables. *See* Reference tables
Lucid labels, 47–49

**M**

Message
    clarity of, 38–41
    determination of, 39
Multivariate data, 69, 74
Motion charts, 74

**N**

Negative bar chart, 60
Nightingale, Florence, 104
Nonnumerical charts, common
    problems, 96–97
Numbers
    handling, 7–23
    illustrating cause and effect, 88
    memory and mental arithmetic
        with, 16–17
    and PowerPoint, 113
    presenting, 7
    selecting specific, 88–89
    working with, 87–93
Numbers in order, 8–12
    by average, percentage and total,
        10–12
    comparisons, 9–10

size order, 10
Numerical communication, 2
Numerical tables, 107–108
Numeric chart, 37

## O

Organizational charts, 100
    design, 100–101
Outlier, 72–73

## P

Page design, 107
Paired bar charts, 57–58
Paper, tips for using, 112
Parallel coordinates, 79–80
Percentages, 12
Pie charts, 64–68
    comparing, 67–68
    constructing, 65–67
    history of, 104
    problem with, 65
Plain figures, six rules of, 7–8
Playfair, William, 104
Plots, scatter, 72–73
Positive correlation, 72–73
PowerPoint, numbers and, 113
Print, 112
Process charts. *See* Flowcharts

## R

Radar charts, 74–75
Rand, Paul, 3
Readability standards,
    improving, 2–3
Readable tables, checklist for, 108
Reference tables, 27–28
Rounding numbers, 16–21
    accuracy, 17–18
    exceptions, 19–20
    making decisions, 17
    memory and mental arithmetic,
      16–17

misleading, 18
variable rounding to two effective
    digits, 18–19
Rounding totals, 20–21

## S

Scale, integrity, 50
Scatter plots, 72–73
Size order, numbers, 10
Software and charts, 109–110
Sparklines, 80
Specialist charts, 79–81
    functions of, 70–72
    Spider graphs. *See* Radar charts
    Stacked bar charts. *See* Component
      bar charts
    Star charts. *See* Radar charts
    Statistical Breviary,
      The (Playfair), 104
    Stock charts, 80
    Sub-divided bar charts. *See*
      Component bar charts
    Superimposed graphs, 77–78

## T

Tables
    clarity of wording, 33–34
    components of, 26
    demonstration, 29–30
    designing, 27
    labeling columns and
      headings, 34
    numerical, 107–108
    readable, 108
    reference, 27–28
    selecting specific, 88–89
    selection of, 83–86
    successful, 26–27
    titles, 33–34
    types of, 27–30
    using, 25–35
Technical charts, functions of,
    70–72
Technical integrity, 50–51

Text boxes, 103–104
Timelines, 101–103
    digital, 102
Titles
    charts, 39–41, 96, 100
    definitive, 59, 60
    explanatory, 60, 62, 73, 101
    table, 33–34
Totals, 10–12, 20–21
Tree maps, 80
Tufte, Edward, 3

## V

Variable rounding, digits, 18–19
Vertical bars, 54
Visual Explanations (Tufte), 2

## W

"Web-safe" colors, 112
Web pages, design, 112–113
Written summary, 21

# Allworth Books Page

Designer's Guide to Presenting Numbers, Figures, and Charts.

---

**AIGA Professional Practices in Graphic Design**
*By Tad Crawford* (6 x 9, 336 pages, paperback, $29.95)

**Business and Legal Forms for Graphic Designers**
*By Tad Crawford* (8 ½ x 11, 160 pages, paperback $29.95)

**Career Solutions for Creative People**
*By Ronda Ormont* (6 x 9, 320 pages, paperback, $27.50)

**Careers by Design**
*By Roz Goldfarb* (6 x 9, 240 pages, paperback, $19.95)

**Creating the Perfect Design Brief, Second Edition**
*By Peter L. Phillips* (5 ½ x 8 ¼, 240 pages, paperback, $19.95)

**Design Thinking**
*By Thomas Lockwood* (6 x 9, 304 pages, paperback, $24.95)

**The Education of a Graphic Designer**
*By Steven Heller* (6 x 9, 368 pages, paperback, $29.95)

**The Elements of Graphic Design, Second Edition**
*By Alex White* (8 x 10, 224 pages, paperback, $29.95)

**Graphic Designer's Guide to Pricing, Estimating, and Budgeting, Third Edition**
*By Theo Stephan Williams* (6 x 9, 256 pages, paperback, $24.95)

**How to Grow as a Graphic Designer**
*By Catharine Fishel* (6 x 9, 256 pages, paperback, $19.95)

**Legal Guide for the Visual Artist, Fifth Edition**
*By Tad Crawford* (8 ½ x 11, 304 pages, paperback, $29.95)

**The Profitable Artist**
*By Artspire* (6 x 9, 240 pages, paperback, $24.95)

**Starting Your Career as a Freelance Web Designer**
*By Neil Tortorella* (6 x 9, 256 pages, paperback, $19.95)

**Teaching Graphic Design**
*By Steven Heller* (6 x 9, 288 pages, paperback, $19.95)

To see our complete catalog or to order online, please visit *www.allworth.com*

# The bestselling suspense novels of
# LINDA FAIRSTEIN
## win nationwide acclaim!

### COLD HIT

"A sure hit! Linda Fairstein writes tough, beautiful prose about a world she knows firsthand. . . . Moves with a deftness only a true insider can manage."

—Lisa Scottoline, bestselling author of *Mistaken Identity*

"A shining protagonist, comfortable in the upper echelons of New York society but eager to roll up her sleeves at work, her heart aching for her staff and the victims they defend."

—*Publishers Weekly* (starred review)

"Fairstein is dazzling in her third Alexandra Cooper mystery. . . . Smart, sexy, and indefatigable, Alex is relentlessly likeable. . . . Fascinating and fast paced."

—*Library Journal*

"Thoroughly tension-filled and pulse-pounding."

—*Midwest Book Reviews*

### THE DEADHOUSE

"Darkly woven, with a shocking history of New York asylums, penitentiaries, and plagues, *The Deadhouse* conjures up a horrid past to solve a baffling modern murder."

—Patricia Cornwell

"*The Deadhouse* offers, along with the author's usual beguiling mix of murder, romance, and suspense, an intriguing history lesson. . . . Fascinating. . . . An extraordinarily well-knit mystery that the author wraps tightly in suspense before unfolding it with a flourish. . . . The crime novel easily make[s] my list as one of the best of the year."

—Dick Lochte, *Los Angeles Times*

"Linda Fairstein writes tough, beautiful prose about a world she knows firsthand."

—Lisa Scottoline

"Like its predecessors, *The Deadhouse* allows Fairstein to display her first-hand knowledge of crime and investigation. . . . The storm-toss'd, struggle-to-the-death finale . . . is superb."

—*The Washington Post*

"The city that never sleeps is ably guarded by Linda Fairstein's Odd Couple, sex-crimes D.A. Alexandra Cooper and Detective Mike Chapman. . . . Their emotional bond anchors Fairstein's absorbing and well-plotted [novel]. . . . Fairstein excels at conveying the reality of Coop's days. . . . Four stars out of four stars."

—*Detroit Free Press*

## LIKELY TO DIE

"An authoritative and scary view from one who has battled evil and locked it away."

—Patricia Cornwell

"Step aside, girls. Here comes Manhattan sex-crimes prosecutor Alexandra Cooper in a red Escada suit, trailing a cloud of Chanel No. 5. . . . Fairstein gives her sleek—and single—D.A. a whopping whodunit. . . . There are plenty of suspects to keep Alex clicking along in her Manolo Blahnik heels . . . and sizzling sexual tension between Alex and NYPD detective Mike Chapman. With its taut plot and classy setting, *Likely to Die* is an uptown act."

—*People*

"This gritty, harsh book has a strong sense of authenticity."
—*Chicago Tribune*

## FINAL JEOPARDY

"Raw, real, and mean. Linda Fairstein is wonderful."
—Patricia Cornwell

"Put down *Final Jeopardy* and you almost expect to find crime-scene grit under your nails. Dead-on details are no surprise in this taut mystery."
—*Us* magazine

"If it is authenticity you demand, *Final Jeopardy* has got it in spades. . . . There is an anger and a passion in Alex Cooper that is clearly not fictional."
—*The Times* (London)

"From its *Laura*-like opening, which hooked me completely, to its astonishing denouement, I was held hostage by *Final Jeopardy*."
—Dominick Dunne

## BOOKS BY LINDA FAIRSTEIN

### The Alexandra Cooper Novels

*Cold Hit*
*Likely to Die*
*Final Jeopardy*

### Nonfiction

*Sexual Violence: Our War Against Rape*

# Linda
# Fairstein

# COLD HIT

**POCKET BOOKS**
New York London Toronto Sydney Singapore

POCKET BOOKS, a division of Simon & Schuster, Inc.
1230 Avenue of the Americas, New York, NY 10020

Copyright © 1999 by Linda Fairstein

Originally published in hardcover in 1999 by Scribner

ISBN: 0-671-01955-4

First Pocket Books printing October 2000

11  10  9  8  7  6  5  4  3

POCKET and colophon are registered trademarks of Simon & Schuster, Inc.

For information regarding special discounts for bulk purchases, please contact Simon & Schuster Special Sales at 1-800-456-6798 or business@simonandschuster.com

Front cover photo by Brian Velenchenko

Printed in the U.S.A.

I am spellbound by the mystery of murder.

—Weegee (Arthur Fellig)

# 1

It was after eight o'clock, and all I could see of the sun was its gleaming crown as it slipped behind the row of steep cliffs, giving off an iridescent pink haze that signaled the end of a long August day. Brackish gray water swirled and broke against the large rocks that edged the mound of dirt on which I stood, spitting up at my ankles as I stared out to the west at the Palisades. The pleats of my white linen skirt, which had seemed so cool and weightless as I moved about the air-conditioned courtroom all afternoon, were plastered against my thighs by the humidity, and I swatted off the mosquitoes as they searched for a place to land on my forearms.

I turned away from the striking vista across the Hudson River and glanced down at the body of the woman that had snagged on the boulders less than an hour earlier.

The detective from the Crime Scene Unit reloaded his camera and took another dozen shots. "Want a couple of Polaroids to work from till I get you a full set of blowups?" I nodded to him as he changed equipment, leaned in above the head of his partially clothed subject, and set off the flash attachment.

The old guy with the fishing rod who had made the grim discovery was twitching nervously while he answered questions hurled at him in Spanish by a young uniformed cop from the Thirty-fourth Precinct. The officer pointed at something bulging in the man's pocket, and the fisherman's free hand shook uncontrollably as he pulled out a small flask of red wine.

"Tell him to relax, Carrera," Detective Mike Chapman called over to the rookie. "Tell him this one's a keeper. Catch of the day. Haven't seen anything this clean pulled out of these waters since Rip Van Winkle used it as a bathtub."

Chapman and his good friend Mercer Wallace had been talking with each other from the time Mercer and I reached the site ten minutes earlier. They had walked away from me so that Lieutenant Peterson could fill Mercer in on what he and Mike had learned since being called to the scene, while I stood at the woman's feet, staring down at her from time to time, half hoping she would open her eyes and speak to us. We were all waiting for one of the medical examiners to arrive and take a look at the body so it could be bagged and removed from this desolate strip of earth on Manhattan's northernmost tip before onlookers began to gather.

Hal Sherman rested his camera on top of the evidence collection bag and wiped the rivulets of sweat off his neck. "How'd you get here so fast?" he asked me.

"Mike was reaching out for Mercer to help him on

this one and got me in the deal. Mercer was down in court with me for pretrial hearings in an old case when Mike beeped him. Said he had a floater with a possible sexual assault, and he wanted Mercer to look at her."

"Tell the truth, kid. You couldn't resist a night on the town with the big guys, could you, blondie?" Chapman asked, after coming over to check whether Sherman had finished the photography. "Hey, Hal, who's the guy seems like he's about to lose his lunch over there?"

We all turned to look at the man, not more than twenty-five years old, who was leaning against a large boulder, taking in deep breaths of air and cupping one hand over his mouth. "Reporter for the *Times,* fresh out of journalism school. This is his third assignment, tailing me around to see how we process a crime scene. Two burglaries in the diamond district, one arson in a high school, and now—Ophelia."

Chapman went into a squat next to the right side of the woman's head, impatient with the presence of amateurs as he set to work on what was clearly the start of a homicide investigation. "Tell him he ought to look into getting the gig for restaurant reviews, Hal. Much easier on the gut."

I stepped closer to watch Chapman go over the corpse again, this time as he concentrated on details that he had observed before our arrival and explained them to Mercer Wallace. The two had been partners for several years in Manhattan North's Homicide Squad, where Chapman still worked, until Mercer had transferred over to Special Victims to handle rape cases. Despite the differences in their backgrounds and manner, they came together seamlessly to work at a crime scene or on a murder investigation.

Mercer, at forty, was five years older than Mike and I. He was one of a handful of African American detectives who had made first grade in the department, a detail man whom every senior prosecutor liked to count on, in the field and on the witness stand, to build a meticulous case. He was as solid as a line-backer but had passed up a football scholarship at Michigan to join the NYPD. Slower to smile than Mike Chapman, Mercer was intense and steady, with a sweetness of disposition that was, for those shattered victims who encountered him, their first lifeline back to a world of normalcy.

Mike Chapman was just over six feet tall, a bit shorter than Mercer. His jet black hair framed his lean face, momentarily somber as he reviewed the dead woman in front of him. A graduate of Fordham College, where he worked his way through school as a waiter and bartender, Mike had never wavered in his determination to follow the career path of his adored father, who had been a cop for more than a quarter of a century. He had a grin that could coax me out of almost any mood, and an encyclopedic knowledge of American history and military affairs, which had been his major concentration while in school.

"Four-point restraint," Chapman began, focusing his pen like a pointer in a college classroom. The slender body was resting on a wooden ladder about eight feet long. The victim's ankles and wrists were bound to narrow rungs above her head and below her feet.

The cord used to hold the woman in place was firmly knotted and secured. Longer pieces of a thicker rope dangled from parts of the frame, and two of them still had rocks attached to their tips.

Mercer was bending over now, looking at the extremities from every angle. "Somebody went to an awful lot of trouble to make sure this body didn't come to the surface anytime before Christmas, wouldn't you say?"

He tugged at one of the loose lengths of rope, holding up the ragged end, from which it appeared a weight—perhaps another rock—had torn free.

Over the top of his head I could see Craig Fleisher, the on-call medical examiner, walking toward us. He waved a greeting and added, "Better move quickly, the vultures are gathering." Next to his parked car the satellite dish sitting above a Fox 5 television truck was suddenly visible. The first field reporter had already picked up word of the unusual find from a police scanner, and it would take only minutes before other camera crews joined him to try to get the most salacious shot of the corpse.

"What have you got, Mike? A drowning?" Fleisher asked.

"No way, Doc. Throwing her overboard was just a means of disposing of the body." We all leaned in closer as Chapman placed his hand on the crown of the woman's head and moved it slightly to the side. He slipped his pen beneath her matted black hair, which was still wet and splayed against the wooden crosspieces of the ladder, then lifted it gently to expose the scalp. "Skull was bashed in back here, maybe with a gun butt or hammer. I'd bet you'll find a fracture or two when you get in there tomorrow."

Fleisher studied the gaping wound. He was stone-faced and calm, running his fingers over the rest of the rear of the head. "Well, she wasn't in the water very long. Only a day or two at best."

He repeated what Chapman had told us when Mercer and I arrived. There was no putrefaction or decomposition, and the bruises he noted on her body were probably antemortem. "Fish and crabs usually get to work on the soft tissue pretty quickly," he explained, "but the face is completely intact here. Seems like they didn't have much of a chance."

Fleisher had trained in San Diego, so although he was a recent hire in New York, he was quite familiar with marine deaths.

"Could be our lucky break, Doc," Chapman said. "The killer—or killers—couldn't have picked a worse place to dump a body if they expected to keep it from surfacing."

The doctor straightened up and scanned the area—a barren headland, just thirty feet long, that sat at the end of a city street, nestled between Columbia University's Baker Field and below the toll bridge leading north out of Manhattan, to the Bronx. "That water sure looks angry, doesn't it?"

"Spuyten Duyvil," said Chapman. "Welcome to the neighborhood. It's an old Dutch name for this tidal strait that connects the Harlem and Hudson Rivers, separates us from the mainland."

Mike knew the background as well as I did. Settlers in New Amsterdam had called it that in the early

1600s. *In spite of the devil,* they said, because the waters were so very rough, rocked by the tides in both directions. Passage through it had been impossible for centuries, until the government cut a canal almost one hundred years ago.

"Not that you'll see any Dutchmen around here now, Doc. Rice and beans replaced Heineken's a few years back, if you know what I mean. But they named it well."

The kid reporter had gotten to his feet and come up behind me, out of direct view of the body but close enough to listen to the conversation and jot down what we were saying.

"You mind not putting anything on paper for the time being?" Chapman asked, in a voice that was more of an order than a question. "You'd be required to give your scribbled musings to Miss Cooper here. It would become discovery material for the trial and she'd have to turn your notes over to the defense, once we catch the prick who did this."

"But, but I'm—uh—there's a privil—"

"You want to wait in the car while we do this, or you want to stand here quietly like a good scout and count on your memory to get this right? The local history you can find in a book, the current events are off the record. Start with the fact that she's got a crater the size of a teacup in the back of her head and that nobody planned on her doing any laps once she hit the water. Now keep out of my way. Understood?"

Chapman turned back to our small group, which was huddled around the body. Only the police divers, dressed in their scuba gear and holding for directions, stood off to the side as the rest of us waited for Fleisher to finish his inspection. Wallace had sent Officer Carrera up to his radio car to get a blanket, and he and another cop were holding it open as a shield between the dead woman and the curious busy-bodies who were gathering on 207th Street. He opened his cell phone and called the local precinct for crowd control backup as the news crew moved up within feet of our operation.

"Who's the blonde?" I heard the Fox 5 news reporter ask his cameraman.

"Alexandra Cooper. District Attorney's Office. Runs the Sex Crimes Unit for the D.A., Paul Battaglia. Probably means the cops think the deceased was raped. They always bring her in on those cases."

I wanted to hear what else the cameraman was going to say about our work, but Fleisher was talking again and I focused back on his remarks.

"You've got a female Caucasian who I'd guess to be in her late thirties." I had recently turned thirty-five, and I peered down at the frozen gaze of the woman, wondering what had brought her to this violent end, so prematurely. "I'm not going to turn her over or do any more work here, gentlemen. Too many eyes. But I'm certain the cause will be blunt force trauma—that blow to the head which Chapman located for us. I don't think we'll find any signs at autopsy that she was alive when she was submerged."

Fleisher went on. "Possible sexual assault. We'll be checking the vaginal vault for abrasions. I would doubt there'll be seminal fluid of value, once the sea-water invaded. Hard to tell whether the missing clothes suggest rape or the rough current ripping them out of place."

The well-toned body of the young woman still had a beige silk shell covering her bra, and a skirt of the same material. Both had tears and rips in the fine fabric. But there were no underpants, and I noticed what appeared to be finger marks embedded in the skin of her inner thighs.

"Doesn't look like a local girl, does she, Mercer?" Chapman remarked. The Thirty-fourth Precinct still housed some elegant old apartment buildings, but it was not one of the tonier neighborhoods of the city. "Check out the fingernails and pedicure. From the shape she's in, I'd bet she spent a lot of time on the StairMaster."

The vermilion polish on her toes and nails had been slightly chipped by her struggle with her assailant or by the tides. It was clear that she had taken good care of herself, until this week.

The Eyewitness News truck had joined the posse. "Hey, Mike," I heard a voice call out from the far side of the blanket Carrera was holding, "got anything for us?"

"Gimme a break, Pablo. Have a little respect for the dead. C'mon, Doc. Can we get her out of here now?"

Fleisher told him to cover the body, move the waiting ambulance in, and load up the ladder as it was, its cargo still lashed to the wood. "Need anything else from me?"

Chapman shook his head and said he'd be at the morgue for the autopsy proceeding the next day. He bent over and noted the name of the manufacturer on the underside of the ladder before an attendant loaded it onto the van.

"Summer backlog," Fleisher said. "I won't get to this one until two P.M., and that's with jumping her over a few unclaimed souls I've got in the cooler."

Four new arrivals from the precinct formed a human chain to separate the growing crowd from the diminishing group of us who were standing where the lady on the ladder had been.

Chapman walked over to talk with the lieutenant, who was watching the scuba team members tether themselves to huge pieces of equipment that Emergency Services had ferried to the scene. They were going to attempt to crawl around the border of the whirling passage in the unlikely possibility that they could feel for any evidence or weapon. It was obvious that there would be nothing to see along the silt-lined sides and bottom of the treacherous waterway gap.

"Don't waste their time or energy, Loo," Chapman urged Peterson, using the informal nickname that rank evoked from all detectives. "She didn't go into the drink anywhere near here. Could have been Yonkers, could have been the Bronx. It's just my good fortune that she stubbed her toe and washed up on a little piece of Manhattan North. I haven't picked up anything except drug shoot-outs in weeks."

Only Mike Chapman would consider this discovery to be his good fortune. I looked around the neglected plot that had become this woman's temporary graveyard, its surface littered with broken beer bottles, empty crack vials, scores of spots of pigeon droppings, and a few dozen used condoms.

Mercer Wallace came up beside me, grasping my elbow in his enormous black hand and guiding me out to the street, running interference for me through the rows of news teams and the neighborhood cronies who were looking for excitement now that darkness had fallen. He unlocked the passenger door of his car and I ducked into the seat.

People moved back to the sidewalk as Mercer made a U-turn on the narrow road, and we drove off. He turned in and out of a maze of one-way streets, accelerating when he reached Broadway, taking me downtown and across Central Park to my apartment, on the Upper East Side. I was silent for blocks.

"Where are you, Alex? Talk to me. I can't let you go upstairs alone just thinking about that body. She'll be with you all night. You'll never close your eyes."

I knew that without being told. But I was deeply distressed and much too wired to sleep after what we had just seen, despite my exhaustion from a couple of weeks of hard-fought courtroom battle in front of a demanding judge. "Thanks, Mercer. Just wondering about the obvious, knowing that there aren't any logical answers. I'll be fine."

"We'll get him, Alex. It doesn't seem very likely tonight. But Chapman and me, we'll get him. In spite of the devil, Miss Cooper. In spite of the devil."

# 2

A cold blast hit me as I opened my apartment door. Thank God I had forgotten to turn down the air conditioner. The coolness felt good as I moved into the bedroom to take off my wilted suit.

The green light flashed on my answering machine. I smiled at the thought of hearing a friendly voice or two, someone who would ease my transition from a scene of violence to the peace of my home, secure and comforting, on the twentieth floor of a high-rise apartment. I pressed the playback button as I began to undress.

I was on my way to the shower when I heard the voice that I had been waiting for, so I walked back and sat on the side of my bed. "Alex? . . . Alex? . . . It's Jake . . ." The telephone connection sizzled and faded. Before I could move, it started again. "Don't know if you can hear me . . . still in China . . . and . . . must be about nine o'clock your time. Sorry I missed you . . . I'll see you . . . and just wanted to tell you that . . ." I pushed the replay button. The machine hadn't captured any more words than I had heard, but it was

Jacob Tyler's voice that I wanted to listen to over and over. We had been dating for only a couple of months and the newness of the relationship still got me tingling when I heard him speak. I pushed the save button and went in to shower.

I lifted my face up to the steaming water that poured out at me and drizzled down the length of my legs. I reached for the bar of soap and stared at my fingernail, noticing the chip of polish at its tip. My eyes closed and all I could see was the bright red on the nails of the dead woman's hand. I opened my eyes and shook my head, willing myself not to call up other memories of that body on the ladder. There would be all night for such visions, as I knew too well from past experience. I scrubbed the day's grime off my face and body, then dried and wrapped myself tightly in a warm, thick terry robe.

I toweled my hair as I played Jake's message once more. I was smiling again, imagining what he might have said in between the snatches of words that were actually recorded and not gobbled up by the satellites. I'd have to phone my best friend, Nina, and tell her about Jake's call. I could guess what her response would be: "What good is it to have a guy half a world away when you need him to put his arms around you right now?"

Maybe I'd wait and call her tomorrow. She wasn't wrong about my needing Jake, but I had been dealing with images of victims for more than ten years. Most of the time, my work was with women who survived their assailants and who would triumph in the courtroom. But very little could soften the shock of seeing firsthand the destruction of a human life—a life as young as my own, as full of promise and hope as I dreamed mine would be.

I shook the dampness off my hair and looked at my watch. It would be morning in China. I had no idea where Jake was at the moment and no office number abroad at which to call him back. I wished he were here with me now. This was not a night to be alone.

My head ached and my stomach was making noises, demanding to be fed. I pressed the telephone button to speed-dial the deli on the next corner and order a turkey sandwich. I could nourish the body if not the soul.

"Sorry, Alex. It's almost ten o'clock," said Clare at P. J. Bernstein's delicatessen. "We're just closing up."

I never cooked at home, so I knew there would be nothing in the refrigerator. I had cans of soup in the cabinet, but it was too warm out to entertain the thought of hot soup. I put some ice cubes in a glass, moving on to the den to fix myself a stiff Dewar's. A mystery novel waited for me next to my bed, but there was nothing like the sight of a real corpse to alienate me from the genre for a couple of weeks. Jake had left a dog-eared Henry James on my dresser. Perhaps I'd start that instead of trying to go to sleep.

I hadn't bothered to turn on the lights before I sat on the sofa, drink in hand, and gazed out over the city. Soft music from my CD system distracted me until Linda Ronstadt began to sing about the hungry women down on Rue Morgue Avenue. I flashed again to the body on the ladder and visualized the setting where it rested tonight.

The sharp buzz of the phone startled me. I caught it on the third ring.

"You almost sound happy to hear from me for a change."

"Mike?" I asked, having hoped it would be Jake.

"Wrong voice, huh? Don't go getting dejected 'cause it's me. It's not like I'm the Unabomber or Ted Bundy calling you for a quick squeeze. The lieutenant asked me to get hold of you. Says he'd really like you to be at Compstat in the morning."

Compstat—comparative computer statistics—the NYPD's hot new demonstration for leadership accountability. Meetings held at headquarters several times a month, in the War Room, to show off the commissioner's ability to identify and solve the city's crime problems.

"What time do I have to be there?"

"Seven o'clock sharp. Seems the brass went berserk over this one tonight—it screws up all the mayor's statistics for the month. The commish may even call on you if he gets frisky and wants answers for all his questions, or wants to blame your boss for refusing to prosecute some of the quality-of-life cases."

"Thanks for the warning."

"You sound really flat, kid. You okay?"

"My head's still back at Spuyten Duyvil, if you know what I mean. Want to grab a pizza and come on up here for supper?"

"Sorry, Coop. It's almost eleven o'clock. We'll be working most of the night, trying to figure out who this broad is and when she got popped in the river. See you at reveille. Better sleep with the night-light on."

It wasn't the dark that frightened me. It was the fact that moving around out there, below my window, were creatures capable of splitting open the head of a young woman and throwing her body into the water. I stared out at the lights of Manhattan for the next hour, watching them gradually go off as people went to sleep. And all the time, as I sat awake, I thought about the monsters who walk among us.

# 3

There were still a few cars parked on Hogan Place near my office, most of which belonged to the lawyers working the midnight shift in night court, when I pulled my Jeep into a reserved slot behind the district attorney's space at six forty-five on Friday morning. I took the shortcut over to One Police Plaza, cutting behind the Metropolitan Correctional Center and alongside the staggeringly expensive new federal courthouse, which made our digs, complete with oversized rodents and roaches that obviously thrived on Combat, look like judicial facilities in some third-world country. I stopped at a cart being wheeled into place by one of the regular street vendors and bought two cups of black coffee, remembering that the brew served in the hallway outside the meeting room was too weak to start me up for the day.

One by one, black Crown Vics with red flashers mounted on each dashboard pulled into the tightly secured parking garage beneath Police Headquarters, marking the arrival of bosses from all the commands in Manhattan North, the upper half of the island. I continued past that underground entrance and jogged up the two tiers of granite steps, walking around in front of the building to display my identification to the cop at the door and run my shoulder bag through the metal detector.

"Eighth floor," the guard said. "Elevator's behind the wall to the back."

I knew the way well. In over ten years as a prosecutor, I had come to this building more times than I cared to count. Some days I was sent to sit in at meetings called by the commissioner in which the district attorney himself had no interest; on other occasions I came to brainstorm on investigative strategies in cases the department was struggling to solve; frequently I was there to plead for manpower in a matter that was not getting appropriate police attention; and every now and then—under this administration's budget-driven oversight—I walked over to attend the promotion of a friend to a higher-ranking post.

Compstat had revolutionized the accountability of precinct commanders when it was introduced to the department in the early nineties. Several times a month, at seven o'clock in the morning, bosses from one of the city's geographic divisions were summoned to appear at One Police Plaza, to spend the next three hours being grilled by the chief of operations and two of his trusted henchmen. There was only one direction in which this mayor wanted the crime rate to move, and each man was called upon to answer for the evil that crossed his borderlines and played havoc with the numbers regularly released to the press by the Public Information deputy.

When the elevator doors opened on eight, I was facing a wall of blue-uniformed backs of the commanding officers, pressing ahead against each other as the invited guests who were not members of the department turned the corner to enter the Operations Room and take their seats in anticipation of the arrival of Chief Lunetta.

Chapman called out to me before I noticed him, wedged between two full inspectors who were laughing at whatever tale he was spinning. "Hey, Coop! Meet Lenny McNab. Just been transferred over to clean up the Three-three. Take a good look at him now, because after this meeting I doubt he'll be able to sit down for a week."

McNab shook his head and my hand at the same time. The newspapers had been full of stories about the string of bodega burglaries in McNab's territory. If he couldn't account for progress in the investigation by this morning, he'd be made to look like a fool by the three grand inquisitors.

Lunetta's voice boomed out at us from the stairwell door. "Let's get it going, guys. We've got a lot to cover this morning." His entourage brushed past us and we dutifully followed.

Room 802 was a cavernous space, with double-height ceilings and state-of-the-art electronic equipment, that had been designed to become Command Central in case of any terrorist takeover or natural disaster in New York City. Three gigantic media screens filled the front wall of the room, which was lined on one length with concealed booths—to hold the crisis solvers at more critical points in time, and observers on more benign occasions—while the other wall was decorated with police shields and murals featuring flags of various law enforcement agencies. Two tables ran through the center of the room from forward to rear, around which the commanders seated themselves with the personnel who ran their investigative and uniformed forces, as well as a few detectives who might be called upon to explain the status of a particular case that had attracted media attention.

Directly beneath the huge screens was the podium, to which speakers would be called at the whim of the chief of operations. Lunetta would tell the computer programmer who sat beside him which graphics to display over their heads on the three screens—usually starting with a map of the precinct, a chart of the previous month's crime statistics, and a graph plotting the most recent week's violent crime activity, with robberies flagged in red, rapes in blue, and burglaries in green.

Lunetta and his superchiefs sat in the rear at a table perpendicular to the array of well-decorated men spread down the center of the room. He was tall and lean, with angled features and black hair that was drawn sleekly back and trimmed at the neck in military fashion. He looked great in the dark navy blue uniform, and knew it.

My seat was in one of the three rows of folding chairs behind the chief's position, which were reserved for non-NYPD spectators. Each chair was labeled with a scrap of paper torn from a legal pad. Excusing myself, I tried to slither into place, passing over two lawyers from the United States Attorney's Office and four guys from upstate police departments, before sitting down next to a woman who introduced herself as a trend researcher from the Department of Justice. I opened the lid of my coffee cup and took a slug as Lunetta called the first group of officers to the podium.

Frank Guffey moved forward to the mike, flanked by his supervising staff. He was smart and well liked by police and prosecutors, a tough boss who had been moved from the East Harlem area a year earlier down to the cushy confines of Wall Street, and now back to the high-crime neighborhood of the Twenty-eighth Precinct.

"G'morning, Chief. I'm reporting on the period that closed July thirty-first." Guffey smiled and paused briefly, weighing whether to add a personal pleasantry. "Nice to be here again in the North, after a brief visit to Manhattan South, sir."

Lunetta shot back, "I hope you can say as much *after* the meeting."

"First of all, the decrease in overall crime continues." Clearly, Guffey knew the drill. That's what these guys wanted to hear, right out of the box. "Now, we do show an increase in robberies, but—"

Forget the "buts," buddy. I watched as Lunetta turned his head ninety degrees and gave a command to the computer programmer sitting at his right shoulder. Seconds later, the three overhead graphics changed. A

map of the Twenty-eighth Precinct's territory domi-
nated the middle screen.

Lunetta barked, "Break them down for me,
Inspector. I want them by day of the week, and then by
the time of day of the tour."

Before Guffey could lift his papers and find the correct answers, we could all see the numbers in the pro-
jections that the chief's team had prepared for this
attack.

"I want to get right into these spikes, Guffey. Take
us through them. Give me reasons."

I could see the color rise in Frank's cheeks, as most
of the bosses around the tables seemed to squirm in
sympathy.

Guffey started to respond. "Several of them seem to
be the work of the same team, Chief. The numbers
started to spike when a pair of male Hispanics began
to hit a couple of apartments on Broadway, just north
of McDonald's. Same M.O. Gain entry with a ruse—
female knocking on the door for the perps and asking
for her sister. Then she disappears while the guys tie
up everyone inside with speaker wire—"

"Drug related?"

"Probably. Only, the one last week, on the twenty-
ninth—"

"You mean the restaurant manager they burned
with an iron?" Lunetta thrived on displaying to the
crowd how well he could learn the detail of hundreds
of these cases, outlined for him in his briefing books,
and talk about them as familiarly as if he were working on them himself.

"Yeah. We figure that was a mistake. They went to

the wrong apartment. I got Louis Robertson here. They're his cases, if you'd like to hear from him."

"Not unless he's got answers for me, Guffey. Excuses I got plenty of. It's answers I want. You guys doing the obvious? Running fingerprints through Safis?" The new, automated fingerprint-matching system was solving scores of cases that used to require tedious hand searches. "Checking with surrounding precincts to see if they got anything like this going? Parole—probation—informants? I assume you'll study these charts and decide how to redeploy your manpower to address the situation more aggressively."

Guffey said his men had been doing all of the above and that he would certainly make use of the time charts. He got through the other crime categories fairly gracefully and back to his seat without a great deal of damage.

Inspector Jaffer was next up. A real breath of fresh air for the department. As I ran my eyes around the table, Joanne Jaffer and Jane Pearl were the only two women inspectors I noted in the room. They were both young, bright, and attractive, and were changing a lot of opinions about female bosses in the department, held by too many of the hairbags, those dyed-in-the-wool old-timers who were petrified in their traditions.

Jaffer's numbers in the Twentieth Precinct were excellent. The Upper West Side had always been one of the safest residential areas in Manhattan. Robberies, burglaries, and car thefts continued to be lower than ever. No homicides in over six months. Her only problem was a serial rapist who had been operating for more than two years—hitting sporadically, and not even linked to a pattern until DNA tests on the rape kits had confirmed that the most recent attack was committed by the same assailant as the first one, which had occurred more than twenty months ago. Battaglia had been asked to address a community meeting about the case in a few days and would be pleased if I could come back to him after this morning with a sense about the chief's role in the investigation.

Jaffer gave her report and began to answer Lunetta's questions about the rapist.

"How many cases you up to now, Inspector?"

Jaffer answered sharply. "Eight, sir. That we know of. Eight with an identical M.O., and two of those have been linked to each other by DNA. Serology is working on two others this week."

"What took you so long to put this pattern together? Somebody asleep in the station house?"

She started to answer, as a hand went up on the right side of the room. Sergeant Pridgen, who was assigned to Special Victims, was responsible for the task force handling the investigation. He had been running the cases long before Jaffer became involved and was trying to jump in to take some of the heat.

Lunetta ignored Pridgen's waving arm. I knew he'd like to see Jaffer sweat, and I kept my fingers crossed that he would fail to make it happen.

"Serology finally came up with a cold hit, Chief. That's what broke it for us."

Her answers were clipped, to the point, and good.

The investigation had floundered until the Medical Examiner's Office made a computer match—known in the still-evolving language of genetic fingerprinting as a "cold hit"—between DNA samples left by the rapist in his victims' bodies more than two years ago and those found in the most recent case. Cops who had argued about whether or not the older attacks bore any connection to the current crimes were silenced by the stunning ability of the database to definitively link an assailant's targets to one another.

"Why can't serology match it to a perp in their data bank?" Lunetta asked.

"Because the bank is just up and running in New York. It's only been in operation since last year, and they've got fewer than a hundred samples from convicted rapists and murderers."

Legislation created genetic data banks in most states across the country during the late nineties, but few of their labs were equipped to process the information collected from inmates and create the pools from which to search for repeat offenders, until quite recently. It would be unlikely to get a hit on this serial rapist, who had been operating on the streets of Manhattan since the days before the law enabled the collection of blood samples from incarcerated prisoners.

Jaffer continued to describe the team's approach. Last week the department sketch artist, working with several of the victims, had completed a composite that was being distributed to stores and residences throughout the precinct—the "generic male black," as Mercer liked to describe the suspect. Medium complexion, average height, average build, between twenty-five and thirty-five years old, possible mustache, close-cropped hair, no distinguishing features, scars, or marks. Before too long, every African American adult male who set foot north of Sixtieth Street and south of Eighty-sixth Street, between Central Park West and Riverside Drive, would be stopped and questioned. Neighbors would be turning in their deliverymen or elevator operators, and good citizens would be frisked by anxious and weary cops, each one hoping to get a lucky break and catch the compulsive rapist.

"Stop dancing around, Pridgen. I'm getting to you. What else is your crew doing about this one?"

The sergeant stood to answer. "We've got Traffic giving out summonses on the midnight tour, tagging all the unregistered and uninsured plates. Mounted's working the area on weekends, which is mostly when he hits."

I could see Lunetta rolling his eyes even as I stared at the rear of his head. Mounted cops riding up and down West End Avenue at midnight on a Saturday. Not the most subtle way to patrol the neighborhood. Even the rapist might catch on and change his movements.

Pridgen continued. "We've called in the Profiling Unit at Quantico and—"

Say the magic word and the duck comes down, hitting Lunetta square on the head. "Feds? *Feds?* Whose stupid idea is that? Aren't you guys up to handling this one yourself? Answer me, Pridgen. Whose idea was it?"

Lunetta saw Pridgen flash a glance in my direction. "District attorney calling the shots on this one, Sarge? You just sit back and let them take right over and run the show, huh? Maybe you're moonlighting on the side, too busy to do major investigations? We got an opening over at the auto pound, looking after towed vehicles, if you think this is too tough for you. What does Cooper use on you guys anyway, a nose ring? Just leads you around on a leash all day? Let me know if you start rolling over on your back or baying at the moon."

The woman researcher from Justice bit into her lip and looked at me for a reaction. I didn't know whether I was blushing for Pridgen or for myself. I ripped some paper from my legal pad and dashed off a note to Lunetta, passing it forward, in which I asked his permission to explain where we were going with the investigation. By the time it reached him, was opened and read, he had continued to pepper the sergeant with questions and then kept on going at Pridgen even harder, choosing to ignore my offer. If he had intended to call on me before I asked to speak, I had just sealed my fate by assuring him that I wanted to give him answers to these questions.

"Last week's attack—was this girl coming from one of those Columbus Avenue bars, too?"

"No sir," Pridgen answered.

"Where from, then?"

"Actually, her boyfriend drove her home, just before two in the morning. Let her out of the car about half a block from her apartment, up at the corner. She walked to the front of the building alone. The rapist pushed in behind her, after she unlocked the vestibule door."

"So much for the boyfriend. I guess chivalry's dead, wouldn't you say, Sergeant? I want some progress on this one before the next time you come back here. Take your seats. I want the Three-four up now. Let's hear about last night's homicide."

Chairs pushed back and the podium assembly changed over, with Lieutenant Peterson and Chapman accompanying the CO up to the stand.

The general precinct figures were good. Lunetta was pleased that the deputy inspector in charge had taken the story of one of his burglary patterns to a local cable TV program, *¿Que Pasa NY?*, which resulted in an informant breaking the case. He liked that kind of creative policing, as he would call it. What he never had liked was wisecracking, not even back when he had been Chapman's boss in the Street Crime Unit, almost a decade earlier.

"Who's going to bring me up to speed on the new case?"

Peterson pointed at Chapman and stepped aside. Mike rested his notes on the podium and ran his fingers through his thick dark hair. He dug one hand into the pocket of his blazer, then started his description of how he was summoned to the scene. He was thorough, detailed, and professional—the best homicide cop in the business—but I fidgeted and recrossed my legs when he got to the end of the narrative and closed his description with Dr. Fleisher's directive to load "Gert" into the EMS van.

"'Gert'? I didn't know she'd been identified."

Lunetta was annoyed. His head whipped from side to side as he checked with each of his aides to see if they had failed to give him the morning update on the city's most visible crime of the moment. The case was the cover of both daily tabloids, and he should have had the newest information about the unfortunate victim before the public did.

"She hasn't been identified yet, Chief."

"Well, *is* her name Gert, or isn't it?"

Don't go there, Chief, I urged quietly from the peanut gallery. All of us who worked with Mike knew that he named his victims in every case. Always did it, and often stuck with his nickname, no matter what the eventual I.D.—his own perverse way of personalizing his cases.

"I call her that, Chief, so she's not just some number, some cold statistic for the mayor to get off on. I named this one in honor of Gertrude Ederle—three Olympic medals and the English Channel. I figure, given the way somebody tried to send her to sleep with the fishes for keeps, she must have had the soul of a great swimmer to stay afloat."

There were a few snickers around the room, but most of the group knew it wasn't the safest direction to follow.

Lunetta wouldn't bite twice. He moved away to the next questions. "What are you looking at here?"

Chapman went on. "After the autopsy results today, we'll work on a press release and sketch."

"Can't you give the papers a photo from the scene—a close-up? Get an I.D. more quickly?"

"I don't think the way she looked coming out of the

water is the way any of her loved ones would want to see her featured. We're working with Missing Persons and each of the precincts."

"You checking every area that borders the creek? May turn out to be a Bronx homicide after all, Chapman. The numbers get tallied in the precinct where the crime occurred, you know."

"I don't care where she dove in, Chief. *We* got her now."

Fat chance, Lunetta. Count it as an outer-borough murder so we keep the Manhattan numbers down? Nope, I'm with Chapman. She landed here, and no matter where she was killed, that gives us jurisdiction.

"I see from the newspapers that you had Miss Cooper up at the scene last night. You throwing in the towel, too, Detective? Ready to call in the Feds? I can't help but wonder what it is you need a pet D.A. for at all these crime scenes and station houses. D'you carry her lipstick case for her, or her hairbrush?" The chief smirked at his put-down, jabbing the detective and me in the same thrust.

But trying to embarrass Chapman that way wouldn't quite work. He'd simply use the opportunity to get more laughs, even if they would be at my expense. "No, no, sir. She never lets me near the makeup. You know me, Chief—I'm strictly a leg man. I'm in charge of her spare panty hose. Each time there's a run in one of those suckers, I pull out a replacement pair. Best I can do at the moment."

A couple of my friends around the room raised their eyes cautiously to meet mine, to make sure I was rolling with the flow. Not a problem. Battaglia had trained me well. I could control my short fuse with the knowledge I'd get some shots back at the chief eventually. The district attorney might even take them on my behalf.

Lunetta's number-two man leaned over and whispered something to him, flipping through the briefing book to an earlier page. He scanned it and looked up. "Is that case of the body that came out of the East River last month related to this one, you think? That's still open, isn't it?"

"Yeah, but no connection. That one, a homeless man was fishing, hooked up and pulled an arm out of the water. Right out of its socket, actually. Scuba went in and found the rest of the body, weighted down with concrete blocks. She'd been in the water more than half a year. Feet bound, ligature round the neck. That's a mob case—got a good snitch who's working with us. We know who we're looking for, just haven't been able to find him yet."

Great restraint, Mikey. He had resisted the temptation to tell Lunetta that he had christened that victim "Venus." A one-armed Italian woman in a cement overcoat didn't lend herself to any appellation except Venus de Milo.

The aide whispered to Lunetta again. "We had Bronx South here on Wednesday of last week. They've got a rape pattern as well in a couple of the housing projects. You might check over there to see if there are any similarities."

Chapman looked less than interested. The likelihood that the well-groomed, silk-clad woman he had dubbed Gert had anything to do with ghetto dwellings in a run-down neighborhood that wasn't his official territory didn't engage him very seriously.

Lunetta listed off a punch list of places to go and things to do that would have been elementary for a rookie homicide detective. Mike listened patiently and assured the chief that as soon as they figured out who the deceased was, he'd be off and running. "I assume we'll know who she is by the end of the day."

"That's great, Chapman. Then I'll expect an arrest within the week. Maybe next time you'll do a better job keeping the shutterbugs away from the scene you're working. No reason for a case like this to be front-page news, except for the photo opportunity you gave them. Now it'll take a couple of days to make these headlines go away."

Lunetta finished snapping at Chapman, looked around the room, and announced to the bosses, "I think you gentlemen realize how much the commissioner hates it when this kind of thing happens. Tourists aren't scared away by drug dealers killing each other off on their own turf or gang members shooting other gang members to death. But if this woman turns out to be an innocent victim of violence, I don't think I have to tell you what it means to the city. Last night, at a fund-raiser, the mayor was just telling his supporters that murders in New York had dropped to their lowest numbers in more than a quarter of a century—when he got word of this mess." Lunetta scanned the brass arrayed in front of him. "That's the point of all these exercises—in case it's slipped your minds. Letting everyone know how safe this city has become. Our homicide rate hasn't been this good since nineteen sixty-one."

Chapman made sure he muttered into the microphone as he picked up his notes and pocketed them. "I hate to burst Hizzoner's bubble, but I gotta tell you his numbers are small comfort to the broad who's laid out in a refrigerator up at the morgue, waiting for her last physical."

# 4

Mike spent most of the short walk over to my office, three blocks north of One Police Plaza, trying to worm his way back into my good graces. I was used to being the butt of Chapman's humor and had long ago stopped letting it get to me. It was not even ten thirty and I was already more bothered by the oppressive heat that had blanketed the ugly stretch of asphalt that ran in front of the city and state buildings along Centre Street.

"Aren't you going to be late for court?" he asked me as we rounded the corner and I stopped at the cart to buy us each another round of coffee. Mike called up to the vendor to throw in a cruller for him, too. "Couldn't eat a thing last night. Kept looking into that hole in the back of Gert's head every time I closed my eyes."

"No court on Friday. The defendant's a Muslim. Today's his holy day," I answered, hanging my identification tag on a chain around my neck as we approached the entrance to the District Attorney's Office.

"Reggie Bramwell's a Muslim? I collared him on a gun case five years ago, and he was a full-press Baptist then. I'm sure of it."

"Jailhouse conversion, Mike," I said, pushing through the revolving doors and holding the security gate open for one of my colleagues who was on her way out of the building, headed toward the other courthouse, pushing a shopping cart loaded with evidence. "A week ago Thursday, in fact. Must have been a deeply religious experience. Someone at Rikers Island convinced him of the joys of the three-day workweek. The judge uses Wednesday as a calendar day, and the prisoner—Reggie Bramwell, now also known to the court as Reggie X—gets to worship on Friday. Just prolongs my agony for a few days. In fact, I think he's just doing this because he knows I wanted some vacation time this month—and if he can't go to the beach, why should I?"

We waited for one of the three elevators to return to the lobby floor, while a small commotion started behind us. "Alex, tell this jerk who I am, will you please?" a familiar voice called out.

My colleague Pat McKinney was standing in front of the security counter dressed in his running clothes, which were drenched with sweat, arguing with the officer on duty. Pat's already reddened complexion was deepening and appeared to spreading to the tips of his ears and down his neck.

"I'm telling you I left my I.D. on top of that pad next to the telephone before I went out at nine thirty. Now, if somebody moved it or walked off with it, that's *your* problem and not mine."

The cop, obviously a summer replacement who was stuck with this security detail, didn't recognize the deputy chief of the Trial Division. Most of us who jogged from time to time during our lunch hours had taken to leaving our photo identification tags at the entrance desk and picking them up on our way back in. The officers from the Fifth Precinct who regularly worked the desk knew most of us by sight and held the tags in a pile on the corner of the counter, behind the bank of telephones. I had no time for running these days, because of my hearings, and no inclination either, because of the intense heat. McKinney, who liked to take his daily jog earlier than the lunch hour break during the hot summer months, was probably more aggravated by the fact that this police officer didn't recognize him than that the officer had misplaced his only means of official access to the building.

I held the bucking elevator door open with my left arm and started to explain to the officer that I would vouch for McKinney, despite the fact that he hated my guts.

Chapman nudged me out of the way by bumping his hip up against mine and clamping his hand on the button that said *Close*. He was also calling out to the cop as the doors came together in front of my face. "Hey, Officer. Don't let that guy in. He's a whack job—comes around here all the time, looking to get in. The real McKinney has a huge wart on the tip of his nose and foams at the mouth a lot."

"That'll do wonders to break the ice between me and my supervisor, don't you think?" I asked as I pressed the button for the eighth floor and replaced my sunglasses in their case.

"What's the difference? McKinney hasn't had a decent word to say about you in the entire time you've been here. Screw him. Who's going to miss him for the next half hour, his girlfriend?"

"What girlfriend? You mean Ellen? She just works for him, she's not his girlfriend."

We got off the elevator and headed for my office.

"Don't tell me you're as gullible as his wife, Coop. All that platonic crap? 'Beep me, darling, I'm working on a gun bust tonight with the cops. Field assignment. Midnight grand jury.' You know anybody else in the Trial Division who gets the kind of close supervision Ellen does? One on one, behind closed doors? Trust me. Next time he gives you any trouble, I'll run interference for you."

My secretary, Laura, had a smile on her face by the time we came into view, no doubt hearing Mike's voice as we made our way down the hall together. He broke into his best Smokey Robinson imitation as she began to go through the morning's messages with me. She sailed through the first six, all of which could be returned later, accompanied by Mike's humming and finger snapping. When he broke out his modified lyrics—"And in case you go to court, then a lawyer is the one you want to see . . . but in case you want love, Laura . . . call on me"—I gave up the battle and went in to my desk to see what else awaited me.

I opened the desk drawer and took three extra-strength Tylenols. The fatigue of the trial schedule on top of my usual duties supervising the Sex Crimes

Prosecution Unit had been wearing me down. Sarah Brenner, my close friend and second in command, had been ordered by her obstetrician to stay at home, since she was already three days overdue with her second child. I had all weekend to complete the legal memorandum the judge in the Reggie X case expected from me on Monday, so I decided to focus first on the queries from the other lawyers in the unit.

"Who sounded more critical?" I called out to Laura.

"If I were you, I'd get Patti down here first. Want me to call her?"

"Yeah. Then back her up with Ryan, please."

Mike took off his navy blazer and hung it on the back of one of the chairs before picking up the pile of morning newspapers that had been delivered to my desk. He was looking to see whether any clever reporter had scooped him on some aspect of the Gert murder that he might have missed.

Patti Rinaldi was one of my favorite young assistants—a solid lawyer with sound judgment and dogged courtroom style. Her enthusiasm for her work, and for resolving the plight of her victims, seemed to emanate from her when she entered my small office carrying the case file of her latest problem.

"A vision in lavender, Ms. Rinaldi," Chapman said, eyeing the tall, thin brunette carefully over the top of his *New York Post*. "You look ravishing today. You're not cheating on me, are you?"

"Cooper doesn't leave me any time to even think about it, Mike. I worked the four-to-twelve shift on intake last night. Thought you'd want to know about this one, Alex. Have you had any cases at a sleep disorder clinic yet?"

"Not so far."

"I think we got our first."

Mike's interest was piqued. "What's a sleep disorder clinic?"

"Latest psychobabble moneymaker. Almost every medical center has one at this point. Patients who have trouble with sleep—insomniacs, sleepwalkers, snorers, you name it—come in to be 'examined' while they sleep. Idea is to find a cure for the problem."

Patti added to my description. "And they pay dearly—a thousand, fifteen hundred dollars per visit—just to spend the night on a cot and let somebody 'watch' them sleep, measure their dream time and the intervals between dream segments."

"Are there job openings?" Mike asked. "I suppose by now someone's come up with my time-tested solution. Two cocktails, get laid, roll over, and smoke a cigarette—guaranteed to put you out for hours. Maybe I could be a consultant."

"Is this one of the legitimate operations, Patti?"

"Yes, Alex. It's affiliated with Saint Peter's Hospital. It's located in a large office building which houses all their clinics up on Amsterdam Avenue. This is actually run by the head of their Department of Psychiatry, so they treat the whole thing very seriously."

"Your victim?"

"Her name is Flora. Very fragile twenty-two-year-old who lives with her mother in Flatbush. Met the defendant a couple of years ago when he was her psychology professor at Brooklyn College. She began to see him for therapy after the school year, but was smart enough to stop the sessions when he started coming on to her sexually.

"Now, almost two years have gone by and she was suffering from depression. Found his number in the book, called him, and he made an appointment for her to come in to the clinic, where he told her he's currently working. Said he still did therapy on the side."

I was taking notes as Patti continued the narrative.

"Flora got to the office at eight o'clock on Tuesday night. Paid the therapist—his name is Ronald—for the session, and at the end he advised her that she needed to get a job, to engage herself in something serious. He offered her a position as a computer analyst at the clinic. Took out a contract for one year's employment from his desk, signed it, and had her do the same."

I had dozens of questions to ask, but rather than punctuate Patti's story, I would let her tell it and assume she would cover most of what I needed to know.

"Finally, Ronald took the contract back and told Flora that he wouldn't make his boss, the chief physician, enforce it unless she thanked him right now by performing oral sex."

"I am definitely in the wrong line of work," Chapman mumbled.

Patti went on. "Ronald waved the contract back and forth in front of her and kept repeating, 'No blow job, no job.' He reduced Flora to tears in about five minutes, and she complied with the condition.

Meanwhile, in a few of the cubicles attached to Ronald's module, people were sleeping—naked, of course, with monitors attached to measure their breathing, their blood pressure, their REMs, and so on. So when Ronald handed her back her half of the contract, he told her this was better than usual. He said that most of the time he stood there and masturbated while he watched the struggling sleepers try to find the Land of Nod."

Chapman was on his feet. "You mean these idiots are paying big bucks to have this frigging pervert get his rocks off watching them toss and turn? That'd cure my insomnia instantly. I'd like to tie him to a chair by his testicles and make him listen to lullabies for twenty-four hours. See how he sleeps. I don't get it, Coop. This stuff you people work on makes murder look comprehensible."

"How'd she come forward, Patti?"

"When Flora called Ronald yesterday to ask when she could start to work, he told her that there was no job because he really didn't have any power to hire or fire employees. She stormed right into the clinic and showed the contract to the physician in charge, who said it was bogus. So she went directly to a pay phone on the corner and called the cops. I thought you ought to know about it before I did anything on the case."

"Good thinking." Brownnosing worked with me almost every time. Patti knew that if we, as prosecutors, could direct the course of an investigation pre-arrest, we could usually build a stronger case for trial.

"What's to think about?" Chapman asked. "Cuff him and put him in the can, now."

"What's the crime, Mikey? What does Patti charge him with?" I stood with my back to the air conditioner, trying to cool down as we talked.

"Sodomy in the first," Mike suggested.

"I didn't hear you describe any force, did I?" Patti shook her head in the negative in response to my question.

"Public lewdness," Mike spat out at me.

"It's not a public place. Ronald's sitting right in his own office when he's playing with himself. Expectation of privacy and all that," I countered.

"I told you murder is easy. You got a dead body, an unnatural cause of death, and it's one kind of homicide or another. You girls gotta sit here and play Find the Crime."

"Here's what you do," I suggested to Patti. "Bring Flora in and get all the facts. See if you can make out a coercion charge. Try section 135.60 of the Penal Law, sub 9—compelling her to perform an act which might be harmful to health, safety, reputation, et cetera.

"Also, there's a good chance he's been holding himself out as a doctor or some other licensed position at the clinic. Figure on next Wednesday—that's my calendar day, so I'm free to go with you. You can have a search warrant prepared and ready by then. We'll have a couple of guys from the squad take us up to the clinic, and we'll go in that morning with the warrant. That way we can seize all his personnel records, Flora's files, his appointment book, any documents he has on his walls—with credentials that can be checked out—and any other information you can develop during your interview with Flora. No one will be on notice that we're coming, so none of the records will be destroyed. Let's keep this one quiet. No need to embarrass the legitimate part of this operation at Saint Peter's, okay?"

Patti picked up her folder and was gone. I found my list of topics I needed to update Battaglia about and added this one to it. I had to remember to ask his executive assistant, Rose Malone, whether he had accepted the invitation I heard he had received to be Saint Peter's Hospital Humanitarian of the Year, for his charitable work on behalf of underprivileged kids.

"Don't you have anything to do?" I asked Chapman after I told Laura to get Ryan Blackmer over to see me. Mike was lifting things up from the piles on top of my desk and reading them. Some were complaint reports and investigation updates, others were personal notes and messages.

"Nothing till the autopsy this afternoon. I was hoping you'd come with me to Forlini's and grab a bite to eat. I'm always more content in the morgue when I've got a full stomach."

"I don't have time to go out for lunch today. Call Kindler or Holmes—just get out of my hair for a while so I can catch up on everything here."

"Have you returned yesterday's call to Jacob Tyler yet?" Chapman asked, fanning out a handful of messages from Laura's telephone pad. "And does that one have anything to do with the fact that the white lace camisole you ordered is out of stock but will be shipped by FedEx as soon as—"

I lurched across the desk and ripped the papers from Mike's hand as Ryan entered the office.

"Well, I can't imagine that the underwear delivery would upset you, so there must be something about the call from the newscaster that has you jumping, Ms. Cooper. Go easy on her, Ryan, it's been a long morning." Mike always liked to tease me about my social life, but I hadn't yet told him that I had been dating Jake and knew this wasn't the right moment to explain the relationship to him.

Ryan was as good-natured as he was competent, and for every serious case that he indicted, five or six more bizarre situations wound up on his desk. "You got any time next week to help me with an interview?" he asked me. "I'd really like your opinion."

"Sure, which one?"

"Remember the Cruise to Nowhere you assigned to me? Four girls from Jersey celebrated their high school graduation by taking a weekend cruise," Ryan reminded me. "Boarded the ship in New York harbor, then it sails out past Long Island for three days. I didn't know there was anything that could float capable of holding the amount of liquor on board this thing. Or that any land-roving mammal could imbibe as much as these kids did and still be alive."

"I don't remember any of the facts. Sorry, but I've been preoccupied with my hearings."

"The girls started drinking mimosas at breakfast Saturday morning. Stacey, the victim—and I am using that word loosely, Alex—got seasick and went down to their cabin to throw up for a couple of hours. Bounced back in the afternoon for some Bloody Marys and beer. Wine and champagne with dinner. Doesn't remember anything after ten P.M. She was a bit surprised to find the ship's magician in her bunk with her—starkers—when the ship pulled into the dock on Sunday morning. She's screaming rape. And by the way, suing the cruise ship."

"The *Love Boat*," said Mike.

"Well, that's what her bunk mates say, but she's insisting she would never have done anything like that if she were sober. Personally, I don't even think we have jurisdiction if this happened more than three miles out of the harbor, but I know you believe in seeing everybody who makes a complaint."

For far too long, when rape laws prevented prosecutions and the system was not open to its survivors, women had no place to turn for justice or advocacy. One of our goals in setting up a special unit was to see all those women who wanted to report cases, and give them the appropriate guidance—whether their matter belonged in the criminal court or elsewhere.

"Make an appointment with her for the Friday after next and have Laura put it on my calendar. Just give me all your witness interview notes before then, so I know where the inconsistencies are when we start talking to Stacey. Be sure you check with Laura on Thursday, 'cause if I'm still tied up with this new homicide, I'll have to move you back a couple of days. And Ryan, what are you doing for lunch?"

He brightened and looked back at me, waiting for the offer. "Take Chapman across the street and feed him. Stick it on my tab. I've got work to do."

"I'll give you a call when we've taken care of Gertie, Ms. Cooper. Personally, I'm a little bit worried about *you*, though. I think your father's right—listening to

45

stories about all this sex and violence day in and day out can't be very good for you. C'mon, Ryan." Mike was almost out the door when he turned back and threw me the last question. "Whatever happened to romance? Doesn't anybody believe in dinner and a movie anymore?"

# 5

Alex Trebek told the noisy crowd of prosecutors and cops packing "Part F"—the name affectionately given to the bar at Forlini's, since at many points on a Friday afternoon it was likely to have more office personnel in it than most of the dozens of court parts across the street—that the Final Jeopardy category would be New York State History.

I could see Chapman's dark head positioned beneath the television that was hung in the far corner of the room, surrounded by six of the guys from Trial Bureau 50, celebrating the end of another workweek.

"Get it up, blondie!" Mike shouted down the bar at me as I squeezed through friendly packs of coworkers who were reliving their cross-examinations and telling one another about their latest triumphs and travails. "How are you on the Empire State?"

"I'll go the usual ten," I said, sliding into the space cleared for me by Ed Broderick and Kevin

Guadagno. Dempsey had seen me arrive, too, and my Dewar's on the rocks was already on the counter-top.

"All right, then," Trebek continued, fighting for our attention over the noise of the jukebox and the banter of more than a hundred of law enforcement's thirstiest troops. "The answer is: City that was the site of the largest Confederate prison camp during the Civil War."

I shook my head and rested it in my right hand, ready to acknowledge defeat, while I sipped my scotch with the left. Chapman was writing furiously on the back of a cocktail napkin. "I've been had. This isn't a New York question—it's military history," I moaned.

Mike Chapman had majored in history at Fordham College and amassed a limitless knowledge of battles, gunboats, warriors, and even the names of the stallions on which they rode. Our long-standing habit of betting on the Final Jeopardy questions—whether in the middle of a crime scene, a good meal, or a round of cocktails—had taught each of us to stay away from the categories that were the other's strong points, and I was about to be taken down in front of my colleagues on Chapman's principal strength—much to his delight.

As the timer ticked and the theme music jingled on, my mind sped through lists of upstate names, but all I could think of were prisons to which my convicted rapists had been sent over the last decade—Green Haven, Ossining, Clinton, Auburn, and so on. Nothing conjured up the Civil War. Mike was singing an Irish ballad in my ear, confusing me further, and substituting the name of one of the grimmest institutions for the town in the classic song. "How are things in Dannemora?" he crooned as I tried to brush him away from me.

Trebek picked up the card lying on the podium in front of the septuagenarian wallpaper hanger from Minnesota, saw that it was empty, and commented that it was too bad he hadn't ventured a guess.

"Take your best shot, Cooper?" Mike said.

"What is Attica?" I asked, stirring the ice cubes with my finger.

"*Bzzzzzzz.*" Mike imitated the penalty buzzer as the show's second contestant bombed with her answer, too. "What is Elmira?" he said, loud enough for everyone at our end to hear.

The Stanford professor who had won on the show four days this week also had the correct answer, and was beaming no less proudly than Chapman as Trebek congratulated him and announced that his five-day total was $38,000.

"Cooper's got the next round, Dempsey. For me and everybody in Trial Bureau 50. Elmira, the flower of Chemung County. Treaty of Painted Post proposed there in seventeen ninety-one, to end the settlers' war with the Iroquois. Wouldn't expect you to know that, kid. But three thousand Confederate soldiers are buried there. Actually, called it 'Hellmira' during the war, 'cause the conditions were so bad. What'd you think they were going to ask, Coop— where's Niagara Falls? Who's buried in Grant's Tomb? Too much time wasted at Wellesley with those Elizabethan poets and that Chaucerian crap you're so full of."

"I'm going back to the office, Mike. You want to talk autopsy before I go?"

"You gotta be kidding. We got a table in the back room—we're all having dinner together. Aren't you going to stay for that?"

"I'm taking a salad back with me. Honestly, I'll be in the library all weekend. Just tell me what happened this afternoon."

Chapman and I walked out of the bar toward the rear of the restaurant and sat at an empty table for two. "Still no I.D. Dr. Fleisher makes her out to be about forty years old, and in very good health—except for that crater in the back of her head. No kids—never given birth. He was also right about the cause. Blunt force injury—dead long before she hit the water."

"Does he know what's responsible for the laceration?" I asked.

"You can start with the fact that this wasn't a 'slip and fall.' Whatever she was hit with was hard enough to cause a skull fracture. Could have been a gun butt, a brick, a rock. Doubtful that it was a bottle or anything like that—no residue or fragments in the wound," Mike went on. "The impact was probably a glancing blow, but it was so deep that the subcutaneous tissue separated from the underlying muscle fascia."

"And the internal exam?" I asked.

"Fleisher didn't find anything remarkable. Sexually active adult female. Only thing that will interest you is that there were abrasions on her upper thighs, close to the vaginal area."

"Nobody mentioned them last night at the scene," I commented.

"Doc said it's typical with a body that's been immersed in water. That kind of injury—scraping of the skin and removal of superficial layers—only becomes noticeable after the body has dried out," Mike said.

"Were those actually finger marks I saw?" I asked, wondering if the abrasions had been caused during an attempt at a sexual assault.

"Looks consistent with that. They took lots of close-ups, so you can study them."

"How about rope burns from the ligature marks?"

Chapman described the autopsy proceeding, in which Fleisher cut the skin directly under the wrist and ankle restraints, looking for that answer. "Not enough hemorrhaging to suggest she was alive when they tied her up," he answered. "It was probably just the means of securing her body to the ladder, for the purpose of disposing of her. That's it, except for the toxicological workups, which won't be ready for another week."

"Any reason to think there'll be findings of significance?" I wondered.

"Yeah, Fleisher thinks she's had some problems with cocaine. He didn't like the looks of her nasal septum. Could be just one more of those uptown drug deals gone sour," Mike said. "She looked classy, but she undoubtedly liked to stick that sugar up her nose."

"What's next?"

"Gert just stays tucked in her fridge until somebody figures out who she is. Tomorrow morning, she's out of the newspapers, and I start looking for who-done-it."

"Give me a call over the weekend if anything develops, will you?" I asked. "I'll be down here most of the time, either in the library or at my desk."

"Don't you want a ride home later?"

"Thanks, no. I've got the Jeep right in front of the office. Ciao." I said my "Good nights" around the bar, picked up my take-out salad, and walked the quiet block back to the office.

It was after midnight when I locked up my files, rode the elevator down to the lobby, and drove home to park in the garage and drag myself upstairs to go to sleep. I played the messages left by friends on my answering machine throughout the day and evening, and made a list of calls to return at some point on Saturday. Most of my pals got out of the city on the steaming summer weekends—to beach houses they owned or rented, borrowed or shared—and I was just as anxious to get this court proceeding behind me so I could disappear to my home on Martha's Vineyard for some rest.

I bathed, ignored the usually appealing pile of magazines next to the bed, and read a chapter of *The Ambassadors* before falling off into a sound sleep. On Saturday morning I went over to the west sixties, where I took a two-hour ballet class with my instructor, William, who tried to remove all the knots that several weeks of courtroom tension had worked into my shoulders, back, and thighs. When I left the dance studio I headed directly downtown to the office, to continue researching and crafting my arguments for the complicated presentation I had to make on Monday.

It was close to eight o'clock when I realized that my eyes were bleary and my thought process was getting fuzzy. As I neared home on the FDR Drive, I was trying to decide whether there was anyone in town I could call on such short notice to meet me for a light supper. The beeper went off while I was still a few blocks away from my apartment, and when I glanced down and noted that the number on the lighted display was unfamiliar, I decided to wait until I got upstairs to return the call.

"Hello?" I said tentatively.

The accented voice of an older woman spoke into the telephone. "One moment," she said, and I heard her say something inaudible while passing the receiver to someone.

"Yeah?" It was Mike Chapman's voice.

"Hi. Got your beep on my way home."

"Hey, Coop. We got an I.D., just an hour ago. Housekeeper came back from vacation. Says the lady of the house was supposed to be here all week but nobody's seen her. Noticed the sketch in yesterday's news, then she put it together with the fact that 'Madam' is not around. Called the precinct, and they notified us. I grabbed one of the guys and we ran down here with a couple of the head shots from the M.E.'s Office, and the housekeeper breaks up on us as soon as she sees the photos."

"Who is—"

"Lady's name is Denise Caxton. Lives—well,

lived—at 890 Fifth Avenue. Ever hear of her?" Chapman wanted to know.

"No. Why?"

"She and the husband own an art gallery, same place where you get your roots done."

"The Fuller Building?" I asked. Madison Avenue at Fifty-seventh Street—the crossroads of the art world, as the owner of my salon liked to call it.

"Yeah, the Caxton Gallery occupies the entire top floor."

I could hear the background conversation between Mike's partner and the tearful woman as Mike whispered into the phone. "You wouldn't believe this apartment—five-bedroom duplex, with a modern art collection that most museums would kill for."

"So, *did* they? And where's Mr. Caxton?"

"The housekeeper doesn't know. Denise split with him—Lowell Caxton—a few months back. They both still share the apartment—separate entrances and living quarters—but there's no sign that he's in town. And she says there's nothing to suggest any foul play in the apartment, either."

"Want me to come over and—"

"Forget about it. Hazel's giving us the boot. Won't let us look around or touch anything. Not till she gets her orders from Monsieur Caxton."

"Any date book, calendar—to trace back the deceased's movements?"

"All on computer, Coop, and she's not letting us anywhere near that room or any of the equipment."

"Can you secure the apartment until I can get a warrant to search it?" I asked.

"You bet your ass we'll have to. Any of this stuff disappears, we'll all be nailed to the wall. I've sent for some uniformed guys to watch each of the entrances, just to keep the place buttoned up tight.

"And get your beauty sleep, blondie. I have the distinct feeling that you and I will be dancing together on this one. If there's one motive for every million hanging on these walls, we're gonna be busy."

# 6

"Think about it for a minute," Chapman urged me. "*Rebecca*? Domestic violence. *Notorious*? Domestic violence. *Gaslight*? Domestic violence. *Dial M for Murder*? Domestic violence. *Niagara*? Domestic violence. Every one of your favorite movies has some kind of spousal abuse in it, you know? What does that say about you, blondie?"

I was staring at a Monet hanging in the Caxton living room. I had never seen any painting from the water lily series in private hands, and here was a glorious canvas, practically as large as the triptych that hangs in the Museum of Modern Art, stretching the length of the wall.

"*The Postman Always Rings Twice*? Domestic violence. *Double Indemnity*? Domes—"

"Yeah, now you're getting to the good ones. The ladies strike back, Mikey. Those are the ones I *really* enjoy." I walked over to Mercer, who was studying the signature in the corner of the painting.

"Is this for real?" he asked me.

I smiled and shrugged my shoulders. "I assume so. I played around on the Internet for a couple of hours last night after Mike called me with the I.D., and it seems the Caxton collection is world famous. A lot of it has been in the family for generations."

Mercer and I were moving around the forty-foot-long room like it was a gallery in the Louvre. Each painting and object was museum quality, and I was fascinated by their beauty and number.

Chapman was sitting on a sofa facing the stunning view of Central Park, watching as the housekeeper delivered coffee and English muffins to the table in front of him, pouring from a Georgian server that was worth our collective salaries for at least the next couple of years.

"Thanks, Valerie. I was starving." Chapman gave the red-eyed woman his best grin and began slathering butter on the toasted morsel he had picked up from the plate. "Valerie makes these from scratch, Coop. Got her own nooks and crannies—better than Thomas'. You oughta take a lesson from her."

Mercer shook his head and walked over, spreading a napkin across the knee of Chapman's jeans. The dripping butter would have been an unwelcome accent to the delicate design of golden Napoleonic bees on the peach silk fabric of the sofa. "How'd you get Valerie to let us in?"

"We bonded last night over a bit of Mr. Caxton's Irish whiskey. I've frequently found it helpful in periods of bereavement. Basically I told her I wasn't going anywhere until she located him for me."

Chapman had called me again at midnight to tell

me that Valerie had reached Lowell Caxton at his home in Paris and that he would be taking the Concorde back to New York. It was Mike's idea that the three of us await him in his home, to deny him the opportunity to alter or destroy any evidence before we could interview him.

Air France flight 002 from Paris had been due in at 8:44 A.M. on Sunday. Chapman had returned to the building at six, and Mercer had picked me up at home two hours later. "Why'd she let you back in today?" I asked. "The boss won't be too happy about this, I'm sure."

"Let's just say she was encouraged by the doormen. One thing they frown on in these snooty buildings, Miss Cooper, is scenes. The sight of me alone in the lobby wasn't all that upsetting to them at first, but it was probably when I asked Frick and Frack if they thought it was gonna be necessary for me to get the Emergency Services Unit over here with battering rams that they called and suggested to Valerie that I might be more comfortable waiting in Caxton's salon. I'm telling you—doormen despise scenes."

So much for any evidence that we might be lucky enough to come up with in the apartment. The kind of pressure that Mike liked to apply to get his way more often resulted in a consent under threat than the freely given consent necessary for a lawful entry or search.

Valerie returned to the room with another ornate tray and porcelain cups for Mercer and me. Her hand trembled slightly as she poured the coffee, and I wondered whether it was because of grief over her mistress's death, the effects of a hangover, or fear of

Caxton's reaction when he found us settled in and enjoying his hospitality. She replaced the silver pot on a small table beside a large ormolu clock that bore an engraved seal depicting a royal crest I couldn't identify.

"Hitchcock had it right, Coop. Think of how many movies it's the husband or wife who offs the other spouse. Just because this guy was in Paris all week doesn't mean he isn't a prime suspect. Shit, we don't even know exactly how many days she's been dead. Besides that, someone with this kind of dough could hire a killer with his pocket change."

"Well, what did you get out of Valerie during your fireside chat last night?"

"Precious little. Seemed to genuinely like the late Mrs. C., who hired her personally and relied on her for all kinds of intimate service. But the husband pays the bills, and she's not about to throw that out the window so fast." Mike was almost finished with his second muffin, the buttered topping covered over with some kind of strawberry preserve. "Hey, Mercer, might as well lift the lids on those little—Coop, what does your mother call useless little dust catchers like that stuff over there? Tchotchkes? Maybe Denise stored her coke in one of those."

Chapman pointed at a gilt-trimmed *bureau plat,* only half in jest. It was completely covered by miniature porcelain snuffboxes. Half a dozen of them would have fit at once in the palm of Mercer's hand, but he lifted the lids of several of them individually. I sipped on my coffee as I walked beside him, noticing that each box was hand painted with portraits of cavalier King Charles spaniels in a variety of regal back-grounds.

Above the table was a Degas, familiar to me from my Wellesley introductory art course and close enough in detail to the famous *Foyer of the Dance* that it had to be the study for the great painting that hangs in Paris.

Chapman was on his feet, wiping his hands with the heavy damask napkin. He was standing in front of a Picasso about four feet by six, his head cocked as he tried to make some sense of the Cubist representa-tions. "I just don't get it. Why would somebody pay millions of dollars for something like this, which isn't supposed to look like anything anyway? I must have spent too much time in church. I haven't liked any artists since Michelangelo and Leonardo da Vinci. Just give me a Madonna—I mean, the old Madonna—and I'm happy."

I had circled the room and was back in front of the lilies. "You'd like Monet. Impressionism got its name from one of his paintings—*Impression of a Sunrise*." Chapman joined me to look at the vast canvas, one of the endless images of the same subject portrayed at different hours of the day in different variations of light.

"That one you're looking at was painted at Giverny, just before his death. He was nearly blind." Caxton's voice startled us as we turned to look toward the entryway of the long room.

"Looks to me like most of the stuff painted in this century could have been done by a blind man. Mike Chapman, Homicide," Mike said, advancing to shake

Lowell Caxton's hand and show his identification. "These are my colleagues—Detective Mercer Wallace, and Alexandra Cooper from the District Attorney's Office."

Caxton extended a hand to each of us. "I hope Valerie has made you comfortable. Perhaps you'll allow me to step inside and freshen up for a moment before we get on with what you need to do."

It was a reasonable request after a trans-Atlantic trip, and although Chapman would have liked to tail him into the private quarters of the apartment, we had no choice but to let Caxton disappear to his suite of rooms.

Fifteen or twenty minutes later he returned to the living room, opened a set of sliding pocket doors, and gestured the three of us into the library. The walls were lacquered in a rich shade of Chinese red, strikingly showcasing another Picasso, this time from the artist's Rose Period. Bookcases were lined with sets of leather-bound volumes, valuable and rare, and assuredly untouched and unread. Some decorator's idea of a complement to the art.

Lowell Caxton seated himself in the largest chair in the room as we took our places around him. "It's a bit more intimate in here," he said to no one in particular.

As he looked each of us over to size us up, waiting for Valerie to bring him the tea he had requested, we examined him as well. The articles I had seen in Lexis-Nexis gave his age as seventy-four. But he was trim and vigorous, with a full head of thick gray hair, and I would have guessed him to be no older than sixty-five. He remained in the clothes in which he had traveled—

gray slacks, loafers without socks, a tennis shirt, and a pink cashmere sweater looped around his shoulders. The solid gold Cartier Pasha on his wrist was the only jewelry he wore.

Valerie delivered the tea on yet another small silver tray. "Close the doors after you, will you, Valerie?" Caxton asked. Her hands were still shaking as she backed out of the room, sliding the doors together by pulling the brass knob on each of the sections.

"Am I supposed to open this session by telling you how distraught I am by Deni's demise?" he went on. "Or have you already found ample fodder in the tabloids to know that it wouldn't be a very sincere way for me to begin? The flight home—even with the abbreviated flying time of a supersonic transport— was more than enough for me to shed whatever tears I had left. I didn't kill her, although there'll be plenty of her friends to suggest as much to you. But I certainly didn't love her any longer, so you might as well know that from the outset."

"You want to ask us anything, before I get started?" Chapman queried.

"I know everything about how and where she was found, Detective. After Valerie reached me with the news last night, I had my assistant make all the inquiries he could. I'm sure you'll tell me whatever else you think it's necessary for me to know."

I had worked with Mike often enough to get inside his head. You couldn't look at a situation like this without thinking you could easily find a motive for the husband to want the wife dead—money, business, infidelity, and in this instance, even more money. A contract hit in this kind of marriage would be cheaper than any alimony decision made by a judge or jury. But it was also so obvious that we were each thinking that it was too easy. Now the guy plays right into the theory by not even expressing interest in how his estranged wife was killed. He probably had more channels of access to whatever information he wanted than I had pairs of shoes.

Mike had two short-term goals. He needed to get as much information about both Caxtons, personal and professional, as he could, and he wanted to shove open the pocket doors so he could see whether anyone was coming or going into the private rooms of the apartment.

"It's warm in here, Mr. Caxton," Mike said, taking out his notepad and loosening his tie as he rose and walked toward the doors. "Mind if I open these for a little air?"

Caxton lifted a remote control panel from the table beside him. "Not necessary, Detective. I'll simply adjust the room temperature. It stays much cooler in here without the summer sun beating through those glass windows off the park. Carry on. Tell me what you need to know."

Whether we needed it all or not, the Caxton family history and the building of the art fortune had to be explored, in case they proved to be links to the murder.

Lowell Caxton III was the grandson of the Pittsburgh steel baron whose name he bore. The grandfather had been born in 1840 and was one of those great American success stories—a poor kid from a large family who rose from menial mill jobs to running a production plant before he was thirty. When he recognized the growing demand for steel, needed to build the railroads across the country, he borrowed all of his working-class relatives' money and purchased a factory. In 1873, when another young fellow, named Andrew Carnegie, came along and began his acquisition of businesses which he later consolidated into the Carnegie Steel Company, Lowell Caxton never had to work again. He became an investor and speculator, and thereafter a philanthropist responsible for helping Carnegie build libraries and art museums all over the Northeast.

In the mid-1880s, Caxton became enamored of the bohemian lifestyle of many of the young artists living and working in Paris. He bought several apartments in Montmartre and let some of the struggling upstarts live there rent-free, in exchange for paintings that he took to America.

On one of his trips, drinking in the nightclubs with Toulouse-Lautrec, Caxton took up with a dancer, whom he married and brought back to the States. Their son, Lowell II, inherited the entire fortune—the money and the art—when both of his parents died in the sinking of the *Lusitania,* in 1915. He was thirty years old at the time.

As though the passion for art had been genetically transmitted, the junior Caxton carried on his father's interests, patronizing the creators and expanding the family collection. He was a popular figure at Mabel Dodge's "evenings" in her home at 23 Fifth Avenue, where he championed the Post-impressionists to Lincoln Steffens, Margaret Sanger, John Reed, and the other intellectuals who gathered to exchange ideas while Dodge puffed on her gold-tipped cigarettes. It was at one of those soirees that he met his wife, a guest of Gertrude Stein's named Marie-Hélène de Neuilly, who was a well-known patron of avant-garde art before the First World War. Our host, Lowell III—or Three, as his father liked to call him as a boy—also had the love of art in his blood.

"The first artist I ever met was Picasso," Caxton continued, "at our home in Paris, before he went off to Spain to fight. He was having an affair with my mother at the time, although I was much too young to pick up on that. And in case you're wondering, it was perfectly all right with my father. Got him some stunning paintings for his collection. You might like to see them someday. They're in my bedroom—never been shown publicly."

"Do you mind if we talk about your wife, Mr. Caxton?" Chapman asked.

"I've had three, Detective. I assume you mean Deni?"

"Well, actually, why don't you tell me about the other two first? Then, yes, I'd like to know as much about Denise as possible."

"Not much to say about them. Rest in peace." Caxton looked over at me, daring a smile. "I married Lisette in France at the beginning of the war. She died in childbirth. Tragic, really. I adored her. My second wife was from Italy. She raised Lisette's child and then two more daughters of our own. Killed in a boating accident in Venice."

"Aha!" Chapman said under his breath, shifting in

his chair and leaning across to me. "*Rebecca*. I told you so."

I ignored the crack and went on. "Where are your daughters now?"

"All grown, married, living in Europe. And if you want to know whether or not they liked Deni, they didn't. She was younger than all of them, and they never got along very well. But they've had absolutely nothing to do with her for years."

"I understand," Chapman said. "We will, of course, need to get in touch with them at some point."

"I'll have someone from my office get you all their information."

"Back to Denise, if we may."

"Certainly, Detective. I met Deni nearly twenty years ago, in Firenze. She was—"

"You were widowed at the time, Mr. Caxton?" Mercer asked.

"Widowed once, Mr. Wallace. My second wife was alive and quite well. Her mishap occurred several years thereafter. In any event, I had flown over to look at a Bernini sculpture that I wanted to bid on. It was at the gallery that I first saw Denise, and I was more infatuated with her than with the statue. That hadn't happened to me in years."

"And she was there to bid on the same piece for the Tate?" I ventured, having found that item of her biography on-line the previous night in an old magazine clipping about a museum opening.

Caxton smiled. "I should think you'd know better than to believe everything you read in the newspapers, young lady. Deni was just off her year as Miss

Oklahoma, and a very-distant-second runner-up in the Miss America Pageant. You were probably too busy with your nose in your schoolbooks," Caxton said, with a nod in my direction, "to be watching that year, but she was the kid from Idabel with great looks and no talent to speak of—traded in baton twirling in favor of reading a soliloquy from *As You Like It*. Not exactly a crowd pleaser. She took her ten-thousand-dollar scholarship prize and escaped. Worked her way over to Florence to study art, which she didn't know the first thing about at the time. Figured if Andy Warhol could fool the world with what he was selling, she could catch on and find a niche.

"I decided to follow my grandfather's route, Miss Cooper. What Denise lacked in breeding, she made up for in—shall we say?—élan. She was a marvelously quick study and I enjoyed teaching. All she needed from me was to create a provenance for her, no different than a clever forger would do for a fine painting.

"I gave Deni a vague and somewhat mysterious background—orphaned as a young child, with a trust fund. Raised abroad in a series of boarding schools. Moved her from the *pensione* she was living in to the Excelsior, where I was staying when I came to town. Had her tutored in French and Italian—she was adequate in the former and tolerable in the latter. Most of the men who met her were intrigued and forgave her the minor incongruities. She didn't care much about what the women thought of her. Denise was never a contender for Miss Congeniality."

"What did your second wife think of her, Mr.

Caxton?" Mike clearly was fascinated by the circumstance of the thrice-widowed husband.

"I'm not sure she ever knew about Deni, to tell the truth. She was riding in a cigarette speedboat when it flipped, killing her instantly. I had only known Deni a few years at that point. The whole arrangement was working perfectly for me. And yes, Mr. Chapman, there was an inquest when my wife died. Accidental death. I'm sure Maurizio, my assistant, can get you all the records that you need."

"How long have you had the gallery in the Fuller Building?" Mercer wanted to bring this story up to the present.

"Deni and I moved back to New York twelve years ago. We bought this apartment so that she could open our gallery. For me, the satisfaction has always been in finding and collecting the great pieces—more than a century of Caxton taste that I can surround myself with in the privacy of my own homes. Not entirely selfish, mind you. We frequently exhibit portions of the holdings, whenever asked, and many of my mistakes have wound up permanently on the walls of museums all over America and most of Europe.

"But Denise also liked the game itself. It wasn't enough to gift her with unique art or jewels, which worked very well at the beginning. She had come from nothing—her father was a soybean farmer—and she really needed to prove she was as smart as any of the rest of us out there. She liked the hustle of the art world. She adored being a tastemaker, if you will. But I suppose your research has revealed all of that."

Now I was doubly sorry that I had suggested I

knew anything about either of the Caxtons. "Not at all, Mr. Caxton. Forgive me, but I only tried to acquaint myself with information about Mrs. Caxton's business when I learned that it was she who had been killed. It's always helpful to me if I can get as close to the victim as possible—to try and understand why she might be a target for someone. That is, if her loved ones allow me that kind of access."

"Anything you'd like, Miss Cooper. Perhaps it would help if we took a walk into Deni's quarters, to give you an idea of how she lived. Would you like that?"

Chapman was on his feet before I could answer. Caxton moved to the double doors as Mike leaned in behind me and whispered, "Very smoothly done, blondie. Keep batting those eyelashes and you could be the fourth late Mrs. Lowell Caxton. A very temporary position, from the looks of it."

As the doors slid apart I could see the back of a man carrying a black leather suitcase as he walked out of the entryway that led from the living room to the elevator. Mercer nudged Chapman. "There goes Kardashian with Simpson's bloody clothes."

"Mr. Caxton," Chapman said, "I'd appreciate it if you could hold that gentleman before he leaves here with any property that we might need to look at."

"Is it safe for me to assume, Detective, that you don't have a warrant to search my luggage?"

Mike and Mercer were silent. Caxton continued. "That was Maurizio. He simply unpacked the bag I returned with this morning and is taking it down to the storage area in the basement of the building. Sorry to disappoint you." We heard the heavy door swing closed.

He led us past the Picasso and pointed at three doors across the room. "That far exit goes to the kitchen and the servants' quarters. Unless you think the butler did it, Mr. Chapman, that portion of the household needn't take up your time. These other two are—rather, were—our separate apartments. Nothing new about that. Even when we were getting along very well, we always had distinct living spaces. Different lifestyles, different tastes in art.

"I didn't approve of the drugs, and I didn't much care for Deni's current passion for modern painting—some of the very abstract, jarring works she'd developed an interest in recently." We followed Caxton as he opened the door to Denise's wing.

"You know, gentlemen, this may sound a bit peevish in light of the fact that I'm standing here with you while my wife is being fitted for a coffin, but if your department had taken *my* shooting a bit more seriously, perhaps this wouldn't have happened to Deni."

Mercer, Mike, and I couldn't conceal our puzzlement as we exchanged looks.

"Are any of you with the Nineteenth Precinct? That's the unit that's handling the investigation," Caxton explained.

"No, we're not. Could you tell us what happened?"

Chapman was plainly annoyed that we had come here without such an important piece of information. "Just crossing Madison Avenue, six weeks ago, on my way home from the Whitney. Holding a Styrofoam coffee cup in my hand. A car driving past slowed down, and the man in the passenger seat pointed at me—it was happening so quickly that all I saw was his hand—then I heard the sound of a gunshot and felt a stinging on my scalp. I found myself sitting on the curb, people running over to help me. Never even dropped the coffee."

Caxton bowed his head and parted his silver hair with his hands. "I'm sure you can still see the scar, like a seam across my scalp. At that moment I was quite sure I was dead. This must be what it's like to die, I thought to myself. No pain at all. It took me a few seconds to realize, as the blood dripped onto my face, that I had been grazed by the bullet and not seriously injured at all. If someone had actually tried to kill me, they'd hired the gang that couldn't shoot straight.

"I trust you'll be able to figure out whether Deni's death had anything to do with that, won't you?"

He pivoted away and walked on ahead of us to turn on the lights in the dim hallway. "The only thing I trust," said Chapman, "is that some ass-kissing lieutenant in the Nineteenth was trying to make his numbers look better for the commissioner. When I call over for the case report on the assault on Lowell Caxton, I'll probably find out that they're carrying the investigation as disorderly conduct instead of attempted murder. Heaven forbid you alarm the good citizens of the Upper East Side by suggesting a violent crime could happen here—they might confuse the place with Harlem."

# 7

"Here's another Degas," Caxton said to me, stopping in front of a painting. "Perhaps you remember from your college days that after the Napoleonic wars, it was presumed of firstborn sons of a certain class that they would become lawyers. Edgar dutifully followed his father's wishes and enrolled at the Faculté de Droit. Fortunately for the rest of the world—if not his parents—he dropped out in favor of doing something more creative than litigation after only a month."

He walked on. "Cézanne spent almost three years at law school in Aix, replete with boredom. And Matisse actually clerked for a lawyer for quite a while, drafting briefs and keeping files. It was only when he was forced to stay at home with appendicitis that he was given his first paint set by his mother. A decade later, he changed the history of the art world with the birth of Fauvism—exuberant colors and wildly distorted shapes. Imagine our loss if any of these giants had become mired in the law. You don't paint by any chance, do you, Miss Cooper?"

Lowell Caxton managed to summarize a bit of art history while making clear his disdain for the legal profession. I got the point.

So far, the hallway lined with Impressionist paintings was as breathtaking as any gallery in the finest museums. Caxton opened the last door, which had been Denise's bedroom. The contrast was stunning.

"A bit self-involved, would you say?" he asked rather facetiously.

The room was like a shrine to its former occupant, with almost every painting in it a portrait of Denise. "Gifts from the artists, of course. Thankful for her ability to turn their talents into gold, in some instances. Quite like alchemy. The Warhol is the great irony, in that he started this whole odyssey for her, without his ever knowing it."

Displayed above the headboard of the king-size bed, covered in an exquisite set of antique linens with countless throw pillows layered on top, were the four-colored Warhol images of a younger Denise Caxton. The youthful bride with a swanlike neck and beauty queen smile was deserving of a few portraits, I conceded, but this accumulation was a bit frightening.

The three of us circled the space, looking at signatures and taking in the variety of styles. I recognized some of the names—Richard Sussman, Emilio Gomes, and Aneas McKiever among them—but Caxton pointed out the rest of those I had never encountered. There were Deni Caxtons fully clothed and bejeweled, and there were Deni Caxtons completely nude and erotically posed. There were torsos without heads and limbs, and there were heads without body parts.

"How'd she let this one slip in?" Chapman asked. He pointed at a yellow canvas, three feet square, with a small pink rectangle in the upper right corner.

Caxton laughed. "That *is* Denise, Detective. According to Alain Levinsky. Even she had a sense of humor about it. She managed to sell about a dozen Levinsky 'portraits,' Mr. Chapman. One each to Bardot, Trump, and Ted Turner—can't remember who sat for the others. A few rectangles, a few oblongs, a few squares. *Et voilà,* a portrait."

"This is all like 'The Emperor's New Clothes,' if you ask me," Chapman said.

"Precisely," Caxton responded. "I couldn't agree with you more. Denise mocked me for my traditional views—too representational, she used to argue, too old-fashioned. I wish P. T. Barnum had lived long enough to encounter this trend. Nowadays there are two or three suckers born every minute, if you ask me. He might have gone into partnership with Deni."

Mercer was scouring the surfaces of the furniture— bedside tables, dresser top, lingerie chest—for any signs of notes or papers, names or phone numbers. But there was nothing loose and nothing casually laid about. Either Mrs. Caxton lived that neatly or Valerie had removed every jotting or message pad before we arrived.

"Would you—or the housekeeper—know whether any belongings are missing?" Mercer asked. "Jewelry, clothing, anything like—"

"I couldn't begin to guess," said Caxton. He stepped to the only other door in the room and pulled the handles back to reveal a walk-in closet, which was probably larger than half of the studio apartments in Manhattan. Clothes were assembled by category—dresses, slacks, suits, evening gowns—and then again by colors within those groupings. "The lesser jewels are kept in that safe at the rear. The more important things, from my mother and *grand-mère,* are all safeguarded in a vault. We'll certainly check for you during the week.

"If you've seen enough here, we'll go inside to Deni's office."

I wasn't sure that I was ready to leave the boudoir, but we were given no choice, and the three of us dutifully followed Caxton, retracing our steps back up the corridor and into the next room.

Denise had constructed a thronelike encampment for herself at one end of this huge home office, centered around a fifteenth-century table that Lowell told us he had found in an Umbrian monastery. The table had become her desk and was ornamented only by a Fabergé clock. There were two chairs placed opposite Denise's high-backed leather seat, and four more scattered around the room that matched that pair. Here the walls were decorated with paintings that were completely unfamiliar to me—all contemporary and none bearing signatures that I recognized.

Caxton walked behind the table and lowered himself into Denise's chair, looking around the room as if for the first time from that perspective, and invited us to sit down and ask him whatever questions we wanted to pose about her.

"When do we reach the point at which you ask me who her enemies were, gentlemen?"

"We're ready anytime you are. How long's the list?" Chapman said.

"Depends on where you are in the art community, I would think. A disgruntled 'artiste' who thinks his dealer has taken too great a commission for his work. Just glance at the walls and see how many of those there might be. Then you've got the clients, who've found they've paid too much for a painting, on the dealer's advice, that they neither like nor will be able to resell for anything remotely near the price they put out.

"There isn't anyone in the business," he went on, "who hasn't been accused of selling a forged piece, by accident or design, over the years. And then there's the current brouhaha in the auction houses, with the government charging sellers with rigging the bids to knock up the prices. On the surface, gentlemen, it's a world of exquisite beauty and refinement. But it's every bit as filthy and cutthroat as any other commercial enterprise, as soon as you get beneath the top layer of gouache."

Mercer was leaning forward, balancing his pad on his knee while he reviewed subjects he wanted to ask Caxton about. "We'll need a client list, then, as well as contact information for the painters she represented."

"You'll have to talk to her partner about that tomorrow at his office."

"I thought you were her partner," Mike said.

"As I mentioned, I set her up in the gallery in the Fuller Building originally. Without the Caxton name, I doubt she would have been able to sell the *Mona Lisa*, had it come on the market. I was the entrée to the uptown world in Manhattan—old money, large walls, deep pockets. But once she got involved in the New York scene, she had her own separate business—a thriving one at that—with a silent partner who mirrored her taste much more directly. Perhaps you've heard of him—Bryan Daughtry? They called their business Galleria Caxton Due."

Mercer and I certainly knew Daughtry's name. He had been a suspect in a very bizarre murder case in a neighboring county—beyond our jurisdiction but right up our alley. Chapman went for the bait. "Dead girl in the leather mask? *That* Daughtry?"

"Indeed, Mr. Chapman. That's why I was so grateful that he was a silent partner. The scandal didn't alarm Deni at all. Might even have helped, with her type of clientele. But none of the stigma ever stuck on Bryan. I haven't spoken with him yet today, but he knows all the players in their professional life."

"Does he have any part of your Fifty-seventh Street business?" I asked.

"Not a dime. Not a speck of paint."

"Where was their operation? SoHo?"

"You're not keeping up with the trends, Detective Wallace. SoHo is dead. It's a commercial mall these days, not a creative zone any longer."

The area south of Houston Street and north of Canal had been claimed by the avant-garde art community in the sixties and seventies. Abandoned lofts and warehouses, uninhabitable and overrun with rodents, had been renovated, populated, and gentrified by the struggling artists who were unable to afford midtown rents and needed the cavernous space to house their oversized canvases. The old meat district known as Washington Market became chic with its new infusion of hip locals and its redesignation as "Tribeca," the triangle below Canal. By the late eighties, galleries there were being displaced by designer boutiques, chain store branches, and bed-and-bath shops with their ubiquitous supply of votive candles.

Caxton described the exodus. "In the mid-nineties, Paula Cooper moved her business up to Chelsea, the west twenties between Tenth and Eleventh Avenues. Have you been over there lately?"

"You won't be asking Alex questions like that after you get to know her a little better, Mr. Caxton," Chapman said. "She doesn't eat, shop, or sleep outside of her zip code. Makes her skin crawl soon as you say the words 'West Side,' doesn't it, Coop?"

"We have a lot in common," Caxton replied, smiling back at me. "Paula Cooper—no relation, I take it?"

"No, I know her only by reputation." And because my father had bought some paintings from her, I thought to myself, remembering a Jennifer Bartlett I particularly loved.

"Well," he continued, "she's the real class of this business. And its bellwether. I don't actually know the reason she moved, but it's a safe guess to say that it's because of what happened in SoHo. This district in Chelsea was full of enormous warehouses. Fifty years ago, when the ocean liners docked on the piers all along the Hudson and connected to the railways there, it was a commercial hub. Lately, the warehouses have been used for auto repair shops and taxi dispatch centers—vast and utilitarian, but not terribly attractive.

"Paula found a fabulous space on Twenty-first Street. Cleaned it up, put in some skylights, white-washed the interior, and everyone who thought she'd been out of her mind realized what a genius she was. Deni and Bryan started buying up land on those blocks a couple of years ago, planning to open a new venture together. Real estate's gone through the roof over there. Kind of sorry I ignored them in the beginning. I could have made a killing on the property alone." Caxton paused. "Bad choice of words today, isn't it?"

Remorse wasn't his strong suit.

"And the cocaine? What were her sources for that?"

"The problem only started four or five years ago. About the time that her taste in art changed so radically. Deni knew how strongly I disapproved of her drug use. I could only joke that one had to be stoned to appreciate the work she was trying to hawk to the great unwashed."

"Do you know who her dealer was?" Mercer asked.

"I think she used to get it from the kids who hung around the galleries. Then, as she got hooked, she'd just beep whoever wasn't in jail at the moment, and a delivery would arrive, brought up to our home by the white-gloved doormen. Usually camouflaged in pot-pourri or packaged in a bag with assorted foodstuffs from Dean & Deluca."

"Did she owe money to anybody? Any suppliers?"

"No reason to. More than enough money to support all her habits."

Mercer was working the drug angle with good reason. Deni's body had been found at the tip of the

Thirty-fourth Precinct, which was the heart of Manhattan's illegal drug operations. Colombians, Dominicans, and African American street gangs—Santiago's Sinners, Latin Kings, and Wild Hightops—mixed it up with one another night and day as they pumped the streets of the city full of heroin, cocaine, and all their derivative forms. Even if Deni had been thrown in the water from the Bronx side of the creek, the odds were overwhelming that the site of the dumping was heavily infested with users and sellers of every kind of controlled substance.

"Had either of you started divorce proceedings, Mr. Caxton?" I wanted to know.

"Yes, yes, I had. More than a year ago. No rush about it, and not that I had any plans to go to the altar again, but the marriage was over and I wanted to be sure that I got out of it with most of the treasures I came in with, you see. The money was irrelevant to me, but I needed to protect the collection and keep it intact, as well as I could."

"What was the status of the legal action?"

"Our lawyers were negotiating, Miss Cooper. I'm sure you know what that means. Trying to run up their bills at hourly rates with endless phone calls and meetings and suggestions—and general nonsense."

"I assume there was a prenup—"

"Certainly there was. But most of its contingencies were useless after the marriage survived ten years. You must realize how much older I was than Deni. I thought a decade with her would be bliss. It's like the salesmen who try to sell a man my age a watch with a lifetime guarantee," the septuagenarian went on. "I always tell them that I'd be interested in a similar piece, but for a lower price and with simply a ten-year guarantee."

"So what was she fighting about?"

"It wasn't money, Detective Chapman. I've offered plenty of that, and she made quite a lot of it on her own projects. But she wanted more of the art, some of *my* pieces. Claiming an entitlement for many of the things I'd bought since we'd been together. As though I needed her judgment to lead me to a Titian or Tintoretto. Perhaps next time you're here," Caxton said, making it obvious that we were coming to the end of his hospitality, "you might like to see what it is I want to hold on to.

"Unlike that mishmash of styles my wife favored, I've hung my favorites each in its own salon. My bedroom is devoted to van Gogh—Deni thought they were minor, but they're quite wonderful, really. My office is the Poussin room, and my—"

Chapman had just about had it with the self-importance of Caxton and the arrogant cataloguing of his wealth. "How about your inamorata's bedroom, sir? How'd you decorate that one?"

"Not a stupid guess at all, Detective. Yes, I've been seeing someone. She's in Paris, and quite content to be there. And if you think it bothered Denise at all, you'd be wrong. We've been leading separate lives for a long time."

"Do you know who she's been seeing?" I asked.

"Perhaps the help would know that, Miss Cooper. They change the linens here—I don't."

That last exchange brought him to his feet, as he

81

ushered us out of his wife's office and back to the living room.

Chapman wasn't quite done. "When was it, exactly, that you left for Paris?"

"Maurizio will give you all that infor—"

"I'm sure Maurizio would give me oral sex if you told him to, Mr. Caxton. I'm not talking ancient history, here. This is Sunday—what day did you leave New York to go to Paris on your last trip? I'd like to hear it from *you*."

Caxton's veneer had worn thin, and Mike's patience even finer. "It was Tuesday, Tuesday evening at seven o'clock."

"Any other homes that you and Denise owned? Any place that she might have gone if she left this apartment for a few days and you were holed up in Paris?"

"Well, we've got a house in Saint Bart's, but it's not the season there, of course. I doubt it's even opened up this time of year."

Chapman couldn't resist the cheap shot. "Yeah, I know you two wouldn't be caught you-know-what there off-season, would you?"

Caxton ignored him.

I knew the small Caribbean paradise well. My parents had bought a home and begun spending winters there after my father retired from the practice of medicine. The Cooper-Hoffman valve, which he and his partner had invented as young physicians, had revolutionized the then-new field of open heart surgery and made possible a lifestyle that allowed him to live in that French-owned resort while continuing to travel for his lectures and conferences all over the world. It would be easy for me to get information about the Caxtons from my connections on the island.

"I'd suggest that when you speak with Bryan Daughtry you ask him about the truckload of paintings—mostly Della Spigas, I think, and quite ghastly—that was hijacked at the end of June. I don't know if the art was ever recovered, but the hijacking had Deni completely crazed when it happened."

Mercer added the truck incident to his list.

"May we spend a few minutes with Valerie?" I asked, hoping to get a closer handle on personal life in Denise's wing of the house.

"I'm so sorry I didn't think of it before I excused her for the day. I told Maurizio to let her go after she prepared my tea. She'll grieve enough for all of us, Miss Cooper. I'll let her know you'll be contacting her, of course.

"Now I've got to ask you to leave so I can get ready for tomorrow. I must arrange for the services at Frank Campbell. Find a minister. Suggest an appropriate psalm. That sort of thing. I'm afraid the closest Deni ever got to a church was her frantic scrambling to buy that incredible Velázquez of Innocent the Tenth."

Caxton opened the door to the landing that put us at the elevator. "You know, Miss Cooper, there's a poignant fact about values in the world in which Deni and I lived that very few people realize. More than ninety percent of the art sold in America will never again fetch anywhere near the same price when the buyers attempt to resell it." He paused, not quite ready to turn his back on us. "It was like that with Deni, too, and I think that fact was even beginning to dawn on her. She had invented herself once—brilliantly—and sold the stunning result at the very top of the market. I'm not sure she could have done as well—repeated her success, if you will—the second time around. Very sad, that, don't you think?"

This time he closed the door behind him without waiting for us to be gone.

# 8

It wasn't even noon when we emerged from the lobby of Caxton's building onto the pavement in front of the Fifth Avenue co-op. The temperature was already over ninety degrees and the humidity was best measured by the tiny ringlets that formed instantly at the nape of my neck.

"Hate to say it," Mike remarked, "but even this feels like fresh air after an hour with that pompous jerk. Where to?"

"I've got to spend the day at my office. I'm supposed to finish up the hearing tomorrow, and I need to put the finishing touches on the brief I'm submitting after the argument."

"Is P. J. Bernstein's air-conditioned?"

"Yeah." The delicatessen near my apartment was my morning hangout on weekends.

"Let's grab some breakfast while we break up my to-do list. Then one of us can shoot you down to your office, okay?"

I rode the short distance to Third Avenue with

Mercer, who parked at a meter in front of the deli, a feat that could be accomplished only in August. Midtown Manhattan was a ghost town on summer weekends, between vacationing New Yorkers, others who commuted to beach houses and shared rentals in the Hamptons or on the Jersey shore, and day-trippers who made their way to Jones Beach or the suburban pool of a friend or relative.

The three of us sat at a table in the rear, near the kitchen, each of us taking out a pad to make lists and notes for the next week's work.

"Any point in my gracing the funeral?" Mike asked, after we ordered.

"The best reason to go," Mercer offered, "is to try and get a look at—maybe even a copy of—the list of attendees. See if you can scope the sign-in book. They've always got one of those at Campbell's. Might give us a jump start on some of the people in her business, beside what we hope we'll get from her friend Bryan Daughtry."

"Already thought of that. There's always some sweet old mick used to drink at my father's bar who runs the show at that funeral home. If I spread a little cash around, I'm sure they'll make a copy of the guest list."

The beeper attached to my waistband went off just as the waitress returned with my iced coffee. Mercer saw me slip it off the belt of my slacks and lift it to check the callback number. "Trouble for us?" he asked.

I laughed when I read the dial. "It's Joan Stafford, and she even added a nine-one-one after Jim's number." Joan, one of my closest friends, was vacationing with her fiancé on the Outer Banks off the coast of North Carolina. "Either of you want to guess what she thinks is so urgent she's got to talk to me immediately?"

Mike grabbed the cell phone from my hand after I dialed and heard it ringing. "Get your skinny ass out of bed with that foreign policy wonk and c'mon home to me. It's lonely here without you—just the Cooperwoman to give me orders all the time. What's with the emergency beep, kid—half-price sale at Schlumberger you gotta tell her about?"

Chapman looked up at Mercer and me as he repeated Joan's answer. "You wanna dish about a dead woman? Well, now that it's been on CNN this morning, I guess all you art mavens will be calling in with useless information." He paused to listen to something Joan was telling him, then glanced back at us as he said good-bye and turned off the phone.

"It's not enough we gotta deal with *you*. Nancy Drew's on board, too. Joan just gave me the names of three of Deni's clients and a couple of her lovers," he said, writing in his notepad as he talked, "and also has the story about why Caxton was no longer welcome at Sotheby's. She'll be up this week—dinner on Tuesday. Y'think this is some of her fiction, or should we run with it?"

Joan was a playwright, just back from London, where her latest satire had opened to brilliant reviews and full houses. "Go to the bank with her on this one. It's the world she was raised in. It wouldn't surprise me at all if she knew most of the players in the gallery scene—she's got a marvelous collection herself, plus she's been shopping the auctions to redecorate Jim's place in Washington."

I looked at the list on my pad. "I need to do a search warrant for some of Deni's things and have it ready in case you connect with her partner by tomorrow. The appointment book and calendar, records of sales and purchases—"

Mercer interrupted me. "We've got to assume a lot of this stuff is on computers. Be sure you draft the warrant so we can walk out of there with the hard drives, disks, and anything else in the office. The guys can download the data and get information that way, too. We'll search the gallery first to let you know what's there."

"I can always amend the warrant if you see more than we've thought of by the time you go in," I said.

"I'll reach out for Daughtry," he continued, "and call the funeral home for details on the memorial service."

I finished my Raisin Bran while Mike worked his way through an omelette, home fries, a side order of bacon, and toast and Mercer picked at a bagel with cream cheese. "Who's going to check out Lowell Caxton's shooting incident in the Nineteenth?"

"I'll swing by there later tonight," Chapman said, barely coming up for air between bites of his breakfast. "I'll also take care of the ladder manufacturer— see how common the brand is and who sells it." He aimed his fork at Mercer. "You see if you can run raps on all the employees at both galleries, and work on the art hijacking in June. What was it—Della Spigas? Who's Della Spiga, Coop?"

"I've got to go back to the books for that one. Ask me again at the end of the day."

"What's your schedule like this week?"

"Once I knock off the brief on Reggie X this afternoon and argue it tomorrow, I'm free. It'll take the judge a couple of weeks to make a decision and write his opinion. The sooner I get downtown, the faster I get it out of the way."

Mercer pushed off from the table and took the check from the waitress, while Mike dredged the last few fries through the ketchup.

"No point in you taking me," I said. "My car is right up the street. Just keep me posted." I waved good-bye and walked to my garage. I pulled the Jeep out and made my way over to the FDR Drive, while the all-news radio station wedged the story of Denise Caxton's identification as the murder victim between the Yankees' doubleheader victory last night and reviews of the Spice Girls' concert in Central Park. Maybe Chapman wasn't entirely crazy—live fast, die young, and be a good-looking corpse. Deni's fortune hadn't seemed to offer her very much more.

I escaped the rest of the hot afternoon and evening by immersing myself in completing the court papers I had to submit on Monday morning. The case was an old arrest of Mercer's, and my adversary had used his skills to challenge every aspect of the police procedures used in the investigation. The hearings we had just ended included the propriety of the arrest tactics, the legality of the search and seizure of evidence linking the perp—Reggie Bramwell—to the beating and rape of his estranged lover, and the admissibility of statements that Bramwell made to Mercer in the hours after he was taken into custody.

The case was pending in front of Harry Marklis, a jurist from the old school who didn't get domestic abuse at all. My last pretrial motion was an effort to convince the judge to allow my victim, Mariana Catano, to testify to two earlier episodes that involved the same defendant. One was an attempted assault that he had pleaded guilty to a year before, and the other was a confrontation in which he had threatened to set fire to her so that she'd look ugly enough that no other man would want her.

I had argued myself blue in the face, but Marklis was clueless. "So, why didn't she just leave him, Miss Cooper? What the hell'd she take him back for?" If I hadn't been able to explain the complex dynamic of a relationship of battering to a justice of the Supreme Court of the State of New York, I could only imagine how the average juror would respond to the same issue. Yet over and over again, my colleagues and I would see the cycle of violence escalate in these cases, and attempt to understand the complicated panoply of emotional, familial, and economic binds that kept the partners in place.

Mercer Wallace joined me in my office at nine o'clock on Monday morning. He was keenly interested in the outcome of Mariana's matter and wanted to hear my argument on this final pretrial issue. Marklis had directed our appearances for 10 A.M., although he was known for taking the bench late in the morning and quitting early in the afternoon.

"Anything develop last night?"

"Nope. Wasn't able to reach Daughtry anywhere. Gallery's closed on Sunday and Monday all through the summer, and his answering service just kept telling me they'd given him my message several times. Trying to get his home address so we can pay him a visit, but I'll wait till you're done upstairs. Allnighter?"

"Not too bad. I was home before midnight. Polished this off and started a rough draft of a warrant on the word processor, ready to go when you guys come up with something."

"All work and no play . . ."

"Don't go there, Mercer. You're as bad as Mike." I gathered up my file folders and motioned to him to move so we could head upstairs to Marklis's court part. "I'm fine. Got stood up for the weekend 'cause this guy I've been seeing was sent out of town on assignment. But thanks for asking."

The only people in Part 59 were the three court officers and Rich Velosi, the court clerk. I placed my files on the counsel table and asked if there was any word from the judge.

"Yeah, Ms. Konigsberg just called," Rich answered, referring to the judge's law secretary. "He's working in chambers, she says, so he won't get up here for another half hour."

The court officers all laughed, knowing that "working in chambers" was just a euphemism for "The judge hasn't arrived yet." But neither had my adversary. "Prisoner produced?"

"He's in the pens."

Mercer began to schmooze with the officers while I

reviewed my notes. From baseball they went to golf, from golf to the first pro football exhibition games, and from the games to the Bramwell case. "Y'think Cooper's got a chance to get a decision on this motion before Labor Day?"

"Marklis make a decision? Listen, he's got two toilets in the robing room and it usually takes him twenty minutes to figure out which one he wants to use. All depends on the troll factor."

Mercer and I both smiled. The officers referred to the petite law secretary, Ilse Konigsberg, as "the Troll." Whatever she whispered in Marklis's ear was bound to be the law of the case.

It was exactly eleven twenty-eight on my watch when Marklis, short and stout, waddled through the door and took his seat at the bench as the clerk called us to order and asked everyone in the courtroom to rise. The defendant had been brought out from the pens minutes earlier, when his lawyer had entered the well.

"Good morning, gentlemen. Miss Cooper. Why don't you all state your appearances for the record, and then we'll get started."

"Alexandra Cooper, for the People." I spoke aloud and remained standing while the defense attorney, Danny Wistenson, spelled his name for the stenographer.

"It's now nine thirty-five, and we're going to resume argument in the Bramwell case."

I glanced over my shoulder at Mercer and rolled my eyes in disgust. Marklis had long protected himself by making a phony record of the time of the proceedings. My colleagues and I had challenged him on any number of occasions, but I knew that if I tried it today, it would seal my fate in the argument I was about to make. His arrogant grin confirmed that he knew he had me.

"I have the papers you submitted in support of your *Molineux* application, Ms. Cooper. Do you have anything to add this morning?" It was clear that he was hoping I did not.

"I do, Your Honor." I rose to my feet, but before I started to lay out the law that supported my position, Marklis went on.

"You know, evidence of a defendant's prior crime can't be admitted at a trial for the sole purpose of showing that he has the propensity to commit the crimes he's now charged with."

"I do know that, Judge Marklis." He'd obviously done the minimum amount of homework necessary to get through this process. "But *Molineux* makes it quite clear that it's admissible when it's probative of his motive, his intent, and a common scheme or plan.

"In the instant case, Bramwell's prior threats and assaults on Ms. Catano are 'inextricably interwoven,' using the language in the *Vails* opinion, and—"

"You got that cite, Counselor?" Marklis swung his chair around and pointed at Wistenson.

"It's in Ms. Cooper's brief, but I'd like to be heard on this, Your Honor."

"I'm not finished, Judge."

"Yeah, well, I've got about all I need on this point, dear."

I turned away from the bench, steaming at Marklis's laziness and choice of appellation. At some point during the argument, Chapman had slipped into the courtroom and joined Mercer in the front row on the far side of the rail. I read his lips as he mouthed to me, "I love it when you're angry."

As I walked toward the detectives, I asked over my shoulder, "Judge, may I have a few minutes?" and kept moving without waiting for a response.

"When you put your hands on your hips, blondie, it's a dead giveaway. Temper, temper."

The diminutive judge stepped down from his seat and walked over to whisper to Ms. Konigsberg. Chapman couldn't resist another crack, looking at the huddle of two small figures, like conspiring Munchkins. "What's going on, Coop? Looks like a wrap party for *The Wizard of Oz*."

"Don't get me in any more trouble with Marklis. How come you're down here so early?"

"Caxton played cute with the memorial service. Ten o'clock this morning. Invitation only—just a handful of friends, and Daughtry wasn't among them. My guy inside says the husband wants to wait until the fall, when everyone is back from summer vacation, before he holds a real memorial. Wouldn't want to slight all the artists and clients who couldn't get here on short notice. But you better cut this exercise in futility short, 'cause we need some help."

"With what?"

"Looks like we found the car Deni's body was transported in. Need you to do a warrant."

"Great. How'd you get it?"

"Uniform cop in the Bronx noticed an abandoned station wagon this morning. Not far from the water.

K-9 Unit took a dog up there a little while ago and got a positive hit. Looks like there's blood on a canvas tarp in the back, too."

"Any plates? Whose is it?"

"Stripped clean. VIN number's been scratched out a bit, but the computer still came up with a list of possibilities."

"And?"

"One of them comes back to an employee who works in Deni's Chelsea gallery. Bingo."

I stepped back and smiled at the judge. "That's it, Your Honor. No further argument. We'll rest on our papers." I grabbed my files off the table and followed Mercer and Mike out of the courtroom.

# 9

Laura tried to pass the telephone to me as I swept through her alcove. "It's Rose. She just wants to warn you that Battaglia said he'd like an update on the Caxton investigation."

"Tell her that he'll have it by the end of the day."

Mike was at my desk, using the private line. "It's a girl!" This time I grabbed the receiver out of his hand. Sarah's baby had been born during the night, and she was calling to tell us about it, urging us to come visit Janine as soon as possible.

"You okay?"

"Much easier this time. When are you coming up to the hospital? I'll only be here until Wednesday."

"Don't worry. We'll come see her tonight or tomorrow. Give her a kiss and tell her we'll all be up the first break we get." I placed the phone back in its cradle.

"See, Alex, that's what you should be doing with your life instead of chasing around after scumbags like we do all day."

"You're beginning to sound like my grandmother."

I turned to Mike as I sat down at my desk. "Have you ever done one of these before? I mean, a search warrant based on a *dog* as the informant?"

"No, but I got the officer right outside who knows how." He walked to the door of my office and signaled to a plainclothes cop who was reading the *Daily News* on a chair in the hallway. "This is Detective Loquesto," he said, introducing me to a sandy-haired man with a crooked smile that seemed to align with his long, hooked nose. "Armando, meet Alex Cooper."

"Good to meet you. Thanks for the break."

"Don't thank me," he said. "Tego did it. Latin word for 'I protect.' I'm just the handler; the dog does the heavy lifting."

"Can you walk me through the affidavit?"

"No problem—do it all the time."

I pulled up my standard search warrant application form on the computer, quickly punching in the information Chapman fed me about the target automobile, a '91 light blue Chevy wagon, partial vehicle identification number 6683493, registered to Omar Sheffield.

"How'd you connect Sheffield to one of the Caxton galleries?" I asked.

Mercer spoke up. "Caxton's aide, Maurizio, faxed me a list of all the employees. It was on my desk when I walked in today. Also had the names of some of Denise's clients—said we'd have to get the rest of them from Daughtry."

I fleshed out the paragraph delineating that there is reasonable cause to believe that we might find blood, hair, fibers, fingerprints, and other evidence of the presence of the body of Denise Caxton. Then I added in the "moreover" clause, asking the judge to believe that this property was used to commit or conceal the commission of a crime.

It was essential to explain to the court how, when, and where the body of the deceased had been found, and that her death was the result of a homicide. When I finished that paragraph, I looked up at Armando for help. "Now what?"

"You gotta throw in some background about me and Tego."

I typed in his name and shield. "Your command?"

"NYPD Emergency Services, K-9 Unit." He told me how many years he'd been on the force and what his training had been to qualify him for this special duty. "Tego's got four years on the job—specializing in cadaver duty."

"What?" I knew German shepherds were used to great advantage in police work, trained to identify the scents of bomb materials and controlled substances. This one was new to me.

"True. He's like Chapman—death is his specialty. Sniffs it out and loves it."

"How do you train them for that?"

"There are a couple of chemicals that simulate cadaver odors—"

"Yeah, Coop, and Chanel doesn't make 'em," Mike cut in. "So don't try and seduce me by dousing yourself in 'em."

Armando continued. "They're called Cadaverine and Pseudocorpse—both are artificial commercial scents. The dogs practice by smelling body parts, corpses, crime scene areas. Then we sprinkle some of the fake stuff on items like you'd find at a scene and let them go to work."

"Tell her what you give them when they come up with a body."

"Three treats and a rawhide pull toy, just like if he'd brought home your missing slipper."

I improvised a few paragraphs about Tego's training and the fact that he had completed more than sixty tests in the company of Detective Loquesto.

"What else do I need?"

"You gotta say what the dog did when he got to the target. The Chevy was parked in a row of nine cars. In training we call it a 'marked reaction,' which——"

"What'd he do, exactly?"

Chapman was impatient and anxious for me to complete the warrant. "He went ape, like you do when you see Alex Trebek. Drooling, panting——"

"Pretty close," Loquesto said. "He sniffed next to the right rear passenger door, then ran around to the back of the wagon. He jumped up against it and began pawing at it, whining and scratching like it'd get him inside. I looked in—window was slightly tinted—and there's a dark stain on a canvas-colored matting. Then I pulled Tego away and took him one at a time to the doors of each other car. No reaction at all."

I finished the application with the routine language, respectfully asking the court for a warrant and order of seizure. "As soon as the lunch break is over, we'll go down and get the judge who's sitting in the arraignment part to sign it, okay? Anybody want me to call in something to eat?"

"Nah, we'll grab a bite on our way to the Bronx."

"Okay. I'll open a grand jury investigation this afternoon so I can start some phone company subpoenas for muds and luds on the Caxton telephones—home and galleries." Contrary to what most people thought, prosecutors have no power to subpoena people or evidence to their offices. It was only the authority of the grand jury in New York, not the district attorneys, that enabled the request for a witness to produce documentary evidence. "Who's looking for Omar?"

"*My* job," Mercer said. "Since the gallery's closed today, there's no activity at all. The address on the Motor Vehicles Bureau records—for Omar's residence—is in Brooklyn."

"Before I came up to the courtroom," Mike went on, "I called the boss at the Eighty-fourth Precinct and asked them to do a drive-by of that address. Desk sergeant beeped me back and said it's a burned-out building. Mercer'll be working on it this afternoon."

My paralegal, Maxine, came into the room and greeted the trio of cops. "This looks like the wrong time to ask, but what do I do with a walk-in who just arrived now for her ten-thirty appointment?"

"Who is she?" I looked at my watch, noting that the woman was more than three hours late.

"Her name's Unique Matthews. Says she's here to see Janice O'Riley, but Janice has to do a preliminary hearing all afternoon."

"This one's the prostitute who was raped at gunpoint by the trucker on Houston Street, right?"

"Yep." Maxine smiled and motioned discreetly with her thumb for me to look out the doorway to Laura's desk. A young woman was towering over my secretary, balancing on four-inch platform sandals with straps that wrapped up to her knees. The cheeks of her buttocks were hanging well below the bottom of her shorts, and her cleavage strained against the skimpy cut of her fuchsia cotton tank T-shirt, exposing a tattoo of Mickey Mouse on her inner left breast, outlined against her dark skin. Unique was chewing a wad of gum and sipping from a large bottle of Yoo-Hoo.

I called out to the witness, knowing that there would be no particularly good reason for her tardiness. "Unique, how come you're so late today? You were supposed to testify this morning."

She took the straw out of her mouth and sneered at me, certain that I could not understand how hard it had been to rouse herself for something as relatively unimportant as her court appearance. "I overslept."

"Why don't you take her across the street to Catherine's office?" I said to Max. This was going to take more experience and a firmer hand than Janice had with these cases. "Let her work with Unique for a couple of hours."

Chapman patted Max on the back. "Remind O'Riley of Cooper's basic commands. Never make a morning appointment for a hooker. Like vampires, they don't thrive in daylight. C'mon, blondie. Let Mercer get on his way. Me and Armando'll come down to court with you to get the warrant signed."

"Armando and I."

"What else do you do in your spare time besides give grammar lessons? Wellesley meets the NYPD. Now *that's* an exercise in futility."

I stopped at Laura's desk and asked her to check the docket assignment sheet. "Who's sitting in arraignments this week?"

"You've got Roger Hayes in AR1 and John Reick in AR2."

Mercer chided me. "Judge shopping, Alex? My money's on AR1. I'll check in with both of you as soon as I get back from Brooklyn."

Mike, Armando, and I took the circuitous route to the first-floor arraignment parts, down the interior stairway one flight and over to the elevator bank that serviced the courtrooms and stopped on only a single floor of the District Attorney's Office, as a security measure. As usual the wait for a functioning elevator going in the right direction seemed interminable. And walking the hallways with Chapman was more of a social occasion than a business trip. He had worked with and partied with every senior assistant in the office at one time or another. He was a legendary storyteller, a great foil for people's jokes, and the best investigator that most of us would ever encounter in the NYPD.

The double swinging doors of AR1 pushed open as I entered behind Mike. Families and friends of prisoners arrested within the last twenty-four hours and awaiting their first appearances before the judge filled rows of benches on both sides of the room. Some mothers looked tearful and anxious, waiting for word from the Legal Aid attorneys that their sons would be coming home today, while other relatives slept soundly despite the noise and activity, clearly accustomed to the routine of this process.

We made our way down to the front row, saved for attorneys and police officers, and I scooted into the only available seat, between two uniformed cops who were dozing until their cases were called. Mike and Armando sat behind me, scrunched between an elderly Hasidic Jew dressed in his traditional black overcoat and an obese Latina woman who was whining some kind of prayer over and over again under her breath.

The air-conditioning wasn't working and the windows were so tall in the two-story room that there was no way for the crew to open them for fresh air. Everyone in the well of the courtroom—lawyers, stenographer, officers, and clerks—was fanning with different files or sheaves of papers. The stench was unbearable.

As soon as Judge Hayes made eye contact with me, he waved me up to the bench. As I rose, Chapman grabbed my shoulder. "I'm coming with you. This place smells like a broad I used to date."

"May we approach, Your Honor?" I asked as I closed the swinging gate that separated the benches from the counsel tables.

"Absolutely, Ms. Cooper. We'll take a ten-minute recess, folks," Hayes announced, eliciting groans from almost everyone in the gallery. "Why don't we all go into the robing room? Will we need a reporter?"

"Yes sir."

Hayes had been one of my first supervisors in the District Attorney's Office when I started there, more than ten years ago. I respected his judgment and valued his guidance and friendship enormously.

Mike, Armando, and I followed Hayes out of the

courtroom and into the small chambers behind it that served the arraignment part. He normally sat as a trial jurist in Supreme Court but was serving a week's rotation in this duty since so many of the judges took vacation time during July and August. Hayes greeted Mike and me warmly, and we introduced him to Armando.

"I'd tell you to make yourselves comfortable, but that's obviously not possible."

The small room was bare except for an old wooden desk, three chairs, and a black rotary telephone that hung on the wall. It was painted the institutional green that must have been bought in vatloads by the city of New York fifty years ago and was now chipped and peeling from every corner and molding. Next to the phone, written on the wall in ink, were the numbers of most of the delis and pizza joints within a mile's radius, jotted there by lazy court officers who called out for deliveries during the meal break of night court.

I explained our visit to the judge, and we went on the record with the stenographer so that he could make the appropriate inquiries before signing the warrant.

"Everything seems to be in order, Alex." He initialed the papers and chatted with Mike while I went back to the clerk to have the official seal put on the documents. As the court officer gaveled the crowd back into order and Hayes resumed his position on the bench, we left the courtroom with exactly what we needed to move the investigation forward.

The rear entrance of the immense Criminal Courts Building was adjacent to AR1. Mike took his copy of the paperwork from me, and he and Armando headed for the door while I started to retrace my steps back up to my office.

"I'll call you as soon as we're done checking out the wagon. Wanna meet Mercer and me for dinner?"

"Sure. Cocktails and *Jeopardy!* at my place, then we'll go somewhere in the neighborhood."

Upstairs on the eighth floor, Laura greeted me with word that Patrick McKinney, deputy chief of the Trial Division, wanted to see me. The chief, Rod Squires, was on summer vacation and McKinney would use all the muscle he could to make me answer to him and try to micromanage my case. I thanked Laura for the message, then did my best to ignore that she had given it to me. I knew I could deal directly with Battaglia on something as major as the Caxton murder.

I called my friend Rose Malone, in the D.A.'s suite, and told her that I was ready to update the boss whenever it was convenient for him. Things looked good, I assured her, since the cops had already found a critical link to the deceased's disappearance. I was optimistic enough to think this early break would signal a speedy conclusion to the investigation. Battaglia was on his way to Albany for a meeting with the governor on the legislative agenda, so I knew I was off the hook for the rest of the day.

The intercom buzzed. Laura reported there was a woman on the line who refused to give her name and would speak only to me. She said she had some things to tell me about Denise Caxton.

"Put the call through on my private line and close the door so no one interrupts me." I pressed the flashing light on my dial pad. "This is Alexandra Cooper."

"Thank you for taking the call. I thought you might be interested in some personal information I have about Deni Caxton."

"Yes, but it would also help me if you would tell me with whom I'm speaking."

My request was met by silence.

"Hello?" I asked, getting no response. At least she hadn't hung up, so I didn't want to push her too hard. "I hope you can understand that we get an awful lot of crank calls whenever our names appear in the paper on a sensational case. It just helps me to know that I'm dealing with someone who really has something useful to say." And who isn't wasting my time.

Still a pause. Then, "I'll give you my name, but I'd like a few assurances first."

"That's not unreasonable. May I ask what they are?"

"I can't have my name connected with this case in the papers. Not in any way. Can you promise me that?"

Impossible. "All I can promise is that no one will get your name from *us*. You have my word that it is not the kind of thing we would ever give to the press. But obviously, since I have no idea what your connection is—either to Denise or to the investigation—I simply have no idea how you figure in the matter at all. Perhaps reporters already know who you are."

I was clearly fishing now, and she was just as clearly getting agitated. "I have nothing to do with the case. I'm a friend of Deni's, that's all. One of her oldest friends. I know things about her that I doubt anyone else knows. Very intimate things. Perhaps they'll be useful to you, perhaps they won't. But I thought I'd be more comfortable talking with you than with a bunch of detectives."

"And your other requests?"

"Just one other, really. Lowell Caxton must never know I've spoken with you."

"That's easy. He's a witness in this matter. We'd have no business telling him where or from whom we get our information."

"He's terribly well connected, Ms. Cooper. I'm afraid it's more difficult to keep secrets from him than you might think. That was one of Deni's biggest problems."

"Would you be willing to meet with me this afternoon?" I glanced at the clock on the wall, and it was already after three. "Or this evening?"

"I'm coming into New York late tonight. I can meet with you tomorrow."

"Let me give you the address of my office—"

"No, I won't come there. I don't want some tabloid photographer camped out on your doorstep snapping witnesses as they go in and out of the building."

*Rivera Live, Burden of Proof,* and Court TV had been real wake-up calls to the public about the way high-profile cases frequently spin out of control.

"We're closer to a solution than you might think," I said to ease her concerns, sure in my own mind that Omar Sheffield would be the key to Deni's disappearance. "But I'll be happy to meet you at your home, if you prefer."

"My hotel, if you don't mind. I'll call you during

the day, and perhaps you can meet with me by late afternoon. The name is Seven. Marilyn Seven."

"Thank you for that, Ms. Seven. I appreciate it. Where will you be staying?"

The click on the other end of the phone reminded me that she didn't trust me or the system all that much. I went back into our office E-mail and sent one of my regular messages to my colleague who ran the computer section's Investigative Support Services, Jim Winright.

CooperA to WinrightJ: Can you please run me a background check on a woman named Marilyn Seven? Sorry, I've got no date of birth, no social security, no residential address. Nothing but a name. It's a long shot, but could you see if you can come up with anything before I meet with her tomorrow? Thanks, as always.

With Jim's skills and a bit of luck, the not-so-common-name search might call up something on his database, whether out-of-state driver's registration records, licensed professional information (if her occupation required some kind of government control), property ownership records, or even a Dun & Bradstreet report. It would help me not to go to the meeting blind, so that I could better evaluate whatever it was that Marilyn Seven had to barter.

When I finished drafting the subpoenas, which Laura could format and print, I ran upstairs to the ninth-floor grand jury room, to open an investigation into the death of Denise Caxton. Several of the jurors whispered to one another as I spoke, recognizing the deceased's name from the newspaper accounts. I was out of the chamber as quickly as I had entered it, and on my way back to my desk.

"Call Catherine or Marisa," Laura told me. "They want to make arrangements to go to the hospital tomorrow to see Sarah and the baby. And Kim McFadden, from the U.S. Attorney's Office, called. Here's her extension."

I took the slip of paper from Laura and dialed the number immediately. I hadn't seen Kim, who was a federal prosecutor, in months. Our offices often tangled when investigations crossed jurisdictional lines and our bosses became territorial, but she and I had been friends since she started to date one of my colleagues, several years ago.

"Sorry I've been so out of touch," I began our conversation. "Can we make a lunch date for later in the month, when things slow down here?"

"That'd be good, Alex, but it's not the reason I'm calling. Got the clearance from the top to give you a heads-up on this, once I saw you were handling the Caxton case."

"Just when I was beginning to think this was a ground ball, don't tell me it's going to get muddier. My guys think it's a disgruntled employee—raped and dumped her in the water. Probably just hired the wrong guy. I'm waiting for the results on his rap sheet now, with a team of detectives out looking for the subject."

"That's probably what you've got, then. Just thought

that you should know—and I'd appreciate it if you didn't tell anyone other than Battaglia—that we've had a major investigation under way with Justice. Price-fixing by auction houses and art dealers. We've had subpoenas out for months—you may have seen the story in the *Times*."

"Well, if I did, I didn't pay any attention to it. I don't remember a thing about it."

"We're looking at it as an antitrust matter. Know what bid rigging is?"

"Not in the art world. Bring me up to speed, Kim, and the next time you get a sexual assault on federal property, I'll walk you through it." I said it only half in jest, since once every few years their office actually claimed jurisdiction for a rape in a Veterans Administration hospital or on a military base.

"The claim has been that some of the biggest art dealers in the city have formed a ring agreeing not to bid against each other on paintings in which they all have an interest. That collusion keeps the price down at auctions—an illegal restraint, really. Then the participating dealers hold what's called a 'knockout.' "

"Which is . . . ?"

"That's a second auction—but a secret one. The dealer who got the piece at the public auction sells it off for a much higher price, and then the members of the ring all split the profits. The agents who've been investigating this for years can lay out the whole thing for your team."

"Any direct connection to Denise Caxton?"

"Nothing certain yet. But records have been subpoenaed from both Lowell and Denise Caxton, Bryan

Daughtry, and quite honestly, a cast of thousands. All the big dealers are being called down here—Leo Castelli, Knoedler, Pace Wildenstein. They're all in the contemporary field. David Findlay and Acquavella in modern and Impressionist works. Even Sotheby's and Christie's have gotten those unfriendly little slips of paper. I'm not saying any of these places are targets—there's no allegation they did anything wrong or participated in the knockouts—but we're trying to get a handle on the nature and extent of the scam."

"Any results yet?"

"We're getting buried in an avalanche. Travel logs, phone records, invoices from business transactions, correspondence between the auction houses and some of the dealers."

"Can I bring my detectives over later in the week if we don't settle everything in the next twenty-four hours?"

"That's why I called. No reason for you to reinvent the wheel. If you're going to have the legal authority to request the same kind of documentation, maybe we can shortcut some of this for you."

"Thanks a million, Kim. I'll call you in a day or two."

There was enough to keep me busy at my desk until after six, so I successfully avoided contact with McKinney through the end of the day. I drove home, went upstairs, turned on all my air conditioners, and filled the ice bucket in anticipation of the arrival of Mercer and Mike. I called Lumi, who owned the wonderful Italian restaurant over on Lexington Avenue, and made a reservation for the three of us at eight o'clock, after confirming that she had Mercer's favorite pasta on the menu tonight—cavatelli with peas and prosciutto. I settled in to watch the end of the evening news, knowing that very little would keep Mike from missing the Final Jeopardy question at seven twenty-five.

I had told the doormen that they didn't need to announce either of the detectives, who were well known to the staff in the building. Mercer was the first to come through my front door, and we decided there was no reason at all to wait for Mike before we poured our first drink. I fixed him a Ketel One with two olives and lots of ice before filling my own glass with Dewar's.

"What'd you find out in Brooklyn?"

"I found out that the last time anyone lived at the address given on Omar Sheffield's automobile registration, he wasn't even a glimmer in his momma's eye. The whole block is a wreck. The Eight-four squad had some informants in the 'hood that they rousted for me, but nobody ever heard of Omar. I spent three hours pounding that hot pavement and every minute of it was wasted time. Hope Chapman did better than I did. Zip, zero, nada."

He sipped on his vodka while I started to tell him about my phone calls from Marilyn Seven and Kim McFadden.

Mike came in minutes later and walked straight to the den, checking the screen and pouring himself a drink before he took over the conversation with the results of their search.

"I think I'm asking for a new partner. Gimme one of those four-legged sniffers any day. Man, I've worked with detectives so bad they couldn't find dog shit at the pound."

Mercer smiled over at me. "I guess this means Tego was on the money."

"Emergency Services broke into the car. No question about it—there was definitely a body in there. Backseat is down, and there's a big piece of sailcloth laid out full length, with a bloodstain on top. It was folded over, so we opened it up—you know what I mean? It was like the body had been sandwiched in between. Huge bloodstain, kinda matching the hole in Denise's head. Even some hair. And a pair of lace panties—beige, size four."

"What did you do with them?"

"Everything's vouchered. Going directly over to the lab. They'll run the DNA tests at the M.E.'s Office. We could have preliminary results within forty-eight hours."

In the mid-1980s, when the lawyers in my office had first been introduced to DNA technology and the science of genetic fingerprinting, it took three or four months to obtain results from the private labs to which materials were sent for testing. Now the city had established its own laboratory, and the methodology had changed so dramatically that we could include or eliminate suspects and match samples to victims or defendants in a matter of several days.

"Tonight's Final Jeopardy category is Bob Dylan's Music," announced Alex Trebek as he led into a commercial break and Mike *sssshush*ed us into silence.

"I'm out. I do not know anything about this one," Mercer said, standing to freshen his drink.

"I'll go twenty," I offered, comfortable with the category.

"Let's keep it at ten," Mike said. That was a sure sign that he didn't have a clue.

"Nope, it's twenty or I'm not betting."

He reluctantly put his money on the table.

"Let's show our contestants the answer, ladies and gentlemen." Trebek read along with the words that were revealed on the screen: "Famous rock musician who plays the organ on Dylan's 'Like a Rolling Stone.' Ooh, that's a tough one, folks."

The theme music played as Chapman cursed, noticing the smile on my face. "Double or nothing?" I asked.

"Talk about obscure, how could you possibly know this? No way."

The bioethics professor from Oregon shook his head and didn't even attempt an answer. The mother of eleven from Nevada and the crab farmer from Delaware both guessed wrong, as Trebek was sorry to tell them.

Mike's beeper gave off with a loud series of noises as I put my response in the appropriate question form. "Who is Al Kooper?" I asked. "Impossible for me to forget, right?"

"A Jewish organist, no doubt," he said, squinting at the number after he took the device off his waistband. "Turn to Comedy Central. Let's watch *Win Ben Stein's Money* before we go eat."

We had a new quiz show favorite in the seven thirty time slot, so I switched channels and passed Mike the portable phone. "Who's the beep from?"

"It's the lieutenant's line," he said, dialing the number at the squad. "Hey, Loo, what's up?"

"*What?* How certain are they?"

I muted the television sound while Mercer and I waited to hear what seemed so surprising to Mike.

"Mercer Wallace is with me. We'll get over there right away. No, no—we're just ten minutes away." He hung up the phone and handed it back to me.

"I'll start with the good news. They found Omar Sheffield."

"Where?" Mercer and I spoke at once.

"In the culvert next to the railroad tracks, between Tenth and Eleventh near Thirty-sixth Street. Dead. Very, very dead. Run over by a freight train."

# 10

"Death Avenue," Chapman said flatly.

"Seems like an appropriate name after last night."

Mike and I were standing on Eleventh Avenue at the edge of the Thirtieth Street rail yards at eight thirty in the morning. He had called to suggest that I meet him there on my way into the office so he could show me where Sheffield's body had been found.

"Forget last night. That's what this stretch was called a hundred years ago." His sweeping arm gesture took in all the property north and south of the tracks that had once been owned by the New York Central Railroad. "My old man grew up here—Hell's Kitchen. Used to tell us stories about this neighborhood all the time."

After the Civil War, when a large area of Manhattan's West Side was thick with slaughterhouses, factories, lumberyards, and tenements, it housed one of the worst slums in the city. Cops who covered its beat called it Hell's Kitchen, from Thirtieth Street north to Fifty-ninth Street, and from Eighth Avenue west to the Hudson River.

"Freight trains rolled through here every day and night. The place was notorious—for its filth and for the dangerous gangs that controlled its everyday life. The kids who weren't killed by disease or driven out by dust and noise were just as likely to be flattened by one of the trains. Big Mike was around long before they elevated the tracks, after nineteen thirty, to get them off the street." Mike grinned as he thought of his father's stories. "Used to fascinate me, 'cause he said that every time a train came through, there was a 'cowboy'—a guy who actually rode on a horse ahead of the engine, waving a flag to get people out of the way. Can you imagine that—in the middle of Manhattan, in the twentieth century? When he was four or five, my dad dreamed about being that cowboy when he grew up. By that time the trains were raised above street level. But Death Avenue is what they called it, even then."

"Here's Mercer," I said, pointing to the corner of the next block, where I saw him parking his car. "What's the plan?"

"We're meeting Daughtry at the gallery in a few minutes. Thought you'd want to be along for the interview."

Mercer greeted us with, "What's the word from the morgue?"

"I was just telling Coop. Train messed up Sheffield's body pretty well. But there's no way he just happened to be crossing these tracks. Fleisher says it'll take a few days for the toxicology reports to come in. My guess is somebody probably filled him up with dope or tranquilizers and left him here in the dark to make it look accidental. And by the way, it didn't happen last night. Omar was lying here a couple of days—out of sight, out of mind."

Mercer held up a roll of papers he was clutching in his left hand. "Let me tell you about Mr. Sheffield. Forty-six years old, three felony convictions—worked his way up from burglary to gun possession to armed robbery. Released on parole about eight months ago. Needless to say, he reported faithfully to his parole officer, who didn't have a clue that Omar's residential address simply didn't exist."

"You think Deni Caxton knew that when she hired him?" I asked.

"Let's hope we're about to find out. Daughtry returned my call late last night. He's waiting for us at the downtown gallery. Ready for this?"

Mike and I left our cars parked near the rail yards and rode down to Twenty-second Street between Tenth and Eleventh Avenues in Mercer's department car. I had never met Bryan Daughtry but knew well the story of his involvement in a murder in Westchester County almost ten years earlier, even though he had never been charged or prosecuted.

In the late eighties Daughtry had a gallery in the Fuller Building, where Lowell Caxton still maintained an upscale presence. Daughtry was forty years old at the time and had worked his way up quite rapidly from apprenticing with another successful dealer to owning his own business, once he became the personal business associate of the wealthy Japanese collector Yoshio Tsukamoto.

Daughtry was buying and selling major works—

Jackson Pollocks and Franz Klines—and living a lifestyle that matched his newfound ability to afford it. A town house in the east sixties and a grand Victorian country place south of the highway in East Hampton. He was intensely private about his personal relationships, but rumor had it that he preferred teenaged girls—young, lean, fond of drugs, and dressed in leather.

By 1992 his professional life seemed to be unraveling just as quickly as it had taken off. Creditors had trouble collecting money from him—even small amounts—and auction houses as well as other prominent dealers began to sue because of misrepresentations Daughtry had made about ownership of some of the works he sold. Then the IRS piled in after a disgruntled accountant whom Daughtry had fired reported that Daughtry had withheld tax payments on more than $5 million of income. Informants told the Feds that he was buying almost fifty grams of cocaine a week, at $100 a gram. His lawyers were working on a deal to get him out of his legal problems.

And then, the body of a fifteen-year-old Swedish girl, a would-be model, was found in a wooded area surrounded by enormous private estates in a suburban town north of Manhattan. The bird-watchers who stumbled on the carcass were stunned to find that the only part of the remains that had not been consumed by rodents was the stunning head of the child, her faded blue eyes staring out from a black leather mask that tightly covered her skull.

I reminded Mike and Mercer of the rest of the story. Posters of Ilse Lunen had been plastered all over the Village, where she had last been seen at a leather bar, one frequented by Daughtry and his crowd. Although no one had placed the dealer there the evening of the girl's disappearance, his closest personal assistant, Bertrand Gloster, had been at the bar for hours and was known to pimp for his boss when Daughtry was too wrecked to appear on his own.

In fact, it was rare for Bryan to come on to his subjects face-to-face. His preferred mode of pickup was to sit in a private room on the third floor of the building in which Cuir de Russie ("Russian leather"), as the bar was called, was situated. He'd stare out the window for hours, doing an occasional line of coke. When he saw a girl who was young and nubile enough standing on the sidewalk for a chat with a friend or a smoke, he would call the number of the pay phone outside the bar, talk to his target, and invite her up to the owner's lair.

Long after the death of the Lunen girl, people in the art world told stories of visiting Daughtry in his office, where he often had sex toys casually displayed on his desk and cabinet tops—handcuffs, collars, studded bands, and even leather masks like the one found on the corpse. In those same encounters he would refer to the ever-subservient Bertrand as "my executioner," the enforcer who had been brought in to serve as a bodyguard against the rough characters Daughtry encountered in this underside of his life. No one took his words seriously at the time.

Also later, acquaintances admitted hearing stories of the sadomasochistic games that Bryan and his pals had favored, wild evenings of drugs and sex, complete with whips and chains, during which Daughtry increasingly lost his self-control.

Bertrand Gloster was picked up within days of the discovery of Ilse Lunen's body. He had once been employed as a caretaker on one of the neighboring estates, and his borderline intelligence level made him an easy subject for police interrogators. He admitted killing the young girl, who had gingerly agreed to participate in the S&M activities in return for Daughtry's promise of an airline ticket home to Sweden.

In Gloster's chilling confession, he described Ilse Lunen putting on the leather mask and zipping its mouthpiece shut before Daughtry handcuffed her behind her back and directed her to kneel behind a large boulder in the woods. Then, Gloster said, the already floating art dealer snorted a few more lines and leaned over to whisper to Ilse, "You'll be going home, all right—in a wooden box," before he ordered Gloster to shoot her in the back of the head.

"End of story?" Chapman asked.

"Not exactly. Gloster's doing twenty-five to life for murder, and the Westchester D.A. has never been able to nail Daughtry." The testimony of an accomplice has to be corroborated by some other evidence—it's not sufficient in and of itself to charge the coconspirator with the crime of murder. "There has never been a single other thing to link Daughtry to the child's death."

"So this friggin' lunatic did eighteen months for tax evasion and now he's back in business like he's a normal guy, right? Man, I'd like just five minutes alone with him while you wait in the car. Whaddaya think, Coop? No loss to society, I promise."

Mercer parked in front of Galleria Caxton Due, the newest Chelsea outpost, which Deni and Bryan had just been setting up for a fall premiere at the time of her death. It was too early in the day for the galleries to be open, so there were few other cars and little pedestrian activity on the street.

Mike paused briefly to read the sign that was posted below the bell: "*Service entrance in rear on Twenty-third Street.* Hope that doesn't mean us."

The front door was unlocked, so Mike pushed it open and we followed him in. The cavernous first-floor space of the former auto repair shop had been completely whitewashed and gutted of all signs of its earlier life. New Age music played on speakers tucked up high in corners of the room.

"Guess they're not set up for the exhibition yet."

"You're about to step on a masterpiece, Mikey. Read the sign." I pointed to a piece of gray string, about twelve feet long, that extended out from the wall to form a triangle and was tacked to a point on the floor near my left shoe. He ignored me, looking around, instead, at similar strands of colorless yarn spread across sections of the gallery like giant cat's-cradle forms. I called out the words written on the placard describing the display: "*In these string sculptures, the space takes on an incorporeal palpability, concentrating on the planar or volumetric components. Illusion and fact are interwoven, with overlapping linear trajectories.*"

"This is *art*?" Mike responded. "You think some horse's ass is going to pay money for these things? I never saw anything so useless in my entire life."

Bryan Daughtry's voice called down to us from a high balcony area off to the side of the airy room. "Don't be so quick to declare this one the most absurd, Detective. There are several more floors above you might like to see. Why don't you take the lift up here to my office?"

"Can I make it up there without hanging myself on any of this string crap you call art?" Mike said to Daughtry, rolling his eyes at the bizarre exhibit of yarn sculptures that stretched across the mostly bare space on the ground floor. Then he turned to me. "Let's head up, blondie. Maybe if I dangle my handcuffs in front of him he'll get a hard-on. You're certainly much too old for his taste."

There was a small lift in the far corner of the wide room. When the doors of the elevator opened on the sixth floor, I was struck in the eye by a blaze of light. The southern exposure of the building was a wall of glass, which let the bright midday sun flood into this most unexpected setting.

From this point, with no tall buildings in the immediate area, I could see over the rooftops of nearby galleries and garages and out to the Hudson River, which curved in toward the east just a few blocks below us.

The most striking surprise was that about three floors beneath where we stood, running from the north end to the south side of the airy atrium, was an actual stretch of railroad track. It was heavy, thick, covered with rust, and overgrown with weeds.

I stared down at it. "Is that real?"

Chapman was rapt. "I wish my old man could see

*this.* Sure it's real. Look," he said, pointing to an open-ing where the track ran out of the glass-sided building and across the street, directly into a warehouse facing the Galleria Caxton Due.

I leaned against the railing to see that in similar fashion, the grass-filled ties also ran back out of the converted garage, crossing over the double width of Twenty-third Street and rolling on between two build-ings on its north corner.

"What is it?" Mercer asked.

"The old Hi-Line Railroad. Another Hell's Kitchen special. When they raised the tracks off Death Avenue north of the rail yards, they still needed trains to get down to the meat markets in the Fourteenth Street area. So, south of Thirtieth Street, this became the ele-vated line. Haven't you ever noticed the old tracks?"

Mercer and I looked at Mike blankly and shook our heads.

"Just drive uptown on Tenth Avenue and look to your left. The air rights over the railroad tracks were sold off, so all these warehouses were allowed to build above and surrounding the actual path of the Hi-Line. Between every block in the twenties and even below that, till you hit the old Gansevoort Market, you can see the great tracks right from the street."

Daughtry stepped out of his office, on the south-west corner of the floor, and looked across at us. "Amazing space, isn't it? We're the only gallery in the city smart enough to incorporate this bit of history into our design. Glad you appreciate that much."

He invited us into his chilled office, and despite the temperature in the climate-controlled gallery, I was surprised to see that beads of sweat were pooled on Daughtry's forehead. He repeatedly dabbed at the streaks running down the side of his neck.

Mike, Mercer, and I introduced ourselves, and he invited us to sit opposite his desk. There were no signs of his former indiscretions here, and although he resembled the photos I had seen in the press during the Gloster trial, Daughtry was paunchier now, and jowls had replaced the even line of his pointed chin.

"I'm sure you know all about my background, Detective," he began tentatively, as his eyes darted back and forth between us, trying to measure our level of hostility or the extent of our familiarity with his past. His fingers trembled when they were at rest on the desktop, so he kept wiping at his head and neck, even before it was necessary. "But you need to know that I adored Deni Caxton, and I'll be glad to help you in any way that I can."

Chapman was unmoved by Daughtry's effort to set a cooperative tone, so I sat back quietly, like a guest privileged to be at the interrogation but not encouraged to participate. Mike was aware of his witness's vulnerability, so, in contrast to his meeting with Lowell Caxton, he knew he could control the conversation.

Mike let Daughtry think that if he bared his soul about the tax fraud matter, we'd get off the old case and move on to the mystery of Deni's death. It seemed to calm him to tell us what we already knew about the tax matter, as though we would think better of him for admitting his wrongdoing aloud.

Then Mike moved his chair directly across from his target. "Now, Bryan," he said, knowing the use of his first name would bring Daughtry down one more notch, "tell us about *her*."

Daughtry seemed relieved to be off the subject of himself and onto his friend. "Oh, Deni. She's the only reason I'm still in business today, after getting out of—"

"No, no, no, Bryan. Not Deni. I want to know about the *girl*—about Ilse Lunen."

The moisture gathered again on his pasty skin, and now he looked from me to Mercer and back again, hoping one of us would intercede with Chapman and call him off.

"I had nothing, nothing to do with that girl, Detective. I've never been charged with any crime. That sick little bastard should have been strung up and—"

"And stringing *you* up would probably have given you more pleasure than any pervert like you deserves, Bryan. Just keep in mind that there's no statute of limitations on murder. You play with us on this case, you tell me even one little white lie about you or Denise Caxton or Omar Sheffield, and—"

"Omar? What does he have to do with any of this?"

The collar of his hunter green sport shirt was soaked through, and the underarms matched it. His surprise about Sheffield seemed genuine to me.

Chapman continued. "The slightest misstep with us, and I'll go to the ends of the earth to find the nails for your coffin, the evidence that'll stick you in a jail cell right next door to Bertrand Gloster. So, now—you tell me, Bryan. What's this operation all about? And sit on your hands while you're at it—

you're making me crazy with all your mopping and dabbing. Take a shower after I leave—you need it anyway."

Bryan responded like a three-year-old child and literally put his hands under his thighs. He explained how he and Deni had met in 1990, when both of them had galleries in the Fuller Building. They discovered their similarities early on—both from poor families and with invented histories, each with an untrained eye but great instincts. Deni and Bryan delighted in the big sale to a famous client, and both would do almost anything—testing the boundaries in a fairly sedate business—to stumble upon a sleeper, a lost masterpiece that had suddenly come back on the market, and then find a Streisand or a Nicholson to buy it.

"Don't forget the candy. You still sniffing, Bryan?"

"Not really."

"No such thing as 'not really' when it comes to cocaine addiction. You and Deni had that in common, too, didn't you?"

"May I wipe my mouth, Detective?" Chapman nodded and Daughtry lifted one of his hands and wiped his face and neck with the sleeve of his shirt. "We got high together occasionally."

"Who's your source?"

"Actually, Deni was. With my felony conviction I couldn't take chances buying off the street. I relied on my—well—friends to give me coke. Artists, dealers, even the guys who work in the warehouse. There's no shortage of the white stuff on the streets. You know that."

Chapman stood and looked out through the glass wall of Daughtry's office, down over the tracks to the string-lined display that we had seen on entering. "Did Denise really go for this garbage? I mean, you've seen the paintings in her home, and in Lowell's gallery, haven't you? They've got an amazing collection."

"Detective, van Gogh only sold five of his paintings in his lifetime. Relatively speaking, merely a handful of artists have ever been recognized by their contemporaries. Deni wanted to get in on the next wave, pick the giants of the future, take some chances. What Lowell does with his collection of masters takes no brains at all, no imagination. Just money."

"Let's talk about your business."

"It's Deni's business, not mine. I've put some money into it, but she couldn't risk attaching my name to a venture like this. Too many people seem to remember too much."

"D'you know she was having problems? Legal ones?"

"Of course I did." Daughtry looked down at his desk. "I mentioned van Gogh a moment ago. I'm sure you knew about the controversy over *Vase with Eight Sunflowers*."

"Let's say we know *our* version of it," Mike bluffed. "Why don't you tell us yours?"

"There's a bit of a storm in the market these days. Vincent van Gogh only painted during the last ten years of his life. He's been credited with completing 879 oils, 1,245 drawings, and a single etching." Daughtry was talking to me now, as though Mercer and Mike wouldn't be able to understand the story.

I glared back at him. "Talk to the detectives, Mr. Daughtry. They're much better at this work than I am. They're really quite intelligent."

"The brouhaha is that a great many experts now believe that some of the most famous paintings, and even the one etching, are fakes. In fact, they suspect that many of van Gogh's contemporaries created them and others passed them off as the real thing. Since his work is fetching higher prices than almost anyone else's, it's a rather hot debate these days."

"And Deni?"

"Well, Deni recently sold *Eight Sunflowers* to a client in Japan. I don't know his name offhand, but it's a matter of public record. He's now made a claim with the United States government—"

I broke in. "I don't get it. There are supposedly fake van Goghs everywhere from the Musée d'Orsay to the Metropolitan."

"Yes, Ms. Cooper, but the gentleman's claim is that Deni sold it *after* she had sent it to Amsterdam to be authenticated by the curators there, and after they'd told her its value was questionable."

"So, after she'd been told it was a copy?"

"An opinion she fought vigorously with the Dutch Ministry of the Arts."

"But rather than waiting for the outcome," Chapman said, "she stiffed the client anyway. How much?"

"Four-point-six million."

Chapman let out a whistle. "Not a bad day's work, Bryan. What's your cut of that? And what do you know about the bid-rigging investigation the Feds are doing?"

Daughtry was shaking his head. "I didn't have a piece of the van Gogh. I'm only involved in buying the contemporary works."

Chapman was pacing the small room, looking through the glass panel at the space below. "Phew. You musta had that leather mask wrapped too tight around your brain. This junk'll never bring you a nickel."

"Deni wasn't the least bit worried about the auction investigation. She was above all that—it never occurred to me to even mention it. And about your eye, Mr. Chapman," Daughtry said, "if what you're referring to as junk is that single oblique line of string you saw downstairs, I just sold the artist's last piece—*Red Yarn as an Octagon Half*—for a quarter of a million dollars."

"To some yupster Cooper went to school with, no doubt. When's the last time you saw Denise Caxton?"

"I think it was Wednesday of last week, before I went to the Hamptons. Things were very slow here—there's really nothing that goes on in August in our business. I invited Deni to come out to the house with me, but she said she had errands to get done in town. I left her here late in the afternoon, and we never talked again."

Daughtry was more emotional about Deni's death than her husband had been, but this reaction could just as easily have been a function of his nervousness and discomfort.

"Alex, you got a couple of subpoenas for Bryan? Why don't you give 'em to him now?" Mike turned back to Daughtry. "We'll give you a few days to get this stuff together. Two other things. I assume you were printed when you went in the can, right? We'll be pulling those out for comparisons with some of the evidence we've found. And you'll also notice that there'll be two cops parked in front of the gallery in a patrol car for the next few days. Nothing—and I mean nothing— goes in or out of here until we've been through the place with a fine-tooth comb. Ms. Cooper here will draft one hell of a warrant that'll cover my ass in court, and I'll expect your complete cooperation while we execute it."

Daughtry stood up. "But, Detective, there'll be art shipments coming in and out all the—"

"I don't think so, Mr. Daughtry. From what I read in the newspapers, I take it you liked to be the top in your little S&M games. Well, I'd like nothing better than to make you the bottom—for me and for some eight-foot-tall, three-hundred-pound convicted rapist waiting for you in a very crowded cell upstate, if I can get you there. So don't misbehave too badly, 'cause you may go back into prison a tight end, but I know you'll come out a wide receiver."

I turned to face Mercer, biting my lip to suppress a laugh. "Get me out of here, will you?"

"Mr. Daughtry," Mercer said, standing up and towering over the rest of us, "when's the last time you saw Omar Sheffield?"

He looked up at the ceiling. "I'd guess sometime that same afternoon, last Wednesday, almost a week ago."

"Who hired him to work here, and what'd he do for you?"

"Deni did all the hiring—and firing. Omar's a sort of handyman—moves exhibits, hangs the artwork. Painted the gallery with a couple of his friends. Ask him yourself. He'll be here within the hour."

"Don't count on it, Bryan. Omar's feeling a little sluggish this morning."

Mercer said, "Did you know that Omar had a record? That he was on parole?"

Daughtry hesitated, and I sensed that he was starting to filter his responses to us.

"I'm not sure. I may have heard something about that, but didn't pay any attention."

"Didn't pay attention?" asked Chapman incredulously. "What was this place, one-stop shopping for the parole board? You know that there are restrictions about who you do business with, don't you? What if I tell you that you gotta hire a new whipping boy—oops, damn it, there I go again with that dominatrix crap. Omar Sheffield is the latest casualty in the Caxton-Daughtry partnership. He's as dead as Deni. What do you think of *that*?"

Daughtry drew in a deep breath, and his hands started trembling again, uncontrollably. "I think, actually, that it's not such a bad thing, Mr. Chapman. Would you like to know why Deni hired Omar to work for her?"

"Let me guess. A direct pipeline to a cocaine source, right?"

"Well, that was just a lucky coincidence. Denise actually had a special job for Omar," Daughtry went on, clearly banking on his betrayal of his dear friend and partner to get Mike Chapman off his own back. "She put him on the payroll for a single purpose. And now that she's gone, I don't suppose there's any harm in telling you.

"The sole reason she employed Omar Sheffield was to kill Lowell Caxton."

# 11

The three of us settled into a booth at the Empire Diner, the sleek-looking chrome-fitted slice of a Deco eatery on the northeast corner of Tenth Avenue and Twenty-second Street, to regroup over a late-morning cup of coffee.

"I'll take a mushroom-and-cheese omelette, too," Chapman told the waitress.

"How many breakfasts have you had today?" I asked.

"I try to fortify myself in advance whenever I know I'll be hanging out with *you*. And throw in an order of crisp bacon and some sausage, okay?"

Mercer was doodling on his napkin, connecting stick figures with arrows and seemingly going around in circles. "Someone killed Denise Caxton. I assumed it was Omar Sheffield. Someone probably kills Sheffield—I don't think he just walked under a boxcar after forty-six years of careful living, but we'll know for certain in a day or two. Denise had hired Sheffield to kill her husband—so maybe Omar's the guy who screwed up the job and caused Lowell's scalp wound. Deni seems to have all the money in the world, but keeps scamming for more. Plus, she's got a class A dirtball pervert for a business partner. Where are we going here?"

"Nowhere, fast. I'll feel better after some more caffeine," I said.

I called Laura on my cellular phone. "I hope you picked up the voice mail I left at seven this morning, telling you I wouldn't be in till we finished uptown. Any messages for me?"

"Jim Winright found nothing on the Internet about the woman you asked about in your E-mail. He doubts it's her real name," Laura said. "And someone called Marilyn Seven phoned to say she could meet with you at noon in the restaurant at the Four Seasons Hotel, on Fifty-seventh Street. Then the M.E.'s Office wanted you to know that there was indeed seminal fluid on the canvas piece taken from the Chevy, and they'd probably have DNA results by the end of the day tomorrow. Last one is from Jacob Tyler. He expects to be back from China by the weekend, and hopes you can get away to the Vineyard."

I repeated the first three messages to my companions, omitting Jake's call and my hope that we might find Deni's killer so I could be with him by Friday.

"Good," Chapman said. "I already told the M.E. we'd need a comparison DNA print for Omar, so he should have that one under way, too. One of us oughta take that meeting with Marilyn Seven and you."

"It doesn't sound like she wants to have this conversation with police around. I think the Four Seasons is still a pretty safe place to be."

"Let Mike get on with what he's got to do, Alex. I'll take my car up there and sit in front of the hotel, in case you need me for anything."

Mike took us back to where we had parked earlier in the morning, and I drove uptown, throwing my parking permit in the windshield and leaving the Jeep near the entrance to the building.

The only woman in the lounge was a slight, serious-looking brunette whose long hair was wound into a French braid. Her tortoiseshell eyeglass frames held tinted lenses, and as I stood in the entrance to the room she dipped an ivory cigarette holder in my direction.

A bit dramatic for my taste, but I approached her and introduced myself. She stood and shook my hand, smiling openly and inviting me to join her. "Sorry for the dark glasses. I've had some vision problems lately, and even the softest light bothers my eyes. And I also apologize for being so mysterious. With all of Deni's problems, I just don't know where to turn and whom to trust. I called the lawyer who handles all my business affairs here in New York yesterday—Justin Feldman—and he assured me that I could rely on your judgment and your discretion."

"If he's your lawyer, then you're in very secure hands. Justin's the best in the business." Although I had been put off by her phone call, I liked this woman immediately. "Are you also an art dealer?"

"No, but my late husband was a collector. I live in Santa Fe now, but we bought a lot of our paintings from Lowell in the old days."

She was wearing a dark blue sweater, probably silk,

with a dark blue skirt that extended to midcalf, showing a bit of her thin ankle above the tops of her delicate blue sandals.

"Like Deni, I was married to a much older man, and a very rich one. Unlike her, I had inherited a lot of money, too—an automobile fortune—well, automobile parts, actually." She smiled at me. "And Lowell had sort of put Deni in my hands, to help polish her up a bit. I was ten years older than she—I'm forty-nine now—but we became friends, best friends. I'm sure you know how important that is to a woman."

"I can't imagine going through life without one," I said. Nina Baum, my Wellesley roommate, had taught me everything there was to know about friendship and loyalty. And even though she lived in Los Angeles and Joan Stafford was spending more and more time in Washington, I counted on the intimacy of our relationships to bolster me through the sometimes dark days and nights of my chosen work. "May I ask you to tell me about Deni—what you know, as well as what you think was going on recently?"

"Certainly. Would you care for something to drink?"

"No, thanks." I watched as she sipped at a glass of white wine.

"At the very beginning, it was as though Deni had walked into the pages of a fairy tale. Lowell was amazingly seductive, and Denise was like a magnificent jewel that he wanted to place in the center of his crown. His dinner parties were legendary—has anyone told you about them?"

I shook my head in the negative.

"Not that it was *his* idea, really, but he copied a page out of Gertrude Stein's ingenious recipe for entertaining. The living room—perhaps you've seen it—was hung with old masters and works from many of the greatest artists who ever lived. Then, with a handful of the richest collectors at the ready, he'd sprinkle the guest list with whoever was hottest in the art world—and seat the artist opposite his own paintings. Brilliant, wasn't it? Those often surly and sullen personalities couldn't help but smile as they were reflected in their own canvases and assured of almost immediate sales.

"Imagine at one table having Ellsworth Kelly, Keith Haring, David Hockney—all sitting amidst their creations while they debated each other about style and talent as well. Those were the days that Deni loved."

"How long did life at the Caxtons' go on like that?"

"Quite a good while, actually. Beyond Deni's youth and exuberance, Lowell seemed to love everything about her, not least of all how eager she was to learn everything there was to know about his life's passion. She was a tireless student, and though she had an untrained eye, her hunches could be brilliant. Lowell called her 'my budding alchemist.' First, he tempted her with really fine paintings that he'd search out in the châteaux of Bordeaux and the palaces of the once-rich in Venice. She'd a gift for knowing there was something lurking beneath the crusted dust and oil, and she would coax Lowell to take the gamble.

"More often than not she was right. They came home with a Canaletto and two amazing Delacroix that way. Stole them, in a sense. Paid practically nothing for the works, then turned around and sold them for a fortune to several of the Caxton stable—Lowell's devoted followers. He was less amused when she turned the same talent on the current art scene. He thought she was wasting her time."

"Chicken or egg, Ms. Seven, which came first? Do you know how the marriage began to unravel or come apart?"

"That's a bit too quaint a description. I'd say it came to a screeching halt.

"It was when Lowell had gone to Bath, a year ago this past June. There was to be an auction for the estate of Gwendolyn, Lady Wenbotham. She was the ninety-four-year-old dowager who'd owned a fabulous collection of portraits—lots of minor royalty and major military figures. Lowell and Deni were feuding, rather mildly, because she was too busy to go with him on the trip. Not only did he value her eye, but he wanted her there to show off at all the social events— Ascot, if they could get away early enough, staying on for Wimbledon, dinners, and balls. Kind of thing she usually loved to do."

"What kept her away?"

"I'm not sure, really." Ms. Seven stopped, as though considering whether or not to tell me what she guessed had been the reason. "She was vague even with me at the time."

"Another man?"

"No, up to then she'd been quite faithful to Lowell. So he left for England—did the tennis and the horse races—and Deni was quite aloof for those weeks. Finally, she called and said that if I would go along with her, she'd surprise Lowell in Bath. We packed our trunks and off we went. I had a driver pick us up at Heathrow the morning of the auction and take us directly to the Royal Crescent. Do you know it?"

"Yes, I do." I had stayed at the charming old hotel when one of Joan Stafford's first plays was staged there before opening at the Lyric Theatre in London.

"Denise went to the desk and announced that she was Mrs. Caxton and would like the key to the room. I had one of those suites facing the crescent, but to get to Lowell's room she had to pass through that quiet little garden, where half of the guests were having high tea.

"Five minutes later I heard Deni yelling as though she were standing in my very room. Language I doubt many of the hotel guests had heard before. Lowell, as I later learned in exquisite detail from Deni, was in the middle of some kind of acrobatic sexual maneuver with Gwendolyn's great-granddaughter, a twenty-five-year-old local beauty who was no doubt trying to up the ante on the family fortune. She had captured Lowell's attention and was hoping to keep his bids high that evening."

"Any point in asking what happened next?"

"Deni used more four-letter words than I thought I'd ever find in Webster's. The young lady came downstairs wearing a hotel bathrobe, and Deni tossed her underwear out the window, probably landing it on someone's scones and crumpets. Gwendolyn's eighty-nine-year-old sister, Althea, watched the whole episode unfold from her wheelchair in the middle of the courtyard.

"When Lowell stormed through there, fully dressed, about fifteen minutes later, Althea lifted herself up with her cane, reached it out to stop him in his path, and announced for all the family friends to hear, 'I applaud your courage, Mr. Caxton. Must have been something like trying to fit an oyster into a parking meter, having your way with my great-grandniece? Lovely to have met you. Sorry you can't stay for the evening.'"

"He didn't go to the sale, after all that?"

"No. In fact, he had our driver take him directly to the airport for a flight back to New York."

"And Deni?"

"She and I went to the auction. She was furious, and determined to do something to show what he had taught her professionally. Everyone in the room, of course, was impressed that she showed up at all. To them it was pure American moxie. She dressed elegantly, beamed at everyone—flirting with the men and being unusually courteous to the women—and focused her attention on every item in the sale."

"How'd she do?" I asked.

"Like a dream. She bought a portrait of the Marchesa Cecchi for sixty-seven thousand dollars. It had been unattributed in the catalogue. But Deni brought it back to her restorer, Marco Varelli—have you encountered him yet? He's a genius. And after he cleaned it up, they actually found Sir Joshua Reynolds's signature under a couple of centuries of grime. She sold that piece for more than a million and a half. And just for fun, she bought a small piece of garden statuary, some kind of wood nymph if I remember correctly. I don't think it cost her two thousand dollars."

Marilyn Seven took a breath, put out one cigarette and lighted another, and reminded the waiter to bring her another glass of Saint-Véran.

"I'll tell you, Miss Cooper, I was sitting in the same room, looking at the same objects. I thought the sculpture was too kitschy to put in my own backyard. Turned out to be an original by Giambologna, the great Florentine artist. Worth close to ten million. Deni refused to sell it. Just shipped it home and installed it in Lowell's bathroom. She wanted to remind him of the entire experience. Make it indelible."

"I take it that was the beginning of the end?"

"*Basta. Finito. Terminato*. Neither one of them was willing to forgive the other, and for Lowell it was a confirmation that they had been moving in separate directions for a couple of years. Deni had no idea if that was his first indiscretion—although I really doubt it. He'd finished the Pygmalion thing with Deni. He was ready to take on someone new."

"Why didn't she just walk away from him? Certainly she'd made enough money to go out on her own."

"I suppose when you come from a background like Deni's, there's never quite enough to erase the fears that you're going to find yourself back on the farm sowing soybeans in the dirt for the rest of your life."

"With what she was sitting on? I can't believe that."

"It wasn't a very attractive side of my friend, but she also wanted to take Lowell to the cleaners. Deni wanted some of the Caxton treasures as well, and she had no plans to walk away without them."

"But she had no right to them, Ms. Seven. They're clearly Lowell's, aren't they, except for some of the works acquired during the marriage?"

She looked at me as though I were an absolute idiot. "I'm not talking about the art in their home or in the gallery. Don't you know anything about the Caxton operation? Because if not, you've got a lot of catching up to do.

"The Caxtons have been at this now for three generations. Lowell has such a tight grip on the collection that not even his employees know the extent of what he owns, or more importantly, where all the art is. Deni knew there were paintings stashed in Swiss vaults and even in an old Cold War bunker on a hillside in Pennsylvania. He moves his pieces in armored cars and by private jet."

Deni's friend was certainly devoted to her. I could see she was going to go on bashing Lowell as long as I'd listen.

"Are you aware that Three—you probably know it was his childhood name, and it made him crazy when Deni called him that—was never invited to join the Art Dealers Association of America?"

Again, I shook my head to tell her that I was not.

"In seventy-five, I think it was, and certainly before Deni, he was caught bugging the telephones of the most prestigious galleries in New York, long before hi-tech spying became a tool of the business world. He was checking on their inventory, as well as trying to get an idea of what their customers were searching for on the market. Lowell's father had used a lot of his money to pay scholars to write catalogues raisonnés."

"Sorry, you've lost me. I don't know what they are."

"They're the key to individual artists and their works. Good ones are well researched and documented, and by controlling the catalogues of a particular artist, you control the price and value of his work. Many experts think there's an aura of questionability about the Caxton catalogues, that histories and pedigrees have been altered for the family's private gain. Several art historians have denounced the works publicly, which made Lowell furious. It threw into question his Vermeers, his Légers, his Davids."

"But Deni thought she could get her hands on those paintings?"

"Well, yes—in part. She was also terribly frightened that she knew too much about them for Lowell to let her go. His first two wives had never really participated in his professional world. But once Deni learned it and loved it, he let her in. She knew things about Caxton and his father, and their manner of doing business, that Lowell regretted having told her once the bottom fell out. Her greatest fear—and she spoke of it to me often—was that he'd never let her walk away from him, knowing what she did about his dealings. She couldn't stay with him, Ms. Cooper, but he wouldn't let her go."

I wondered if Marilyn Seven knew anything about Deni's partnership with the late Omar Sheffield. "Do you have any idea how desperate your friend was to get rid of her husband?"

"About as anxious as you or I would be, if your life had been threatened like hers had."

"How and when was *she* threatened?"

"Well, that answers that. I didn't suppose Lowell told you about the letters Deni got last year, which practically drove her insane."

"No, so far he hasn't mentioned any letters to us at all."

"I've brought you a copy of one of them, if you'd like to see it."

Marilyn Seven withdrew a xeroxed paper from her slim purse and passed it across to me. The copy was a page of lined white paper, covered with neatly printed handwriting and addressed to Denise Caxton. I scanned it quickly.

My name is Jennsen, and I live in Brooklyn. I know you don't know me, but I have been watching you since you got home from England. I know how you look like, and I know how to find you. Listen, if you go to the police about this, I will hurt you bad, or go back to Oklahoma and kill someone you really love. I know when you leave your house and go to W. 22nd St., so I could follow you. I know you get your hair cut at La Coupe and you eat dinner twice a week at Fresco on 52nd St. Your husband pays you $125,000 a month for your expenses. Are you getting this yet? I know where you buy your underpants and how much you pay for your wine. Now here's what I want. Listen close. I want you to send $1,000 to my

friend, who is in jail, and who's address is on
this letter. This is to show you that I am not
kidding, by two ways. One is that I know every
move you make, and the other is to show you
that my best friends are locked up doing time,
so you know I am not playing games. We know
how to hurt people very bad. Lowell also told
me who the five men are who are your lovers.
Now you think I'm jiving? Send a check or
money order to my friend Omar Sheffield, 96B-
1911, Box 968, Coxsackie Correctional Facility,
Coxsackie, New York 12051.

REMEMBER NO POLICE. If you don't
send my friend the money, I will take charge by
getting you in the near future. Include your
phone number so we can talk.

I looked up at Marilyn Seven. "What did she do
about this?"

"Certainly not call the police."

"Did she do what this guy wanted?"

"What would *you* have done?"

"Look," I said, my impatience growing. "It's not a
contest about us trying to match wits. *I* didn't get this
letter."

"These letters, Ms. Cooper. A shoe box full of
them. It was obvious to her that this man could only
have gotten the detail about her from Lowell, and that
Lowell had hired him to kill her. She knew she was
being scammed, but of course she did as he told her."

"She sent money up to the state prison?"

"You bet she did. Early and often. The faster she

sent it, the faster the ante was raised. By the time the guy finally called her, she must have already sent him twenty thousand dollars. She was terrified, and asked him point-blank whether her husband had hired him to kill her. He confirmed it for Deni. Told her that Lowell was trying to torture her first, mentally, and that's why he'd given this guy Jennsen so much information about her movements and whereabouts. They were planning a way for the hit to happen sometime when Lowell was abroad and Deni wasn't in her apartment—almost exactly the way it *did* happen—so it couldn't be traced back to Lowell."

"But she kept the correspondence going, of course," I said.

"To stay alive, and to turn the tables on her beloved husband. It was her idea to outbid Lowell on this deal, too—and to get the Jennsen fellow to kill Lowell before he murdered her." Marilyn Seven leaned in and put her hand on top of mine. "I told her over and over again that she was insane, and that it would be a deadly mistake for her to play with fire. She wouldn't listen to me, of course, and my insistence that she abandon her plan took her further and further away from me. I don't think, in the end, that she really had anyone left that she could trust."

"Bryan Daughtry?" I ventured.

"You'll forgive me if I don't dignify that question with a response."

"Do you have any of the other letters that she received?"

"No, I never saw them. And I have no idea where she would have kept them. The first one was the only one she sent to me, when she wanted my advice. I don't know if they're at her home, or office, or in a safe deposit box. I felt you should know about them."

She removed a fifty-dollar bill from her pocket and summoned the waiter to bring a check. "I'll be at the hotel for a few days before going back home, if you need me for anything."

"Under the name 'Seven'?" I asked.

"Yes, of course." She smiled. "Why, I suppose you tried to check up on me before we met, Ms. Cooper. It's close enough to my real name—the Italian word for 'seven.' I used it briefly, almost thirty years ago, when I attempted a career on the stage. Did I stump you?" she asked, seemingly pleased by the idea.

"In fact, you did. We came up blank. Much too blank for someone of your means."

"That *is* my name, in a fashion. I was actually born Marina Sette, in Venezia. My mother abandoned me when I was eighteen months old. Left my father and ran off with a very dashing American—Lowell Caxton."

I suppose that I was unable to stifle a slight gasp.

"My father left Italy and came to the States, where his parents raised me while my mother raised her stepchild and had two more of her own with Lowell. She never glanced over her shoulder, not even to stop from being run over in that boating accident."

I had grown up with the most loving mother on the face of the earth and could not comprehend how any woman could leave a child to take off with another man.

Marina Sette went on. "My father turned his automotive parts factory in Michigan into an integral part of the Ford Motor Company—Sette Moto—by the time I was six. If you can measure wealth in material ways—and believe me, I can't—money has never been an issue."

"But Lowell Caxton—surely he knew who you were."

"Perhaps he'd have recognized me if I were as breathtaking as my mother must have been. But he never caught on. Not for a moment. Then, after the fireworks in England, when Deni was looking for every conceivable way to hurt him, she couldn't resist telling him exactly who I was."

"And his reaction?"

"I wanted it to be rage, of course. I wanted it to cause him to agonize over me—or at least, if he didn't care about my feelings, he should regret the loss of my husband as a rather substantial client. As I should have expected, all I got was indifference.

"Surely you can understand why I thought Deni was on such a treacherous course with her pen pal. After all, there was no need to go outside the family." Marina Sette removed her cigarette from the holder and crushed it in the ashtray on the table. "I could have killed Lowell Caxton myself."

# 12

Laura stopped me on my way back to my desk, half an hour after I had left Mercer in front of the Four Seasons Hotel. It was almost three and I was making my first appearance of the day at the office. "McKinney was looking for you. He's assigned someone to the investigation of the dead guy they found in the rail yards last night."

"Tell him to listen to his voice mail. I called him this morning to tell him it's part of my case. As nicely as you can say it, Laura, tell him to keep his hands off my corpses, okay? Boss back from Albany yet?"

"Rose said not to worry. He's in a meeting all afternoon with some of the lawyers on that foreign bank scandal. They're offering millions of dollars of forfeitures—Battaglia hasn't even asked about your case since he returned. But you've got an unexpected visitor, Alex. Mrs. Braverman is back. I've had her in the waiting area since lunchtime, but she won't leave and she won't talk to anyone else. You're the only one who can help her."

"Tell Max to bring her in. I don't think I've seen her in six months, have I?"

"Got that search warrant ready for me yet?" Chapman asked. I knew he'd come down to meet me when he had finished at the M.E.'s Office, but I hadn't expected him to walk through my door quite so soon.

I lowered myself into my chair and groaned. "Slow down. I just walked in and I've got some social work to do. Just stand by for a few minutes. You're about to meet my favorite witness."

"Do not ever go to an autopsy of someone run over by a freight train. I've seen some pretty gruesome sights, but this was like chopped—"

"Spare me the details. The photographs will be more than I need to know." It was mandatory for one of the assigned detectives to be present during the medical examiner's autopsy proceedings on a possible homicide victim.

Max walked in, leading a very obese elderly woman on her arm. Mrs. Braverman was wearing a garishly colored sundress and a chartreuse straw hat with an enormous brim.

"Alexandra, darling, I'm so glad you got down here in time to see me." The octogenarian dropped Max's hand and waddled across the room to embrace me as I came out from behind the desk. "And who's this handsome young man?"

"Michael Patrick Chapman, ma'am, Miss Cooper's favorite detective," he replied, giving her his best and brightest grin.

"Is he on *my* investigation now?" she asked me.

"He's the man. I brought him in specially for you.

He's solved hundreds of these cases. What's been going on since the last time you were here?"

She plopped into one of the leather armchairs opposite me, while Mike leaned against a file cabinet and listened to her story. "You were right about Christmas and New Year's, Alexandra. They must have gone away for the holidays because I didn't have any problems after I saw you. Then, of course, I went to Boca to be with my son and grandchildren for a few months. Now, ever since I'm back, they're making life miserable for me."

"Tell Detective Chapman who they are, Mrs. Braverman."

"Extraterrestrials, son. In my day we used to call them Martians. But I've done a lot of reading up on this, and now I know they could be from anywhere out there."

Mike kneeled by her side and looked her directly in the eye. "What are they up to this time?"

"They've moved into the apartment upstairs, where old Mr. Rubenstein used to live before his daughter shipped him off to a home," she said, now slipping into a whisper as she talked to Chapman. "They've been flashing signals at me, beaming them through the ceilings and the walls. They're trying to control my brain waves."

"Are they doing it through the toaster and the television set, too?" he asked, with the same degree of intensity that I had seen him question murder suspects.

"Exactly!" she replied emphatically.

"I told you he was good, didn't I?"

"Nobody in my family believed me, Mike—I could

call you Mike, couldn't I, sweetheart? The precinct wouldn't do nothing about it. They sent me down here to see Alexandra after I told them about the time one of them fondled my breasts while I was napping. She's been wonderful to me, really. I feel better every time I see her." She cocked her head and looked over at me. "I try not to be a nuisance to her. Then, as soon as I saw her picture in the paper with this lady in the water, the rays became even stronger. I got worried that maybe the same people are after you, sweetheart."

"We're gonna solve this for you, Mrs. B.," Mike said, rising up and pointing to my top desk drawer. "Coop, gimme a couple of boxes of clips, right away."

"Clips, of course," I repeated, sliding it open and removing two boxes of paper clips.

"Not those, the giant-size ones. Those ordinary ones don't work with E.T.'s."

I took two boxes of large clips out and Mike ordered me to make it four.

"Now, here's what you do. When you get home, take a couple of dozen out of the box, make yourself comfortable, and start to string them together, know what I mean?"

Mrs. Braverman's eyes were gleaming with delight at the attention she was getting. "Sure, sure. This I can do." She nodded as Mike looped the metal pieces together to demonstrate to her.

"Then, you take the top one and you attach it to the belt on your dress. You gotta have enough clips to make the chain reach to the floor. Then—you're grounded. You're completely safe because the signals run right through the chain and onto the carpet, missing you completely. Who lives beneath you?"

"Mrs. Villanueva. Dominican, but very nice."

"No problem. Sometimes the waves go through to the apartment below, but Dominicans are immune to extraterrestrial interference. She'll be fine."

Mrs. Braverman got up from her chair while I put the four boxes of clips in a plastic bag and handed them to her. "Costs the city a dollar forty-five, but it's worth every penny for your peace of mind. Just call Coop if you need a refill."

"I'm gonna kiss you for this, Mike." She puckered her lips and reached out for his face, planting herself firmly on his mouth. "Could I make a *shiddach* with you and Alexandra here?" I recognized the Yiddish expression for a brokered marriage.

"Hey, Mrs. B., you'll excuse me, but I don't have the balls to take on a broad as tough as this one. Don't you have a daughter for me?"

"Three sons. An oral surgeon, an accountant, and one we don't talk about. Plays the horses, best I can tell. I'll leave you two to your business now. And you, don't use that kind of language in front of my girl here," she said laughingly. "Someday she's gonna meet a nice man who'll take her away from all this, right, Alexandra?"

"Right, Mrs. Braverman." I walked with her and Max to the door so that I could accept another hug and sent her off to the elevator.

"Wouldn't it be great if we could solve two percent of our cases that simply?" Chapman asked. I came back to my desk and waved him out of the way so I could get to the word processor to work on the search warrant for the Galleria Caxton Due. I told him about Marina Sette and showed him the letter she had given me.

"Looks like we need another visit with Lowell Caxton. And you'd better do a subpoena for Omar Sheffield's prison records. Be sure and include the visitors' log. Let's check to see when Deni made her appearance there."

"Make yourself useful," I said, as I filled in the facts to establish probable cause for a search of Daughtry's gallery, from all of Deni's property through the contents of Omar Sheffield's locker. "Go tell Laura what you want and she can type up the subpoenas for me to sign. And ask her to hold all my calls for an hour so I can knock this thing out. That way you can execute it tomorrow."

I had almost finished the application when Chapman came back in the room and reached across the desk to pick up the blinking phone line of a call that Laura had put on hold.

"She assured me you'd want to be interrupted for this one. Jake Tyler, with an overseas operator patching him through."

I took the receiver from Mike's hand and spoke into it. "Hello? . . . Hello?" I waited for a response but there was none.

"I thought this technology worked all over the world."

"So did I. My luck, he's in the one little village in the middle of nowhere that can't pick up the signals." I held on for several more seconds and then hung up the phone.

"So, what's all the secrecy about this romance with Jacob Tyler, blondie?"

"For one thing, I only met him last month—Fourth of July weekend, at a clambake on the Vineyard. It's still very new. And for another, you know what a gossip mill this place is."

"Jeez, you'd think Mercer or me was gonna slit our wrists if you were getting laid."

The next look I flashed at him wasn't so pleasant.

"Mercer or *I*?" he asked.

"It's not the grammar I'm so worried about this time, it's the sentiment."

Mike's feet were up on my desktop now. "What do you hear from your friend Drew? I felt kinda sorry for that guy."

"He just wasn't ready for anything that intense yet. As much as we liked to be together, he was still getting over the death of his wife. When Milbank offered him a transfer to their new law office in Moscow, he took it."

"Like my pal Scanlon says, 'The camel shits. The caravan moves on.' I agree with little old Mrs. B. You need to get a life before this job sucks everything out of you, kid."

"Don't start with me, Mike. It's everyone else I know outside these doors who can't understand why I love what I do and who just doesn't get it. From my pals, I at least expect that you agree that this is the most fascinating job in the world. How many people get up in the morning and look forward to going to work? You and I have never had two days that have been at all predictable in our entire careers, and no two that have been even remotely alike. And on top of it, you do a little bit of good for somebody else in the mix." I knew I was preaching to the choir, but Mike was just in one of those moods that swept over each of us from time to time.

"Jacob Tyler. Isn't he the guy who's like a baby Brian Williams?"

"I don't think that's quite the description he'd favor."

"But he's the one who sits in for Brian Williams when Williams sits in for Tom Brokaw, right? Anchorman-to-be. Deep voice, lots of hair, best-looking striped shirts on the airwaves."

"When you're ready to tell all about *your* love life, I'll buy the drinks and we'll compare notes for an entire night, if you'd like."

"All I need is half a minute. The story of my love life'd fit on a matchbook cover. C'mon, let's get this thing signed so I can rattle Bryan's cage tomorrow morning."

As we returned to the office from the courtroom, Catherine Dashfer and Marisa Bourges, the two senior members of the Sex Crime Unit, were waiting for me. "Did you forget that Rich was on trial?" Marisa asked, referring to one of our colleagues, who was in court with his first date-rape prosecution.

"Damn it, I forgot completely. I'm so wound up in this that I'm not paying attention to the daily routine."

"That's okay. When he heard you weren't in, he called and we went over to help him. The medical testimony was on today, and his witness handled it extremely well."

In more than 70 percent of reported sexual assaults, the victim suffers no gross physical injury. And even though physical injury is not an element of the crime of rape, most jurors expect that they'll hear evidence of bruises and lacerations. Frequently we need an expert physician to explain the absence of visible trauma, as well as the elasticity of the vaginal vault.

"Thanks for covering for me. Michael Warner is such a prick, I thought he'd make mincemeat of Rich's doctor." The defendant's attorney was a mean-spirited character as well as a screamer, and though the physician who had examined the victim was an experienced practitioner in an emergency room setting, he had never testified in a courtroom before.

"I think Rich has a lock. Dr. Hayakawa held up beautifully. Every time Warner went back at him, he held his ground, described his findings, and concluded that they were consistent with the victim's version of the events. Finally, Warner was halfway across the room and yelled out at the doctor at the top of his lungs, mocking him for dramatic effect. 'I want you to tell the jury why it is, Doctor, that you did not expect to find any lesions or tears, even though this woman had described to you an absolutely brutal and life-threatening encounter.'

"Dr. Hayakawa never lost his cool. He just looked straight at the jury and said, 'Because actually, penis not so awesome weapon, ladies and gentlemen.'"

Catherine broke in. "The foreman cracked up and the rest of the jurors followed. I never saw anyone run for his seat as fast as Warner. Rich is going to sum up tomorrow. We took him through it when we got out of court tonight and he's going to do fine. You still have time to go to the hospital to visit Sarah and the baby?"

It was after six. "Sure. I told Nan Toth to be downstairs at my Jeep at six fifteen."

"You two ride with me," Chapman said to Catherine and Marisa. "They can meet us up there."

I finished returning phone calls before going out to meet Nan. We headed up First Avenue to New York University Medical Center and parked the car on Thirty-fourth Street, stopping to buy flowers before going in. Keith Raskin was getting off the elevator as we waited for it on the ground floor. A brilliant orthopedic surgeon, he had painstakingly reconstructed the bones in my right hand after they were shattered in a horseback riding accident several years earlier. I flexed my fingers and made a fist to demonstrate how successful the operation had been.

"After that Dogen murder case you worked on this spring, I never thought I'd see you inside a hospital again," Keith remarked, referring to the tragic slaughter of a neurosurgeon inside one of the city's largest medical centers.

"Just a visit to the obstetrical floor, Doctor. In and out as fast as I can make it." We caught up with each other briefly, and Nan and I continued on our way to Sarah's room.

We arrived in time to join Catherine, Marisa, and Mike in admiring the baby as she squinted up at us through teeny brown eyes. The room was well stocked with bouquets, Beanie Babies, and oversized stuffed animals, and the phone rang constantly while we each took turns holding Janine in our arms.

When the aide came to take her back to the nursery, Sarah put on her slippers and padded down the hall for a few laps of exercise around the maternity floor. Mike grabbed the clicker and turned the television on to *Jeopardy!*, having timed his visit to be sure to get in for the final question. The screen lit up just as Trebek displayed the category for the night, which was Famous Quotations.

We looked at each other and I shrugged my shoulders, knowing this could go any which way, depending on the subject of the quotation. "You guys in for ten?" Chapman asked all four of us.

Marisa, Catherine, Nan, and I each dug in our pocketbooks to match the ten-dollar bill that Mike had thrown on Sarah's bed.

"And tonight's answer is: John Hay referred to it as 'a splendid little war.' "

"So much for all your fancy degrees and the twelve years of law school among you. This is the quickest fifty bucks I ever made," Chapman said, scooping up the money and fanning it in our faces.

There was not much about American history—and nothing about military history—that Mike Chapman didn't know. I looked at the other women and told them I conceded defeat. Not one of us had a serious guess.

Before any of the contestants revealed their answers, Mike announced, "The Final Jeopardy question is: What was the Spanish-American War?"

"That's exactly right," Alex Trebek said, remarking

on the answer given by the poultry inspector from Lumberton, North Carolina, which earned him $8,700 and the evening's championship.

"Eighteen ninety-eight was the year. And John Hay, ladies," Chapman continued, "was our ambassador to Great Britain during that conflict. Later he was secretary of state. His comment may have seemed appropriate at the time, since it was a very short and one-sided war. Now, more than a hundred years later, we're still dealing with the fallout—Cuba, Puerto Rico, Guam, and the Philippines.

"A little less time shopping at the Escada sample sales and a bit more with your noses in the books—and I don't mean Dorothy L. Sayers or Anthony Trollope, Mrs. Toth—and you'll be able to hold on to your husbands' well-earned money. C'mon, blondie, we got work to do."

"We're meeting my friend Joan Stafford for dinner. She claims to have some inside poop about the deceased. See you in the morning."

We said good night to Sarah and the others near the nursery. It was a quick ride up to Forty-sixth Street and the quiet elegance of the best steak house in Manhattan, Patroon.

Mercer and Joan were already seated at the front corner table when we entered. I kissed the top of her head before sliding into the banquette and told her how much I missed having her in town, now that she was spending all her time in Washington with her fiancé. Ken Aretsky, the owner, sent a round of drinks over to the table.

Mike was already buried in the menu and banking

on Joan's inimitable generosity. "I'm starting with a dozen oysters. Then the veal chop with the garlic mashed potatoes. Let's order so we can talk business." He raised his glass in Joan's direction. "Cheers. So whaddaya know that we don't?"

"Here's the thing. I never knew Deni personally, but a lot of my friends did. And I've met Lowell more times than I can remember—at his gallery, at auctions, and even dinner parties. But there have been stories floating around town for years, for whatever they're worth."

"You gave Mike the names of two of her lovers when you called. Any significance to that?" I asked.

"I ran rap sheets on both of 'em," Mike broke in. "Came up clean. Look like legit businessmen."

"There's Preston Mattox, who's an architect," said Joan. "Not much talk about him. The other one nobody really gets. He's Frank Wrenley, an antiques expert and dealer. Scratch a bit below the surface on him and I'm not quite sure the kind of guy you'll find. Maybe it's just that he's such new money. Sprang up on the art scene out of nowhere, and suddenly he's in the big leagues, running side by side with Deni Caxton."

"I'm telling you, Coop. This case has everything for an art caper except Nazis," Mike said, eschewing the dainty shellfish fork in favor of slurping up an oyster.

Joan Stafford picked at her warm foie gras. "So it's Nazis you vant, Herr Chapman? Then it's Nazis I shall give you."

# 13

"Have you ever heard of the Amber Room?"

The three of us shook our heads in the negative.

"I'm sure I don't have to remind you about all of the art that was seized and stolen by the Nazis during the Second World War," Joan said.

My father had insisted that my brothers and I learn about the Holocaust from our childhood on, both to understand the magnitude of its atrocities and to know its historical and cultural importance. As a Jew, and also as an art collector, he had followed the stories of families fleeing Europe before the war, and those sent to the death camps, whose personal treasures became the property of their conquerors. Recent years had seen a series of legal wrangles to reclaim such confiscated artworks and restore them to the survivors or the rightful heirs of their owners. I knew of many of the cases that had been brought in the courts as paintings surfaced at auctions or institutions after half a century of being secretly held, but I had never heard of something described as a room.

"In seventeen seventeen, King Wilhelm I of Prussia gave the tsar—Peter the Great—a unique gift. It was a set of gilded oak panels that were decorated with more than six tons of amber, elaborately carved and inset with Florentine mosaics and Venetian glass mirrors. The walls were installed in the Catherine Palace in Tsarskoye Selo, and had actually been dubbed the 'eighth wonder of the world' by the British ambassador. So far as I'm aware, only a single photograph of this breathtaking creation was ever known to have been taken in its two-hundred-year history.

"When Nazi troops invaded Russia in nineteen forty-one, they brought their own art experts along to aid in the plundering of the Soviet bounty. The priceless Amber Room was taken apart and shipped off to a town called Königsberg, which is on the Baltic coast. But by the end of the war, as some of the treasures began to appear, there was not a sign of this enormous chamber."

"Any theories about it?" I asked.

"Dozens. I researched it carefully because I intended to write a play about it." She glanced across at me, knowing that I always chided her about her abandoned efforts. "Had to stick it in a drawer once your DNA buddies matched the Romanovs' bodies. I had it all set to be reconstructed for Anastasia, who was found alive and well in—never mind.

"I take it you want the leading theories and not the obscure ones. Some professional treasure hunter showed up a few years ago with Xeroxes of documents signed by Himmler, claiming he could prove that the room had been redirected to Quedlinburg but that the general transporting it had made an independent decision to change the route in the face of the Allied advance."

"Quedlinburg," Mike said. "That was a major Nazi stash, wasn't it?"

He reminded us that in 1996 the Feds tried to prosecute two Texans for the return of several hundred million dollars' worth of medieval reliquaries, stolen by their brother—an American soldier—at the end of World War II. German troops had looted the religious treasure—everything from ninth-century prayer books and lavishly painted manuscripts to gem-encrusted vases and figures. And in the process of the American liberation of Europe, lowlifes in our own army had made off with the already stolen cache of goods.

"So, one school has the amber buried in the quarry beside a seventh-century castle, while the latest claim is that the son of a German military intelligence officer who helped with the actual logistics of the move has used his father's papers to establish that the stuff never even got to Germany, but is still buried in the Russian system of underground tunnels and mine shafts."

Mercer had been unusually quiet throughout the meal. "Connect this to Denise Caxton for me, will you?"

"This all goes back to the Second World War. Lowell Caxton's father lived in France, as you may already know by now."

"Yes," I said. "He made some reference about how his parents met, and his being raised in an apartment in Paris."

"Although the senior Caxton spent the war years in the States, he never severed his ties with a guy called Roger Dequoy, who was later identified as one of the worst collaborators in the art world. Dequoy was selling paintings to all the Nazi leaders, and they in turn were trying to dump the Impressionist works they had stolen. Thought it was all too degenerate, if you can imagine that.

"The French government considered bringing charges against Caxton's father for selling to the Nazis, but they were never able to build a case. What *is* quite clear is that the Caxtons were positioned—both financially and politically—to have had access to an unbelievable number of the pillaged works. What they also had was the ability to move them around Europe pretty well, too."

"It seems to me," Mike said, "that with all the wealth they had already accumulated, the old man could afford to sit on the stuff until the millennium. No need to try to sell it and show his hand, like most of the others who got caught."

"The Caxton thing has never been about selling or making any more of a profit. That's just sport for them, father and son. It's all in the possession—sheer, unadulterated greed. You've been to the apartment, right?"

"Yeah. We were there over the weekend."

"Lowell has suites, as you may know, each done in a favorite painter or period. Of course, I've never seen it myself, but rumor has it that somewhere, in one of his properties, he has rebuilt the Amber Room. It's not complete—some of the wood was warped when the mine shaft was flooded. But he got most of the jeweled pieces out of Europe somehow, and found craftsmen to regild the mirrors and panels in separate units, so none of them had reason to suppose that he had actually found a whole room. It must be as close as anyone in the world is going to come to feeling like a tsar."

"And Deni?" I asked.

"She certainly knew about it. Each of his wives did. That's what Liz Smith was alluding to in her column this morning."

"You'll forgive me if I tell you I didn't have a moment, between autopsies, to read the friggin' society pages, won't you?" asked Chapman.

"Sorry. Liz wrote something about how getting to Caxton's inner sanctum was certainly the kiss of death for each of his three lovely wives. You know, like Bluebeard's castle. Once he got them in his secret lair and made love to them there, he had to kill them."

"Don't lose me here, Joanie. Are you suggesting that Lowell was trying to shut her up about the Amber Room, or that someone else was trying to use Deni to get to it? And please don't tell me that your personal trainer is the source for this." I knew that half of Joan's best gossip came from the guy who worked her out at home every morning when she was in Manhattan, where she still kept an apartment. He had a fantastic client list, and something about lifting weights and doing inversions seemed to cause these well-toned, tight-lipped women to reveal their deepest secrets to him.

"The way I heard it, the Russian mob was pushing

its way into the Chelsea art scene, hoping to put pressure on Deni to lead them to the amber so they could return it to the palace, which has been under restoration for twenty years. They've got a patron, a Soviet businessman who hit it big in the telecommunications industry, willing to pay the tab for what they assumed she could lead them to."

"Ever been to Brighton?" Chapman asked Joan.

"Sure, my play had tryouts there and in Bath before it opened in London."

"Not Brighton, England. Brighton *Beach*. Home of the Russian mafia."

"You think *I* don't do the West Side, Mikey? Well, Joan doesn't do the outer boroughs. Forget Brooklyn, Queens, the Bronx. They're just places she has to drive through to get where she wants to go."

"So she's not coming with us when we go poking around for double agents looking for Nazis looking for stolen art, huh?" Mike asked me.

Mercer picked up the thread. "What do you know about Bryan Daughtry?"

Joan laughed. "More than anyone needs to know, that's for certain. Denise Caxton didn't create that monster, but she was certainly feeding him."

"Why was she so attached to him, do you think?"

"She was the classic underdog, Alex, and there was something in her that must have made her reach out to characters with the same background. I'm sure you remember that I used to buy from Daughtry, in the old days, before any of us knew about the dark side with the leather and young girls. Like Deni, he's basically a dreamer, trying to create a fantastic life out of whole cloth. His business was riskier than anything that Lowell did, and she apparently liked that. I mean, it doesn't take much skill to sell a Picasso, right?"

"Got any suggestions for who we talk to about their commercial enterprise?" Mike asked.

Joan thought for a moment. "Marco Varelli, perhaps."

"I just heard that name today, but where?" I was tired, and confused as well.

"Sweetest little old guy you'd ever want to meet. He's a restorer, perhaps the most respected in the field."

Now it came to me. Marina Sette had mentioned him to me during our conversation at the Four Seasons this afternoon.

"I mean, if I tripped over something like the Amber Room, Varelli's the person I'd go see to make sure whatever the treasure might be is not a fake. He looks like a gnome—must be well over eighty by now. Varelli might have known some of Deni's secrets. You'll find him in a small atelier he keeps in the Village."

"We expect to be getting as many of the gallery records as we can. With a little luck, maybe she kept notes about her love life, too," Mercer said.

Joan shook her head. " 'Good girls keep diaries; bad girls don't have the time.' Tallulah Bankhead, by the way. I don't think that's very likely."

"You said you were going to tell us why Lowell Caxton wasn't welcome at the legitimate houses any longer," I reminded Joan.

"The Gardner Museum heist, almost ten years

ago. Has that come up in any of your interviews yet?"

"You should stick to your fiction, Joan," Mike said. "Wanna pour me another glass of that red wine?"

I knew that around the turn of the century Boston socialite Isabella Stewart Gardner had built a Venetian-style palazzo to house one of the country's most spectacular art collections, which she had put together with the aid of her close friend Bernard Berenson. I had been to the museum many times when I was in college, and even once last year on my way through the Fenway section of the city.

"I remember the break-in, but it was years ago. Hasn't that ever been solved?" I asked.

"Never. Listen, guys," said Joan, telling the story of what remains to this day the costliest art theft in United States history, "this is where Lowell may have gotten his hands even deeper in the dirt.

"In March of nineteen ninety, two men disguised as Boston cops presented themselves to the museum's security officers at the side door of the building, and were let in. The robbers locked up the guards, disabled the unsophisticated alarm system, and made off with about ten paintings. Estimated value? Almost *three hundred million dollars.*"

"Are you serious? What was in the place?" Mercer asked.

"A few Impressionists—I think a Manet and a Degas—an ancient Chinese bronze work, a finial from a Napoleonic flagstaff, a Vermeer, and most importantly, the masterpiece that all the fuss has been about. It's a three-hundred-and-sixty-year-old Rembrandt that hung in the Gardner's famous Dutch Room. The title of it is *The Storm on the Sea of Galilee,* and it was the only seascape that he ever painted.

"Nothing from the heist has ever been found. Not a trace. The Gardner had so little insurance at the time of the theft that the reward they offered was only a million dollars. Just a year or two ago, the FBI upped it to five million. There have been rumors in the art world for years, but not a clue to follow up on. Except the chips."

"What chips?"

"I'm just being dramatic, Alex. Paint chips, of course. Most of the works were small enough to be taken frame and all. But—maybe because of the way the Rembrandt was fastened to its mountings—the robbers actually *cut* it out of the frame. Isn't that awful? Anyway, the varnish on it—and its great age— must have made it so stiff that literally dozens of paint chips fell onto the floor, and that's all that was left behind."

"Get me from there to Caxton," Mike said, licking the chocolate sauce from the profiteroles off the side of his mouth.

"Everyone knows the painting is too hot to handle. Over the years, several mobsters who've turned up dead in the Boston area have been linked to the robbery. And each time there's been a buzz in the galleries and auction houses that the Rembrandt's at the heart of it. If anyone could hide this kind of booty, or better still, transport it anywhere in the world, it could only be an individual with the means of a Lowell Caxton, or someone who flirted with danger as freely as Deni.

"There was an opening at Lowell's gallery in the Fuller Building a few months ago. Deni had left before I arrived. Everyone said she was high and kind of mouthing off about this astounding coup she was about to make that would turn the art world on its ear. Be sure and ask Lowell about it when you see him again."

This time it was Mercer's beeper that went off before the end of the meal. He rejected my offer of a cell phone and stepped away to return the call from a booth at the top of the staircase.

When he came back down the flight of stairs, he approached the table and tapped on it with his knuckles. "Off to Chelsea, m'man."

Mike threw back his head and chugged down the La Tâche '86 as though it were a Budweiser. "More string sculptures at this hour of the night?"

"Nope. Denise Caxton's car."

"Where?"

"Right under our noses the whole time. In a chop shop one block away from her gallery. About to be dissected and shipped overseas, from Chelsea Road Repairs, Ltd."

"Anything in it?"

"Crime Scene's going over it now for fingerprints. And it looks like there's blood. Could be she was abducted from her car and then finished off in Omar's wagon."

Mike stood up from the table and thanked Joan for the meal. "How about we pick you up in the morning and drop in on Lowell at the Fuller Building?" he asked me. "Be downstairs at nine."

"Don't rush off before I finish with the news from the Medical Examiner's Office," Mercer said, putting a hand on Mike's shoulder. "DNA isn't in yet, but they did a basic ABO typing from the sperm sample found on the canvas where the body had been. We got a new ball game, ladies and gentleman. Omar Sheffield did *not* rape Denise Caxton."

# 14

" 'Lovers,' Mr. Chapman? It's not the term of art I would have chosen," Lowell Caxton said, standing behind the desk in his office in the Fuller Building and seemingly looking out at the view northward on Madison Avenue. "Personally, I referred to them as Deni's 'shareholders.' Each had a piece of her at some point in time. But it was a very volatile market."

"You're not suggesting they were interested in Deni because of her money, are you?" Mike reeled off the names of the men Joan had told us about—Mattox, the architect, and Wrenley, the antiques dealer.

"Come, come, Mr. Chapman. You're brighter than that. Not her money, certainly. *My* money. The Caxton fortune has attracted all kinds of maggots to Deni as well as to me." He turned back to face us. "Something I've had to deal with all my life. And no, as I've told you, I was spared a proper introduction to either of those gentlemen you've mentioned."

Morning sunlight was beaming in and hitting Caxton directly in the eye, so he came out from behind his desk and gestured for us to sit in the overstuffed leather chairs grouped beneath a pair of Boudin beach scenes.

"How come you didn't tell us anything about the letters Deni had gotten? The threatening ones, the blackmail?" Mike asked.

"Ah, do I sense the presence of a little guttersnipe?" Caxton groaned.

"What?"

"*La povera Signorina Sette,* am I right? Poor little Miss Sette, still peddling the same nonsense at the drop of a hat. Let me guess, gentlemen—when you sell the movie rights to your ridiculous fantasy here, you'll be played by Arnold Schwarzenegger," Caxton said, grinning at Mike. "You'll be Denzel Washington, Marina Sette will be some two-bit Shirley Temple look-alike, and as for me—if only they could bring Bela Lugosi or Vincent Price back to life. I'm always to be cast as the villain, am I not? At least, it's usually such a richly textured role."

There was a knock on the door and an assistant entered with a tray holding a Baroque silver coffee service and a mound of croissants and Danish. Caxton was silent as she put the heavy load on the table in front of us and walked out of the room.

"Why don't you help yourselves, Detectives?"

"Nah, I'll just let Sharon Stone over here pour for me. That's why I bring her along. Not very useful, but sometimes decorative." Mike jerked his thumb in my direction as I was leaning forward to pour the coffee.

"What made you connect Marina Sette to the letters Deni received?" I asked.

"This isn't the first time she's tried to bring me down, Ms. Cooper. Did she take the trouble to come all the way here just to stir the same old pot again? You know why she hates me, don't you?"

There wasn't much of a way to protect Sette in all this. "I know what she told me."

"Her story is nonsense, of course. There's no way for her to prove it, but sadly, there's no way for me to *dis*prove it, either." I remembered that the woman Marina claimed was her mother, Lowell's second wife, was killed in a boating accident. "Buried at sea, as it were."

Caxton flashed one of his more loathsome smiles at me as he said that, and went on. "Even these latest scientific techniques of yours—genetic fingerprinting— are useless in this instance. I can't convince anyone that this waif was not the child of my wife."

"So, why does she hate you so much?" I didn't bother to tell him that the DNA of Marina's half sister could indeed prove the claim that she was his stepchild.

"I think it has more to do with her husband. He was a substantial client of mine until we had a falling-out over a serious acquisition I made. Richard tried to claim a piece of the profits, but he wasn't successful. Soon they were coming at me from all directions."

"But the letters were real, weren't they? I've seen one of them."

"Quite real. I can give you copies of all of them, if you like." Caxton removed a microrecorder smaller than a matchbook from his shirt pocket and spoke into it, reminding himself to ask his lawyer for a set of the correspondence.

"They played quite a dramatic role in the matrimonial sparring. Deni's lawyer tried to use them to show that I had hired someone to take a hit on her life."

With good reason, I thought to myself. "In the letter I saw, the information was strictly private in nature, Mr. Caxton. It had to come from someone who knew Deni intimately. If not you, then can you suggest who it might have been?"

He looked through me as though I were a complete idiot. "I guess when my attorney charges me four hundred fifty dollars an hour, it's worth the results. *He* got to the bottom of it rather quickly. Once you check this fellow out, this—what was his name?"

"Omar Sheffield," Mercer offered.

"Yes, Omar. You'll find, as my lawyer did, that Omar had developed quite a scheme for himself in state prison. He's got a file six inches thick, just up at the jail, blackmailing women the same way. Every single one of them in the middle of a divorce."

"I know I'm only a dumb cop, but where'd he get his information?"

"The library, gentlemen. The law library. Would you believe, our pen pal Omar is a regular little scholar, though you'd not know it from his crude language."

We still didn't get it.

"When the divorce proceedings began, Deni applied for temporary alimony. I don't know if you're familiar with these civil actions, but they tend to involve a lot of mudslinging. I was prepared to be more than generous with Deni. After all, she'd given me a great deal of happiness for ten years.

"Either she or her lawyer got greedy. Suddenly her bills for hairdressing and entertaining escalated to ridiculous numbers. She claimed more for facials and massages during the last year than most people in this city spend to eat."

"So, what book did Omar find in the prison library?" Mercer asked.

"It wasn't a book at all. It wasn't even the tabloids. Surely you can guess by now, Miss Cooper, can't you?"

I was dumbfounded.

"What's it called?" Caxton went on. "The *Law Journal*? Have I got it straight?"

All three men looked at me, and finally the lightbulb went on in my head. "Of course, the judge's opinion in the matrimonial case. It would have everything—details and facts—in it."

"Thank you. Vindicated at last."

The *New York Law Journal* was printed every weekday and subscribed to by most law firms and libraries in the state. It was my daily tool for keeping up with case law in the criminal field; I clipped and filed articles about court decisions and issues related to my work. It rarely interested me to read write-ups of divorce matters, but I had seen enough of them to know that every detail mentioned in Omar Sheffield's letter was likely to have been referenced by the judge in reaching conclusions about the case at hand.

Caxton continued. "My lawyer was furious—even took it up with the editor. After all, there's no reason not to have redacted some of the confidential information, because of precisely this kind of escapade."

Mercer had never read any of the decisions. "So, how did Sheffield get your address?"

Caxton seemed almost exasperated by our collective density at this point. "My dear fellow, the judge practically spoon-fed the whole scam to him. You'll read it for yourself, but I can pretty much paraphrase it for you. 'The couple live in separate apartments in the matrimonial residence, which is located at 890 Fifth Avenue.' And so on down the line, chapter and verse, hairdresser, masseuse, pedicurist, and psychic all included.

"Go visit the warden, as my lawyer did. Omar Sheffield is a more prolific letter writer than Winston Churchill. The bastard had done this operation a dozen times. Check with him—he was quite candid with my lawyer."

"Omar ran out of ink not too long ago," Mike said.

Our intentions of putting Caxton on edge by confronting him with the threats against Deni that we had assumed would be linked back to him had failed dismally.

Mike was noshing on a cheese Danish and took a swallow as he looked over at Caxton. "So, is there really an Amber Room?"

"You don't look the gullible type, Detective. Have they suckered you in with all this nonsense, too? Is this another Marina Sette story?" He was looking back and forth at each of us, to see if one of us would make a telltale slip. "Willing to sacrifice one nubile young prosecutor? Legend has it, I think, that once I let a seductress in that secret chamber with me and make love to her, I have to kill her."

It did sound a lot sillier than it had when Joan told us about it last evening, and I absorbed it on one Dewar's and two glasses of superb red wine.

"Keep them coming, gentlemen. Your questions get easier to answer all the time."

"Why didn't Deni go to England with you in June of last year? What was so important to her that she needed to stay behind, until you went on to Bath?" I asked.

Caxton stiffened noticeably, perhaps because the reminder of the scene in Bath rankled him. "Well, *you're* the ones they pay to do the investigation, aren't you? Suppose you get on about your business and get an answer to that for me. It's puzzled me for quite some time now."

He tried to bring the meeting to a close now, but Mike and Mercer weren't entirely ready.

"Got any Rembrandts in stock, Mr. Caxton?" Mike was on his feet, walking to the far side of the room to study the portrait hanging on the opposite wall. "A little something with water in it, for a change?"

"No, Detective, not on hand. But I'd love to buy one from you, should you come across it. The Caxtons, going back a couple of generations, have been known to squeeze every penny worth of value out of a fine painting, but we simply don't do armed robberies. Not my style.

"*The Storm on the Sea of Galilee*, painted in sixteen thirty-three. Probably the most famous missing artwork in the world, Mr. Chapman. And I would be delighted to get my hands on it."

"Did Mrs. Caxton ever talk to you about it, or about the theft at the Gardner?"

"Everyone in my business talked about it at some time or other. Quite frankly, it fascinated all of us. Such a bold undertaking, and then to be stuck with a treasure that no museum would dare touch, despite the fact that eighty percent of the things you see in European collections have been stolen or looted over the centuries.

"Once a year thieves pull off a caper at some institution or other—even the Louvre has had its share of embarrassments. Deni was a free spirit. Not exactly, shall we say, to the manner born. Would it intrigue her to be the one to find the lost Rembrandt and make her mark on the world? No question in my mind. Would she sleep with the enemy to do that? Two years ago I would have been confident in saying no. Now I'm really not sure."

"Tell us about the opening you gave here a few months back. The party that Deni came to—she might have been high that night."

"There haven't been any shows this summer—not enough of my clients stay in town to make it worthwhile. Perhaps you're referring to the eighteenth-century Italian landscape collection that was installed here in May? Yes, Deni showed up. No problem with that."

"People have told us she was talking openly about some great thing she was onto, some kind of coup that she was going to have."

"Nothing I heard. But after all, I was hosting the party and there was a rather large crowd around."

Mike was expressing his skepticism that Caxton hadn't observed or heard what Deni was up to. "So busy that you didn't notice what your estranged wife was saying to your clients?"

Again a snide look. "Well, Detective, I wasn't out in the kitchen with the Ritz cracker box open, making the appetizers by myself. I simply had no interest in anything she had to say at that point."

"We located Mrs. Caxton's car last night," Mercer said. "She might have been attacked while she was in it. We still haven't found a witness who knows where she was or what she did from last Thursday on. I realize you were away, but have you heard from anyone who saw Deni?"

"Not a soul."

"She have any trouble with the car, that you know of? Any reason to bring it in the shop?"

"The car was a dream. Never a moment's worry. I gave it to her several years back. Mercedes 500—E Class. A collector's item. Only about a thousand of them in total. Benz body with a Porsche engine. Deni could fly in that car.

"It only had one dangerous feature. Got her in trouble once before."

"What's that?"

"The lid on the gas tank was controlled by the door locks. To fill it with gas, you had to unlock the car doors. In case you haven't noticed, most gas stations in Manhattan are in fairly unsavory parts of town. One time, over on Eleventh Avenue late at night, Deni had to unlock the doors. After the attendant stepped away from the tank, a man with a pistol opened the rear door and got into the car. Held the gun to her head and took her a few blocks away, where he robbed her.

Took her cash, her jewelry, the Chopard watch I'd just given her for our tenth anniversary—none of it insured. Cost me a bloody fortune. Tried to make her get rid of the car after that, but she refused.

"Anything further?" Caxton asked. "I'm sure you'll excuse me. I've got a condolence call to pay this morning. One of the most respected figures in our business, and a dear friend both to me and to Deni, passed away yesterday." He stood up, walked to his desk to retrieve a pair of sunglasses. "I've really got to be going."

"They're dropping like flies around you, Mr. Caxton. Hope it isn't contagious," Mike cracked. "Anyone I knew?"

"I sincerely doubt it, Mr. Chapman." Caxton lifted the *Times* off his desk and passed it to Mike. "A lovely gentleman. A very distinguished art restorer called Marco Varelli. Read the obituary page if you think I'm deceiving you yet again."

"Marco Varelli?" My lips moved as Mercer said the name aloud with disbelief.

"How'd he die?"

"A heart attack, in his studio. Eighty-four years old. I'm off to console his widow."

# 15

Battaglia was drinking apple cider and puffing on a cigar as he waved me into his office an hour after I left Lowell Caxton on Wednesday morning. I could tell there was no urgency to the district attorney's questioning of me by the fact that he removed neither the cigar from the corner of his mouth nor his feet from the edge of the desk.

"Any progress in this art dealer's murder?"

"Developments, yes. Progress, no."

"I've got to give a speech at the Department of Justice next week on the significance of the drop in the crime rate in New York. Rose is typing it up today. Any figures you can give me to throw in on sex crimes?"

"Nothing that will help you. Rape is the only crime in which the rate of reporting has increased in the last three years. Stay away from those numbers, unless you think Justice will give us more money if we can show how the volume has gone up."

"Suppose they ask me why it hasn't dropped like the other violent crime categories?"

"Not complicated at all. A lot of the credit for the reduction goes to aggressive community-policing policies, right? Most people don't realize that almost *eighty percent* of reported rapes occur between people who know each other. The stranger rapist—the guy who jumps out from behind trees in the park or breaks into homes—he's only responsible for about twenty percent of the cases. But he's the guy most women fear.

"So, while violent street crime is way down, the acquaintance-rape victims aren't at all affected by the presence of the cop on the beat. They trust their assailant—so they walk right past the officer into the apartment or dorm or hotel room of the man they're with—and then the attack occurs."

Battaglia went back to the report he was reading. "Get me a memo on that before the end of the day, will you? Flush it out a bit so I can use it in Washington."

I was almost out the door. "Hey," he called after me, "what's with you and this news guy, Jacob Tyler? I'd like to meet him. Maybe we could get him to do a story on the new Welfare Fraud Unit we're setting up."

It was impossible to keep a secret from Paul Battaglia. He never even had to leave his spacious office on the eighth floor of the building to get the most complete intelligence—professional and personal—from a cadre of loyal and talented men and women who served him in his distinguished career in public service.

"I'll be sure to let him know, Paul. May I ask how—"

The cigar was parked squarely in the middle of his gritted teeth now. "Tell him I said I never divulge my sources. He'll appreciate that, as a good reporter."

I stopped at Rose's desk, knowing that I could learn from her what Battaglia had been told about the status of my new romance, but she had stepped away, so I went back to my office.

"Mike's on hold. I tried to transfer him over to Battaglia's wing but they said you were on your way back," Laura said.

I went into my room and picked up the phone.

"Just checked with the morgue," he said. "No autopsy done on Marco Varelli. Didn't have to. He was eighty-four, with a serious heart condition, and under a doctor's care. Once his own physician signed off on the death certificate, that's it. By the end of the day he'll be resting at a funeral parlor down on Sullivan Street. We'll go over for tonight's visiting hours and see if we can turn up some employees or friends.

"Also," he continued, "spoke to the Feds on the auction-bid-rigging investigation. Can you meet us at Kim McFadden's office at five? They'll fill us in on that, and update us on the Gardner Museum heist, too."

The United States Attorney's Office for the Southern District was a four-block walk from my office, set back behind the old federal courthouse, near Police Headquarters, and the New York City offices of the F.B.I. "Fine, that gives me the rest of the day to catch up on the things I need to do. See you at five."

"Is this a bad time?" Carol Rizer asked as she stood in the doorway. She was new to the unit, and although her skills were good, it was important that she be supervised on complicated matters.

"If I told you to wait for a good time, your witness is likely to die of old age. What do you need?"

"I'm having a lot of trouble with a victim in a case I picked up last night. The defendant's got a really bad record—three felony convictions—but there's something wrong with the victim's story and I just can't break her on it. Can I bring her in for you to talk to?"

"Yes. Give me the background."

"Her name is Ruth Harwind, and she's nineteen years old. Lives in Queens with her mother. Has a boyfriend named Wakim Wakefield—he's waiting up in my office. The defendant is Wakim's roommate, and his name is Bruce Johnson. Ruth claims that she stayed in their apartment one day after Wakim left for work. She says Bruce forced her bedroom door open with a knife and dragged her into his room. That's where she says he raped her."

Carol knew how I handled these interviews. She had written out a list for me identifying all the inconsistencies in the story Ruth had told, first to the police and then to her. She had also highlighted for me the facts that didn't make much sense.

"What do you find troubling?"

"Start with the point that in the middle of the rape, the boyfriend came back to the apartment, knocked on Bruce's bedroom door, and asked where Ruth was. Bruce said he didn't know, and Wakim left. My first problem is why she just didn't scream out for help when Wakim was right there in the next room.

"Now, if she'd told me it was because he'd threatened her again with the knife, it might have been credible. But all she says is that it didn't occur to her."

"What else?"

"The cop examined the door that she claims was

pried open with a knife. There's no sign of any disturbance on the paint or to the wood. Also, there's no immediate outcry. When she left the apartment and went outside on the street, she ran into Wakim. She went back upstairs with him, showered, and made love. Nobody mentioned the word 'rape' until Bruce's girlfriend came home and told Wakim that Ruth had been cheating on him. He's the one who challenged her to go to the police if the story was true."

Frequently the motive in a false report can be gleaned from the circumstances of how and why a sexual assault gets related to the police. In many cases like this, an angry boyfriend dares the victim to prosecute if the crime really happened.

"Did Bruce make any statements?"

One of my favorite bureau chiefs, Warren Murtagh, had a list of training rules, and Murtagh's Rule #3 was a good one. "No defendant ever says absolutely nothing." Everyone arrested makes some comments to the cops, spontaneously or in response to questioning, which is usually useful in sorting out the facts.

Often the perp's remarks can be discarded as self-serving and of no value, but just as often there are kernels of truth that can be used to shed light on the victim's version of events. Every now and then, the real story lies somewhere right in between.

Carol answered, "Johnson says it was consensual. Says he gave her ten dollars to come in his bedroom and have sex with him. Even told us they watched a porno movie together. And that he used a condom, 'cause she asked him to.

"Also, Alex, she's lied about some of the basic stuff. Said she worked at the Victoria's Secret store in the World Trade Center for six months. I called over there and got the woman who's been the manager for two years. She's never heard of Ruth."

"Bring her in." Once a witness has lied about facts that are *not* essential to the case and that can be easily verified or disproved, there is reason to be suspicious about the underlying allegations in the criminal complaint. Until caught in a direct lie, every witness who walked in the door was presumed to be telling us the truth.

Ruth Harwind was not happy to be ushered into my office. At five foot eleven she was a couple of inches taller than I, dressed in jeans and a T-shirt and directing her defiant pout toward the floor.

I began with a series of pedigree questions to get as much background knowledge about the young woman as I could. "Why you need to know all this business about me?" she asked, balking at the personal information for which I was probing.

"Because I need to know as much about *you* as Bruce Johnson knows, as much about you as he's going to tell his lawyer to use against you. It may be the only way that Carol and I can protect you when you go to court.

"Who do you live with in Queens?"

"My mother."

"What's her name?"

Ruth's annoyance level was growing. "What's that got to do with me being raped?"

"Like everyone else who's been the victim of a

crime, you walk through my door and tell a story that could keep Bruce Johnson in jail for the next twenty-five years of his life. That's longer than you've been alive. And that's what he deserves, if everything you told the police about him is true.

"But Carol doesn't know you and I don't know you, so I'm going to ask you a series of questions that are really simple to answer and that are a very easy way for us to be able to prove that things you tell us are true. So, let's start over. Would you please tell me your mother's name?"

"No, I won't." Ruth had dug her heels in. Slouched down in the chair, she stared at a small vase of flowers on my desk, refusing to make eye contact with me.

"Why won't you tell me?" I asked. "Look at me when I'm speaking to you, please."

" 'Cause I don't want my mother to know I'm here, that's why."

"That's fair. I can accept that." Since Ruth was nineteen, there was no legal requirement that her parents be notified. "Why don't you tell me what you do? Do you go to school? Do you have a job?"

"Like I told her," Ruth said, jerking her head in Carol's direction, "that's nobody's business but mines. This is about me and Bruce. Why don't y'all ask me questions about that, huh?"

"You're not going to be able to give the answers you're giving me to the judge, when he asks the same things in the courtroom. He's going to insist on a little respect and make you respond to whatever he needs to know."

"Well, let's just drop the whole thing and lemme

outta here." Ruth slammed her hand on my desk and stood up. "Wakim can take care of Bruce."

"Sit down, Ruth. You're not going anywhere. There's a man who's been held in jail since last night, and based on what you tell me today, the judge is going to decide whether to keep him in on high bail any longer."

We glared at each other for a couple of seconds before she took her seat again. The questioning continued at the same pace and with similar results. When we got to the part at which Bruce forced Ruth into his bedroom, I asked whether he had turned on the television or a movie.

"Yeah, he put on the VCR, but I wasn't watching."

"That's not what he says."

"Well, who you gonna believe, him or me? Whose side are you on, anyway?"

"What kind of movie was it?" I asked, ignoring her questions to me.

"I seen it before, at Wakim's. Some kind of dirty movie with two girls sucking on each other. I only looked at it from time to time."

Great. Already Bruce's version was making more sense than Ruth's.

My intercom buzzer went off and Laura asked me to step out to her desk. "If there's anything else about your story that you remember now that's different than what you told the police, this is the time to tell Carol. Once we put you under oath and you swear to the judge about something, if it turns out not to be true, then it will be too late for Carol and me to help you." I excused myself and said I'd be right back.

"Alex, this is Mrs. Harwind, Ruth's mother. One of Ruth's friends told Mrs. Harwind that her daughter was coming down here today, and she's asked to talk to you."

The middle-aged woman in the hallway outside Laura's cubicle was agitated and tearful. I introduced myself and took her into the conference room to explain what was going on. Since Ruth had asked me not to tell her mother about the case, I was avoiding the fact that her daughter was fifteen feet away, inside my office.

"Miss Cooper, you've got to help me find my child. I've got a warrant for her in Queens Family Court, 'cause she ran away from the group home they put her in."

"How long ago was that?" I was confused, since Ruth was too old to be a candidate for court placement in a group home.

"Just back two weeks. This guy Wakim, he's got her hid in his apartment. My girl *looks* big, but she's only fifteen."

"Fifteen?"

I sat Mrs. Harwind down and explained that Ruth was with me. Since there was a warrant issued in her case, I was legally obliged to return her to court.

"Laura, call the D.A.'s Squad. Ask for Sergeant Maron, and tell him I need a detective down here immediately. Get two, and tell him to make sure that one is a female."

This would not go down easily, and I expected that the girl would get confrontational. With Ruth and Carol in my office, and Mrs. Harwind in the conference room, I waited at the foot of the staircase for the detectives from the squad to come downstairs. Before they appeared, a man who seemed to be forty years old got off the elevator holding two cans of soda and headed straight for Laura's door. I heard him ask for Ruth.

"Excuse me, are you Wakim? I'm Alex Cooper, one of the D.A.'s working on Ruth's case. We're almost done, but I'm going to need you to go back to Carol's office until we finish the interview, okay?" Without protest, he handed me a soda and asked me to give it to Ruth, and walked back to the elevators. I didn't want him anywhere around when I explained to Ruth that she wasn't going home with her boyfriend.

Sergeant Maron and Detective Kerry Schrager arrived within minutes. "This could get ugly. I've got a very unhappy teenager here who needs to make a court appearance in Queens. Just stand by while we break it to her, okay? And then you can help me get transportation for her."

I opened my office door to walk in. Maron and Schrager stayed in the doorway, and Ruth immediately sensed this was trouble.

"Why don't we go back to a couple of basic questions, Ruth. What's your date of birth?"

"I told you, I'm nineteen," she said, glancing back over her shoulder at the cops. "Why are these people here?"

"I didn't ask how old you were, Ruth. Tell me the year you were born."

She was smart, but like many of us, lousy at math.

The subtraction was off, and the year she gave would have made her sixteen.

"Your mother tells me that you're only fifteen. Is that true?"

Ruth picked up a copy of the Penal Law from the top of my desk and threw it toward the window, missing my right ear by a couple of inches. "I *hate* my mother. All right, y'all, is this what you want to hear? Bruce Johnson didn't rape me, okay. Bruce Johnson gave me ten bucks to get him off, and you know what? I did it. And you know what else? It wasn't the first time."

The tears began to flow. "Wakim woulda killed me if he caught me in that room with Bruce. And Wakim don't ever give me nothing. No money, no clothes, no presents. You woulda made up a story, too, if it was your ass that woulda got broke."

I spoke softly to Ruth as I tried to give her some tissues. "You just can't go into a court of law, swear to tell the truth, and then lie about something. I realize Bruce is a bad guy, but you can't put him in jail to save yourself. How old does Wakim think you are?"

She was sniffling. "He know the truth. He know I'm fifteen."

"You understand that *he* can be arrested for having sex with you, because you're underage? When you try to act like a big girl, Ruth, you're gonna get stuck with the consequences." I paused. "Your mother's down the hall."

She got up from her chair, shouting curses at the top of her lungs and trying to push past the detectives. I told Kerry to stop her. I made her sit down and explained that she had to go before the judge in Family

Court, since she had absconded from the program and was wanted, AWOL.

"You can do this the easy way, like a young lady. I'll let you leave here with your mother, and put you in a taxi to go to Queens. Or you can do this the hard way. That means the detectives would have to handcuff you and take you there like a prisoner."

"Well, you can all go screw yourselves, 'cause I'm not going anywhere with her or with any of you." She was screaming again and kicking the side of my desk. "I don't care what you do with me, 'cause I'll just run away again and Wakim'll take me home."

Sergeant Maron raised a pair of handcuffs and looked at me questioningly. "I guess that's the way our customer wants to go."

Ruth looked me straight in the eye and spat across the desk, hitting an old indictment on top of a pile of papers. "And you, you bitch, I hope you get what's coming to you. I hope you—"

"Attitude," I said. "Attitude from a fifteen-year-old. Save your breath, Ruth. You know how lucky you are to have a mother who cares about you and who—"

"Where's Wakim?" She was screaming now, at full pitch. "I wanna go home with Wakim."

While Kerry Schrager cuffed Ruth behind her back, I called Witness Aid to make sure that Margaret Feerick, one of our social workers, could go with the detectives and Mrs. Harwind to Family Court. Pat McKinney came to my doorway and started yelling over Ruth's wail. "What the hell is going on in here? This is an office, Cooper, and the rest of us are trying to get some work done."

I asked Sergeant Maron to go to Carol's waiting area, find Wakim, read him the riot act about hanging out with a minor, and send him on his way.

Eventually, the miserable troupe of characters was ready to leave the office, with Ruth Harwind in tow. By the time I got them off to court, contacted Bruce Johnson's parole officer to find out if we could have his parole revoked for statutory rape—the sexual acts with an underage teen—wolfed down a light yogurt, and dealt with the stack of messages on Laura's desk, it was a quarter of five and time to go to the U.S. Attorney's Office.

With summer vacations in full swing, the elevators were practically empty as I rode down to the lobby. I chatted with some of the secretaries who were walking out onto Hogan Place with me, then made the left turn onto Centre Street for the short walk to McFadden's office.

The area in front of the Supreme Court, Civil Division, had been under renovation for almost a year in an effort to convert a cement triangle into a small green park.

I crossed with the light and had just passed in front of the plywood frame of the construction area when a dilapidated livery cab with tinted windows veered across the sparse line of cars moving north on Centre Street. Brakes squealed and horns blasted, so I picked up my head to see what was happening.

The gypsy cab was coming directly at the sidewalk, where I was trapped between a parked police car and the wooden fencing behind me. The driver slammed into the patrol car, which jumped the curb and was catapulted toward me, as I flattened myself against the plywood boards. The marked police vehicle caught its right fender on the fire hydrant in its path, but as the left fender made contact with the lumber, the fencing gave way and I fell backward into a small ditch.

My embarrassment was greater than my discomfort as I lay on the ground in the dirt, my heart racing and my lip quivering. Three court officers had seen the accident from the steps of the courthouse and came running down to check if I was all right.

"Are you a juror, ma'am? You're gonna have some great lawsuit against the city," the first one to my side remarked.

"I'll be fine," I said as they helped me to my feet. I wiped pebbles out of my hair and brushed the soot off the rear of my pale aqua suit. There were long scratches on my calves and one of my elbows was bleeding.

"Did you get a license off that car?" one of the men asked me, as onlookers gathered to see what the disturbance was about. "We'll help you make out the police report."

"No, thanks. I couldn't see the plate at all." But I had no trouble making out the face of the driver.

"Must've been a madman," the second guy said. "Did you hear him?"

I shook my head to indicate I had not. But as I thanked the officers and continued on my way to Kim's building, the driver's words—"You're dead meat, bitch"—were still reverberating in my ears.

# 16

I walked into the conference room after clearing security on the ground floor. Mike and Mercer were exchanging war stories with four very buttoned-down federal agents while they waited for me to arrive. I didn't need a mirror to tell me what was obvious from the expression on Mike's face as he looked up to see me.

"Mother of—jeez, what the hell happened to you? That picture's got 'line of duty' written all over it. Someone messes *me* up like that and I could go out on three-quarters disability pay tomorrow."

Mercer came over to examine the scrapes on my arm and ask whether I was all right.

"Yeah, I tripped into a hole on my way over from the courthouse."

"All those years of ballet lessons and you're a regular twinkletoes. You got four city blocks to walk here, what kinda hole we talking about?"

"I'll explain later. Let's get going here."

"You'll explain now, blondie."

"Ran into somebody who doesn't like me. Wakim

Wakefield, a forty-something ex-con. Took his fifteen-year-old plaything away from him this afternoon and he didn't appreciate it." I told them a short version of the story.

"Just another friggin' Ponce de Léon looking for his fountain of youth," Mike said. "Let's call in a police report on your hit-and-run attempt."

"No," I said firmly. "Just leave it alone. I'm not hurt. And this'll blow over by the time he goes out tonight and finds himself another teen angel. It couldn't have been anything more than chance that he saw me on the street as I was leaving and took out his frustration on me. I hate to tell you, but some cop's going to walk out of Central Booking later tonight and find a radio car that got bashed up worse than my pride. Point me to the ladies' room and give me a little time to make myself presentable."

Special Agent Rainieri chose not to delay the discussion until my return, since I had already kept the group waiting an extra twenty minutes. He seemed to be speaking in answer to a question one of the detectives had asked. "Yeah, we had a turncoat. That's what started the whole investigation. Seems he got cheated out of a very big sale and decided to rat out some of the other dealers in the pack.

"The point of these rings, you know, is to keep the prices of the artworks at auctions way down. One of them buys the painting at the public sale, then resells it at a vastly greater price—usually to a private client—and splits the big profit with his—or her—small clan of coconspirators."

"Denise Caxton?"

"She was a player all right. Don't forget, not only do we have ordinary business receipts and phone records, but we've got tapes of all the telephone bidding that goes on during an auction house sale. And the expense statements and each gallery's credit agreements."

I had to remind Mike that beyond the social cachet and great expense connected with the grand auctions, art was one of the only objects in the world that could be purchased in any currency and from any location.

"Do you know who her cohorts were in these deals?"

The only female agent present, Estelle Grayson, answered. "She moved in and out of a few partnerships. Lowell Caxton didn't mess much with auctions, and didn't run with the pack. He has always had his own sources and paid dearly for them. Doesn't leave much of a paper trail, and didn't mix well in the sandbox with the other kids."

"Bryan Daughtry?" I asked.

"He's everywhere in this. Not up front, not sitting there with a paddle in the air. But he was pumping cash into her operation and trying to guide her into play with some of this very contemporary art inventory."

"Any names you can give us connected with the auction investigation?"

"Denise Caxton spent a lot of time at events this year. Sometimes she was with a personal client, a big collector." Rainieri referred to his file and gave us a list of names, none of which sounded at all familiar. "Often she brought a friend or escort, and it's hard to tell if there's any business purpose instead of a social one. Chapman says you've been talking to Mrs. Caxton's friend Marina Sette. She's a figure at these things. Could be she's just a big spender.

"Two of the men Denise had been socializing with also show up—Frank Wrenley and Preston Mattox. Again, one's an antiques dealer and one's an architect, so we've got subpoenas out for their records, too. Nothing in on them yet. We just don't know if they're around for the fun or the profit."

"Well, do they buy anything?"

"Wrenley does. But that's a new twist, new buzzword in the auction world. It's called 'cross-marketing.' So, when Sotheby's has a sale of Impressionists, for example, they don't start the program off with a Monet. Last spring at their big show, the first piece sold was a pair of silver soup tureens made by a French silversmith in the eighteenth century. Used to belong to J. P. Morgan. Went for more than seven million bucks. The houses are trying to lure art collectors into new passions."

"Wrenley bought those tureens?"

"No, no. But he's shown up often and bought a lot of silver pieces—old French royalty. And Denise Caxton had Preston Mattox bidding on a set of murals out of an old Scottish estate. So we haven't reached a point of figuring whether this was business or romance.

"Anyway, Kim asked us to start making connections between Mrs. Caxton and anyone who'd have a reason to do her in. We're looking, and a few months down the road, when we have all the paper we need, something might leap out at us. In the meantime, if you guys have subpoenaed some of the same phone and business records that we did, we can cut through a lot of this and give you our copies. Maybe you'll find things that wouldn't mean anything to us."

I fished through my overstuffed pocketbook to pull out copies of the file folders with the subpoenas inside. The bag had turned upside down in my fall and was even more disastrously messed up than usual.

"I don't know how she finds anything in there," Chapman said as I clasped lipstick, a compact, a handkerchief, Tic Tacs, four pens, and a wallet in my left hand, trying to free up the folder with my right. "What do you know about the Gardner Museum heist?"

"Not our turf. We've talked to the team who've worked it for practically ten years, just 'cause they're figuring the stolen items have got to surface somewhere before too long. So they're watching the auction houses pretty closely, too. D'y'all know about Youngworth and Connor?"

More than anything, Mike hated telling a Fed that there was something about which he was ignorant. He wouldn't say no to them, so I did.

"There are two guys in Boston, William Youngworth and Myles Connor. Youngworth's an antiques dealer—been in and out of the can on minor things—and Connor's a master art thief. Both of these men were in jail when the Gardner job was pulled, but word is, if they weren't the brains behind the theft, they certainly knew about it.

"Last year Youngworth claimed that he could broker the return of the missing Rembrandt for the five-million-dollar reward the FBI put up, along with immunity for him and his pal. You know about the chips?"

Another thumbs-up for Joan Stafford. "Sure," said Chapman, puffing. "Know all about the chips. Those assholes cut the painting right out of the frame."

"Yeah, well, Youngworth gave some Boston news reporter a few chips to support his claim that he could produce the goods. Our experts looked them over. Not authentic, not from the missing painting. That's the latest on the Gardner case."

"Who was your expert? Got a name for us?"

"No idea who it is. We'll get it for you tomorrow."

We spent the next half hour sorting through documents to see which ones I was legally entitled to examine at this point. At six fifteen, Mercer suggested we close up. "Let's get over to the funeral parlor before the seven o'clock visiting hours. Maybe we can chat up some of Marco Varelli's friends and family."

Varelli's wake was in a small, dark funeral home on Sullivan Street, in the narrow block just north of Houston. I had been in the neighborhood before, which had been home to Vincent "the Chin" Gigante, whom I had often seen there walking up and down the street in his bathrobe, feigning insanity, before his recent conviction and trip to federal prison.

I stepped out of Mercer's air-conditioned car and onto the steamy pavement in front of Zuppelo's funeral parlor. "You think they got a TV in there?" Mike asked.

"You are *not* watching *Jeopardy!* in front of the

mourners," I said. "Call your mother when we leave here and ask her what the question was, okay? Live without it for one night."

The three of us presented ourselves to the manager of the mortuary. "The only one here at the moment is Mrs. Varelli. You're a little early. Are you friends?"

"Distant relatives," Chapman answered.

Mr. Zuppelo looked skeptically from Chapman to me, then frowned at Mercer Wallace's dark skin.

"Northern Italian," Mike said. "With a trace of Sicilian."

He flashed his badge at Zuppelo, who led us into a dingy sitting area. The odor of more than thirty flower arrangements—mostly orange gladioluses and yellow carnations—was especially stifling in the intense late-summer heat. The open casket was in an alcove at the far end of the room, and Mrs. Varelli sat beside it, clutching a set of rosary beads. The jacket of her gray suit seemed to overwhelm her delicate shoulders, and she looked as if she had cried all the tears she was capable of shedding in the past twenty-four hours.

Mike nudged me and told me to introduce myself. "See if you can get her outta this hothouse and away from her husband's body. Bond with her, Coop. Be sensitive—if you still remember how to do that."

I left Mike and Mercer at the doorway and approached the widow. "Mrs. Varelli, I'm Alexandra Cooper. I'm—"

"So nice to meet you, Miss Cooper. You were, perhaps, a friend of Marco's?"

"Actually, no, Mrs. Varelli. Would you like to come

inside with me, to another room, and I'll explain why I'm here?"

"Sixty-two years, Miss Cooper. Never apart for one night in sixty-two years. What am I going to do without him?" She grabbed the side of the coffin and started to talk to her husband. "I'm just going to be a few minutes, Marco. I go with this young lady to see what she's going to try to sell me."

She extended her hand, and I grasped the white cotton glove and braced her elbow, helping her to her feet. "Everyone thinks I just got off the boat from Napoli. Do I want a mausoleum, do I want a condominium, do I want a ticket back to the old country? I was born in Newark, New Jersey. Lived here all my life. These people think I'm stupid. Think I'm going to give away Marco's paintings or turn his studio into the YMCA.

"All I want is for Marco to get up and walk around the corner with me to have our dinner at Da Silvano, sitting on the sidewalk, like we did almost every evening in the warm weather. Artists would look at Marco with respect, Marco would look at the young ladies with longing, I'd have a couple of glasses of wine, and together we'd go home very happy. It's awfully lonely after sixty-two years, Miss Cooper. You want to sell me something, or you want to buy?"

As she talked, I walked her past Mike and Mercer and into an empty room decorated in somber, waiting-for-the-next-body tones of neutral palettes. There was an elegance to the old woman, with her perfectly erect carriage, fragile body, and very keen mind.

"I'm an assistant district attorney, Mrs. Varelli. A prosecutor."

"Somebody make a crime here?"

"I'm working on another case, a murder case. A woman who was killed last week. I understand that Mr. Varelli had done work with her. We—the detectives and I—had planned to come see him later this week. Then we learned about his death. I'm so sorry for your great loss. I don't mean to burden you now, but maybe you could give me the name of your husband's assistant, who could tell—"

Her back was straight as a rod as she poked herself in the chest. "I am the only one he trusted with his work, Miss Cooper. He had several workmen who helped him with the physical labor, the movement of large pieces, the arrangement of supplies, and from time to time he had an apprentice. But there is nothing *I* didn't know about his business. Who is this lady who was killed?"

"Caxton. Denise Caxton."

Mrs. Varelli turned her face ninety degrees, away from me. She was silent.

"You knew her, then?"

"It's not good to speak ill of the dead, is it?"

"What kind of business did she have with your husband?"

"The same as everyone, Miss Cooper. You know about Marco?"

"I have to admit that I had never heard his name until this week. But all the people I've talked to say what a wonderful man he was."

"A genius. Did they say that, too? Mostly, he was a genius."

I nodded to her.

"As a boy, in Firenze, he studied art at the Accademia. Paint is what he loved—not the canvas, but the substance that made color—and he had even more passion for that than for beautiful women. But he never did it so well himself—the drawing or the creation. What he did brilliantly was to find the beauty in the paintings of others who had gone before him.

"Marco could stand in his atelier for hours, some eager dealer at his heels watching, working on what appeared to be a dirty old piece of burlap. He'd fasten his binocular headset on—that was the only thing that even looked like it connected him to this century. Gently, ever so gently, he would swab at the tired colors with a little touch of cotton.

"Behind him, some greedy collector or dealer would be urging him on. 'What do you see, Marco? Who do you think it is, Marco?' You have no idea what treasures he has found over the years. Even so recently, his eyes saw things through the filth of centuries that no one else could dream possible."

"And his illness—he was still working until recently, even with his heart condition?"

Mrs. Varelli snapped at me. "Illness what?"

"I, uh, I knew that a doctor had come when he collapsed."

"A touch of arthritis, that's what the doctor was for. Marco's skill depended on two things, his eye and his hand. Neither one of us—no pills, no machines, no medicines. He only had a doctor to help him when his hand ached from the arthritis and it hurt him to hold a scalpel for so long. *Un po' di vino*, Marco believed in. The medicine from the grapes."

"It was his heart that gave out," I said, hoping it was gentle enough a reminder of what the doctor had told the M.E.'s pathologist.

"There was nothing wrong with Marco's heart. His heart was so good, so very strong." Mrs. Varelli became tearful.

"Were you always in the studio with your husband?"

"No, I was rarely there. We have an apartment in the same building. We had our coffee together in the morning, then he would go upstairs to work. Back home for lunch and a nap. Then more work, always. Sometimes into the evening, if he found himself in the middle of a surprise or a painting he had come to adore. Then he would come home to bathe himself, to get rid of the oil and varnish and streaks. Together we would go off for dinner, alone or with friends. A simple life, Miss Cooper, but a very rich one."

"Had you ever met Denise Caxton?"

"It was her husband I met first. I can hardly remember when, it was so long ago. He was not a warm man, but he was very good to Marco. Lowell Caxton bought a portrait at an auction house in London, maybe thirty years ago. It had been miscatalogued in England and sold as an unidentified portrait of a young girl. Lowell bought it only because he said it reminded him of his wife, whichever one that happened to be at the time. He didn't believe it had any value, and he brought it to Marco simply to clean it up to be hung.

"But Marco thought she was a beauty, too. 'Overpainted,' he complained to me every time he came downstairs. He didn't use many words, Marco. He didn't need to with me. Days and nights he worked on it, until there was life in the child's face and her petite blue dress had texture and the warm glow of silk. One afternoon, Marco came down for lunch. I give him his soup and he looks across the table. 'Gainsborough,' he said to me, 'it's a Gainsborough.' Every museum in England wanted to buy it back.

"Many people would just have paid Marco the price he asked for the restoration, and still my husband would have been happy. Lowell Caxton did that. But then he came back the next week, when Marco had come home for his lunch. I let him in the house—that's when I met him. He had under his arm a small package wrapped in brown paper. It was a Titian—very small, very beautiful. We have it still. You come to my home, you'll see it."

"In your apartment? A Titian?"

"But so very little. It's a study, just a piece of one of his great works. You know *The Rape of Europa*?"

Of course I knew it. Everyone who had ever taken an art course in college had studied it. Rubens had called it the greatest painting in the world. And I had seen it many times because it was part of the collection at the Gardner Museum. Was this just another coincidence? "When did you say Mr. Caxton gave you the Titian?"

Mrs. Varelli thought for a moment. "Thirty, thirty-five years ago."

Before Denise, before the Gardner Museum theft.

"And Denise Caxton, was she a client of Mr. Varelli's?"

"First she came many times with her husband. Then alone. Then with other people—maybe dealers, maybe buyers. I never met them in the studio. Sometimes Marco would tell stories about them."

"Did he feel the same way you did about Mrs. Caxton?"

Mrs. Varelli tossed back her head and laughed. "Of course not. She was young, she was quite beautiful, and she knew how to make an old man feel wonderful. She'd practice her Italian on Marco. She'd flatter him and tease him and bring him fascinating paintings to examine. Always looking for gold where there was none. Wasting Marco's time, if you ask me."

"Do you know who the men were that she brought recently?"

"No, no. For this, I give you the names of my husband's workmen. Maybe they were introduced or can tell you what these men looked like. You give me your card, and next week I call you with their telephone numbers."

"Is that the only reason you didn't like Denise?"

"I don't need many reasons. She was trouble. Even Marco thought she was trouble."

"How, Mrs. Varelli? What did he tell you about her?"

"Like I said, Miss Cooper, Marco didn't use a lot of words. But these past few months, on the days that Mrs. Caxton came to see him, he didn't come home smiling like he used to. She was trying to get him to work on something that upset him, gave him *agita*. That he did say. 'At this age, I don't need any *agita*.'"

"But didn't he get any more specific than that?"

"Not with me. I was just glad he didn't want to work with her any longer. He didn't seem to like the people she was bringing around."

"Did Mr. Varelli talk about Rembrandt ever?"

"How could one make his life in this world and not talk about Rembrandt?"

I was grateful that she had not responded by saying what a stupid question I had asked. "I mean recently, and in connection with Denise Caxton."

"You don't know, then, that Marco is"—her chest heaved visibly as she breathed deeply and changed the wording. "Marco was the world's leading expert on Rembrandt, no? Perhaps you're too young to know the story."

Mrs. Varelli went on. "Rembrandt's most famous group portrait is called *The Night Watch*. Have you ever seen it?"

"Yes, I have. It's in Amsterdam, at the Rijksmuseum."

"Exactly. Then maybe you know that originally, more than three hundred years ago, it had a different name."

"No, I've only heard it called by this one."

"When he painted it, it was entitled *The Shooting Company of Captain Frans Banning Cocq*. Over the decades, it became so covered with grime that people assumed that the setting was at nighttime—the name you know it by. Well, after World War Two was ended—in about nineteen forty-seven—when Marco was just getting a reputation as a restorer, he was part of the team of experts put together to restore the enormous painting. During the cleaning, it lightened brilliantly. That's the first time anyone in the twentieth century realized that it wasn't a night scene at all.

"Marco was the only member of that restoration group still alive fifty years later. When anyone—and I mean *anyone,* Miss Cooper—has a question about the attribution of a Rembrandt today, it was only my Marco who knew the truth. Monarchs, presidents, millionaires—they all came to see Marco Varelli about their paintings."

"Denise Caxton, did she ever bring him a Rembrandt?"

"This I don't know."

"Did your husband ever say that she or anyone else asked him to look at paint chips recently?"

Again Mrs. Varelli looked at me as though I had no brain at all.

"That's what my husband did every day of his life. Paint, paint chips, paint streaks, paint fragments. From this, Miss Cooper, come masterpieces."

"Excuse me, Alex. Could I see you a minute?" Mercer was speaking to me from the hallway.

"May I go back to Marco now?"

"If you'd give us another few minutes, Mrs. Varelli, we'll be out of your way," he said to her.

I thanked her for her graciousness at such a terrible time and walked back to the room in which the coffin rested. Mike was standing next to the dead man's head.

"I hope by paying your respects to the deceased you got more than I did from the widow," I said to them as I reentered the room. "A bit of art history and a hunch that Denise Caxton was nothing but trouble."

"Then I'd say Mrs. Varelli's got great instincts. Remember that case I had a few years back in Spanish Harlem? The Argentinian dancer, Augusto Mango, who died prematurely during a sexual encounter with a rabid fan?"

"Very well."

"You know how we found out it was murder and not a bad heart?"

"No."

"Some doctor declared him dead at the scene. I think he must have been a podiatrist. Then, at the funeral parlor, while they were combing his hair into place, the mortician found a bullet hole in the back of his head. Small caliber, barely the trace of an entry. The fan's husband was the killer. *Post* headline was *Don't Tango with Mango*.

"Well, Mr. Zuppelo wouldn't make such a good barber."

Mike carefully turned Marco Varelli's head away from us and smoothed the thick white hair back from his left ear, much as he had done at Spuyten Duyvil when we first saw the body of Denise Caxton. There was the unmistakable mark that a bullet had pierced the skull of the gentle old man.

# 17

"Criminal court press room—where every crime's a story and every story's a crime. Mickey Diamond here." The veteran *New York Post* reporter had covered the courthouse for longer than anyone could remember, and answered the phone with his usual élan on Thursday morning.

"What did you think you were doing by running that story this morning?" I asked when I called, trying to control my temper.

Pat McKinney had left a copy of the page-three clipping on my desk, quoting me in an article about the Caxton murder investigation. Battaglia had an inviolable policy about assistants talking to the press. He enforced it rigidly, and he was right to do so. With more than six hundred lawyers in the office and three hundred thousand matters a year coming through our complaint room, it would have been insane to let prosecutors comment on cases they handled. First I had called Rose Malone, urging her to let Battaglia know that Mickey's feature was pure fiction, and then I had dialed the newsroom.

"Slow news day, Alex. My editor was begging me for a story."

I looked at the lead paragraph in the piece, in which Diamond attributed to me a statement about a major break in the case.

"If we're close to a solution, as you say I say, then it truly is news to me," I told him. The story reported that, working closely with detectives from the Manhattan North Homicide Squad, I had discovered the motive in the Caxton killing and an arrest was imminent. "Battaglia will be furious when he reads this. It's bullshit, but now he'll get pressure from the mayor to make an arrest, and we don't even have a suspect yet."

"The truth is so rare, Alex. I like to use it sparingly." He laughed at his own joke, knowing that I wouldn't. "Straighten me out. Give me some real scoop to go with. Maybe this'll make the killer show his hand—he'll think you know more about him than you do."

"Thanks for the help, Mickey. When he turns himself in because of your story, I'll make sure you get the reward money." If nothing else, I confirmed that word of Marco Varelli's murder had not yet leaked to the press. Diamond would have been all over me if he'd heard what we had discovered last night.

We had broken the news to Varelli's widow just as mourners had gathered for the evening visit to the funeral home. Her initial shock at the fact that her husband had been assassinated was replaced with her proud resolve that she had known he had not died of natural causes. Bravely, she composed herself and greeted their friends and associates for more than two hours, while we mingled with the small crowd in the room.

She had finally thanked Chapman warmly and then turned to tell me good night. "You see, Miss Cooper, I was sure that Marco Varelli would never have chosen to leave me. Such was his love, such was his life."

The funeral was to be on Friday, after the second night of the wake, and she invited us to come to her nearby apartment the next week.

Mike had gotten her permission to seal Marco's atelier last night and secure it with patrolmen. He would go back later today to process it with the detectives from the Crime Scene Unit. We needed her, or one of Varelli's workmen, to help discover whether any artworks or valuables were missing. That might have to wait until after the burial.

Finally, when everyone left the dingy funeral home, Mike and Mercer had arranged for the Medical Examiner's Office to pick up the body of Marco Varelli for an autopsy.

I had come downtown to work, busying myself in the review of new cases till I could meet Mike or Mercer in Chelsea. We were going back to Galleria Caxton Due to talk to Bryan Daughtry again, as well as to oversee the execution of the search warrant.

It was Mercer who phoned at eleven thirty to tell me he was leaving his office to go to West Twenty-second Street. Mike had witnessed the proceeding on Varelli at the morgue, which had validated his discovery at the funeral parlor, and would join up with us in Chelsea.

I drove my Jeep up to the gallery thinking about Denise Caxton, Omar Sheffield, and Marco Varelli. What common factor in their lives so closely linked them in death?

I parked right in front and walked to the Empire Diner, where I sipped another cup of coffee until the guys arrived a few minutes later.

"You got the warrants?" Mike asked, slipping into the booth along with Mercer, who had met him at the front door.

"Everything we need."

We walked across the street and down the block, where the entrance to the gallery's garage was blocked by a radio car. One of the uniformed officers saw us coming, recognized Mike, and got out to say hello.

"Hey, Chapman, how's it going? Been a long time. I thought you did steady midnights?"

"Used to be, Jack. Now I'm afraid of the dark— doing day tours. Any action here?"

"He ain't givin' us any trouble. A little pedestrian traffic around, but no packages going without gettin' searched, and no trucks in or out. Same report from yesterday."

A receptionist met us inside the front door. "Mr. Daughtry thought you might be coming in sometime this afternoon. He's upstairs with a client. I can make you comfortable down here, if you'd—"

"No thanks," Mike said, ignoring the young woman and leading us to the elevator in the far corner. When we reached the top floor and stepped out onto the landing, there was no sign of Daughtry on the walkway. Mercer headed over to see whether he was in his corner office, while Mike and I looked out at the old railroad tracks again.

"My father used to tell me the stories about the gangs from Hell's Kitchen who terrorized the train lines—the Hudson Dusters, the Gophers. When he was a kid, he hung out in a saloon right up the street here, running errands for a guy named Mallet Murphy. Called him that 'cause he'd crack disorderly customers over the head with a meat hammer."

Mike leaned back against the waist-high iron rail as he looked out at this view of Chelsea. He couldn't have been any happier if you'd sat him at the top of the Eiffel Tower. This was his father's home turf, and the neighborhood held his family roots.

"This view could change my whole opinion of both Denise Caxton and Bryan Daughtry. It's really cool that they left the old tracks in place." He turned and noted the Plexiglas doorway that led out of the gallery onto the tracks.

"Hey, Coop, someday after me and Daughtry have put our differences aside, I'll walk you and Mercer out that very door, onto the tracks, and take you as far downtown as it goes. Tell you stories about real gangsters and show you where the bones are buried."

"We're down here, Mr. Chapman. As long as you've made yourselves at home, why don't you come tell me what you need?" Daughtry called up to us from somewhere a level or two below. I couldn't see him from where I was standing, but he had obviously been alerted to our arrival.

The catwalk around the edge of the upper floor was about four feet wide. The three of us walked around its perimeter until we came to a metal staircase that led down a level.

Here the space extended out over the track below, and there were couches and sitting areas that faced various exhibits on the vast walls that ringed the gallery.

Bryan Daughtry and another man were seated facing each other in brown leather armchairs. Daughtry stood to reach for Chapman's hand.

"Let me guess," Mike said, looking at two yellow columns positioned next to each other and representing some sort of sculpture. "*The Cat in the Hat?*"

"Shall I read to you from our brochure, Detective? 'A minimal freestanding work, this kinetic fiberglass piece conveys a charming, vertiginous uncertainty.' Like it? Or do you prefer the one behind me? A very creative new fellow—uses beeswax, hazelnut pollen, marble, and rice to make sculptures, as we say, 'of mute yet implacable force.' "

"Come to think of it, my apartment looks fine with a couple of NFL posters, a slightly used baseball signed by Bernie Williams, and an eight-by-ten glossy of Tina Turner that Miss Cooper gave me. Your stuff makes me wanna puke."

"Shall we go back up to my office?" Daughtry asked.

Mercer and I started to follow him. Mike stretched out his arm to Daughtry's companion, who remained seated as I started to walk away.

"Hi. Sorry to break this up. I'm Mike Chapman. Homicide. You are . . . ?"

The attractive dark-haired man, who I guessed to be about forty years old, stood up and smiled, returning the handshake. "I'm Frank Wrenley. How do you do?"

"Well, well, well—Mr. Wrenley. And how do *you* do? Tell you what—c'mon upstairs with us. I got a few questions for you when we're done with Mr. Daughtry."

"Of course. I assumed you'd want to talk to me about Deni. I'm happy to try to help."

Mercer whispered to me as we walked to the narrow staircase, "You and Mike go at Daughtry. I'll baby-sit Wrenley till you're done, so he doesn't make any calls while he's waiting. This is a rare opportunity to get him when he wasn't expecting us."

Mike and I settled into the dealer's office with him. "Like I told you, we got a warrant to go through your gallery and warehouse. A team of detectives will be here shortly to do that. You can make this real easy on yourself if you wanna give us most of what we ask for, which are Deni's business records and belongings, access to the contents of Omar's locker, and things like—well, look at the papers for yourself.

"We'd also like to look through some of the paintings you've got stored here."

"Anything in particular you're looking for? Your taste in art, Mr. Chapman, is so hard for me to define."

"Got any Rembrandts on hand?"

"So you're joining the search for the mythical Holy Grail, too? Everybody's looking for the big score. You've got a better chance of winning the lottery than finding that missing painting."

"Then you won't mind if we look, will you?"

"Certainly not."

"Had you and Deni talked about it? I mean, about *The Storm on the Sea of Galilee*?"

"Many, many times. But so did everyone else in our business."

"Seems to me," Mike said, "that if I were an ex-con sitting on a hot item, my best bet would be to contact somebody else in the same shoes. I wouldn't be likely to walk into a classy operation where they might give me up to the Feds just for talkin' to them, but I'd sure be likely to sniff out some creep who'd done time and was completely amoral."

"What do you want me to say, Detective? 'Sticks and stones'?"

"Look, we know someone offered Deni the Rembrandt. And we even know about her meetings with Marco Varelli, to authenticate the chips."

Daughtry met Mike's stare head-on. "That's the oldest trick in the book, Mr. Chapman. Varelli is dead. Don't expect me to believe he summoned you to his bedside just before he had the big one. I doubt you ever spoke to him. Not much of a talker, that man. Try me again, harder this time."

"Lowell Caxton told us about the hijacking of the Della Spiga paintings last June. Said to ask you why it made Deni so crazy."

"Well, I assume the disappearance of a truckload of any artist's work would make his dealer berserk. Caxton Due represented Della Spiga. The whole thing was rather odd. Nobody ever saw who stole the truck, so we don't even know whether or not the thieves were armed. Deni had actually rented an eighteen-wheeler from a soda delivery company so the truck would be inconspicuous on the highway. After the drivers made a stop for coffee on the thruway, they came out of McDonald's and the truck had disappeared."

"Never found it?"

"To the contrary. It was found the next day, abandoned behind an old factory upstate. Not a thing missing. Either the thieves didn't like Della Spiga or they were looking for cola and not art."

"What did Deni think?"

"That first night? She was wild. Figured it had to be an inside job, someone who knew she was shipping fine art but disguising the delivery truck. When every painting was found intact, she calmed down and assumed the hijacking was just a coincidence. Amateur soda swipers foiled again."

"So maybe somebody did think she had the Rembrandt and was slipping the stolen painting in with the transport of the Della Spigas?"

"One might have thought that to see how upset she got. But of course, Detective Chapman, the police who found the truck went through it and listed every item on it. No Rembrandt recovered. And Deni was far, far too relieved the next day to have been missing one great masterpiece."

Mike jumped back a year in his next question.

"That trip to England that Lowell made alone the June before—the one that broke the marriage apart. What were you and Deni up to that kept her away, that kept her so busy here?"

"Try as you might, Chapman, you won't mix me in

this soup. Whatever it was, Deni never let me in on it. But you're right, it was serious. Whoever called her, whoever contacted her—someone made an offer she couldn't refuse. She withdrew from me completely and was very secretive. It bothered me at the time, but after a few days she changed her mind and went off to join Lowell. You obviously know the rest. I didn't think any more of it. Figured she'd been onto a deal and that it must have fallen through. Happens all the time in this business."

The receptionist buzzed on Daughtry's intercom to tell him that more detectives had arrived.

Chapman stood up. "Why don't you show my guys around?" Then he bent over the desk, the top of his fists pressed against the leather blotter. "Remember, it ain't just me you gotta worry about, Mr. Daughtry. Mess with the cops and you've still got the boys on Eleventh Avenue to deal with—Knuckles Knox, Stumpy Malarkey, One-Lung Curran. They got ways I couldn't get past the Supreme Court in six lifetimes."

When Daughtry left the room, I turned to Mike. I was steaming. "Who the hell are you talking about? Bad enough I don't know what you do when I'm *not* standing next to you. You can't threaten people like that, and I can't stand by and let you do it."

"Not even once? I've waited a lifetime to say that to somebody. 'Battle Row,' this block used to be called. Those guys, Knuckles and Stumpy? Real hoodlums— used to scare my old man to death when he was a schoolboy. Relax, blondie. That gang broke up around nineteen thirty-two. Six feet under, all of 'em. Did I sound like Cagney? Did I scare you?"

Mike stepped to the doorway and motioned to Wrenley to come into the office and sit down. I introduced myself.

He was dressed in black from head to foot—collared polo shirt, linen slacks, tasseled loafers—and his jet-colored hair was slicked back, every strand in perfect placement. I guessed it was his style, not an expression of mourning.

"Hope you don't mind some questions about Denise Caxton," Mike began. "We understand you and she were quite close." The edge in his voice with which he had addressed Daughtry was gone. It was clear to me that he was hoping to get Wrenley's help with more personal information about the past year.

"Not a secret, Detective. I'd met Deni two or three years ago. After she and Lowell had their blowup last year, our relationship became more intimate."

"You didn't mind the competition?"

"Her husband, or do you mean Preston Mattox? I understood what it was about. Deni was just a kid when she hooked up with Lowell Caxton. She'd been faithful to him throughout the marriage, and don't think there weren't lots of opportunities for her to have a fling. After he embarrassed her with that episode in Bath, she was more than ready to spread her wings.

"And besides, she was still married to Lowell. She wasn't very anxious to tie herself down permanently so quickly. We both seemed to get all the pleasure we needed out of each other's company, professionally and personally."

"I take it you're single?"

"Always have been," Wrenley answered.

"How'd you and Mrs. Caxton meet?"

"When I moved most of my business interests to New York—"

"What's the business?"

"Antiques. High end. Furniture, silver, nineteenth-century for the most part."

"Where'd you move here from?"

"Palm Beach, Detective. Grew up in Florida, in the Keys. Set up shop there, but I was always on the road. Auctions in England, France, Italy, and of course, New York. I still keep a place on the water down there, but I live here now.

"I saw Deni long before I met her. She was hard to miss—not just her looks but her spirit and energy. Always in the chase for a great find, and in those days, something to show Lowell how much she had learned from him."

Mike tried the man-to-man thing. "Never came on to her before she split with him? Never asked her out, called her, till after the Bath scandal?"

"I never called her then, Mike. It was Deni who called *me*. We'd been to auctions together and gotten to know each other a bit. I'd asked her for advice about paintings when I was making acquisitions for particular clients. Nothing social. After she flew home from England that time, she was determined to make a statement to her friends back here. Called me and invited me to go to a couple of dinner parties with her. It almost began as a game, for both of us. I never imagined I'd fall in love with her, nor she with me."

"What was the story with the other guys?"

"There were lots of men pursuing Deni. I'd have been an idiot not to think that would happen. I suppose my most serious rival was Preston Mattox. Had an airtight way of getting under my skin."

"Why Mattox more than anyone else?"

"Ever hear of something called the Amber Room?"

"Yeah," Mike answered. "Know all about it."

"Mattox was convinced that Lowell Caxton had smuggled some of the panels out of Europe and had them hidden somewhere. He's an architect, world-class. Deni said he had this dream—you ought to talk to him about it—of creating his chef d'oeuvre with remnants of the room. I don't know whether he was interested in *her* or in what she could lead him to. But that possibility made her furious whenever I suggested it.

"Look, I'm on the road a lot of the time. I never expected her to sit home doing her needlepoint, waiting for me to come back to town. She knows—sorry, she knew—that I dated other women when I was in Europe, and that was fine with her. She'd been tied down too long to care about that kind of thing right now."

"So, what brings you here?" I asked. There was nothing in Daughtry's world that seemed remotely connected to the nineteenth century.

"I wasn't invited to Deni's funeral, as you probably already know. Bryan and I are old friends, and he knows how devastated I was by her death. I just wanted to talk, reminisce, try to make some sense of it. May I call you Alex? When you catch the bastard who did this, Alex—" Wrenley paused, then dropped his head and shook his hand back and forth, as though asking us to wait a few moments before he spoke. "No point in my going on. There's nothing you can do to him in a court of law that would resemble any kind of justice.

"The newspapers said the police thought she was sexually assaulted. Is that true?"

"Probably," Chapman answered.

He lowered his head again. "She was so loving, so—God, I can't bear to think of any animal touching her, hurting her." Again he paused. "There must be something I can do to be useful."

"Let me have your numbers," Mike said, taking his notepad out of his pocket. "There's a lot more I'm gonna need to talk to you about as this thing unravels. As soon as we sort through some of the business records and evidence that's developing, I'll give you a call and set up an appointment, okay?"

Wrenley removed a business card from his wallet, added his home telephone to the number on it, and passed it to Chapman.

"Want me out of the way here? Sounds like you've got things to do with Bryan."

"D'you know that Mrs. Caxton was being black-mailed? Threatened by a man in prison?"

"Sure I did. It terrified her. She was convinced Lowell was behind it."

"Got any idea why she hired that guy Omar and had him working here with her?"

"It made me furious, actually. Bryan can tell you. I had dozens of arguments with Deni about Omar. And I wasn't sorry to see him turn up in a ditch, Mike. But she thought it was her best protection against Lowell, sort of an insurance policy."

"She'd have been a very rich widow if Lowell had died first, wouldn't she, Mr. Wrenley?"

"Take a trip with me to Palm Beach, Mike. You want rich widows? I didn't have to come to New York to catch myself one of those, if that's your implication. They're as thick as palmetto bugs down there."

"Sorry about Denise, Mr. Wrenley." I offered my hand as he stood up to leave.

For the rest of the afternoon, Bryan Daughtry led the detectives through the beginnings of a painstaking search of the art inventory in the gallery and adjacent warehouse. I sat in his office as he produced much of the documentation requested in the subpoena, reading and xeroxing stacks of bills and papers, the endless figures blurring my vision by the close of the day.

"You guys need me for anything?" I asked Mercer at six fifteen. "I'm supposed to go to dinner and the ballet tonight, if you can carry on without me."

"Scat. We'll grab some chow when we leave here, and see if we can catch up with the Crime Scene guys at Varelli's studio. I'll leave a message on your machine if we find anything interesting. You around tomorrow?"

I was tired, dismayed by the dead ends we kept meeting in this case, and glad the following day was Friday. "I'll be in all day. I've got a ticket on the seven-thirty evening flight for the weekend, but I feel guilty leaving you with all this hanging."

"Nothing you can do, Coop, till we give you a perp. Be on that plane. We'll be talking to you before that."

I went out to my car, squared the block, and fought the tunnel traffic of Jersey commuters going north on

Tenth Avenue to begin their ride home. After I passed the entrance, I continued up to Sixty-fourth Street, turning to park in the cavernous garage below the Lincoln Center complex. Although the Metropolitan Opera House was usually dark during the month of August, there was a gala performance this evening, with pieces that the ballet company was staging for an international tour that was about to begin.

There were tiered sections in the underground lot, each identifiable by an enormous band of colored paint that wound around the walls of that area. In my fatigued state, I kept trying to think of a memory device to help me recall that I was directed up the ramp to the red-striped portion of the garage, and parked in the fifth row away from the door, behind a column boldly labeled 5.

I joined the line of patrons to prepay the parking ticket and took the escalator upstairs. Natalie Moody and her party of friends had already been seated in the Grand Tier Restaurant, below the immense Chagall mural looking out over the plaza. The group was ordering their dinners as I arrived, so I chose the grilled salmon and we chatted and ate before moving downstairs to take our seats in the orchestra.

Few things are as capable of transporting me from the images of violence that permeate my working days as is ballet. I have studied dance for almost as long as I have walked, and have continued to take lessons as both a form of regular exercise and a medium of escape from some of the seamy underside of life that I encounter on the street. Had I had the talent, I would rather have been a prima ballerina with American

Ballet Theatre than almost anything else in the world.

So I sat back in my seat, ready to take refuge in this fantasy world, as the crystal chandeliers rose into the ceiling of the opera house and the curtain went up on the first piece. Victor Barbee made a rare appearance to partner the exquisite Julie Kent in a pas de deux from *Swan Lake.* The audience responded wildly with more than six curtain calls, and for half an hour I forgot about Denise Caxton. The second act featured Alessandra Ferri with the dazzling Julio Bocca in the balcony scene from *Romeo and Juliet,* and I lost myself completely in the perfection of their pairing.

There was a sparkling *Rodeo* with Kathleen Moore and Gil Boggs, and a final intermission before the corps was going to perform the "Kingdom of the Shades" from *La Bayadère.* It was after ten thirty, and I told Natalie I needed to get a jump on the crowd and head for home. I was afraid the Minkus music and the endless line of white-tutu'd Shadows would lull me to sleep in my seat.

I dug into my seemingly bottomless pocketbook for the Jeep keys, reminding myself that I had to relocate the red-striped parking area, behind column 5. The walk back to the car seemed farther than it had on the way in, but it was four hours later and I was really dragging. There were plenty of gaping spaces between the automobiles, I noted to myself, and it usually displeased me that so many suburban ticket holders walked out of the theater before the end of the event. Tonight I was one of the guilty leave-takers.

I started the engine, flipped on the headlights, and backed out of the space, heading over to the end of the row toward the ramp down to the exit. As I made the wide turn, a sport utility vehicle larger than my own careened around the adjacent line of cars and came racing at me, head-on.

My foot jammed the gas pedal to the floor and I swerved to the left, speeding down lane Red 4 as the chase car followed closely on my tail. I saw an opening midrow, where two spaces had been created side by side as well as back-to-back, and I barely braked as I nosed the Jeep into a curve and an immediate second left turn.

The dark car in pursuit took the long way around, and I could see that it was skipping two rows to try to cut me off at the top of the ramp.

I was pressing on the horn with my left hand as I steered with my right, hoping that someone would be annoyed by the blaring honk. A Jaguar with two couples in it pulled out in front of whoever was trying to cut me off, and I lurched ahead, hoping to see a security guard at the foot of the incline, where the giant red arrow merged with the equally wide yellow and blue stripes.

Instinctively, my foot hit the brake as a caution, and I immediately recognized that even a second's delay could be a costly mistake. But I had hesitated as I always did when leaving that garage, choosing between the exits on the north and south sides of the building, depending on which one was open at a given hour.

Just as I decided to make the right turn and go out onto Sixty-fourth Street, where there was a bus stop and, always, a posttheater crowd, the dark chase car came roaring down the steep rise of the garage behind me. Its driver passed me on the left side and cut me off. His engine still running, a male figure with a stocking cap over his head opened the door and got out, running toward me with the gleam of something metallic in his hand.

The empty sport utility vehicle was between me and the mechanical arm of the barrier that would have been my escape. As he slammed his left hand on the hood of the Jeep, I juiced the gas again and jumped the curb of the divider that separates the entrance from the exit gate. My Jeep kept going, smashing against the retractable arm of the entry blockade and cruising up the hill to the wide flat pavement of Sixty-fourth Street.

My repeated pounding on the horn cleared the crossing of pedestrians who were out for a summer stroll on Broadway. I paused to make sure the traffic light was with me, then goosed the car across the busy intersection, never stopping for a moment as I raced through the Central Park transverse and reached the East Side.

# 18

"You're not going home alone tonight, Coop. End of story."

It was midnight, and I was sitting at the corner table in the front of Primola with Mike and Mercer. The third Dewar's had failed to calm me.

After I had driven through Central Park, I headed directly across Sixty-fifth Street to my second home, the Italian restaurant where I frequently entertained my companions for dinner. I knew that even at eleven o'clock, Primola would be full of people, so I parked at a fire hydrant in front and ran inside to find Giuliano, the owner. He was my friend, and just as important, he was a soccer player who had competed on a World Cup team several years earlier. If he was between me and the door, I'd be perfectly safe until reinforcements arrived.

I told him that someone crazy was following me, so he sat down at my table, asked Adolfo to get me a drink and Peter to bring over the phone. I dialed Mercer's beeper number and inhaled the scotch as I waited for a callback. He and Mike had just left Varelli's studio and were sitting in a bar in SoHo, eating dinner and enjoying their first cocktail. It took them half an hour to get uptown to meet me. Once they arrived, Giuliano left us alone to talk, and Fenton, the bartender, kept sending rounds over to the table.

"Obviously, I didn't want to go home alone. That's why I called to tell you what happened. But if you two deposit me there and lock me inside, I'll be fine." I live on the twentieth floor of a high-rise building with two doormen, and pay dearly for a great sense of security once inside.

"Why didn't you just go right to the station house, instead of coming here?"

"Because then there'd be a police report, and then somebody would call the tabloids, and then Battaglia would have me under lock and key for the next month."

"You don't even know who you're looking for, blondie. I've had blind victims who've given me a better scrip than you have."

"It's awfully hard to give you a description when the guy's wearing a mask and gloves."

"I think it's time for a slumber party. One of us is gonna hang with you overnight."

Mercer took it a step further. "And besides that, you are on the very first plane to the Vineyard in the morning. That is, if you're not going to be by yourself up there this weekend."

"Clark Kent's booked in for a visit, Mercer. Ace reporter for the *Daily Planet*. She's dumping us for some news jock, m'man. What time of day do they start flying those tin cans?"

Either the liquor or the scare I had just experienced made the idea of a weekend in the country even more attractive than it had seemed earlier in the day. I had completely neglected matters like the sleep clinic investigation for the more pressing problems of the Caxton murder, but I'd push that one back another week as well. "There's an eight A.M. out of LaGuardia. Probably overbooked this time of year. I'm not sure I'll get on."

"Know how much pleasure it would give me to officially bump some investment banker off that flight?" Mike asked. "I'll take you out there myself."

I looked at my watch. "Make you a deal. Let me call David Mitchell. If he and Renee are home," I said, referring to my next-door neighbors, "I can sleep on their sofa, and they can drop me at the airport on their way to the Hamptons in the morning. You two have better things to do, okay? Try solving this mess before anyone else is killed."

My call awakened David, as we knew it would, but he was more than gracious. Renee made up the sofa bed while Mike parked my Jeep in my garage and Mercer escorted me up to my own apartment so I could grab my robe as well as a shirt and pair of leggings to wear in the morning.

"Want me to wait while you pack things to take with you to the country?"

"I've got everything I need up there," I said, as I gave him a hug and opened the door to David's apartment with his spare key, which I kept in my dresser drawer. "Thanks. Call me if anything happens before I see you on Monday."

I undressed, took a steaming hot shower, and wrapped the terry robe around me. I was too jumpy to sleep, but I turned out the light and rested, with their dog, Prozac, curled up by my side.

We left the apartment at seven, and David walked me in to the gate to make sure I got on the flight. There were the usual number of no-shows, and ten minutes before takeoff I boarded the thirty-seat Dash 8 and fell asleep for the short flight to the Vineyard.

I had a monthly parking spot at the airport. It was a brilliantly clear day and a good ten degrees cooler than it had been in the city all week. I put the top down on my little red Miata and drove up-island to Chilmark, to the house.

Once I passed the crest of the drive, where my friend Isabella Lascar had been killed, the gray-shingled farmhouse came into sight and, beyond it, the stunning view of Vineyard Sound, which never failed to take my breath away. This is the one place on earth where every tension I have dissolves, and where I have spent the happiest hours of my life.

My caretaker had unlocked and prepared the house for me, and I went inside to open the windows, settle in, and see what messages were on the answering machine.

The first was from Nina Baum, calling late last night from California. Chapman had phoned to tell her about the incident in the garage, and she was checking on me as well as urging me to get on a plane and come out to Malibu until the investigation was over. Nina, by luck of the draw, had been my college roommate freshman year at Wellesley. She remained my closest friend, and she and her husband were often my refuge when I wanted to hang out away from the problems that my job presented.

The message I'd been waiting for was next, the voice of Jacob Tyler calling from an airport phone booth. "It's Jake here. Can't find you anywhere—all I get are machines. It's Friday morning and I'm on my way to the Vineyard, if that's still the plan. I've gone from China to California, then an overnight in Chicago. I'm due into Boston before noon. And if there's no fog, should be on a Cape Air hop that gets me there at one thirty. I'll try your office in a bit. If you're not at the airport, I'll just take a cab up to the house. Miss you."

I took the portable out onto the deck and dialed Laura's number.

"Alex? Are you okay? Mercer left a message on my voice mail telling me not to expect you today. Is everything all right?"

"It's fine. I'm just whipped. We worked late last night, so I'm taking a long weekend. If people are looking for me, you can reach me on the Vineyard. Anything interesting yet?"

"Jacob Tyler called first thing. He didn't leave a message, 'cause I couldn't tell him what your plans were. And Robert Scott, from University of Virginia Law School. Wants to know if you can do a lecture about public service this fall."

"I'll take care of Tyler. Would you call Bob Scott back and tell him I'd be glad to, if he can suggest some dates?" Maybe I would tell the students about last night's encounter. What the D.A.'s Office lacks in financial rewards, it makes up for in drama and intrigue.

I changed into shorts and a T-shirt, set the dining room table for two, went out to the barn to get bird-seed to fill the feeders, and sat back down on the deck to read the *New York Times* and the *Vineyard Gazette*. The osprey nest at the foot of my hilltop, on the side of Nashaquitsa Pond, had a nestful of babies, being hovered over by their mother. Goldfinches and cardinals fought for the seed I had just put out, and my wildflower field teemed with the pink, lavender, and white heads of cosmos and the cobalt blue of Oriental poppies.

This was the place that I considered my home. Professionally, I thrived and flourished in the fast-paced life I led in New York City. Most of my friends were there, and I had been born and raised in a suburban village in nearby Westchester County, so my parents and brothers were frequently in and out of town. But this island, especially the quiet rural end on which my house was sited, was where I came to relax and to restore the tranquillity that eluded me in the midst of an intense investigation.

Most of my life had been a charmed one. I was one of three children—the only daughter—of loving parents whose marriage was still not only a sound one, but a great romance as well. The trust fund endowed by my father's invention, the Cooper-Hoffman valve, had been used to give me a first-class education, first at Wellesley and then at the University of Virginia School of Law. It permitted me to indulge my dream of working in the public sector without the enormous burden of student loans that forced so many of my colleagues to leave the prosecutor's office for more lucrative careers. And for frivolous interests like travel and my collections of first-edition books and antique jewelry, it was a route to some indulgences that I would never otherwise have been able to afford at this stage in life.

While the Vineyard had offered me some of the most spectacular days of my life, it also held for me my most difficult memories. Adam Nyman, the physician I had fallen madly in love with while I was at law school, had summered here all of his life. When we became engaged the year that I graduated, we bought this house together. It had belonged to the widow of a fisherman whose family was one of the original group of settlers in the seventeenth century. I had delighted in having it redecorated in celebration of our wedding. A local artist had stenciled the walls in pastel designs she had copied from a set of antique hand-painted Limoges plates my mother had given us as an engagement gift. The evocative landscapes by island artists that Adam had collected over the years had been reframed and hung throughout the cheerful rooms.

Our families and friends had been assembled in the homes of friends and country inns around the island for the wedding weekend. The house and its gardens had never looked more beautiful than during that lush summer after an unusually rainy spring.

And then came the morning phone call that ripped my spirit and heart to pieces. Adam had completed his last rounds in Charlottesville and had set off late in the day to drive all night for the trip to the island. It was my mother who took the call from the state police, and it was she and Nina who sat me down on my bed to tell me that Adam's car had been knocked off a bridge in Connecticut by another driver and demolished on the rocks in the river below.

Everything sealed up inside me for years, or so it seemed at the time. I had been afraid to let myself get close to anyone else for fear that something I loved would be seized from me when I was happiest. I went aimlessly from room to room in the house on those rare weekends I could bring myself to come up here, imagining how Adam would have adored what I had turned it into for us.

The ten years that had passed did nothing to lessen the pain of his loss or to make less vivid the depth of our passion for each other. But I had learned to love again, without ever forgetting that I would have sacrificed all the other pleasures and triumphs of my life to have had this time with him.

I had made changes in the house, too. Something had nagged at me to create a different feel, a sense of another phase of my relationships. So the previous winter I added an addition with a larger living room, a huge slate-trimmed hearth, and tall windows open to the handsome sweep of sea and sky. And with Nina's urging, for her upcoming Labor Day weekend visit, I had the architect build a new bathroom, decadently luxurious, with a steam shower and whirlpool tub. Slowly it had become possible for me to be here without any longer feeling that I was betraying Adam's love for me.

Now I found myself looking at my watch every ten minutes, filled with anticipation about the arrival of Jacob Tyler, with whom I had serendipitously become entangled in early July. Less than two months later, I sat here daydreaming about seeing him again this afternoon, excited by the pleasure he gave me, emotionally and physically, and still palpitating from the newness of the romance.

I read the papers, knocked off the Friday crossword puzzle, and called the office to make sure everything was still quiet. I wasn't a cook, but there was an easy trick to serve an elegant Vineyard dinner with no effort at all, and I set about making it happen before Jake arrived. A phone call to the fish market to order a late-afternoon pickup, a stop at the Chilmark store for island corn and tomatoes—at the peak of perfection at this point in the summer—and I was off for the twenty-minute ride to the airport to meet Jake's plane.

Cape Air's one o'clock from Boston was the only flight due in when I arrived. As usual, not many people were leaving the island on a Friday in summer, and several locals waited with me for the nine-seater to come into range. The tiny plane first appeared as a small dot in the cloudless blue sky, and circled out over the south shore before coming in for a landing. I could see the crown of Jake's thick brown hair emerge from the door first as he bent down to get out onto the steps that the pilot had lowered. He picked up his head to look for me behind the arrival gate and broke into a wide smile when he saw me standing on a bench against the chain-link fence, waving at him with both arms. His suit jacket was slung over his shoulder and hooked by the finger of his left hand, and he blew a kiss to me with his right hand when he touched ground.

When he reached where I stood in the waiting area, next to the luggage rack, he dropped his briefcase, took me by my shoulders as he said, "Hello, angel," and kissed me for what seemed like three minutes. My head nestled in the crook of his elbow, and I closed my eyes and stood still to savor the feeling of his embrace.

"Got room in that little car for a duffel full of dirty clothes? It's hard to travel light for ten days in China." Jake had covered the presidential summit in Beijing for NBC and had been traveling for almost two weeks on his way there and back. We had spent a weekend on the Vineyard before he took off, and our communications had been frustratingly erratic since then, between time differences and our unpredictable schedules.

"I'm thinking of giving up prosecution and taking in laundry. I'd be delighted to start with yours, Mr. Tyler."

"Bad week? I couldn't seem to catch you anywhere, no matter when I called."

The suitcases were off-loaded to the luggage rack, and Jake lifted his bag out so we could walk to the car. I carried his jacket and briefcase under one arm, taking hold of his left hand with my right. "You'll get a full report this evening. I've been ordered to take today off, so if you don't talk to me about the gross national product or global warming or the Japanese commodities market, I won't bore you with the twists and turns in my murder case."

"There's nothing boring about it. What's been happening?" he asked, as I opened the trunk to put the bag inside.

I put my index finger up to my lips, whispered "*Ssssss-sssssssshhh,*" and slipped behind the wheel of the Miata. "I'm taking you for a ride. Just relax and enjoy the scenery."

We left the airport and started up-island. After about a ten-minute ride on the South Road, I turned the car off onto a wide-mouthed dirt drive, unmarked and unpaved and full of rutted holes that threatened to devour the small car.

"Am I being kidnapped?" Jake asked, tousling my hair. "Nobody at the network will ransom me, you know. Take me away now and you'll be stuck with me forever."

The brush was thick on both sides of the way, and we bounced along the winding path for more than a mile until we came to a fence attached to two wooden posts, which seemed to be standing on guard in the middle of nowhere. I took a key from the glove compartment, got out of the car to unlock the gate, drove through, and locked it again behind us.

"Where the hell are you taking me?" he asked with a laugh. "I'm exhausted. Quite frankly, I was hoping for a long, hot shower in your fancy new digs, and then—well, something in the way of a warm welcome stateside."

"I promise you'll feel like a new man after this. You've got to trust me."

After a few more seconds I went around a bend, and ahead of us we saw the flat stretch of the dusty

long green grass of the wetlands, and a pond populated only by a handful of swans. Beyond that were the
rolling dunes of South Beach, merging into the wide-
open expanse of the Atlantic Ocean.

There were a couple of other cars parked at the
entrance to Black Point Beach, on one of the most
exquisite summer days. "What's with the gate and
key? Where is everybody?"

There are only two states in the country, Maine and
Massachusetts, in which you can own beachfront
property to the mean low-water mark. As a result, the
Vineyard was dotted by vast lengths of ocean beaches
that were privately held and not accessible to the general public. This was one of them—more than a mile
in length—and I had bought a piece of it when I purchased the house, more than a decade ago.

"Better than a shower. Let's go for a swim."

I parked the car, grabbed two towels from my tote,
and ran to the footpath that led over the dunes, kicking off my moccasins and telling Jake to do the same
with his loafers. We reached the peak together and
stood looking out at the wide belt of white sand and
the white-capped blue water that seemed to go on
forever.

"Great, Alex. You think I didn't see enough of the
Pacific, that I needed this today?"

"Don't be such a grouch. Get those rags off you—
c'mon, hurry up."

"There are people—"

I lifted my sunglasses and peered down the beach.
"It looks like there are maybe four stick figures
between here and Edgartown," I said, turning to Jake

and unbuttoning the business shirt that he had worn on the plane, while he stood with his hands on his hips. I reached for his waistband, drew off his belt, and unzipped his pants.

"Well, I guess if they won't recognize that you're the sex crimes prosecutor from the big city, they won't have a clue that the tired, naked guy you're molesting is a newscaster." Jake finished taking off his clothes while I lifted my T-shirt over my head and dropped my shorts on the sand. I ran down to the water's edge, hesitated for a moment as the cold surf dashed against my feet, then dove into the sixty-eight-degree water and started swimming straight out, away from shore.

By the time I picked my head up and turned back to look for Jake, he had overtaken me with a strong crawl stroke.

"Isn't this glorious?" I asked. I swam to him, wrapped my arms around his neck, and we played our mouths against each other as we bobbed in the endless roll of waves.

"I feel like I'm about fifteen years old—and I like it."

There was nothing quite like the sensation of the brisk salty water against bare skin. Swimming naked in the ocean ranks among the world's best pastimes. I set myself a course parallel to the beach and swam back and forth until I had done almost fifty laps. The undertow was getting more fierce as the tide started going out, so I reluctantly dove under a big breaker and went up on the sand to join Jake, who thought the water was too cold for a long swim.

"I'm exhausted just watching you."

"Harrison High School swim team. Hundred-meter crawl and anchor of the relay. Don't ever try to get away from me by taking a water route." I stood behind him, steadying myself on his shoulder as I put my shorts back on.

"I'm not going anywhere anytime soon," he said, grabbing my knee and kissing the still-damp back of my calf. He pulled on his trousers and we walked slowly over to the car, arms entangled, drying in the breeze as the early afternoon wind shifted and kicked up a bit.

Once on the main road again, I was conscious of driving too fast and tried to slow myself down. The outdoor shower was behind the house, its oversized head curtained only by a couple of old lilac bushes. I soaped up and washed off all the sand before going into my bedroom through the sliding door off the rear deck.

Jake did the same, following me in and pulling me toward him, onto the pale blue cotton sheets that covered the bed. "If dreaming counts, then I've made love to you over and over again all these last two weeks—in hotel rooms, on airplanes, every time I closed my eyes."

"It doesn't count at all," I said teasingly. "I didn't feel a thing." I reached an arm across his chest and he raised my face to his, his tongue reaching in to taste mine. He ran his hands up and down the length of my thighs as I wrapped my leg inside his. We kissed and rolled and laughed and touched for as long as we could both stand to, and then Jake entered me and told me that he loved me.

246

For the next hour we rested on the cool sheets while I explored the surfaces of his body, which seemed so pale next to my own.

"Aren't you going to answer your phone?" he asked me when it rang.

"Let the machine get it."

"Coop? It's me. Are you okay? Nothing urgent, but I wanted to make sure you got up there without any trouble. I started beeping you an hour ago but—"

It was Chapman's voice speaking into the recorder, so I grabbed the receiver from beside the bed. "Hi, Mike. Sorry. Yeah, I'm fine." For some reason that I didn't understand, it made me feel uneasy to be lying in bed with Jake while I was talking to Mike, with whom I had had such a close and complicated relationship for so long.

"For chrissakes, why didn't you call us back? Me and Mercer have been worried about you after last night. Whaddaya trying to scare us for?"

I glanced over at Jake. I hadn't yet told him the story about the week's events. "I apologize. Actually, I never even heard the beep. I stopped off at the beach for a swim and left the beeper in the car. My fault—I won't do it again."

"Don't tell me, Coop. Your new man's into that *From Here to Eternity* crap. Burt Lancaster and Deborah Kerr on the beach, waves washing up over them as they make love on the shore. That it? Too much sand in the crotch for me, kid. I'd rather—"

"Grow up," I snapped into the phone as I slammed it down on the table.

"Friend of yours?" Jake asked jokingly.

"A very good one, actually. One of the detectives on the Denise Caxton case."

"Remind me not to cross you. Why did you hang up on him?"

"Some other time," I said, leaning back and caressing Jake as I did.

"Have you made a reservation for dinner? I'd love to grab a nap before we go out."

"Even better. I thought you might enjoy a good home-cooked meal."

Jake looked over at me and raised an eyebrow. "Now I'm really confused. What time zone am I in? Who *are* you?"

"While you're resting I'm going to sneak out for half an hour, and by about eight thirty tonight we'll have a candlelit dinner for two." I wasn't proud of the fact that I couldn't cook, but it was the truth.

"A little more exercise, and then you might lose me for a few hours," Jake said, pulling me over on top of him and starting to arouse me again. "Put every one of those bad guys out of your mind, Alexandra Cooper. This weekend you're all mine."

When I finally rested in his arms, half an hour later, we both fell sound asleep. Shortly before six o'clock I showered and dressed and headed down the road. In the little village of Menemsha, less than ten minutes away, I could forage for an entire gourmet meal with no more effort than a few phone calls and a quick ride.

My first stop was the Bite, where I picked up a steaming quart of clam chowder and a side order of the world's best fried clams. True to form, the Flynn sisters had the most-up-to-the-moment island gossip.

"Heard you got a real looker with you for the weekend. Is it really that guy on the evening news?" Karen asked.

"He hasn't even been out of my house yet. Who's spreading this one?"

She pointed at her sister. "Jackie's best friend works at the Cape Air counter. She called as soon as you picked him up. Bringing him for lunch tomorrow?"

"What, and lose him to one of you two? See you."

A quarter of a mile farther, I pulled into the narrow space beside Larsen's Fish Market. One of the best services on the island was provided by Betsy and Chris. You could call in the morning, place an order for lobsters, and pick them up at the appointed hour—all cooked, split, and cracked—ready to serve and eat. I could place them in the oven to keep warm, and then serve up the two-pounders anytime I wanted. I went next door, to Poole's, for a few fresh oysters from Tisbury Great Pond. Last stop was the Homeport Restaurant, right on the edge of the harbor, where I stopped at the back door and bought a Key lime pie from Will for dessert.

When I returned home, I shucked the corn and put the water up to boil, poured the chowder into a pot to reheat it later on, and tucked the pie into the refrigerator to keep it chilled.

It was almost eight o'clock when Jake woke up, shaved and showered, and dressed for dinner. The red ball of the sun was setting off to the west as we sat on the deck and sipped our drinks. I listened to the details of the China trip and Jake's descriptions of the meetings he'd had, the personalities he had met, and the opinions he had formed during his travels. For me it was fascinating to get inside a world so foreign to my own, and to contrast the problems of the witnesses' lives in a single criminal case to the global problems he studied every day.

I disappeared into the kitchen to stir the pot, lit the candles in the dining room, and opened a bottle of '91 Puligny-Montrachet. "Why don't you come in and sit down?" I asked, dishing up the thick chowder and carrying it to the table.

With Smokey Robinson singing in the background, we feasted on the delicacies of a Chilmark summer, talking and laughing as we devoured the food. As best as I could I tried to explain the events of the week since Deni Caxton's death, walking Jake through the steps of the investigation to date. "No more of this tonight or you'll have bad dreams," I said, pouring decaf with a serving of the pie.

"Have you made any plans? Outing us to any of your pals this weekend?"

"Everyone, Jake. It's August on the Vineyard—I don't have much choice, do I?" The usually tranquil island more than quadrupled in population with summer people, and it was an opportunity for me to be with friends from all over the country—some of whom I rarely saw all winter—when I came for a weekend or vacation.

"What's the drill?"

"We're teeing off with Janice and Richard at Farm Neck, eight A.M. Louise Liberman and Maureen White are giving a cocktail party in the evening, and we're invited to stay on for dinner." It had amazed me, when

Jake and I first met, to discover how many people we knew in common. Those with whom I had social relationships of long standing, he had gotten to know through his position in the media. Somehow it made us seem even more connected than the short months we had known each other would indicate. I looked forward to letting everyone see how happy I was to be with him.

"Will the president and Mrs. Clinton be there tomorrow night?"

"Not sure, but I know they're invited. I hope so."

"Let's clean up this mess and go to sleep."

I held his face and kissed him on the forehead. "Go inside. This is the part I do really efficiently. I'll join you in ten minutes."

By the time I cleared the table, loaded the dishwasher, and straightened up the kitchen, Jake was spread-eagled, face down on the bed. I folded my clothes and placed them in my armoire, slipping in beside him and raising the comforter over us against the soft night wind that always makes my hilltop such an easy place for sleeping. I don't remember any tossing and turning after my head came to rest on the pillow.

I was startled by the sharp ring of the telephone. Light was just appearing on the horizon as I picked it up and spoke softly into it. It could not have been much later than 6 A.M. "Hello?" I asked somewhat disoriented, perhaps by the hour, perhaps because of too much wine with my dinner.

"Alex, it's Mercer. The lieutenant insisted on me calling you. Said you raised a stink last time you read it in the newspaper without a heads-up from us."

"Don't worry, he's right. What is it?" I sat up as Jake raised his head and rested it on his elbow, massaging his eyelids with his thumb and middle finger.

"West Side—Eighty-sixth Street. Our man just hit again early this morning, about an hour after midnight. Got a twenty-year-old kid going into her building. Raped her, beat her up pretty bad when she tried to resist. I hate to do this, but can you come on back into town?"

# 19

I got out of bed, made the coffee, dressed in jeans and a blazer, and sat on the deck while Jake unpacked his golf clothes from his duffel and got ready to leave the house.

"You sure you don't want me to go back with you?"

"Of course not. It's a sin to leave anything as beautiful as all this unless you have to. You've got a lot of friends on the Vineyard," I said, "and tonight, when I finally crawl into my bed at home, it will give me enormous pleasure to close my eyes and think of you being right here, wrapped in my sheets and looking out at this view.

"I'm the one who feels guilty, promising you a weekend together and then flying off-island to go to work." I was worried that the unpredictability of my job and its all-consuming nature when I was working a big case or a complex trial would put Jacob Tyler off, as it had done other men.

"Hey, if a guy with *my* schedule and lifestyle can't

relate to this, then you'd have something to worry about."

The airport was on the way to the golf course, so he dropped me at the terminal, kissed me good-bye, and I promised to be careful and stay in touch. There was no direct service to New York on Saturday morning, so I took the next Cape Air flight to Boston and called the Special Victims office to tell Mercer that I'd be on the ten-thirty shuttle.

With runway delays and air traffic, it was after eleven thirty when I got through the gate at the Marine Air Terminal.

"Sorry, Alex. Sounds like you were planning a nice couple of days. Hate like hell to pull you away from it."

"You know that's never a problem. How's she doing?"

"She'll be okay. She's got a lot of guts. Tried her damndest to fight him off. She saw the gun but didn't think it was real, so—"

"That's some chance to take," I said.

"You're not kidding. She grew up in Florida, around handguns. So she felt pretty comfortable with her guess. Maybe she was right. The guy stuck it back in his waistband and started to pummel her with his fists."

"Completed rape?"

"Legally, yes. He penetrated but he didn't ejaculate. So there'll be no DNA on this one."

The elements of the crime required penetration of the victim's vagina, however slight, for the charge to be rape. Most victims had no reason to be aware of this technicality, so many would tell us that the assailant "tried" to rape them but hadn't completed the assault. In fact, the insertion of the defendant's penis, whether or not he completed an act of intercourse, was all that was needed, by law, to accomplish the act.

"Where are we going?"

"She's down at headquarters now, working on a sketch. The lieutenant figured you'd want to get as detailed an interview as soon as possible, so that's where we'll do it."

"What time did she leave the hospital?"

"I got called at home and went over to Roosevelt Hospital at three. Treated and released. Had a head-to-toe exam, and one of the advocates stayed with her the whole time." The Rape Crisis Intervention Program run by the hospital was one of the best in the city. Like most others, it was underfunded and staffed by volunteers, but the quality of the care and service was superb.

"I took her home so she could clean up and rest for a while, then picked her up at nine this morning to take her to One Police Plaza."

The NYPD had a unit of detectives whose specialty was the artistic re-creation of likenesses of defendants, the police sketches that were made into Wanted posters and distributed throughout the neighborhood at risk or the city at large. Some preferred to work freehand, and others used computer-generated programs that assigned a particular feature from a description provided by a witness or victim. Every nuance, each subtle distinction, led to a thickening of facial hair or a change in shape of an eyelid. The results in many cases eventually proved to be almost photographic reproductions of the attacker's face.

In this instance, with a serial rapist, the artists had already produced several composites. And although each one resembled the others, there were variations that were reflective of the circumstances under which each woman saw the man who committed the crime. This witness would add her own detail to the pictures that had already been circulated.

"You think it's too much for her if I go back over everything with her today? Can she handle it now?" I asked Mercer, trusting his judgment and knowing the sensitivity that he brought to this work.

"I didn't push her. Thought if you and I did the questioning together at once, we'd get whatever we need, and she'd have to explain it all one less time. She's game, Alex. Determined to get this guy and put him behind bars forever." He had pulled away from the curb and we were headed for the Brooklyn-Queens Expressway and the bridge to Manhattan. "I promised her I'd find him and that you'd make sure he never sees daylight again. She's really eager to talk to you."

So much had changed in this business, just in my professional lifetime. Women, who had traditionally been reluctant to report cases of sexual violence, were now far more likely to come forward, as society lifted the age-old stigma on victims who cried rape, and began placing the blame where it belonged: on the offender. Still, those who were attacked by strangers and not acquaintances were believed more readily and were far more likely to be victorious in the courtroom. Paul Battaglia, who was passionate about this issue, had devoted resources to prosecuting these cases that no other office in the country could match. Whether the assailant was a date, a relative, a spouse, or a professional colleague of the victim, we had a mandate to vigorously investigate and take to trial the case of any credible witness who deserved her day in court.

"Guess you didn't get much rest last night," I said. Mercer looked exhausted. He had worked all week on the Caxton case, which relieved him of other duties at the Special Victims Squad. So he had not caught new cases, but he was still the one they beeped when the West Side rapist struck. He had been assigned to that task force from the outset, and the lieutenant counted on his skill in relating to victims, as well as his ability to remember the similarity in modus operandi—language, actions, order of the sexual acts—that would help coordinate all the cases in the pattern.

He laughed. "First night in weeks I had some companionship in the form of a warm body, other than Chapman. I don't think I'd been home an hour when I got the call." He took his eye off the road for a moment to look over at me. "This job can't do much for your love life either, can it?"

"I'm in no position to complain after you gave me the day off yesterday." I spent the rest of the ride telling Mercer about my evening with Jake and how relaxing a single day away from the city had been.

"Did anything important develop on Caxton?" I asked, as we parked behind headquarters and walked up the long sets of steps from Park Row to the front of the building.

"Bits and pieces. The manufacturer of the ladder

found the lot number of the one that was attached to the deceased. Sold last spring to a hardware store on lower Broadway. We got them checking receipts now. Not going to be any kind of surprise if it came from her own gallery. Wouldn't have been unusual for Omar to have one accessible to him. You'd need to use them to install all the art and exhibits.

"And we located Preston Mattox, the architect boyfriend of Deni's. He was abroad on business all week. Gets back here today. Said he'd give me a call so we could speak to him about her this weekend."

"What did Crime Scene come up with on Varelli?"

"The studio was clean as a whistle. Someone got in and out without leaving a print, or else they polished the place up before they left. Nothing appeared to be disturbed. Only thing that looked out of place was a pair of sunglasses."

"Prescription?" I asked optimistically.

"Not so lucky. Could belong to anybody, but they're just a bit too mod for the old man. And there is a young apprentice who worked for Varelli. He's been home in California all month, visiting his family. He wasn't due back here until after Labor Day. But he's apparently distraught, so he's coming in tonight to see the widow. We can interview him on Monday.

"Also, Caxton's lawyer came up with more of the letters that Denise had received from her blackmailer. Mike didn't see any point in taking them to the lab for fingerprints. They'd already been handled by too many people for us to get anything off them. He copied them for the case folder. Said he'd take a set home to read this weekend."

We had gone through the security checkpoint and were in the elevator heading upstairs to the artists' unit.

Josie Malendez was sitting with two plainclothes detectives, eating a roast beef sandwich and drinking a can of soda. She smiled as she saw Mercer enter the room, and I struggled to show no reaction as I looked at the large purple bruise that had swelled and caused the closing of her left eye. She squinted at me from the good one and held out a hand. "You must be Alex Cooper."

Mercer and I let her finish her lunch. We examined the sketch that resulted from her session with the detectives. "She gives him a rounder face than the last two. Thinner mustache, same eyes, same nose. And she's adamant about the lisp. Slight, but it's there. She's the first one to mention anything significant about his speech."

"She's the first one to engage him in as much conversation, trying to talk him down, talk him out of it, isn't she?" I asked, relying on Mercer's knowledge of the details. "And she was stone sober—unlike the last two—which makes me want to trust her observations even more. They giving this one to the press?"

"Yeah. The commissioner and the mayor want it for the six o'clock news. Any objections?"

"Nope. Ask them to use the same quote from Battaglia's comment, the one he gave last time the guy struck. It got lost in the coverage of the bomb scare story that broke the same night."

We knew that for a rapist to be operating in the same geographic area for more than two years, it had to be, for him, a comfort zone. Clearly he was some-one who lived or worked in the neighborhood and could move about it easily without seeming to be sus-picious. If the police and scientific techniques did not break the case, our best hope was that a neighbor or coworker would notice a resemblance to the sketch and call the hot line with a tip. The most difficult thing to overcome was the stereotypical reaction of most of the public—that the guy who lives next door couldn't possibly be a rapist.

When it appeared that Josie had finished eating and had a few minutes to rest quietly, I went over to sit with her and began to talk, to explain the process. The detectives who had worked with her on the drawing excused themselves, and Mercer replaced them at the table, ready to take notes of our conversation.

Our questions had to be more specific than those that had yet been asked. While the physician who had conducted the physical needed answers to what kind of contact had occurred and what Josie had experi-enced at her attacker's hands, and the uniformed cop who responded to her home had asked for the broad outlines of the criminal event, Mercer and I began our probe in microscopic detail. Things that frequently seemed insignificant to the victim were crucial to our ability to put the puzzle together, and often to link one case to another. I always started the process by explaining to the witness why such seemingly irrele-vant minutiae could be useful to us.

And so we went on, asking Josie to explain her whereabouts all throughout the previous afternoon and early evening. While her actions may have had nothing to do with what happened on her front doorstep, we could not eliminate the possibility that she and her assailant had crossed paths earlier that night, or that he had followed her from one location to another.

The original police report, as in most cases, had summed up Josie's assault in a single sentence: "At the time and place of occurrence, the defendant displayed a pistol, beat the complaining witness about the face with his fists, causing physical injury, and thereby forcibly engaged her in an act of sexual intercourse."

Almost four hours after we began to talk with our victim, Mercer and I were ready to wrap up the interview. We knew exactly how the rapist's approach had been made, where Josie was in regard to him when she was first aware of his presence, the precise language he had used when he accosted her in the vestibule of the building, and how she had responded to him. We knew in which hand he had held the weapon, and what about its design and appearance had allowed her to assume that it was an imitation.

The process was inordinately draining on the witness, and we were keenly aware of that.

"Can you think of anything else that we *haven't* asked you that you think we should know?"

"Not a thing." Josie's fatigue was obvious.

"Are you going home tonight?" I asked. It was almost six o'clock.

"No, no. I'm not ready to go back there alone. My sister lives in Brooklyn Heights. I'm going to spend some time with her till I figure out what I want to do."

"That's smart. I'm sure the counselor at the hospital told you, but these first few nights are going to be hard."

"I know. The doctor gave me something to help me sleep."

"Yeah, but even sleeping doesn't always provide an escape. You may have dreams—nightmares, actually—and flashbacks. You'll see people on the streets who will remind you physically of your attacker, and you may have a visceral reaction—tremble, recoil, cry. All of these things are normal in light of your experience. And believe it or not, time will truly make it better."

"And finding this son of a bitch will be the best of all," Mercer assured her.

One of the detectives who had done the sketch was driving home to Bay Ridge and said he would deliver Josie to her sister's apartment. I walked with her to the restrooms down the quiet hallway, and waited while she went inside. In a few minutes, from where I stood, I could hear her sobs coming from within. I opened the door and found the young woman leaning against the sink, running a finger over the discolored portion of her thin face as she stared at her almost unrecognizable image in the mirror.

I walked to her side and placed my arm around her shoulder. She turned and pressed the unharmed side of her face against me, her chest heaving as she tried to speak but couldn't catch her breath to do so.

"Don't try to talk. Let it go, Josie."

Her body became deadweight in my arms as she cried for several minutes. She pulled away from me and washed her face again in the sink. "Whew. I hadn't shed a tear until now. I was so intent on following everyone's directions and being cooperative, but there's nothing left in me to give. It's like he took everything away from me."

"You're alive, Josie, and that's the most important thing. Whatever you did last night was the right thing, because you walked away from him in one piece. You'll triumph in the end. The hard part is catching him—that's Mercer's job. Convicting him, with a witness like you, won't be difficult at all. We won't let you down—I can promise you that."

I led her back to the detectives' office. Mercer told Josie that he'd be in touch with her on Monday to set up an appointment to look through mug shots of sex offenders, and we said good-bye to her.

"We've got to figure out what to do about *you* for the rest of the weekend. Battaglia thinks you're safely tucked away in the country."

"Drive me home and I swear to you I'll stay at the apartment all day tomorrow. Sleep in, read books, watch old movies. Nobody knows I'm in town. It'll be heaven."

Mercer called his office to see if there were any messages, but there were none. Then he checked the Homicide Squad to see if any of the witnesses expected in town had phoned to leave word for Mike Chapman.

The civilian worker who answered the phones at Manhattan North said there were two calls during the afternoon. Mercer listened to her relay the messages and asked her to let the lieutenant know he was on top of both situations. Then he repeated the news to me.

"Preston Mattox is available to come into the office on Monday afternoon to meet with Mike and me.

"And Marina Sette called. Didn't leave a number, because she said she'd had to check out of her hotel after receiving some threatening phone calls. She didn't know how to get in touch with A.D.A. Cooper, so she asked if Mike or I could meet her tomorrow morning."

"Where? In your office?"

He looked down at the notes he had scribbled in his pad. "Said she's staying with an artist she knows in Chelsea. There's an exhibit being set up for an opening later this week in a brand-new gallery called Focus. It's in a renovated warehouse on Twenty-first Street, a block away from Deni's place. She'll be waiting in the office at the back of the exhibit, Sunday morning at nine. And she wants me or Mike—whoever keeps the meet—to bring you along."

"Why me?" I didn't mean it seriously. But my visions of languishing in bed with the Sunday *Times* crossword puzzle were dissipating quickly.

Mercer looked up from his pad. "Ms. Sette says you're the only one she's comfortable talking to, the only one she trusts. Says she's come up with information about Denise Caxton's murder that she thinks you'd really like to hear."

# 20

I called the Four Seasons Hotel and the front desk confirmed that Marilyn Seven had checked out first thing this morning.

"You want me to invite Chapman to go with us tomorrow?" Mercer asked.

"Let him take his mother to Mass. I think we got on each other's nerves yesterday. If you don't mind doing this without him, I'm game."

"Why the mystery from Ms. Sette, do you think?"

"I don't know. She was very secretive about Lowell Caxton not knowing she was in town. He had no trouble guessing correctly that she was the source of some of our information. Anyway, she seemed to like creating a little suspense. Told me she used to be an actress, and I think she still has a flair for the dramatic. Hey, a little culture on a Sunday morning can't be too bad for either of us."

"On one condition. You let me sleep on the couch in your den tonight—consider it that you're saving me a long ride home, not that I'm baby-sitting. It'll make

Battaglia and the lieutenant happy, and give us a jump start in the morning."

"You're in charge, Detective Wallace. Do I get dinner before you lock me in for the night?"

"Seems to me I haven't had Chinese food in weeks. I could go for some Peking duck at Shun Lee Palace. How about you?"

"My mouth is watering. Give me a few minutes, I've got to make a call." I dialed my house on the Vineyard and Jake answered on the first ring. "How's the sunset tonight?"

"I'm sitting on the deck with my drink, ready to drive to Louise's for cocktails and dinner. How's your day been?"

"Long. We're just about to leave headquarters now. Mercer and I are going to have dinner together, and he's going to spend the night at the apartment. We've got a date in the morning with a skittish witness on the homicide."

"I'm glad he's going to stay with you. It's smart, till somebody knows what's going on. Tell him I'm insanely jealous, will you? I'll call you when I get home tonight."

"Give my love to everyone."

Mercer and I drove uptown and spent a quiet evening enjoying a good meal and the ambiance of the handsome dining room. We parked in the driveway in front of my building and Mercer left his police plate in the windshield so the car would not be disturbed overnight. We went upstairs and settled in, flipping channels on the television looking for something to watch and settling on CNN, until Jake called to give me a rundown on the party. I watched a bit more TV until I got drowsy enough to say good night and go inside.

When I awakened, shortly after seven, Mercer had already brought the newspaper inside and brewed a pot of coffee. "Slim pickings," he said to me as he surveyed the near-empty shelves of the refrigerator.

"Check the freezer. I've always got a package of English muffins in there."

While I showered, he nuked the muffins and put them in the toaster. We sat at the dining room table like a married couple, each coming out of the night's slumber at our own speed, buried in our favorite piece of the Sunday news. Mercer had his head completely immersed in the Sports section. I skimmed the book review, reading the "Crime" column to scout for new mystery writers, and checked the best-seller lists.

"You're not drinking your coffee," I said.

"I hate this flavored stuff. It's really a girl thing."

"It's Colombian cinnamon. I think it's delicious." I picked up the Arts and Leisure section and riffled through to find the write-ups on galleries and exhibits. "Here's a piece about Focus—the place we're going to this morning."

"What does it say?" Mercer was dumping the dregs of his cup into the sink and looking in my kitchen cabinets for a different coffee blend. "Mind if I make another pot of dark French roast?"

"Go ahead. Focus is described as a 'stunning new exhibition space dedicated to long-term installations of works of art that are unlikely to be accommodated by existing museums because of their scale and substance.' Apparently, like everything else in that neighborhood, the place used to be a warehouse building. It's massive—forty-four thousand square feet."

"Is it open yet?"

"Doesn't seem to be. There's a scheduled premiere the first week of September."

"Who owns it?"

I continued to scan the article. "Doesn't mention. This is mostly a description of what it's going to have, why it was built, how unusual it is." I paused to read on. "Hey, we're in luck. Ever hear of Richard Serra?"

Mercer shook his head in the negative.

"He's probably the greatest sculptor alive. Had a superb show at the Museum of Modern Art not too long ago. His work is set up now for the opening. Sounds extraordinary. Want me to read it to you?"

"Sure." Mercer was seated again, waiting for the new pot of coffee to be ready. He picked up the Sports section once more as I tried to describe the show at the gallery.

"It's called *Torqued Ellipses VI.* The concept grew out of Serra's fascination with ships and with steel. Are you imitating Mike Chapman, or are you going to listen to this?"

Mercer put down the paper and I showed him the photograph of the massive steel plates, more than a dozen feet high and several inches thick.

He was impressed. The pieces looked formidably strong, resembling curved hulls of three ocean liners split into a handful of pieces and laid out on the floor of the renovated space like a giant maze, covering more than eight thousand square feet.

"I thought you were talking about tiny little sculptures. These things look like the base of the *Titanic*. How does he do it?"

"The article says Serra contacted every mill in the world, until he found a machine that had been used in World War Two, at a shipyard near Baltimore called Beth Ship, that could roll and bend these huge pieces of steel plate. Each one of them weighs twenty tons."

"So I guess Ms. Sette picked a good spot to hold this conversation. She can tell us about the people running the place. Must be a friend who's letting her use it."

I went inside, ran a brush through my hair, and put on some lipstick. I had on a linen pants suit with ballet flats, casual but professional. The morning was overcast and the air-conditioning in the car and in the gallery was likely to be cool.

It was shortly before nine when Mercer drove into the quiet street. There were no residential buildings, a scattering of still-used warehouses, and four galleries that probably wouldn't open on a summer Sunday until after one o'clock, if at all. As Mercer parked, I pointed out the Hi-Line tracks that sliced through the middle of Twenty-second Street, north to south, rife with weeds, just as they had looked when they passed through the Caxton Due gallery and ran on downtown. It still surprised me that neither one of us had ever been aware of the tracks till we saw them when we were here with Mike the week before.

The entrance to the new gallery was quite discreet, a rectangular white sign with very small letters printed in jet black ink: *Focus*.

Mercer put his hand on the doorknob to test it, expecting to find it locked. It gave at once and opened into the dimly lit space. A young woman came forward and invited us in. "Good morning," she said. "I've been expecting you."

I recognized her immediately as the receptionist who had been at Bryan Daughtry's office on Thursday, when the three of us had gone there with the subpoenas. The face was less distinctive than the four silver studs in her right ear, the three in her left, and the small ring piercing one of her eyebrows.

I followed Mercer inside. "Is Ms. Sette here yet?" he asked.

"I'm not sure who's coming, exactly, but you're the first ones to arrive. I was told to be here to open the gallery and let the police officers in. You're welcome to look around. I'll be up front at the door if you need anything. Hope you don't get seasick," she said to me, smiling. "It's a really weird feeling inside those things."

Mercer and I stood at the prow of the first sculpture, which loomed over us like the hull of a great oil tanker. I rounded the corner and stood in the space between two ends of the first ellipse. When I looked back at Mercer, I couldn't help but laugh. It was so unusual to see any physical thing that dwarfed him so completely.

"What's it like inside?"

I stepped between the enormous curved surfaces and started to walk to the far end. It was immediately confusing and disorienting to the senses. I knew I was standing still on a flat surface, but the arrangement of the pieces made the entire thing feel out of proportion and dizzying. To my left, the structure bowed outward and was wider at the top, more than ten feet above my head. The one to my right sloped inward, and when I raised my eyes to see its top, I had a claustrophobic reaction, as though the entire steel frame might fall on me if I so much as brushed against it.

"Whoa, c'mon in, Mercer. It's almost like a brilliantly artistic fun house. I see what she was talking about—it's a very bizarre spatial illusion."

Mercer paused in the entry while I kept walking, about to exit the first ellipse and trail around its outer side to get to the second one, in which the side shapes were set up in reverse. Each of the five forms was angled in a dramatic fashion, different from the others. He caught up to me inside the third figure, bracing himself against a wall the reverse in shape from the last one, which surprised him so radically.

"Don't lean on it," I said, half jokingly. "Doesn't it seem like it would fall over and crush us instantly?"

Mercer was fascinated with the composition of the colossal steel plates, and stopped to bend and rub his hands up and down against the skin of the sculpture. "This mother isn't going anywhere, Alex. It must have been like moving a bunch of battleships to get it in here. Man's a genius."

He straightened up at a sound coming from the front of the warehouse space. "D'you hear that?"

"Sounded like the door closing. Let's go meet her." I moved to find my way out of the ellipse and toward the front of the gallery.

"Hold it. That noise *after* the door closed, that's what I'm talking about."

"I didn't hear it. I must have been speaking to you."

"Wait here, Alex. Let me see who came in."

Mercer passed by me, motioning me to stay put as he walked out of my line of sight.

I could distinguish the sound of the hard-soled bottoms of his loafers clicking on the concrete floor, moving away from me. I heard him call out "Hello," then pause and call it out again, but the words only echoed in the cavernous expanse of the room without eliciting a response.

"Oh, shit!" he exploded. "Hold still, Alex, stay there. I'm coming to get you."

I heard his first exclamation and started to run, screaming, "What?" as I did, until I heard his command for me to stop.

I was turned around inside this torqued ellipse, not certain where the front or back of the gallery would be when I emerged. I could make out the sound of what I thought was Mercer's shoes pounding toward me, and then something softer, perhaps rubber-bottomed, coming at me from another direction. There was nothing to hide behind or duck under within the shell of the sculpture, and I didn't have the least idea about whether there actually was an office in the rear of the exhibition space, and if so, whether it would be locked or open.

I was frozen in the same spot, accustomed now to the obscure lighting and the lack of contrast between the gray steel mammoths and the interior walls and ceiling. My yellow linen suit stood out against the dark colors like the bull's-eye on a target, and my head whipped back and forth, not knowing from which direction my friend would appear.

At the same moment as I saw Mercer's hand grab the end of the ellipse, I heard him yell, "Alex, DOWN! Now!" The discharge of his gun resounded like a cannon in the open space between the sculptures as he fired at someone I could not see.

I squatted on my haunches as though I were on the starting blocks of a relay, fingertips poised to lift me up and out the moment Mercer gave the next order. His single shot was met by a return salvo of two or three bullets, which pinged off the side of the steel almost even with the level of my head as I crouched and cowered.

Mercer's left hand reached around for me, and I moved to meet it. Without more than a glance, he grabbed me by the wrist and we started to jog in the direction of one of the other structures, Mercer's large frame running interference for me as we searched in vain for something that would provide a shield.

"It's your stocking-mask guy from the garage," he whispered, trying to catch his breath and check the gun that he usually kept holstered on his ankle.

"The girl?" I knew the answer before I asked the question.

"Dead." He stopped to listen for noise and heard none. "At some point I'm gonna signal you to run, and you're gonna move like a gazelle to get to that front door and call in a ten-thirteen."

Word on a police radio that an officer needed assistance was the universal beacon to summon cops to any emergency situation in which another cop's life was at risk.

"Not without—"

"That's movie bullshit, Coop. When I send you, you fly."

There was no point arguing. It was a decision I would have to make if an opportunity even presented itself to us.

Mercer stepped in front of me, practically flattening me against the side of one of the exteriors. He must have heard a sound that I had not picked up. He cocked his ear in the direction of its source and moved in a 180-degree arc as he turned to fire off another round. He swung back in front of me and waited for the return fire, as my sweaty palms pressed an imprint on top of the dark steel.

Now the padded footsteps had drawn closer, and I could actually hear them running across the floor on the far side of this ellipse, toward our position.

"We're moving," Mercer mouthed to me as he briefly turned his head to face mine. Again he took me by the wrist, and we dashed around into the sculpture we had stood behind, and through its far end, bullets chasing us and bouncing off the cylindrical walls as we zigged and zagged together.

I trusted that Mercer was trying to find his way to the front door. Despite the variety in shape and curve, every one of the steel walls looked identical to me. Their height and their solidity had become oppressive, and I tried to steady myself as I ran behind him, praying that he had maintained some idea of the relationship between these gigantic barriers to our freedom.

Pure silence again. Mercer bent his head to peer around the edge, then looked back at me and winked. His lips formed the word "now," and he tugged on my jacket sleeve to try to propel me out in front of him. With blind faith in his instincts, I broke into a trot and sped through the length of one more sculpture. At its far end, I thought I made out the doorway that led to the street and an escape. I looked over my shoulder to make sure that Mercer was coming along with me, and as I did I could see the expression of horror cross his face.

"Down!" he screamed at me again as he saw the gunman run into place behind my back, aiming at me from a site between me and the gallery exit.

Shots were fired from both guns, and someone shrieked in pain. I couldn't tell whose voice had cried out, but in the split second after hearing the noise, I bolted in Mercer's direction.

"Stay right here, Alex. I got him." Mercer's gun was in his hand as he overtook me and raced toward the masked figure, who was bent over from the waist and trying to run to the door. He seemed to be dragging his left leg.

I ignored Mercer's order and chased after him as he let himself out the door. When I was within ten feet of the front wall, I could see the body of the receptionist slumped over in a leather armchair, blood oozing from her forehead a fraction of an inch away from her pierced eyebrow. I stopped in my tracks, turning to kneel and check her for a pulse.

As I dropped to my knees, Mercer was edging himself to the long metal bar that pushed out onto the street. Suddenly daylight flooded into the huge space of the gallery as the door was pulled by someone on the outside. A burst of light exploded close to where I saw Mercer standing, at about the same time as I heard the noise of the discharge. The gunman had swung the heavy entrance open from the sidewalk and let off three more shots into the gallery.

Mercer Wallace collapsed to the floor without uttering a sound.

# 21

I picked up Mercer's hand and spoke his name with an urgency I had never known before. His eyes opened, and he tried to talk but could not.

"Thank God," I said. "Stay with me, Mercer. I'm getting help."

The doorway gave against my push and I was on the street. Three teenage boys were Rollerblading, heading westward to the piers. I had no idea where in the gallery I had dropped my tote and the cell phone I kept inside it. "Call nine-one-one," I shouted at them. "Please call nine-one-one—tell them a cop is shot. Please!"

One of the kids held his index finger and thumb together in an "okay"sign and skated off, I assumed, to a telephone on the corner. The other two came to the sidewalk and were only seconds behind me as I scrambled back to Mercer's side.

I sat on the floor next to his motionless body and tried to find where he was hit. His eyes flickered open and he attempted to follow the movements of my hands.

"Oh, shit," I said, both to myself and to the boys, who stood dumbfounded at my back, not knowing what to make of the dead girl and the dying cop. "Are you sure your friend's going to call nine-one-one? One of you should stand in front of this place so you can point it out when the police car comes." I was barking commands like a general. "Get out to Tenth Avenue. Flag down anyone you can find to get in here to help."

One kid took off but the other watched with fascination as I folded back the lapels of Mercer's jacket and saw the bullet hole that had torn through his clothes and perforated the left side of his chest, terribly close to his heart.

"Bad," Mercer mumbled as I held my ear over his mouth to better hear him. He opened his lips to say more. No sound came out as he turned his head away from me and his eyelids shut.

"Don't close your eyes, Mercer. Don't close your eyes, please." I could hear sirens in the distance and I kept on praying that he wouldn't lose consciousness, that I wouldn't see his eyes roll back into his head. I held one of his strong hands in my own, stroking his face and head, trying to keep him with me by talking at him ceaselessly.

"Listen to me, Mercer," I begged him. "I can hear a siren. They're on the way. We'll get you to Vinny's in three minutes. Stay with me, Mercer. You got that son of a bitch, now stay with me, please." Saint Vincent's Hospital was less than ten blocks away, with an emergency room well equipped to handle trauma like gunshot wounds.

I watched his chest move up and down, his labored

breathing giving off a low, rumbling noise from his throat. "Keep looking at me, Mercer. I'm gonna be with you through everything, just give me a chance. Breathe for me." I was wiping sweat off his forehead with my fingers as it dripped down both sides of his neck and into his eyes.

The smallest blader skated back in the door. "We got a fire truck, okay?"

"That's great, that's excellent. Hear that, Mercer? We got a truck coming in." I turned back to the kid. "Tell them we need an ambulance." He was gone again.

Mercer's mouth curled up on one side, as though he was trying to smile. I pressed the palm of his hand to my lips. Again I started babbling anything I could think of to keep him alert. I talked about Mike and about food and about the department and about how he could go to my house on the Vineyard for his recovery, and as I was rambling on to the next topic, four firemen in all their gear tore into the room and surrounded us.

I got up and stepped back, telling them that Mercer was a detective and that he had been shot at close range in the chest. Before I could finish the explanation, an ambulance had pulled up next to the hook and ladder parked in front of the gallery. I got lost in the commotion as the EMS team started an IV drip in Mercer's arm and loaded him onto a stretcher. As I stood on the sidewalk, five radio cars pulled into the block from both directions, responding to the call for assistance that each cop dreads most of all, for himself and for everyone else in blue.

Now I was just a hanger-on at the fringe of the

growing crowd. None of the officers who arrived knew me, and my identification and badge were somewhere in my bag on the floor of the gallery. I pushed the kids who had helped me out of the way, trying to explain to the cops who Mercer was and what had happened.

The EMS workers lifted the stretcher onto the rear of the ambulance, and as it tilted, I could see that Mercer's eyes were closed shut. "I'm going with you," I shouted over the heads of the firemen who were clustered around the wagon.

"Sorry, lady. You'll have to meet us at the hospital—Seventh Avenue and Eleventh Street." One of the men was getting into the driver's seat and the other was closing the first side of the double rear doors.

I squeezed ahead and climbed up onto the back running board. There was no point telling them I was an assistant district attorney. That fact, without any supporting identification, didn't buy me a ride on the ambulance. "I'm his wife!" I screamed at them. "I'm going with him." I ducked into the van, and the medical technician came in behind me and slammed the door.

I held Mercer's hand for the short ride, ambulance sirens blaring, as we were escorted to Saint Vincent's by three police cars leading the charge downtown.

I couldn't tell if the moisture on the crease near Mercer's left eye was perspiration or a tear, but a big drop formed and hung there until the shifting of the stretcher dislodged it as his body was removed and carried toward the entrance of the emergency room. He didn't open his eyes, not even for a moment.

# 22

"Stop beating yourself up over it, kid. He's a cop and you're not. Aren't we supposed to take bullets for the rest of you ungrateful assholes who delight in calling us pigs? *You* didn't shoot him. Some friggin' mutt who I should have alone in my office for maybe fifteen minutes . . ."

I had beeped Chapman even before I called the lieutenant and the district attorney. "It's my fault we kept the meet without telling you about it."

"Great, blondie. You wanted *me* pumped full of lead too, huh?" Mike had raced to the hospital, arriving within an hour of my call, and was waiting with me for word from Mercer's surgeon. He was white with fear about his friend's medical condition, and his fingers combed through his hair constantly—a sure sign of his agitation.

"What did you tell Spencer?" Mercer's father was a widower, retired from his job as a mechanic at Delta Air Lines. Mike had stopped by his home in Queens on his way to the hospital, to tell Spencer Wallace about the shooting.

"Man, that sucked. Better me than seeing some chaplain on your doorstep, like it was normal for him to drop in every week to pray for Mercer's well-being. I just didn't want his pop to hear it on the news later without some personal contact first. Might be the toughest thing I've ever done." Mike stopped pacing long enough to sit down on one of the institutional beige vinyl chairs in the waiting lounge and rest his head back against the neck cushion.

"Did he want to come here with you?" I knew Spencer had already suffered a mild stroke earlier in the year and had not yet fully recovered. But Mercer was the light of his life, and it tore me apart to think of how the impact of this event would pain him.

"Yeah, but I told him absolutely not. He just looks so weak to begin with, Alex, and I knocked whatever remained right out of his guts. His sister lives down the block, so I called her to come in to sit with him for the afternoon." Mercer had two ex-wives and no current steady. "Spencer was worried about you, too. He just looked at me and said that you and I are Mercer's family now. We're the ones to be with him today."

Mike was on his feet again, first circling the room, then walking out the doorway.

"Where are you going?"

"I got some calls to make. Sit tight."

"There's a phone right here. We can use my credit card number to get an outside line."

Mike ignored me and walked off. I understood the dynamic and knew that, as close as the three of us were, I was an outsider in these circumstances. The fraternity of police officers who put their lives on the line every day for the rest of us circles the wagons pretty tightly when one of their own is harmed. I had been there today with Mercer, but I had escaped injury. Most cops swear they would rather have given their own life than to have failed to protect a partner. I didn't carry a gun and would not have been expected to play the role that a police officer would play in this situation. But my heart was heavy with guilt knowing that I had drawn Mercer into a situation that had, perhaps, cost him his life.

"Are you Miss Cooper?"

The halls were swarming with cops—some of whom had responded to the news of a downed colleague, others of whom Mercer had worked with and had heard of the shooting through the department grapevine. The commissioner was coming back by helicopter from a weekend upstate, and the mayor was expected to arrive at the hospital within the next hour to visit Mercer's bedside.

"Yes, I am."

"Lieutenant Gibbons asked me to bring these to you. Thought you might need 'em." The young patrolman handed me a brown paper bag. Inside were my identification badge, wallet, keys, and cell phone. "Said to tell you that he had to keep the pocketbook and the rest of the contents to send over to Latent to be processed for prints."

I couldn't remember when I had dropped the bag from my shoulder, and even though I doubted the gunman had stopped to touch my belongings, I knew the routine investigation of a police officer's shooting would include the most painstaking details. This gunman would be found.

"Tell him thanks."

Chapman reentered the room. "Man, you don't want to set foot out in the lobby of this place. The hospital is crawling with reporters. Last thing they need to see is a bloodstained prosecutor, and Battaglia'll have you begging for a job with the Legal Aid Society's Baghdad branch office." I glanced down at the pale yellow suit now covered with blood from Mercer's wound.

"Maybe Mickey Diamond was right. Maybe his fictitious story saying we were close to a solution and an arrest made the killer nervous and drove him to the surface."

"Did you call the other emergency rooms?" I asked, pretty certain that the shooter had fled only because Mercer had nailed him in the thigh with at least one shot, and that the wound was serious enough to need treatment.

"That's a waste of time. He ain't walking into that kind of trap, if he's been this smart."

"Just do it. Remember the Trenta story?" I had handled a case a year before in which a burglar had surprised a woman in her apartment and, after stealing her money, demanded that she perform oral sex on him. As she kneeled on the cold linoleum floor in her kitchen and placed her mouth on the defendant's penis, she noticed that he put his knife down on the counter. So instead of acceding to his request, she bit him as hard as she could and kept biting as the defendant howled in pain.

An hour later, Harry Trenta walked into Roosevelt Hospital and asked to be treated for an injury to his private parts that occurred, he told the nurse, when he fell out of bed. She examined what she described in her notes as a "shredded penis"—a condition completely inconsistent with a fall—and contacted the local precinct to ask whether anyone had reported a recent attempt at a sexual assault.

As is often the case, we count on the stupidity of the perpetrators to make our jobs easier. In this instance, that kind of slip had not yet occurred. Mike didn't expect us to get lucky now.

"Someone else can take care of that end of it. I did check out Santa Fe. Marina Sette got back there yesterday afternoon. The airline can probably confirm that for us. In any event, my guess is that she was airborne when that call was made to the squad asking us to come to the gallery. So either she's a part of this—phoned from the plane or had someone else place the call for her—or whoever set it up knew she was unreachable all afternoon and that's why her name was used."

In the hours since Mike had arrived at the hospital, I had also brought him up to date on the contacts Mercer had told me about yesterday. Mike had made appointments to see Preston Mattox and Varelli's apprentice, Don Cannon, on Monday, but I also knew that he would not step outside the doors of Saint Vincent's—no matter how long it took—until he could see Mercer.

Again Mike was pacing. "Your faithful pal Mickey Diamond has a new one for his Wall of Shame." The

*Post* reporter papered the small pressroom in the courthouse with his front-page stories. "News radio's already calling this one 'Slaughter off Tenth Avenue.' No doubt they're gonna run that poor girl's puss all over the tabloids. What a waste of a life—she was just in the wrong place at exactly the wrong time. This guy is a monster."

Mercer had been in surgery for more than four hours at this point. Mike and I were running out of things to distract us. Every half hour brought a new wave of detectives who came by—to console, to pray, to offer blood or whatever aid was needed. The mayor and police commissioner had given their sound bites from the hospital lobby, urged all the citizens of New York to keep Mercer in their prayers, and moved on.

When two men in green scrubs that were stained like my suit entered the room smiling, Mike embraced me before they could speak. "Your partner's going to make it," one surgeon said. "We've just—"

"Well, what the hell took you so damn long to let us know?" Chapman asked. "We'd like to be with him." He was walking to the door while the surgeon was still talking, and I knew he was fighting back tears that he didn't want me to see.

"Mr. Wallace is still in the recovery room. Give him another couple of hours there, and when he gets to intensive care, one or two of you can be with him briefly."

Mike did not turn his face to me but said that he was going down the hall to call Mercer's father and give him the good news.

"I'm Alex Cooper. I was with the detective when he was shot. What was—"

"The bullet missed his heart by less than half an inch. Lodged in a bone just above it. But there was a huge amount of internal bleeding that posed an even greater danger. I think we've got it all taken care of, but the next few hours will be rough." He looked at his watch. "It's almost four o'clock. Why don't you go out and grab some lunch? Give the nurses a little time to get your friend settled in."

"We'll be here for a while, Doctor. I think we'd like to see Mercer before we do anything else." Mike and I weren't moving until we could be with him.

I thanked them for their work and they left me alone in the small room. I lowered myself onto a chair, put my head in my hands, and thought of all the promises I had made to God in these past few hours of things I would do differently and better if only Mercer came out of this okay. Every part of me ached, and I tried to relive the day, thinking of what might have happened had the two of us not gone to the gallery. The throbbing in my head was now a constant, and when it intensified, it reminded me of the sound of the morning's gunshots. I could not even imagine the physical pain that Mercer experienced when the shot ripped through his chest.

I reached into the paper bag and removed the cell phone, dialing Battaglia's home number. I was relieved to get the machine and not the person. I didn't need another rap on the knuckles, and I just left him the good news about Mercer and told him I'd be staying with a friend overnight.

Jake was booked on a seven-fifteen evening flight back to LaGuardia, the same reservation that I originally had. I couldn't find him on the Vineyard, so I left a message on my machine there and one at his apartment, telling him about the shooting and asking if I could stay with him for a couple of days.

Mike came back about fifteen minutes later with coffee for both of us and a deli sandwich. "Wanna split this?"

"No, thanks." My stomach was still roiling. "I need to apologize for snapping at you on the phone on Friday."

Mike's appetite was directly related to his spirit. He opened his mouth wide to get around the hero, which was stuffed with ham and provolone, lettuce, tomato, and onions. He garbled a "Never mind" through the food. "I know you're full of crap, blondie," he said when the first three mouthfuls had been thoroughly chewed. "Hey, you think I haven't been through this before? You just spent half a day praying over Mercer's soul, probably had to swear you were even gonna be tolerant of *me* in the bargain." He winked at me and shoved the sandwich back in his mouth.

"So, I spent yesterday reading Omar Sheffield's file." He was able to concentrate again. "He was really a pro at that scam. Whole bunch of complaints against him to the prison warden. Lowell Caxton may have been right. Looks like Omar hung with the jail-house lawyers. Pulled a lot of the divorce cases directly out of the *Law Journal*. One opinion, the judge even wrote which private school the two kids attended. Omar lifts the name of the school from the judge's decision, threatening that he could have the kids picked off on the sidewalk as they came down the steps after class. Wife went nuts, blaming the husband. All along it was Omar, with the aid of the honorable jurist."

"Didn't anybody arrest him for aggravated harassment?"

"Nope. Worst I can see is that he got box time." Put in solitary confinement for twenty-three hours a day, denied use of the library and any mail service. "Added a few months against an early parole.

"But the warden told me there's an even bigger problem now, with the Freedom of Information Act. Prisoners write to agencies like the Board of Elections, and because of the law they can ask for and get the home addresses of anyone they want. One guy just used it to get the new address of the ex-girlfriend he's been stalking for six years. I'm telling you, the lunatics are really running the asylum when it comes to the criminal courts." The last sentence was muffled by the remains of the sandwich and by Mike licking the mustard off his fingers before wiping them with a napkin.

"Any record of Denise Caxton in the visitor log?"

"Not that they've found yet. But I gotta go through it myself. Maybe she didn't even use her own name. Meanwhile, you given any thought to where you're gonna be spending the next few weeks, when you're not at work?"

I nodded my head. "I'll stay at Jake Tyler's apartment. Maybe you can swing me by my place so I can pick up some clothes."

"I'll get somebody to do it. I'm not leaving here tonight."

There was no point in suggesting that Mike do otherwise. He would be at Mercer's side throughout the critical hours, no matter how long they turned out to be.

It was almost six o'clock when a nurse came to tell us that she would take us to the intensive care unit. "He's sleeping now," she said. "Doctor said you wanted to see him. Then I'll take you to a place where you can be more comfortable."

Mercer had been placed in a cubicle directly opposite the nurses' station. I could hear a gaggle of monitors beeping before we reached the entrance to his room, which was guarded by two plainclothes detectives. I stood in the doorway and looked at his long frame, which filled the hospital bed completely. There were tubes coming out of his nose and intravenous lines attached to his forearm. He didn't move or respond at all to the sound of Mike's voice saying, "Hey, buddy," as he lifted the sheet that covered Mercer's chest to expose the bandaging there and stroked him gently on the blade of his shoulder.

"That's a lot of anesthesia he's got to sleep off," the nurse said. "I'll come get you in a bit. There's a room right over here."

She led us down the hallway and we resumed our vigil with the families of several other critically ill patients. Mike couldn't stand the company and the prattle of the anxious people. "I'll be in with Mercer."

"But there's no room—"

"I'll make room. I wanna talk to him." He shot me

a look that had the same effect as adding the word "alone" to his statement and walked away.

It was impossible to drag my thoughts away from the day's events. I was trying to ignore my pounding headache, and as I covered my eyes with my hands, I didn't notice the approach of the two men who planted themselves in front of me.

"Alexandra Cooper?"

I looked up as they palmed their gold shields and identified themselves. "Sean Iverson and Tom Bellman, Major Case Squad," one of them said, pointing first to himself and then to his companion. "We'd like you to come downstairs with us. Hospital director's given us a room to do interviews in. Just need to go over everything with you."

I stood up, gesturing toward the hallway. "But I'd like to be here with Mercer. We're waiting for him to—"

"We're not going very far, Alex. We'll get you right back up here when he comes around."

"Why isn't Homicide working on this?" I hadn't moved at all, and both men appeared to be annoyed. I knew I was getting paranoid, but I wanted detectives who knew me and loved Mercer to be working on this shooting.

"C'mon," Iverson said, turning his back on me. "They're not gonna give something like this to one of your pals. Chief of detectives brought us in on it." He looked over his shoulder and smiled at me. "He even mentioned that you might be difficult."

"I'd like to have Detective Chapman with me, if that's all—"

"And we'd rather *not* have him, if it's all right with you. He wasn't there, it's not his case, and we'd like to handle this our way, okay, Miss D.A.?"

Clutching my paper bag, I obediently followed the pair down the quiet hallway to the elevator bank and downstairs to a small office with a plaque on the door that read *Security*.

For almost three hours, Iverson and Bellman grilled me about everything that had gone on since my return to Manhattan from the Vineyard the previous morning. I had done this myself to thousands of witnesses in my ten years as a prosecutor, and I was as impressed as I was exacerbated by their demand for precision and detail. Over and over again they pushed me to recall every physical twist, movement, footstep, direction, and sound that had been made or taken in the gallery that morning with Mercer. I strained every one of my senses to re-create the scene exactly, certain from their implacable expressions that I was failing some kind of test that they were giving me.

When Iverson closed his notepad and stood up, I looked at each of them the way witnesses had looked at me so many times, wanting to know if the answers supplied had been good or correct. And I kept my mouth shut, knowing that neither man could give me that assurance.

"Tommy'll take you back up to intensive care, Alex. That's it for now, but later in the week we'll have to get you over to Twenty-first Street with us. Walk us through the place, okay?"

"Sure. Anything you need."

Detective Bellman and I had nothing to say to each

other on the way upstairs. He escorted me around to Mercer's cubicle and shook my hand as he said goodbye. Mike had pulled a desk chair from the nurses' station into the niche next to the bed, with his back to the door. He was leaning forward, his hand on one of Mercer's, and he was speaking in a low voice. I could hear him naming friends they had worked with and knew that Mike was telling war stories and reminiscing, just chatting at his silent partner. The position of Mercer's body had not changed at all since I had first seen him several hours ago.

"Hey, Mercer," Mike said, "Coop's back." Now addressing me, "Where you been, blondie?"

I told him about the interrogation. "These dicks must've worked her over pretty good, Mercer. She looks like shit. I just wish you could open your eyes right now and take a look at her. I oughta borrow one of your intravenous tubes, man—run a little Dewar's through it and give her some juice. Who's the team?"

"Iverson and Bellman."

"Dammit, Mercer. Get your ass outta that bed. I wouldn't let those two lightweights handle a bad check. They treat you okay, Coop?"

I shook my head up and down.

At about midnight, a policewoman from the Sixth Precinct came up to the nurses' station with a few containers of hot soup for Mike and me.

I walked it back over to Mercer's room. Mike was standing now, and I could hear him saying something about an administration.

"What are you talking about now?" I asked. "Can I spell you for a while?"

"Know how they say people in a coma can hear you? Well, if that's true and he's only sleeping off some gas, I'll be getting through to him before too long. I just want mine to be the first voice he hears. Remember my dictionary? I'm going through it with him now. Used to make Mercer so mad—especially if all the other guys were laughing when I did it—he'd be ready to punch me in the face."

Chapman always joked that he was going to sell a reference book to compete with the *O.E.D.*—the *Oxford English Dictionary*. He called it the *C.P.D.*—*Chapman's Perpetrators' Dictionary*—and he thought it should be printed and issued to every rookie in the department.

He took his seat by Mercer's side. "I'm only halfway through the *A*'s. 'Administration'—that's when a woman gets her period." Then he launched into an imitation of the high-pitched voice of a female witness. "'But Detective Wallace, I couldn't let him do the nasty to me. I was on my administration last week.'

" 'Athaletic.' Used interchangeably with the word 'epileptic.' 'Officer Chapman, you can't go arresting my brother. He be having an athaletic fit right now.'

" 'Ax.' What you do uptown with a question. 'Officer, let me ax you this . . .' You ever know anybody Irish or Jewish or Italian who axes questions, do you?"

"Alex, are you in here?"

Mercer's frail voice came at us from the other side of the bed, his eyes still closed, his head still facing toward the wall, and his words barely audible. Mike bounced up from his chair, grabbed Mercer's left ankle—which seemed to be the only part of him not hooked to any kind of medical device—and started kissing the sole of his foot. I answered "Yes," and we both bent over to get close enough to hear Mercer speak.

His lips pulled together to form a smile. "Will you get that racist son of a bitch out of this room?"

# 23

"Cold hit, Coop." I had just stepped out of the shower a few minutes after seven o'clock on Monday morning, and Jake handed me the telephone to take Mike Chapman's call.

"On what?"

"Bob Thaler just called. He said they got a match on the semen found on the canvas tarp that was in the back of Omar Sheffield's station wagon—the one that Denise Caxton's body had been wrapped in. Did it through the data bank."

"Cold hit" was the slang term that scientists used to describe what occurred when a computer made a successful comparison between DNA samples, linking a piece of forensic evidence to an actual human being.

The detectives did not have to submit names, latent prints, mug shots, or vouchers for hours of overtime legwork in order for this technology to work. The computer's ability to make a cold hit took only an instant.

Thaler was the chief serologist at the Medical Examiner's Office and had helped to pioneer this technology. The data bank had been established by the New York State legislature, and there were data banks in almost every state by the late 1990s. New York's was slowly being filled with the genetic fingerprints—DNA developed from a single vial of blood—taken from every prisoner in the state convicted of sexual assault or homicide. Like their latent print counterparts, these unique codes were becoming an invaluable tool in the solution of cases of rape and murder.

"Who's the match?" I asked.

"Anton Bailey. Convicted of larceny three years ago up in Buffalo. Did half of a four-year sentence and was released to parole eight months back."

"Then why was he in the data bank?" His blood would not have been taken for a crime like larceny, a nonviolent theft.

"That's just it. He wasn't in the New York base. Thaler had the Feds run it interstate and, sure enough, got a hit in the Florida data bank." The Sunshine State had passed the legislation before most other parts of the country. "Seems like Mr. Bailey had gone by a different name down South—Anthony Bailor. And Mr. Bailor did some hard time back in Gainesville. Put away at eighteen, for almost twenty years. Rape in the first degree.

"So it looks like Anton Bailey is the man who sexually assaulted Denise Caxton."

"And killed her."

"Talk about cold hits," Mike said. "If this isn't a straight-out sexual assault gone bad, then someone must have hired old Anton to do Deni in. That could be the coldest hit of all."

"Now all we need to do is figure how and where he came into this picture."

"Thaler's the only government guy whose office opens up at seven A.M. I'll get on the horn to State Correction after nine. Just thought you'd like to know first thing."

"How's your patient?"

"Restless night. He was in a lot of pain. But they're taking some of the tubes out today and hope to get him moved into a private room."

"Battaglia arranged a full security crew for me until this thing is over. I told him I already feel like I have a human straitjacket wrapped around me. They're driving me down to the office. Are you doing any interviews today?"

"If they have Mercer set up by the early afternoon, I'll call you so you can come up to the office with me. I'm beginning to think it's safer to let our interviewees drop by our place."

"What did you do about sleeping?"

"Not as cozy as you. Nurses let me curl up on a gurney in the hallway."

"Anybody I.D. the girl yet?" I asked, assuming the receptionist who opened the door for Mercer and me yesterday, whom I had first seen at Deni's gallery, could be a link to the killer.

"Yeah. Name was Cynthia Greeley. Twenty-three years old, from Saint Louis. Bryan Daughtry claims that most of the time she freelanced. He insists that it was Deni who hired the kid, not him. And that Deni met her when she was working for Lowell, on Fifty-seventh Street. Lowell thought Cynthia had too many pierced body parts to be working the uptown scene, so he was glad to let her go."

One more twisted path to unravel. "I'll get down to work and wait to hear from you. Give Mercer's hand a squeeze for me. Tell him I'll come over with you tonight. Need a place to clean up this morning?"

"Nah. I can shower at the squad. Change of clothes in my locker. See you later."

Battaglia had assigned two detectives from the D.A.'s Squad to accompany me from place to place for the duration of the investigation. I didn't like the restrictions it imposed or the waste of taxpayers' money. But he had given me no choice and had sent them to the hospital last evening. They had driven me to my apartment so I could pack a suitcase of belongings that would get me through the week, and then on to Jake's home, not too far from my own. Front-door-to-front-door service.

I had reached there in time to find Jake watching the news on CNN. It was after one o'clock in the morning. "Turn it off and I promise not to tell anyone at NBC that you were checking out the competition," I said to him when he embraced me at the door. "I don't want to hear anyone else's spin on the day, okay?"

I stripped my blood-soaked clothes off right there in the hallway and stood naked, offering them to him with both hands. "Take these to the incinerator and just throw them down the chute, would you please? I'm going to take a bath. I don't suppose you have anything that passes for bubbles here, do you?"

"No, but the bar's still open," he said, kissing the

tip of my nose. "If I can see through the steam, I'll bring you in a drink as soon as I've dumped these."

I soaked in the tub while Jake sat on the floor beside me, sipping his drink while I tasted mine. I told him how Mercer and I had walked into the trap that had been so carefully laid for us at the exhibit, and how terrified I had been at the thought of losing Mercer. Jake didn't interrupt at all as I went on and on, stepping from the tub into the bath sheet that he wrapped around me; then I shivered for the first time in days as I tied the belt of his white terry robe on my waist and sat on the edge of the bed to call my mother and let her know that I was okay.

I stared into the masked face of our gunman—seeing nothing—for what seemed like hours, until I finally fell asleep on my side, with Jake's arm resting on my shoulder.

At seven forty-five I was ready to leave for the office. "What's your day like today?" I asked Jake, watching him knot his tie and ready himself for the crosstown ride to the NBC offices at Rockefeller Center.

"Kind of like yours, in the sense that I won't really know until I get there. I'm supposed to be covering the secretary of state's speech at the U.N. Do I have to worry about *you* as well, or just nuclear warheads, civil wars, and an erupting volcano in the Antilles?" he said jokingly.

"Battaglia has me under lock and key. So, your beeper will call my beeper?"

"Count on it. See you tonight."

I was out the door and down the FDR Drive with

my armed escorts. The early arrival gave me time to catch up on the matters that had come in on Friday, when I had stolen the day to get away to the Vineyard. I checked my appointment book. One of the assistants had asked me to pencil in a re-interview at ten with her witness in a domestic violence case.

That gave me a couple of hours to return phone messages and speak with friends. As my colleagues began to arrive, many dropped by my office to see how I was, express their concern, and ask about Mercer, having heard accounts of the shooting on last evening's news. I finally shut my door to avoid a visit from Pat McKinney. There was enough salt in my emotional wounds without his venom added.

At ten fifteen I called Maggie to check whether her witness had arrived.

"She just called to cancel. Her husband offered to take her on a cruise over Labor Day weekend. She'd like to come see you when she gets back in two weeks. Guess she isn't quite as frightened of him as I thought."

That freed up another hour of the morning, or so I thought until Laura buzzed to say that one of the young lawyers from Trial Bureau 60 had been sent to discuss a new case with me. I opened my door and found Craig Tompkins waiting outside.

"Something different, at least for me. The intake supervisor thought you might have some ideas about how to charge this."

"What have you got?"

"The security guards over at the Javits Center are holding a guy, but I'm not sure they've got a crime to arrest him for."

"What did he do?" The Javits building was the city's convention hall and regularly the scene of large group meetings, trade association gatherings, and exhibitions.

"He signed up to attend this week's Trekkies reunion. Seems to have spent all day yesterday riding up and down the escalators, from floor to floor. Kind of got the guards' attention 'cause he was sort of goofy looking, carrying around a big gym bag the whole time, but never actually went into any of the lectures or conference rooms. When he came back in this morning, the head of security took a few rides up the escalator, right behind the guy.

"This jerk's got a video camera hidden in the bag. What he does is wait for a girl in a short dress to get on in front of him, then he rides up behind her, holding the camera so it shoots the view up her skirt. A thrill a minute, I guess."

"So what did they do with him?"

"Arrested him for harassment. Confiscated the gym bag and the video camera."

"Sounds right to me. What's the problem?"

"Well, they don't have any victims."

"What about the women he was filming?" In order to make out the charge of harassment, there would have to be people who would claim that the amateur moviemaker's conduct had annoyed or alarmed them.

"None of them ever realized what he was doing. They each just stepped off the escalator at the end of the ride, unaware that they had been immortalized on film. Then the security guys played back the videotape. Thighs, knees, lots of underwear—but nobody is recognizable from the angle of the shots. No way to figure out who they are."

I thought for a minute. "How about trespass? That he was unauthorized to be in the center."

"Won't work either. He paid full price for admission and that entitles him to be in the facility."

"Did he make any statements? Admissions?"

"Yeah, he gave it all right up. Married businessman from Connecticut, works for a public utility company there. Started doing this a year ago, just 'cause it turns him on."

"Talk about arrested development. Guess he never got past the sixth grade."

"Now he says he can sell them to a Web site. It's called U.S. Videos—only, the initials stand for 'Up-Skirt.' Lots of videocam voyeurs, he claims. Cops checked it out. Each tape sells for forty bucks."

"And that's exactly what's on 'em?" I asked incredulously. "I'm not sure there's anything criminal to charge him with. Let me call Mark." The usual response for any of us in the Trial Division when we were stuck on legal issues a lot thornier than this was to reach out for the head of the Appeals Bureau, our in-house lawman. We waited for his callback, which confirmed that there was no recourse in the criminal justice system for the Trekkie's actions. Craig used my phone to tell the Javits security force to let the guy go. The Internet was creating more opportunities for perverts than most of us had imagined, and law enforcement agencies were less aggressive than the cyber-geeks in coming up with solutions.

Mike called from Mercer's room at eleven thirty.

"Forget those surgeons you saw yesterday. There's a lady doc here today, and a posse of very attentive nurses, and I think Mercer Wallace is really on the mend.

"I'm gonna scoot up to the squad at one. The pain medication makes Mercer pretty sleepy. His father wants to sit with him this afternoon. Varelli's assistant is going to come in for an interview. Wanna be there?"

"Absolutely."

"I'll swing by and pick you up, since I'm so close to your office," Mike said. "Then I can bring you back here to the hospital tonight. The D.A.'s Squad can take over your chauffeuring duties from that point on."

I called the Special Victims Unit to see who would inherit the day-to-day work on the West Side rapist matter and was relieved to hear it was in the capable hands of two veteran detectives who had worked with Mercer for years.

Then I stopped at Rose Malone's desk so that she could see that I was physically unharmed and tell Battaglia that Mercer's shooting had not unhinged me completely. Now that I was an eyewitness to the attempted murder of a police officer, I knew that the district attorney would assign another prosecutor to take over at least that part of the inquiry, just in case the crime was unrelated to our probe of Denise Caxton's killing.

"Would you ask Paul to let me have a say in who McKinney assigns to Mercer's shooting?" I asked Rose when she told me that Battaglia had just gone to lunch.

"Sure. I know he won't get to it today. He's got to

polish up a speech he's giving tonight, and I don't think he'll have time to speak to Pat McKinney," she said, looking through the crammed schedule sheet that she kept on top of her desk.

"Great. If he wants me for anything, I'll be up at Manhattan North."

When I reached Laura's office to pick up my case folder and wait for Chapman, she told me to call Marjie Fishman, my counterpart in the Queens District Attorney's Office.

"Are you okay?" Marjie began the conversation.

I assured her that I was and gave her the update on Mercer's condition.

"You don't have any racetracks in Manhattan, do you?"

"No." I waved Mike in when I saw him standing with Laura outside my room.

"Well, we've finally got a situation that you haven't seen yet."

"Try me." There were days when my colleagues and I were sure there was nothing left that one human being could do to another that could shock us. And then, without fail, something else came along to prove us wrong.

"Last Monday, out at Aqueduct, a cop patrolling the stables in the middle of the night came upon, shall we say, an intimate encounter between one of the grooms and a horse. The defendant's name is Angel Garcia. The officer heard a loud thud, which was the sound made by the naked Garcia falling off the plastic bucket he'd been standing on."

"How's the horse?"

"The vet says she's fine. If you pass an OTB office on your way uptown, tell Mike to put some money on Saratoga Capers. Last Friday, after a thorough examination and clean bill of health, our horse came in third. That's her best start in weeks."

I hung up shaking my head in amusement, although I couldn't help feeling sorry for the poor creature. Fortunately, there were laws against inhumane treatment of animals, and Marjie's Special Victims Unit was prosecuting Garcia for abusing Saratoga Capers. Mike laughed out loud when he heard the story.

"Just feature sharing a jail cell with Angel Garcia," Mike said. "Every other prisoner has pictures of Cindy Crawford or Julia Roberts or *Penthouse* centerfolds on the wall. Meanwhile, Angel's got giant-size pinups of Trigger and Mr. Ed. Go figure. C'mon, blondie. Let's blow this joint."

"Wait a minute. Has anybody explored that part of Omar Sheffield's background?"

"Whaddaya mean? Horseplay?" Mike asked.

"Cell mates—just what you were joking about. When Omar was in the can doing time upstate, who did he share a cell with? Do we have any names?"

Mike stopped and double-backed to my desk to use the phone. "I don't think I asked that question. I'm not sure anybody did." He dialed the squad and reached Jimmy Halloran, a baby-faced cop who'd been on the Homicide Squad for more than a decade but looked like he was still in high school. Jimmy had been added to the Caxton team last night, after Mercer was injured. He bristled every time Mike called him by the nickname he'd been given by his team—Kid Detective.

"Hey, K.D.," Chapman said. "Squirrel around on the lieutenant's desk. See if you can find the paperwork on Omar Sheffield. You know, the bad boy who forgot his mother told him not to play on the tracks. See if anyone checked the names of his roommates in state prison. Coop and I are on our way uptown. If you don't find anything in the file, call up to the warden at Coxsackie and get some answers. And if they need a subpoena, call Cooper's secretary and she'll crank one out for us and fax it up for her signature. Make yourself useful." He hung up the phone.

"Where are you parked?" I asked.

"Behind the courthouse, on Baxter Street."

"Good. Let's slide out the back door. The fewer people I have to talk to about yesterday's events, the better off I'll be." We went downstairs and took the elevators from the seventh floor to the lobby, walking past the arraignment parts and the roach coach, as the building's snack bar was affectionately dubbed. It was half an hour before the courts recessed for the afternoon lunch break, so we navigated the hallways and went out onto the street without much delay.

As we walked into the squad office, Jimmy Halloran took his feet off the desk and stood to greet us, pointing out a young man who was reading a newspaper at a desk across the room. "That's your one o'clock. The guy from Varelli's studio.

"And those names you wanted from the warden? He said Omar Sheffield spent some of his time in solitary." Halloran looked down at his notes. "Had three cell mates while he was upstate. Kevin McGuire, who's done mostly burglaries, and Jeremy Fuller, who sold heroin to an undercover cop. They're both still in jail."

Again, he glanced at his notepad. "Third one is named Anton Bailey. Does this stuff mean anything to you?"

# 24

The Manhattan North Homicide Squad office was virtually empty. Every man and woman, whether on duty or off, had come in to try to crack the attempt on Mercer's life. Those who were not officially in the field were pounding the pavement, leaning on informants to try to get a lead on which to follow up. The rest were filling the lobby at Saint Vincent's, even though it was far too soon for all but the closest friends and family to visit with him.

"Cooper and I are gonna use the lieutenant's office for this interview. Call Albany, call whoever you've got to, but get every single sheet of paper that exists in this state on Anton Bailey," Chapman told Jimmy Halloran. "And when you're done with that, call the Gainesville, Florida, P.D. and start all over again. Use both names, Bailey and Anthony Bailor."

"Hey, Alex, how'd he get into the system up here without them picking up the Florida case?" Halloran asked me. "How come nobody figured out that Anton

Bailey and Anthony Bailor were one and the same before today, huh?"

"Just lucky, I guess." No one could be arraigned for a felony in New York State without a fingerprint check. But every now and then, all of the automated techniques failed. In some cases, if the interstate computer system was down and the perp used an alias, the fingerprint comparison was never actually made. The fine type at the bottom of the rap sheet, if the prosecutor or judge stopped to read it, said that the results were based on a name check and not a verified latent exam.

If the prior rape conviction had been reflected on Bailey's record, then the larceny case would have drawn a mandatory prison sentence longer than the time he served. He would not have been free to have sexually assaulted Denise Caxton and to have set in motion the chain of deaths that followed.

"You must be Don Cannon," Mike said, shaking hands with the man sitting in the squad room. "I'm Detective Chapman, Mike Chapman. And this is Alexandra Cooper, from the Manhattan District Attorney's Office. Thanks for coming in."

I guessed Cannon to be younger than I am, in his late twenties, perhaps. He was a bit shorter than I, with a serious mien and horn-rimmed glasses. He seemed no more at ease than do most civilians who find themselves in the middle of a homicide case but express a willingness to cooperate, which few mean as sincerely as he seemed to.

"Why don't you have a seat and tell us a bit about yourself?" Chapman asked. "I'd like to know what you did for Mr. Varelli in his business. That kind of thing."

"You probably know by now that Marco was the master, the most meticulous workman in his field. Just about every important restoration project in the last fifty years has been offered to him. Those that excited him most, he worked on himself.

"I'm from Sacramento originally. Went to UCLA, have a graduate degree in fine arts. That the kind of thing you want to know?" He looked from Mike's face to mine, tentatively, to see whether he was proceeding in the right direction. We both nodded.

"One of my professors had worked with Varelli on *Guernica,* back in the eighties. Do you remember, that was the Picasso that was defaced at the Museum of Modern Art by some deranged fanatic?"

"Yes, of course. Our office handled the case."

"The professor knew that I wanted to work in restoration, that I hoped to develop a career, go back to the West Coast, and set up shop at the Getty or one of the other museums. To apprentice to Marco Varelli, well, there's simply nothing better to prepare to learn this business, and no finer credential on a résumé."

"When did you start to work for him?" I asked.

Cannon hesitated. "Nobody worked *for* Varelli. I mean, technical people did—laborers who picked up and delivered the paintings or arranged the studio. But he was quite a loner. Once he had established himself as the virtuoso, more than forty years ago, he was insistent on working alone. If you were fortunate enough to get his attention, and he agreed to work on your project, then he wanted the result to be only *his* handiwork."

"What do you mean, 'he agreed'? Didn't people just pay him?" Chapman wanted to know.

The serious Mr. Cannon smiled wryly. "No, no, no. Mr. Varelli had more than enough to live on. He was paid handsomely for his craft. So, at a certain point in his life, it was easy for him to turn down whomever he pleased. If the painting or the artist was not one he deemed worthy of his effort, no matter what the price offered, he wouldn't touch it."

"How about if the ownership was cloudy?"

"Well then, Miss Cooper, there was simply no way to engage him. I can recall an instance when a collector showed up in the atelier with a Léger. The particular painting had been classified in the Pompidou Center as an R2P, which means that it had been seized by the Nazis during the war and later returned to France. To date, no one had been able to connect it to the original owner or his descendants. Signor Varelli refused to become involved until an effort was made to trace the lineage and try to find the owners. The more money that was offered to retain him, the more offended he became. I'm sure it's a lot like that in the legal profession, don't you think? I mean, with all the ethical dilemmas defense attorneys have?"

He looked over at me for an answer, which came instead from Chapman. "You're watching too much Geraldo. I never met a defense attorney with an ethical dilemma—if the check clears, his client's not guilty."

"You said that no one worked for Varelli. Didn't *you*?"

"I had the privilege of being apprenticed to him, Detective. An expensive privilege."

"You had to pay to help him?"

"I had a grant, actually, from a private family foundation. That's what made the experience possible for me. I certainly wouldn't have had the means to do it otherwise. Consider it like going to the best school in the world. For close to three years I was tutored by a genius. The skills he has given me are qualities I could never have learned anywhere else." Cannon bowed his head. "I still can't believe he's gone. And worst of all, murdered." He looked up at us. "He was such a quiet, benign man. There's not a reason I can think of for someone to hurt him."

"Let me run some names by you. Tell us if you know any of these people, okay?"

Cannon cleared his throat and said it would be fine.

"Start with Lowell Caxton. Ever meet him?"

"Many, many times. I'd guess Marco had known him for as long as I've been alive. I think he was one of the few collectors whose taste Mr. Varelli admired. I've never been to any of Caxton's homes, but I understand there were several generations of a great genetic eye for art. Mr. Caxton used to come by for an opinion every now and then. Do you know about the Titian—the one he gave to Marco?"

"Yes. We spent a few minutes with Mrs. Varelli at the funeral home. We expect to see her in the apartment later this week."

"Marco adored that gift, a real jewel of a little drawing. I think his acceptance of Lowell Caxton had a lot to do with that gesture. It would be hard to dislike someone who had done such a generous thing."

"Any conflict between them, ever?"

Cannon shrugged his shoulders. "Not that I ever witnessed. Keep in mind, I wasn't there all the time. Mostly I was with Marco when he was actually doing the work on his projects, not when he was talking with his clients or when they dropped in for a glass of grappa and some advice about what to bid on a particular piece.

"He was very good at dismissing me. 'Thank you so much, Mr. Cannon. And now, *per piacere,* I think we are finished for the moment.' He'd kind of flutter his hand in my direction, and I'd know it was time to take off."

"To . . . ?"

"The grant covered the expenses of my study, but not an apartment in Manhattan. My girlfriend and I sublet a room in a loft in SoHo. She's here in graduate school at NYU. When I was free to leave I'd head for the library, an art show, or a movie. But I'd get out of his hair, that much was clear."

Chapman checked off Caxton's name on the list he had started and went down to the next line. "Bryan Daughtry. Ever run into him?"

"Yes, he was another visitor. Not so much anymore, with the contemporary work he was trying to sell. But Marco had done ventures with him before I arrived here, which was before Daughtry went to jail. On that tax fraud, not that other thing." Cannon looked at me to see whether I registered any reaction to his reference to the girl in the leather mask.

"What do you know about his background?"

"I don't mean to make light of the story about Bryan Daughtry's involvement in that old case, but it kind of fascinated Mr. Varelli. He never saw the cruel side of Bryan. Met him as a young man who had a rather good eye for art, albeit untrained. I was a bit shocked to meet him myself when Bryan first came to the studio. Marco told me all about him that first day."

Cannon moved in his chair, put the fingertips of his right hand together, and shook them easily in front of his face, imitating the old man's accent. " 'But can you tell me why, Mr. Cannon, *why* a young man wants to tie up a beautiful young girl and cause her pain? This I don't understand at all. From a body like this you should get only pleasure, only sweetness, only—*come si dice in inglese?*—rapture. But maybe I am too old to understand.'

"Quite frankly, I used to think when Daughtry was here to visit and Mr. Varelli kicked me out, it was to ask him questions about his sexual proclivities. Marco was much more curious about that than he was about contemporary art."

Cannon talked for a while about Bryan Daughtry's more recent business focus, but again could think of no incident that unnerved him in regard to Varelli.

"How about Marina Sette?"

Cannon seemed to draw a blank.

"Marilyn Seven?" I asked, adding a physical description as well as telling him where she lived.

"It's quite possible she had been to see Marco, of course. It's just not a name I recognize."

"Frank Wrenley?"

Again, not familiar. Neither was Preston Mattox. Cannon knew the names of some of the workmen, but

Omar Sheffield and Anton Bailey were not among them.

Chapman put down his pen and clasped his hands on the desktop.

"Talk to me about Denise Caxton. Everything you know. When you met her, what she was like, what Marco thought about her. Things that don't seem important to you may be exactly what we're looking for, so give it all to me, okay?"

"This one's a bit complicated, Detective. There was Denise Caxton the woman, and there was Denise Caxton the collector. Marco Varelli's eye was unerring. He admired great beauty, on a canvas or in human form. Nothing inappropriate, nothing unusual. But he would look at a handsome woman's face as though it had been sculpted by Michelangelo. Didn't matter if she were a waitress in a diner or a client with millions. Mrs. Caxton had a real head start with Marco, from the old days. He had met her when she was a kid, just married to Lowell.

"If I'm not mistaken—you might have to check her apartment for this—I think Mr. Varelli once painted her portrait, a full-length nude. He was very proud of it. Told me it was hung in her room at home. I believe she had a collection of self-portraits, right?" He chuckled at the vanity of that idea, it seemed to me.

Cannon continued, "She was a real flirt—Mrs. Caxton, I mean. Knew exactly how to play the old guy, with words. When I first met her, almost three years ago, she could light him up like a flare when he knew she was coming. She would always bring his favorite chocolates, if she had been to Paris, or a chilled bottle of wine to sip with him in the afternoon. She loved to listen to his stories, wanted to know every painting he'd ever worked on—who owned them, what he did to them, what became of them. Marco used to complain that his wife didn't want to hear the old tales over again. Denise Caxton hung on his every word, or at least she let him think that she did."

"Did you ever work on any of the paintings she brought into the gallery?"

"Yes. She had a knack for picking up sleepers, bidding on some incredibly lifeless old canvas that she'd either had a good tip on or had followed with her gut instincts. 'Who is it, Marco? Tell me who's hiding underneath there, *mi amore*.' She'd tease him into playing with almost anything she brought in. And what was funny about it was that most of the time, he wanted me there to watch this game she played with him. As if he wanted me to see that a magnificent young woman doted on him, that it wasn't just happening in his imagination."

"When did his feelings for Deni change?"

Cannon paused. "Is that what Mrs. Varelli said?"

"Yeah. Said she didn't make him quite so happy anymore."

"I can't recall exactly when the change occurred, but she's right. Mrs. Caxton's visits were fewer and farther apart. She rarely came alone anymore, and the games were over."

"Who'd she bring with her, if she wasn't alone?"

"Friends, clients—I don't know. Varelli would shoo me out of the studio. There was no longer any verbal foreplay, so he didn't need me around."

Chapman was annoyed. "You must know who some of them were, don't you? Start somewhere—women? men? young or old?"

"Occasionally she came with people I knew, like Bryan Daughtry. Once or twice she might have been with a woman—maybe even that lady you described earlier, with the French braid. Seven or Sette, whatever you called her. But most of the time it was men, two or three different ones in the past few months, since she split up with her husband."

"Can you describe any of them for us? Would you recognize them if you saw them today?"

Again Cannon shrugged, not attaching any importance to these visitors. "There wasn't anything remarkable about any of them. Sure, maybe I'd know them if I ran into them again, maybe not. You have to understand, Detective, that if Marco Varelli wasn't working on a canvas, I was just as happy to be out of there. It was as much an education for me to spend a free afternoon at a museum as to be a fly on the wall when he was chatting up rich collectors. I didn't need the small talk."

Chapman stood now, walking behind Cannon's back. "In the last three years, is there anybody else who spent as much time with Marco Varelli as you did?"

Cannon thought and then told us, "No. Except for his wife."

"Anybody who knew what he thought about everything and everybody?"

"No, probably not."

"They have any kids?"

"No."

"I bet you were sort of like a son to him, weren't you?"

"Not exactly. But he was very good to me."

"What was the most important thing in the world to him, Don? Leave his wife out of it for the moment. Tell us."

"You know the answer. He lived for great art—for looking at it, touching it, smelling it, dreaming about it."

"And he trusted *you* with his legacy."

"Well, I'm not the only one who ever apprenticed with him. There are dozens of experts in museums around the world who—"

"But *now,* Mr. Cannon. You've spent these last three years joined to him at the hip. I find it really kinda hard to believe that he had many secrets from you." Mike's fist pounded down on the top of the lieutenant's desk. "I'd like you to tell me why he and Denise Caxton had a falling-out."

Cannon started at Chapman's change in mood. "I wasn't his confidant, Mr. Chapman. I was merely his student."

"And you're too damn smart, too good a student, not to have been aware of what was happening in that little garret every day, that's what I think. If you've got a special talent, Mr. Cannon, it's your powers of observation, isn't it? Tell me what you saw up there, what you heard."

Mike's voice bellowed in the small room as Cannon looked at me to call off the angry detective. "She's on *my* side in this, buddy. If I let Cooper cross-examine you for fifteen minutes, you'll forget you ever walked into this room with a set of balls." Chapman was shouting now, and red in the face. "Three people are dead and my partner's lying in a hospital bed with a hole in his chest. Stop wasting my time!"

"Do I need a lawyer?" Cannon spoke quietly and again directed the question to me.

I began to answer but was interrupted by Chapman. "If you're gonna tell me you killed someone, we'll call you a lawyer. Somehow, I doubt that's the problem. Just tell me what's on your mind and worry about that later."

"Well, what if I have information about a crime?"

Mike's open palm slammed the desktop another time. "Whaddaya think I've been asking you to tell me about for the last hour?"

# 25

Cannon had stalled for about as long as Mike was going to let him, and he knew that. "I suppose there are two things that changed the relationship between Mrs. Caxton and Marco. The first problem began about a year ago."

"When, exactly? 'About' doesn't help me all that much."

"I can't give you a specific date. I'm pretty sure it was before she and her husband began to have problems in their marriage. I remember that because I thought it was strange she had come to see Marco about a matter so important but that it was something she wanted to be sure he wouldn't tell Lowell."

"That's a start. Coop, make a list for me. First thing, try to put a date on that visit, okay? What happened that day?"

"Denise was exuberant. It must have been spring or summer, 'cause she wasn't wearing a coat. She was dressed to the nines when she came in, and she looked spectacular. They began the usual flirtation, and

Marco made sure that I took it all in. She handed me a bottle of wine—a very special one, she made sure to tell me—and asked me to open it. I did, and Marco invited me to pour for all three of us."

"Had you known she was coming?"

"Yes, she'd called the day before and told Marco she'd found a surprise. A painting, that is. Asked if he would look at it for her. Of course he agreed."

Cannon took a breath before going on. He rubbed his hands together and talked slowly, as though uncertain he should talk at all. "After half an hour of cajoling Marco, she got up from the chaise and picked up the bag she'd come in with—one of those large canvas sail bags. She removed something from it, and all I could see was a small mound of plastic bubble wrapping. She unwound several layers of it and lifted out a painting. Then she walked to one of the easels and rested it on the stand. 'Come, Marcolino—come play with me.' Mrs. Caxton took him by the hand and stood him before the canvas."

"Did you know what it was?"

"I certainly didn't. It was dark, really covered with dirt, and hard to make out."

"Did Varelli say anything?"

"Then? No. It would have been unusual for him to speak until after he'd gotten to work and made up his mind that he knew what he was looking at."

"What'd he do?"

"What he did best, Detective. He put the glass of wine down next to him, strapped his headset on—sort of like small binoculars—and steadied himself in place to look at every inch of the canvas with the aid of the light from the glasses. You want to know the details?"

"All of them."

"It was obvious that not only was there soot on this one, and varnish, but something had been painted over the original work. That happens frequently with oils, you know, sometimes just because the artist changed his mind about what he wanted to portray. But in this case it looked like it had been put on top to disguise an earlier version of whatever was depicted.

"So Marco got out his acetone, soaked a cotton swab in it, and went about dabbing at a corner of the canvas, sort of the top right quadrant."

"And you, what were you doing?"

"I stood behind him to watch, to be there to assist him should he have needed me to."

"And Deni?"

"Practically breathing down his neck. Not that he minded that, from her."

"How long does this take, what he was doing?"

"Depends. On what's there, how many layers, how easily—or not—it picks up. I would say Marco worked for close to an hour before he said very much. He stopped to tell us that he thought he had gotten through the primary layer. He stood up to stretch, and to have me take a look, which I did."

"What did you see?"

Cannon smiled for the first time in ten minutes. "You sound just as anxious as Denise. 'What do you see, Marco? What can you tell me?' He poured himself another glass and asked me a few questions, ignoring Deni completely.

" 'What century, boy, do you see now? What school, what artist?' He did that with me all the time, delighting in those rare occasions when I could pinpoint a good answer as rapidly as he was able to do."

"Did you recognize anything?"

"Only that Marco had gone back several centuries, between removing the new paint and the grime that had so discolored the original canvas. Wherever this piece had come from, it had been terribly, terribly neglected."

"What then?"

"He went back to work, this time adding some ammonia to the acetone and patiently dabbing away. It's a very slow business. After a while, Marco's touch exposed some bright blue paint trimmed with a very pearly sort of highlight. He almost gasped when he saw the contrast of the two colors next to each other."

"Excuse my ignorance," Mike said, "but why?"

"I didn't know myself, but now I assume that was the point at which he thought he had recognized the artist, perhaps even the painting."

"And Deni?"

"She had seen him do this enough times to know he was reacting to something serious." Again, Cannon slipped into one of his imitations. " 'Go in deeper, Marco,' she urged him. I remember that he hesitated for a bit, then picked up one of his pointed tools, almost like a scalpel, and began to dig at the thick varnish in another part of the painting. More of the picture came into view, near its center, revealing a clear yellow tint that had been almost brown in color in the layer above.

"That's when I was banished."

"By Denise Caxton?"

"By Marco Varelli. That familiar little gesture I told you about earlier, sweeping me away with his hand like you might do to a pet dog you wanted to get out from underfoot? That's exactly what I got from him. 'That's all I'm going to do for today,' he told me. 'You may go home now.'"

"And did you?"

"I left the studio, certainly. But my curiosity had been aroused. I went straight to the library at NYU to do a bit of art research. At that point I was fairly confident that we had been looking at something from the seventeenth century, probably Dutch."

"A Rembrandt?" Mike asked.

"Not bad, Detective. It was an interior scene by a great colorist. I was guessing Vermeer, who was known for his pearl-colored reflections and the fantastically luminous shades of blue and yellow. I pored over textbooks until I found what I was looking for. Have you ever heard of a painting called *The Concert*?"

Neither one of us had.

"You know about the break-in at the Gardner Museum?"

Mike was following the story intently. "Yeah, we do. Why?"

"Along with the great Rembrandt that was taken," Cannon said, acknowledging Chapman as he went on, "which you clearly seem to be aware of, there was one Vermeer stolen that has never been found either. It's called *The Concert*, and it depicts a young woman playing a pianoforte for two others. I believe I'm one of the very few people in the world who has seen that painting—at least, any portion of it—in the last ten years. The other two who saw it with me that day—Mrs. Caxton and Mr. Varelli—are dead. Maybe now you can understand why I'm reluctant to speak about it."

Mike had no sympathy for Cannon's fear. "What's its value?"

"Not as great as the Rembrandt, but still in the multimillions. Vermeer is known to have painted only thirty-five works in his lifetime."

"Was it still at Varelli's studio when you got there the next day?"

"No. I never saw it again. Nor did he mention it to me. We went right back to work on the portrait we had been commissioned to restore for the Tate, the one we were immersed in before Denise Caxton asked to drop by. I came in that next morning eager to hear what he and Mrs. Caxton had found after he had dismissed me. Not a word. But then, the texts I had consulted were written before the Gardner theft, so I had no idea the Vermeer had been stolen. I thought that perhaps the museum was deaccessioning the painting, and it made sense to me that the Caxtons were among the few collectors with the means to acquire it—legitimately.

"It wasn't unusual for Marco to work in silence. Finally, when we broke for lunch, I thought I'd impress him with my knowledge. I'd be the perfect pupil and answer the questions he had asked me when he had started to uncover the picture in my presence."

"Did it work?"

"It backfired colossally. Marco almost took my head off. I told him that not only did I think I knew the century and the school to which the painting could be attributed, but that I also knew the artist and the work itself. He looked surprised and challenged me." Cannon looked up at us rather sheepishly. "When I said the words aloud, he became furious at me.

" 'But why?' I asked him. 'Why are you so angry?' 'You have never, *never* seen that Vermeer, do you understand, my boy? It has *never* been in the studio of Marco Varelli.' He went on to rant and rave about the fact that Denise had brought him a fraud, some lousy copyist's effort to re-create a Dutch domestic scene, that Denise was a rank amateur who had occasionally been lucky but had made a bad guess. He practically made me swear that the event I witnessed had never taken place."

"Have you ever told anyone about it?"

"My girlfriend, sure. No one else. I had gone right back to the library and searched the periodicals. That's when I realized that it must have been the stolen Vermeer, and that Varelli wanted no part of it. I respected him for that, and thought that would be the end of it."

"You mean it wasn't? Did Deni come back?"

"Of course she did. Several times, not too long after, just trying to regain favor, I guess. Lots of good wine, charming coquettishness, gifts. Marco wasn't at all materialistic, but she'd find wonderfully whimsical things—small sculptures, paintings, objets d'art that he couldn't resist—and bring them by to appease him."

"Any talk of the Vermeer?"

"None. And again Marco wanted me around when she showed up and made a fuss over him. So they weren't alone very much those next few visits. Then," Cannon said, rubbing his eyes with his hand, "there was another tempest. Perhaps, if I hadn't been such a coward, I'd have done something about it at the time. Deni came in one day very excited, very flustered."

"When was this, do you remember?"

"Not off the top of my head."

"Months later, Don?"

"No, no. Three or four weeks at most. But I'm pretty sure she had been away, out of the country, in the meantime. I think it was shortly after she and her husband had some kind of huge fight and split up. Anyway, I knew immediately that something different was going on."

"How?"

"As soon as she arrived, it was Denise who asked me to leave. Even Marco looked puzzled, because she dispensed with the usual flirtation. 'You don't mind, do you? I've got some personal matters to discuss with Signor Varelli. It's the middle of the afternoon, Marco—let him have the rest of the day off, okay?'

"For once he seemed reluctant to let me walk out. I think, at that point, he didn't quite trust her anymore. But she was insistent, and he gave me the back of his hand."

"Do you have any idea what she wanted? Was she carrying the same bag?"

"She wasn't carrying any sail bag this time. Just her pocketbook. I took off my work shirt, said good-bye, and closed the door behind me."

"Didn't Varelli ever tell you what it was about?"

"He didn't have to, Detective." Cannon pursed his lips and looked away from us before speaking again. "I'm not proud of this, but I really couldn't help myself. Instead of leaving, I ran down the steps from the atelier door, then I slipped off my sandals and walked back up, sitting on the top of the stoop, so that I could listen against the door.

"It was Denise Caxton at her best, pulling out all the stops. She was pleading with Marco to look at what she had brought with her—coaxing and cajoling him with her limited vocabulary of Italian platitudes. 'My little gems,' she kept repeating. Then I heard her tell him that he was the only person in the world who could know the truth. That this adventure would crown his illustrious career and be his great heritage— to restore a priceless painting to the world."

"Little gems?" Chapman asked. "Could you see what they were talking about?"

"I never saw them, but it became quite obvious. She had a small pouch, which she opened, and placed the contents on Marco's workbench. Chips, a dozen tiny pieces of paint chips."

"From the stolen Rembrandt?"

"That's precisely what she wanted to know."

"I realize Varelli's expertise," I said, "but is that the kind of thing that a restorer would be able to determine with any certainty?"

"I guess you both know that when *The Storm on the Sea of Galilee* was taken in that theft, the burglars were unusually sloppy, just slicing it out of the frame with a knife and leaving behind a dustpan full of chips. That probably means that slivers continued to flake off the edges of the actual painting itself, so whoever possessed the painting would have more pieces like the ones collected by the police. A science lab would have to make the ultimate determination of the authenticity of the age of the chips. They can do it with electron and polarized-light microscopes, like the F.B.I. uses. Specialists have uncovered frauds, for example, by proving that minuscule amounts of chalk in a paint primer were made twenty years ago, not three hundred. That's technology.

"But Marco wasn't a bad place to start, to get a first opinion. What lab technicians do with their tools or their scopes, he did with his nose and his fingers and his infallible eye. It was the trait that made him a genius at restoration. Besides that, Ms. Cooper, Denise Caxton could hardly walk into an F.B.I. office and ask whether the fragments she was holding actually matched the ones that had fallen behind at the Gardner during an unsolved theft, could she?"

"Did Varelli look at the chips?"

"I never found out. When I left, he was still being obstinate and refusing to entertain Mrs. Caxton's request."

"Why didn't you wait?"

"Believe me, I wanted to stay there. But a couple of the workmen were coming back with some large frames that Marco had sent out to be regilded. We had been expecting them earlier in the afternoon. When I heard the buzzer ring from downstairs, I was afraid Mr. Varelli would open the door and find me hiding there. So I left.

"The next day, he carried on as usual. And after what had occurred with the Vermeer, I didn't dare ask him about these paint chips. I don't think I ever mentioned Rembrandt's name to him for a couple of months."

"Didn't he talk about Deni anymore? Didn't she still come to visit?"

"Less frequently, so far as I know. But whenever she showed up, he insisted I stay to help him or have a glass of wine with them. And he was much too discreet to talk about her. After she'd leave, he'd shake his head and say she was crazy. '*Bella pazza*,' my beautiful crazy one. That's what he called her more recently."

"And when she was killed, what did he have to say about her then?"

Don Cannon shook his head at us. "Don't know. I was on vacation with my girlfriend, camping out in Yosemite. My family couldn't even find me to tell me that Marco had died. But those scenes with the Vermeer and then the paint chips were the cause of the breach that developed between him and Deni, I'm sure of it. The other thing," he said, stretching a bit and arching his back, "the other thing was also a bit odd, at least to me."

"What other? I thought you said there were two things that estranged them—meaning the Vermeer and the chips."

"To me," the young man replied, "those two were part of the same headache—the Gardner Museum heist. The other one was something else again."

Mike was jotting notes on his pad, while I added points to my list of questions. "A bit later on, Denise came back to the studio. It was well after she and her husband had separated, I know that. She had another man with her and—"

"Who?"

"Sorry, I can't help you with that. I never got much of a look. He was standing quietly off to the side, and like Varelli, all my attention was on Mrs. Caxton. It wasn't unusual for her to have men with her who were clients. They rarely entered into her conversation with Mr. Varelli and I never paid them much mind. Anyway, she was telling Marco about the breakup, and she said she had brought a gift, this time for Gina—for Mrs. Varelli. It was a necklace of beads—very large amber beads—and a carved figurine that matched them. 'Come look, Dan,' she said to me. She'd met me a few dozen times, but she was a bit too self-centered to bother to learn my name. Always called me Dan instead of Don. 'Come look, you'll never see anything like these. They're quite rare. Lowell gave them to me, and I really don't want to wear them anymore. Might give him too much satisfaction. Gina will adore them, don't you think, Marco? You don't have to tell her they're from me.'

"Mrs. Caxton reached over with both hands to pass them to Varelli, but he recoiled instantly and the strand fell onto the floor. 'Not in my house, *signora*, not under my roof. Too many people have been killed for these trifles with which you amuse yourself.' "

"And she left?"

"She got down on her knees to pick up the beads. One end of the strand had broken and they were rolling across the floor like golf balls. I helped her gather them up and put them back in her purse. Then she and her friend left.

"But they left behind the little amber statue. By accident, I would think. Mr. Varelli didn't even notice it. But when Gina came upstairs the next morning to bring us some tea, she saw it there. She spotted it immediately and admired it. Just picked it up with her and took it down to the apartment."

"Didn't he say anything then?"

"Only to himself, under his breath. He rarely said no to Gina—about anything. But when she carried off her little treasure, Marco muttered something about Nazis. It meant nothing to me then, but a few more hours at the library, and the computer research came up with stories about the Amber Room. I even found a few articles that connected the lost room to Lowell Caxton."

Chapman was holding his notepad in his right hand, tapping it against his other fist. "There must be some way to reconstruct the dates that these things happened, no? You keep any kind of appointment book or calendars?"

"No reason to, Detective. I went to work at the same place every day at the same time. I keep journals about exhibits I've gone to see and I keep loads of sketchbooks, but they don't have any engagements in them."

"How about Varelli?" I asked. "People made appointments with him, there were deliveries, someone paid the bills—"

"Gina Varelli, of course. She was the only one who Marco let control his business."

"The widow, right?"

"Yes. She made most of the arrangements. Marco didn't like to be bothered by telephone calls and mundane things." Cannon laughed. "Like money. Didn't she give you that book when you spoke with her? It's got everything in it—every visitor, client, bill, receipt. I'm sure it would be a great help to you in your investigation."

"No. We'll get it from her when we see her this week," I said, adding to my list and nodding at Mike. "Perhaps we can get her to talk about the amber piece, too. Maybe Marco and she spoke about it at home, privately."

"Yeah. I'll call her tonight and see if I can go over in the morning and pick up the journal and the statue, okay, Coop?"

I didn't have to answer.

Don Cannon spoke. "Not tomorrow, Detective. About two hours before the funeral that had been scheduled for last Friday, Gina got a call from the mayor of Florence. It's where Marco was born. The Italian government offered to fly the body home for burial in the family's church, somewhere up north, in the mountains, alongside all his ancestors. Kind of like a national hero—which shows the respect they have for artists over there.

"Gina Varelli left for Italy last evening. Some little town in Tuscany. I don't even know how to reach her."

# 26

"Your to-do list is getting to be a mile long," Chapman said after Don Cannon left the office and we were eating our sandwiches at the lieutenant's desk.

"I'll call down to my paralegal now and see whether she can get a number for the mayor of Florence. You double-check with the guys from Crime Scene to see whether they took any kind of book when they processed Varelli's studio."

"I'm telling you, Mercer and I were there with them. No such thing anywhere we looked. The only evidence they vouchered was the pair of sunglasses. Whatever this appointment journal or calendar is, it's probably in his apartment, not the studio."

"Well, if we can find the niece who took Gina Varelli home the other night, maybe we can convince her to let us do a consent search. If not, I'll draft another warrant in the morning." I looked at my watch. "It's already almost four o'clock."

The shifts had changed, and detectives working the

day tour were signing out while those doing four-to-twelves were coming on. Even the teams that had finished their official tours were working overtime, without pay, because of Mercer.

Jimmy Halloran opened the door. "Your secretary's on line two. Wanna pick up?"

"Sure. Laura? Everything okay?"

"Just a couple of things you need to know about. Pat McKinney is having a meeting at ten tomorrow with a few of the senior trial counsel. Catherine said to tell you that he hasn't given them any specific agenda yet, but she assumes he's planning to pick someone from the group to assign to prosecute Mercer's case."

"Thank her for letting me know. I'll be there."

"You're not invited, Alex. That's the point. That's what Catherine wanted me to get across to you."

Damn it. McKinney would do everything in his power, as deputy chief of the Trial Division, to make me uncomfortable as a witness to Mercer's shooting. I wanted to have a say in who would prosecute the gunman when he was caught. "Can you find a number for Rod Squires? Scout around for me, will you?" The chief of the division, my friend and ally, was also on summer vacation. If I could enlist his aid before morning, I'd have some control over the selection process.

"Let me call Rose Malone. I'm sure she'll know how to find him. And you also need to know that the man who tried to run you down last week, Wakim Wakefield? Well, he was back here at the building today, trying to get upstairs to file a complaint with Battaglia about you."

336

"Did security let him through?" That's a bit too close for comfort.

"No. His name was on their daily chart." The security crew in the lobby at 1 Hogan Place kept a roster of names of people not welcome in our office—an ever-expanding list of psychos, malcontents, and cranks who were expert at creating disturbances once they got inside.

"Was he arrested?" I asked with some hesitancy.

"No. The guard called up to the squad to get some detectives to come talk to him, but there's only one elevator working today, and by the time somebody got downstairs, Wakefield was already gone. Mr. Battaglia himself called about it. Made me promise to ask you if you were using your bodyguards."

"Don't mention to him that I groaned when I told you yes," I answered. "I'm smack in the middle of a police station right now, and unless Chapman goes ballistic 'cause I tell him to wipe the mustard off the side of his mouth, I'll be perfectly safe. I'll stay with him a few more hours, and then he'll pass me back off to the D.A.'s Squad. Tell the boss I'm being a very good soldier, okay? And please see if you can get a number for any government officials in Florence. We need to find Marco Varelli's widow."

"Alex, it's after ten at night over there. I'll see what I can do, but I doubt I'll have anything for you until tomorrow. And one last thing."

"Some good news, right?"

"Not exactly. Pat McKinney dropped by. He told me to remind you that you are to stay away from the hospital. No visits to Mercer, no talking about the case. He doesn't want you comparing notes and conforming your stories to fit each other's recollections. Sorry, Alex."

"Don't worry, Laura. I know you're just the messenger."

I hung up and Chapman asked what the news was, so I told him about Wakefield.

"Jeez, blondie, if it wasn't for me you'd have no friends at all. Let's take off. Preston Mattox will see us at his office whenever we get there."

"I thought you said everyone else would have to be interviewed *here*."

"What happened to your sense of humor, kid? D'you lose it yesterday? This guy's got his architectural offices in a penthouse suite on Fifth Avenue, overlooking Saint Patrick's Cathedral, with about fifty employees in the surrounding rooms. I'll get you home in one piece tonight."

Mike called the hospital and spoke with Mercer's dad, who told him that Mercer had been sitting up for a few hours in the early afternoon and now was sleeping again. We gathered our things to leave the squad. Jimmy Halloran had been kept over to do back-to-back tours, to man the phone and hot line, since City Hall had announced a reward for information leading to the arrest of the shooter.

"Hey, K.D., give me a beep if anything comes in on Bailey before your shift is done. We've got an interview to do before we stop off at the hospital."

With that we were on our way to the offices of Mattox Partners, and our first introduction to another one of Deni's suitors, Preston Mattox. His secretary announced us and we were led into the stark glass-enclosed headquarters of the prominent architect, which looked south toward the spires of the great church below.

My first reaction was surprise. He appeared to be about fifty years old. He was in good shape and dressed in a navy suit, exuding a much more businesslike air than the art-world denizens we had encountered throughout the last week. But what struck me most about Mattox was that he looked truly distraught, and as though he had been crying for days on end. There was a hollow contour around his eyes and a lifelessness emanating from within, which hit a chord in the core of me that wanted someone to be mourning for Denise Caxton.

Once more Chapman and I made our introductions.

"Why don't you have a seat?" he said, coming out from behind his desk and pulling three chairs around in a circle. "Sorry I didn't get back to you sooner. I really had to get away from here after Deni was killed. Lowell made it clear that I wasn't welcome at the service, and I just needed to be somewhere else."

Mattox was cordial, but he seemed distracted and unable even to muster a smile.

"Have you made any progress in solving Deni's case?"

"Not as much as we'd like," I answered.

"I've stopped reading newspaper accounts, so I don't know what you're up to. The stories about her all made her sound so vacuous and unpleasant. She was a most unusual creature—clever, funny, warm. She craved affection, and I loved giving it to her."

Mike showed unusual restraint in not mentioning Deni's other liaisons. He let Mattox do it for us. "You've probably talked with some of Deni's other friends. Obviously, I wasn't the only man in her life, but I was fighting hard for that slot." He stood up and walked to the window, looking out and not speaking for several seconds. "I had asked Denise to marry me."

"But she wasn't even divorced yet," Mike said.

Mattox rested against the ledge of the windowsill. "No, but I was urging her to speed up the process. Stop fighting with Lowell and walk away from him. Frankly, it made me sick just to think of them living under the same roof. I don't quite have the art collection that her husband does, but short of that, there wasn't anything she wanted that I would not have given her."

"Do you know why she didn't leave?"

"Really why? Probably I don't know. None of the reasons she ever gave me made much sense. 'Just wait,' she used to say. 'Don't rush me.' She was obstinate about it and I was madly in love, so I didn't push her. It was the only thing we ever fought over. And she could fight," Mattox said, almost amused at the memory of it.

"What do you mean?"

"Deni was a battler. She looked so soft, so fragile. But she had an iron will, and if something got under her skin, she'd go to the mats for it. It was one of her best traits as a friend—a tenacious loyalty that endeared her to anyone who got close enough." He took a handkerchief from his pants pocket and held it over his mouth as he cleared his throat, and then tamped the cloth against his eyes. "I keep thinking of how she must have died. I know it wouldn't have been without a struggle."

So many victims of sexual assault had described to me their reactions to the assailant. The greatest number submitted to life-threatening words or display of a weapon. Others chose to attempt to fight back. Some were successful and became survivors. For many, the resistance served only to aggravate the attacker and caused him to use more force, which resulted sometimes in serious injury to the woman, and often in her death. No one could second-guess the decisions each victim had to make in the seconds when she was confronted by a rapist.

Mike tried to direct the conversation back to the areas that interested him.

"Did you have any kind of relationship with Lowell Caxton?"

"A casual one. I'd known him for years—never did any work for him, but we traveled in the same social circles here in town. Always been a perfect gentleman to me."

"How about to Deni?"

"I think I understood him a lot better than she did, to tell you the truth. I don't think she had any business trying to make him let go of some of the artwork that had been in his family for decades. It wasn't the prettiest side of Deni, as you probably know by now."

"What about her concerns that he was trying to have her killed?"

Mattox frowned at that suggestion. "I ridiculed the idea at the time. Sort of makes me crazy to think about that now. It could just as easily be Lowell behind all this as it could be anyone, I guess." He looked up at Mike. "I don't envy your job, Detective. Saw an article in the paper not long ago. Said there are more murderers in the United States than there are medical doctors. More murderers than college professors. It's mind-boggling, really." He talked on about the Caxtons' marriage for more than fifteen minutes, until Mike changed the questions to ask about Bryan Daughtry.

"Never had any use for him, Mr. Chapman. It was a major point of contention between Deni and me. Whenever we talked seriously about the future, I made it clear that there was no room in it for Daughtry. He's a despicable piece of—well, human garbage." Mattox walked along the window on the far side of the room, dragging his finger along the sill. "Why you people never nailed him for the murder of that Scandinavian girl upstate escapes me completely. Whatever he does, he somehow lands on his feet each time. Makes me sick just to think about it."

"Did you spend any time at Caxton Due, their new gallery?" I asked.

"Not when Bryan was around. I'd gone there on several occasions with Deni, when she went to check on shipments that were being unloaded. She found all that very exciting—loved to watch the men break down the packing boxes and lift some painting or sculpture out of them. She was like a little kid on Christmas morning, poring over every inch of the canvas, examining the artist's signature, checking out the condition of the frame.

"I'd go just to see her reaction. Frankly, the art she

and Daughtry were interested in did nothing for me. I'm rather a classicist, as you can see from my work." He pointed at the office walls, which displayed the plans and finished results of some of his buildings. There was an elegance of line and style that didn't mesh with the contemporary works we had seen in Chelsea.

"Do you know Varelli? Marco Varelli?"

"Certainly. I'd actually met Marco many times."

"With Deni?"

"I'd met him through clients long before I started to date Deni. But I'd never been to his atelier until she took me there. He was a genius—a lovely man."

"When were you there—at his studio, I mean?"

"A couple of times this spring. I don't remember exactly, but once or twice, probably in June or July."

"Why did Deni take you there?"

"She usually went when she had a painting that she wanted Varelli to look at."

"Like a Vermeer?" Mike asked.

I wanted to slow him down. I could see Preston Mattox stiffen when Mike mentioned the artist's name. If he jumped into the territory of stolen artworks too quickly, I was afraid he'd lose his cooperative subject.

"So, you two have bought into all the gossip on the circuit. Denise Caxton and the masterpieces from the Gardner heist. When you find the goods, be sure and let me know," he said, scowling at Chapman as though he had made a terrible mistake.

"Deni ever talk to you about the Vermeer? Or the Rembrandt?"

Mattox was angry now. "She wasn't a thief, Detective. Deni made more than her share of enemies, but she was an awfully decent woman when you gave her a chance to be. There was no way she was involved with the scum who've been peddling stolen property. She didn't need that kind of trouble. Between the life that Lowell had built for her and what I was willing to provide when she married me, there wasn't any reason to debase herself with something that would land her in jail."

While Mattox was hot, Mike decided it was a good moment to offer him up the name of his rival. "And Frank Wrenley? Where did he fit in Deni's life?"

"As far out of the picture as I could move him, Detective."

"Why? What did you know about him?"

"Not enough, clearly. But that's because whatever I saw I didn't like."

"More than just jealousy?"

"Yes, Mr. Chapman. Far more than that. Frank moved in on Deni like a vulture right after she and Lowell split. I mean, they had known each other before around the auction houses, but he pounced on her like a panther when her wounds were still quite raw."

"But she loved him, too, didn't she?"

"She certainly liked what he offered her as an immediate alternative when Lowell Caxton brought their marriage to a crashing halt. Wrenley was a vehicle to get back at her husband. First of all, he was young, and youth was something Lowell couldn't buy for himself with all his millions. Wrenley was slick—too slick for my taste."

"Was he a real player in the antiques business?"

Mattox was slow to answer. "He's been making quite a name for himself. Not necessarily someone I'd bring in on a project, but he seems to know what he's doing."

"Would you say that you were closer to Deni in recent months than Wrenley was?" I asked.

Preston Mattox crossed his arms and leaned against the sill. Something he thought of brought a smile to his face. "I almost gave up on Deni before I got started. For a while it wasn't Lowell's shadow that got in the way, it was Wrenley's. Everywhere we went, he'd been there with Deni first. Just your mention of Marco Varelli reminded me how unreasonable I'd been about it. I'd been introduced to the man any number of times, but that last afternoon we were up in his studio, Deni and I walked in with a bottle of wine and some *biscotti* and he embraced me in a bear hug, calling me 'Franco.' Instead of correcting *him,* I took it out on Deni as soon as we left, asking her what the hell she'd been doing there with Frank."

"What'd she tell you?"

"I'm not sure she ever gave me an answer, Mr. Chapman. As with most of our arguments, she got me over them by taking me home to make love. I knew she and Wrenley had been doing the auction scene together, so it made sense that they had taken some work to Varelli to be cleaned up or restored. I just didn't like following in his footsteps wherever we went. But I didn't answer the question you asked, did I, Miss Cooper?

"Yes," he went on, "I was confident that I'd be

spending the rest of my life with Deni. I can't tell you how extraordinarily happy that made me."

"Why had you gone to see Varelli that day?"

"Because Deni asked me to. Simple as that. He'd been mad at her about something, she wouldn't tell me what. So she wanted to take him a gift for his wife, smoke the peace pipe together—that sort of thing. I suppose I was an intermediary. She knew he liked to talk to me about my work—and that I could hold my own, whether it was about the architectural principles of Leonardo da Vinci and Thomas Jefferson or about drawings and art."

Chapman didn't care about the dome on the Rotunda. "What was the gift that Deni took for Mrs. Varelli?"

Again Mattox hesitated before lifting his head to meet Chapman's stare. "It was a necklace, Detective. An amber necklace. But I suppose you knew that already. I imagine you found the small figurine that Deni left behind, and that Mrs. Varelli told you the story."

Neither of us responded to his statement.

"I take it the peace offering didn't go very well, did it?"

"Varelli was furious." Mattox seemed to be open with us, having convinced himself that Varelli had told the story of the encounter to his wife. I guessed that he did not even recall that the soft-spoken young apprentice, Don Cannon, had been in the room when the beads were presented. "He assumed that the amber was part of Lowell's secret cache of looted Nazi riches. The old guy didn't even want to hold the necklace in his hands."

"Isn't that the truth, though? Isn't that the source of the amber?"

"Hardly, Mr. Chapman. All of us who've been looking for the Amber Room have combed the Baltic coast for years. In Lowell's case, for half a century, if you can imagine that. We've each come back with bits and pieces—the area is rich with amber. There are places along the coast where you can pick up chunks of it right on the beach. But no one really knows whether the great room was destroyed in some wartime bombing or is buried in one of the quarries that treasure seekers are constantly drilling."

"How about the rumors that Lowell Caxton has smuggled half the remains out of Europe and re-created the palace room in some hideaway in the Pennsylvania countryside?"

"And that's why I had latched on to Mrs. Caxton, Mr. Chapman? I've heard that one, too. If you could have seen Deni throw back her head and roar at those stories—and the nonsense that she and Lowell had used this mini Amber Room for their trysts—well, then you would have seen the woman I adored. She liked to fuel those absurd tales when she heard they were circulating. The more bold and bizarre, the more it pleased her. She loved outrage, Detective, and if she was at the center of it she loved it even more."

"Were those the only jewels from Lowell that Deni wanted to give away?" I asked, referring to the amber beads.

"Lowell?" Mattox said with some surprise. "I don't think she was parting with anything *he* gave her. His gifts to her were pretty substantial."

"Then why the amber?"

"Those pieces weren't from Lowell."

I was sure Don Cannon had repeated that as part of Deni's explanation when she tried to hand Varelli the necklace.

Mattox thought for a moment. "You know, you're right, though. She told Marco they had been given to her by Lowell." Now he looked up at me. "But you see, that was part of the game she liked to play. By implication she'd let people assume they were part of Lowell's collection. Knowing Deni, she thought it would titillate old Marco to think there really was an Amber Room and that she and Lowell had cavorted in it. She and Varelli may have talked about it on other occasions—I simply don't know that."

"But she wouldn't take anything fake to give Varelli," I said. "I realize that his specialty was paint and artworks, but he had such a great eye. People tell us he had a unique sense of touch, and could identify the age of artworks so precisely. She wouldn't pass off something to him as an antique or a valuable if she was trying to appease him, would she?"

"The necklace and figurine were genuine, Miss Cooper. Very old and very fine amber. The Baltic region is full of great pieces. It's just that these things had absolutely nothing to do with the mysterious Russian palace and its amber. Deni may have tried to create that impression, but she knew damn well where the pieces came from."

"And what was that?" Chapman asked.

"The necklace had been commissioned by King Wilhelm of Prussia for his queen. And the figurine as well. Sold at auction in Geneva several years ago. Can't remember the price they brought, but it was quite high."

"And Lowell bought them for Deni?"

"No, no." Mattox seemed bothered that we hadn't followed his point. "Deni only *said* she had gotten them from Lowell. Actually, they were a gift to her from a friend."

"You know who he was?"

"*She,* Detective. From a woman called Marina Sette."

"Pretty nice stocking stuffer," Mike said.

It seemed even more curious that Deni would relinquish something that her closest friend had given to her. I still had every note card and silly souvenir that Nina or Joan had ever sent me, not to mention the more serious gifts. "But why would she get rid of something so precious, from someone she liked so much?"

Preston Mattox looked at me with a curious glance. "Liked so much? They hadn't talked to each other in a long time."

Chapman spoke before I did. "I thought they were best pals."

"I don't know what gave you that idea. They used to be quite close, but they had a terrible falling-out this spring. I don't think Deni had returned Marina's calls in months."

"What was that about, do you know?"

"The only person who thought she had a greater entitlement to Lowell Caxton's fortune than Denise did was Marina Sette. Deni came to believe that the

349

primary reason Marina had befriended her in the first place was to work herself back into the inheritance—the fortune that would have been Marina's had her mother not abandoned her when she married Lowell. There was nothing logical about Marina's position. I doubt she has a leg to stand on in a court of law. But I think it was more of an emotional attempt to regain some connection to the mother she never knew, by claiming that she had a right to some of the master-pieces acquired during the period her mother was married to Lowell Caxton."

"Seems to me there was more than enough money to go around," Chapman murmured.

"But they'd never argued about that before?" I asked.

"It never was an issue with Deni before this spring. But then, once she suspected that Marina Sette had been sleeping with Frank Wrenley, it became more than an issue. It was the end of the friendship. The worm turned."

# 27

Mercer Wallace lifted his head off the pile of pillows as we entered the room and gave us a weak but warm greeting. The nurse who helped feed him his dinner—still a liquid diet—was moving the tray off the bedside table as we settled in around the patient.

Chapman grabbed the television remote control panel dangling from a cord on Mercer's bed railing and pointed it at the small set that was hanging from a support in the corner.

"Too early," Mercer said, laughing. It was only six thirty-five, and he thought that Mike was looking for the *Jeopardy!* channel. "Let me hear what's going on."

Mike kept clicking until the screen was set on NBC and the national news report. "Don't you want to see Cooper's guy? Has he got a live shoot tonight, kid? Whoops, looks like Brian Williams has the anchor spot." He muted the sound and asked Mercer how he felt.

"I don't remember much about yesterday. Pain's

under control, and they even had me out of bed for an hour this afternoon. One lap around the hallway."

"There he is!" Mike said, rising from his armchair and walking to stand directly under the television set. "Gimme volume, Mercer."

Jake was standing on First Avenue, in front of the United Nations building, and he was midsentence when I heard his voice: ". . . after the secretary of state and the delegate from . . ."

Mike's pen was in his right hand, held up against the screen and tapping at Jake's chest. "Here's the thing, Mercer. The reason you and I will never get to first base with Ms. Cooper is that we don't have these ties that all her beaux wear, know what I mean? Every one of 'em has these itsy-bitsy, teeny-weeny little friggin' animals all over 'em. Grown men, and they got little squirrels runnin' around with nuts in their cheeks, sheep jumping over fences, monkeys swingin' on vines, giraffes standing on tippy-toe. I would be mortified to be here on national television, talkin' about sending troops to the Middle East, decked out in some French necktie—what do you call them, Coop? Hermies or Hermans or Ermies—something like that. Anyway, the thing is, Mercer, that it *works*. 'Cause whatever it is about those ties, every one of the goofballs who shows up wearing one of 'em gets laid.

"Am I right, blondie? Ever do a simple guy with a striped tie? I doubt it. I'm telling you, if Alex Trebek walked in with one of these on, she'd go down on him like a pelican, wouldn't you, kid? You wanna predict who Cooper's gonna get up close and personal with, you check out the tie. That, my good friend, is my Dick Tracy crimestopper clue of the day."

Mercer was holding his hand over his chest. "Don't make me laugh, Mike. Somebody want to tell me what's going on with the case?"

"First of all, forget that you ever saw Alex tonight. Pat McKinney's riding her pretty hard. Doesn't want her to visit with you, so you don't talk about the facts of the case together."

Mercer looked across at me to see if Mike was still kidding. "It's true. He's afraid we're going to conspire and rearrange the events if we talk to each other. I spent three hours last night giving my statement. I'm sure they got one from you today, as soon as you opened your eyes. I don't know what he's so worried about."

"They were here. Two guys from Major Case, first thing this morning. They said they're taking you back over to the scene later in the week."

"Yes," I said, hoping that my involuntary shudder at the thought of revisiting the gallery hadn't been visible to Mike or Mercer.

"That is one spooky exhibit," Mike said. "I stopped there this morning on my way to the hospital the first time. Kind of reminds me of that great Orson Welles scene in *Lady From Shanghai*—the shoot-out in the fun house? Only thing missing was the mirrors. Listen to this."

Mike pulled a wrinkled piece of paper from his pants pocket. "They're already moving a new show into Caxton Due. Somebody probably needed all that friggin' yarn to make a sweater. I'm reading right from the description Bryan Daughtry wrote. It's in *New York* magazine. 'The artist affixes hardened blobs of paint and scraps of paper, hair, and other scavenged materials to her monochromatic canvases.' I'm looking forward to wrapping this case up so I can go back to working something real, like a pickpocket detail."

Mercer winced as he tried to push himself up in bed. I moved to his side to adjust the pillows behind his back and beneath his head. I grabbed one of his enormous arms and pulled on it as gently as I could, but was unable to move him. Mike got on the other side, and together we raised Mercer so that his head rested in a more comfortable position.

"Watch out for the tubes," I said to Mike, lifting the IV drip from where it was caught under a roll of bed-sheet.

"Else you'll get *strangulated* on all those concoctions, Mr. Wallace. That's a word for the *S* section of my dictionary. I got to jot that one down. 'Fixiated'—that goes with the *F*'s, not the *A*'s—and 'strangulated' are two very popular causes of death among perps."

"Have mercy, will you please, Mr. Chapman? I'm supposed to be lying here very still. Don't make me get up and have to hurt you."

We spent the next half hour telling Mercer what we had learned from Don Cannon and Preston Mattox. "Who do you like in all this?" he asked.

Mike shrugged his shoulders. "Nothing and nobody is like what you'd think they'd be. Me, I always thought the international art world was for the elegant and elite. Classy, calm, sedate, cultured. I'm tellin' you, there are more lowlifes in *this* business than all the Hannibal Lecter wanna-bes in the world."

"Between the fakes and the frauds, and centuries of thefts and misrepresentations, I can't imagine now how anyone sets a value that can be trusted on any painting," I added. It was odd that for so many of the people we had encountered, their passions had become obsessions, and their lives as illusory as their art.

Mike reached for the clicker and raised the volume again. "Okay, the Final Jeopardy topic is Sports. Way to go. I'm in for fifty dollars. Partners, Mercer?" Mike gave him a thumbs-up and got a wink in response. "Get your money up, Coop."

I opened my pocketbook and reached in to dig around. Even though I had just taken another handbag from the apartment late last night to replace the one that I had lost in the shooting, I had already filled it with more than any reasonable person would cart around. The heavy wallet, laden with a checkbook, credit cards, business cards, and assorted notes, had sunk to the bottom of the deep tote. On Mercer's tray table I unloaded house keys, car keys, office keys, and Jake's apartment keys. A lipstick case and blusher came out next. Handkerchief, pens, hairbrush, Post-it pads, and my official badge piled on top.

"How the hell do you ever find anything in there? It's really one of life's great mysteries.

"Okay, the answer is: First major league athlete to play all nine positions in the same baseball game. You got sixty seconds, blondie. Mercer and I got this one locked up . . . What the hell is that?"

As I pulled out my wallet, with it came a small plastic bag that had snagged on its clasp, holding an old-fashioned razor and set of double-edge platinum blades, along with a toothbrush and tube of paste.

"I brought a little supply kit for Mercer. Jake has dozens of those travel cases so he can just pack them and go when he gets sent on assignment. Thought maybe you'd be able to use some of this stuff while you're here," I said, holding it up so Mercer could see.

He pointed to his drawer and told me that his dad had brought him everything he needed, so I replaced all my belongings in the bag.

"Enough with the Clara Barton imitation. You either give us a name or just drop the money in my pocket."

I had no idea that anyone had ever accomplished that feat. I took out a fifty-dollar bill and handed it to Mike, at the same time as I said, "Who was Whitey Ford?" As far as I was concerned, if it hadn't been done by a Yankee, then it hadn't ever happened.

Trebek was just consoling the three contestants, none of whom had delivered the correct answer. Before he revealed it on the game board, Mike announced, "Kansas City. Who is Bert Campaneris?"

The television echoed the same question: "Who is Bert Campaneris?"

"I can't believe you knew that."

He'd pocketed the cash before I finished the sentence. "You don't mind if I don't spend it on flowers or candy, do you, m'man? I got some informants who need a little monkey grease to make 'em sing to me."

The phone rang and I picked it up. "Could I speak with Detective Chapman?"

I stepped back and Mike squeezed around the side of the bed and took the receiver. "K.D.? Whaddaya got?" Mike raised his left shoulder to hold the phone in place against his ear while he reached into his pocket for a pen and paper. He listened to Jimmy Halloran for several minutes, occasionally punctuating the conversation with a 'When?' or a 'Who?' while I held a straw to Mercer's lips and helped him drink some of the water that the nurse had directed him to finish. "No, it's not everything," Mike said before hanging up, "but it's not a bad start. Thanks."

Mike began his narrative for us. "Anthony Bailor. Gainesville, Florida. He's forty-two years old now, but back when he was eighteen, he burglarized an apartment. Raped a college student who was living there. Knifepoint. Also I.D.'d in three other cases in town within six months."

"And did less than twenty years?" I asked.

"Three of the victims were too scared to press charges. Hey, it was almost twenty-five years ago. Nothing unusual about that back then."

It was only within the last ten to fifteen years that victims of sexual assault were treated with any dignity in the courtroom. The bad laws that had prevented women from having access to the system had begun to be revised throughout the seventies, but public attitudes about this category of crime had been even slower to change. For centuries, rape was the only crime for which the victim was blamed, and the stigma that attached itself to women who had been forced to experience such an intimate violation kept many of them from seeking justice.

"What didn't show on his sheet was his youth record. Again, Florida. Did time in a juvenile facility, also for rape. Carjacked a woman in a supermarket parking lot."

"So we got a sexual predator on our hands."

"Served his felony sentence in Raiford. They got a prison there, Coop, makes Attica look like a beauty school. Bailor did hard time. *Real* hard time. I'm talking chain gangs and leg irons. Must've been one of the first guys to get himself into the DNA data bank. Even though they didn't exist when he was convicted, by the time he was eligible for parole, no one was let out until his genetic fingerprint was on file."

Mike looked back at his pad and flipped the page. "When he got out of jail, he moved right out of Florida. Can't say as I blame him. If you're gonna foul up again, might as well come north to one of our country club prisons. Be my guest, Mr. Bailor. I love New York.

"Ready for the larceny arrest?" Mike asked. "The original charge was grand larceny, but he pleaded out to possession of stolen property. That's how come he did so little time. Prosecutor had to drop the top count and take the lesser plea 'cause the theft actually occurred in Massachusetts. Anton Bailey was stopped on the New York State Thruway for speeding. When they searched his car, the troopers found a couple of oil paintings. Valuable ones. Seems Anton hadn't saved his sales receipts."

"Massachusetts? From the Gardner?"

"Nope. Right state, wrong museum. Something called the Mead Art Museum, in Amherst. Couldn't pin the actual burglary on Anton. His alibi back in Buffalo held up pretty well. So all they had him for was possession of the goods. They even offered him a deal of no jail time if he gave up his accomplice. But he hung tough. Shit, after the stretch he did in Florida, he must have done this sentence standing on his head."

It was an interesting development. Somewhere along the way, Bailor had connected with art criminals and had perhaps lent his break-in talent to their undertakings. A simple calculation confirmed that he was still in a Florida prison when the Gardner theft had occurred, but he must have more recently marketed his skills to this murky underground world of thieves.

"Do you think he knew Omar Sheffield before they wound up in the same cell?"

"No sign of that yet. We'll have to talk to some of the other prisoners. So far, what K.D. got is only from the paperwork in the warden's files. Could be just dumb luck. Omar's doing his usual scam. Tells Anton about Denise Caxton, maybe even shows him the clippings from the *Law Journal* about the Caxton divorce, which lists every one of their assets and describes all of their dealings in the art business. Anton has bigger plans. Passes off the information to . . ."

"Whom?" I asked. "That's all we've got to figure. He must have been in this with someone else, someone who had his own scam in mind for Denise."

"Or for Lowell," Mike reminded me. "I'm not sure who was out to get which one first."

"You don't really think Lowell was intended to be a victim in all this, do you?"

Mercer had been listening to us without joining the conversation, as he struggled against dozing off. "You said you spoke to that Sette woman out in Santa Fe yesterday, Mike? That she really was back there?"

Mike paused before answering. "It was actually her housekeeper who answered the phone and told me she expected Sette back in an hour or so. She was Mexican, with a thick accent, and hard to understand. No, I didn't speak to Sette directly. And I forgot to check the airline manifest afterward to see if she really flew out there. Sorry, Mercer. I'll get on that tonight."

It was Marina Sette's message—or one that had been left for us using her name—that had resulted in my trip to the Focus gallery with Mercer yesterday and that had set us up to be shot. For good reason, Mike was concentrating more on that intrigue at the moment than on piecing together the puzzle of Deni Caxton's death.

The phone rang again and I answered it. "Alexandra? It's Rose Malone. I thought you might be there with Mercer. I wanted you to know that Mr. Battaglia is on his way home. He's going to stop in at the hospital."

Thank goodness for Rose. She was better than a radar detector. I'd say good night to Mercer before Battaglia arrived, and let the squad detectives take me back to Jake's apartment for the night.

"And one other thing. The police have arrested that Wakefield man who was here at the office looking for you earlier."

"Did he come back?" I asked, alarmed at his persistence.

"No. But that young girl who was in your office—was it Ruth?"

"Yes."

"She showed up at his apartment this afternoon, to try to get together with him again. He beat her up pretty seriously. For admitting to you that she'd been sleeping with his roommate."

"Oh, no." I closed my eyes and gritted my teeth at the thought of the anger that Wakefield must have unleashed at that child. I thanked Rose for the call and hung up the phone.

"You're running on fumes, Coop," Mike said. "I'll sit with Mercer tonight. Let me take you downstairs and send you off. Get a good night's sleep and we'll talk in the morning. Put a double rush on those prison phone records when you get to the office. We gotta figure out who Bailey's connected with, okay? And I think we need to find Marina Sette as soon as possible."

I sat in the back of the unmarked car, looking out at the dark streets as we drove uptown and making small talk with the detectives about the usual office gossip. They discharged me in front of Jake's building, watching as the doorman let me in and then parking at the curb, where they would sit out their shift before they were replaced by the midnight team in a couple of hours.

I turned the key in the lock and entered the apartment. A small lamp was lighted on the vestibule table, where I saw a handwritten note addressed to me.

"Dearest A— My turn to disappear. Running for the last shuttle to Washington. Have a 7 A.M. interview with the secretary of defense. Sweet dreams, see you tomorrow. Love, J."

I groped the walls in the semidarkness of the unfamiliar layout to turn on a light switch in the hallway leading to the bedroom. Once I found my way, I reached for the suitcase I had packed the evening before and laid out some of the clothes for the next day.

The silence and the emptiness made me uncomfortable. I wanted the comfort of my own home, and the warmth of Jake's caress.

# 28

I couldn't find the coffee beans in Jake's kitchen when I got out of bed, shortly before seven o'clock. I showered and dressed, joining the team in the department car for the ride down to 1 Hogan Place. They let me out right in front of the building, and I bought us each some breakfast at the cart on the corner before going up to my office. Now that Wakim had been arrested I felt at least somewhat more secure.

The pile of unanswered correspondence on my desk was growing out of control. There was a stack of indictments on sex crimes cases that needed to be proofread and approved before the end of the August term, which was a week away. Phone messages from friends were taped to the computer screen; a request from Elaine to set a time to come into the Escada store to have the clothes I ordered from the fall collection shortened had been ignored; and solicitations for charitable fund-raisers collected dust on the far corner of the desk. It was still too early to find most people at their offices, so I busied myself in the review of grand jury proceedings to make sure the lawyers in the unit met their filing deadlines.

The first call was from Bob Thaler, the chief serologist at the Medical Examiner's Office. It was not even eight thirty, and I was answering my own phones because Laura would not arrive for another hour.

"Sorry it took me so long for the tox on Omar Sheffield." While autopsy results were available to us quickly, it frequently took weeks to run all the toxicological tests looking for foreign substances in the deceased's brain, liver, tissue, or lungs.

"Find anything?"

"Just about everything. Omar might have been breathing when that train ran over him, but he wouldn't have been aware of very much. He was loaded up with speedballs, more than enough to kill himself with if he'd been attempting to O.D."

"And if someone else was trying to kill him?" Speedballs were a deadly combination of heroin and cocaine, usually mainlined right into the system.

"It'd work like a charm. Just keep pumping it into his arm."

"But the cause of death, what have you put down for that?"

"Gross internal trauma. I mean, he died at the moment the train ran over his body, Alex. But in all likelihood the drugs could have done the trick by themselves. Somebody finds you in a hotel room in a coma, they can still get you to a hospital and try to pump the stuff out of you. Slim chance, with this amount of poison in his veins, but it might have been possible for him to survive. Run a few railroad cars over this perfectly inert body, it's a sure thing he's gone to meet his maker."

"Thanks, Bob. Would you fax over a copy of the report to me?"

Lawyers were beginning to dribble into the office. I had my door open, listening for Pat McKinney's arrival. The click of high heels on the tiles of the deserted hallway caught my attention. Pat's office, like Rod Squires's, was at the far end of my corridor. But there were no other women assigned to this executive wing of the Trial Division, so I stepped out to Laura's desk to see who was walking by.

I recognized Ellen Gunsher from the back. She was junior to me, having been in the office for almost eight years. Bright enough and quite aggressive, she had taken to all of the duties of a prosecutor fairly well—except for the one that counted most. She had never grown comfortable in the courtroom and backed away from trying cases. Her surname lent itself to the unfortunate alias "Gun-shy," and her colleagues teased her mercilessly about her retreat from the kind of professional battle that most of us relished.

Ellen had found a protector in Pat McKinney. As deputy chief of the division, he had taken her out of her trial bureau and created a special unit for her to supervise. Most of us recognized that it was a make-work kind of assignment—to serve as a contact with the NYPD's Warrant Squad, to initiate and oversee active searches for the most dangerous of the thousands of defendants who failed to appear on their cases after bail had been granted. Many of the prisoners for whom Wanted cards had been issued were petty offenders who would turn up in the system before too long on charges of shoplifting or jumping a turnstile. Ellen's job consisted of sifting through court papers and targeting the more violent offenders, then assigning Warrant Squad officers to make an active search for their return.

I believed that McKinney had manufactured that niche because Ellen was a decent lawyer and a nice person who was not otherwise a fit in our division. For two years I had ignored office gossip that they had been having an affair, but now the amount of time they spent together behind closed doors seemed inordinate for the nonessential nature of Ellen's work.

I went back to my desk to gather the notes I planned to take in to McKinney to discuss the latest interviews Mike and I had done on the Caxton investigation. McKinney waved at me as he passed by my doorway. "We gotta talk."

The case papers had outgrown a single folder. I pulled out the sheaf of reports we had worked from yesterday, took my thick legal pad including my to-do list, and headed down to the deputy's office. I knocked on the heavy metal door.

"Come in," Ellen called out to me. Not exactly the welcome I wanted.

She was standing by a hot plate at the far end of the room, boiling water for tea. She had opened a jar of honey and was holding two mugs. McKinney had his back to me and was talking on the phone. It was all a bit too domestic for my taste.

"How's Mercer?" Ellen asked.

"He's in rough shape. It was a very close call."

"You must feel awful. I can't imagine how you handled watching him get shot."

I slowly moved my head back and forth, biting my lip. I had no intention of telling her anything about how I felt, and was boring my eyes through the back of McKinney's sweaty T-shirt as though it would somehow get him off the phone faster.

"Want some tea?" she asked, holding up a third mug with a photo of McKinney's kids under a Christmas tree emblazoned on its ceramic side.

"No thanks," I said, raising my cardboard coffee cup at her.

"Any new leads?"

"I'll wait until Pat gets off the phone."

"Been up to the Vineyard at all?"

"Uh huh." When you're ready for full disclosure on your personal life, I'll be happy to give you an update on my own.

"You really look whipped. Ought to try a little concealer for those circles under your eyes. Maybe you should take the next couple of weeks off. Stay up there until after Labor Day."

Women in the workplace, I sighed to myself. Why is it that Mike Chapman could tell me how bad I looked and I could acknowledge it, but when Ellen eyeballed me and said the same thing, it sounded bitchy? Maybe I could take two weeks in the country if I was as expendable around here as you are, I thought. "I'm fine. I'll take it easy next weekend."

McKinney finished his conversation and sat down opposite me at his small conference table. "I want to talk to you about the case, Alex—I mean, the whole matter. I've been thinking that maybe the best thing—"

"Pat, would you mind if we just do this one-on-one?"

Ellen had poured the water and was squeezing the tea bags now.

"You mean Ellen? She's a unit chief in the division. What's the problem?"

"This discussion is between you and me. I know you've called a meeting for ten o'clock this morning to which I wasn't invited. I'm planning to be there."

"That's a stupid idea, Alex. In fact, I'm not even sure it makes any sense for you to stay on the Caxton investigation."

"Ellen, would you mind leaving the room, please?"

She placed the mugs on the table, and instead of answering me, she looked at Pat, who was looking directly in my eyes.

"I'm *not* having this conversation in Ellen's presence. Last I knew," I said, trying not to let my temper take over my response, "no one in this case had jumped bail, failed to appear, warranted out on a misdemeanor, or otherwise done anything to invoke the awesome power of Ellen Gunsher's irrelevant little unit. This is between the two of us, Pat. You have *no* business talking about it with Ellen. And don't you dare even think about taking me off the Caxton murder. I'll go right to Battaglia and—"

"I've already done that, Alex."

Ellen's head was snapping back and forth between us like it was on a spring. I was infuriated that Pat had spoken to the district attorney about removing me from the investigation.

"I'll bet he told you to stick it. He has absolutely no problem with the work I've been doing."

It was a bluff, but a successful one. McKinney's moment of hesitation revealed to me that although he had raised the issue with Battaglia, he had not been given a green light to take the case away from me.

I pushed my chair back and walked to the door. "I'll be in Battaglia's office. When you and the Lipton Tea lady finish your morning tête-à-tête, feel free to come in, by yourself, to get a bulletin on the case. Meanwhile, I'll leave you to the important matter of how many of yesterday's token suckers failed to show up in AP17."

I doubled back past my office, across the main corridor, and used my magnetized identification badge to buzz myself into the executive wing. Secretaries to the administrative assistant, the first assistant, and the chief assistant were setting up their desks for the day and greeted me with interest and concern.

Rose Malone was already at her word processor when I approached her desk. She was the last to leave the building most nights—sometimes with Paul Battaglia, but never before him. And she was always the first one in place the next day.

She didn't even turn her head to speak to me. "He's not here yet, Alex. There's a community board breakfast meeting in East Harlem."

"Do you expect him before ten?"

"No. He's going from that one directly to the Midtown Court. There's going to be a press release about the new computer system that will track bench warrants in all the borough courthouses and police precincts."

Great. A new technology that will make Ellen Gunsher completely obsolete. "Will he call in from the car?"

"I expect so. Shall I transfer him over to you?"

"Please. Especially if you get him within the hour, okay?"

"Anything wrong?"

"Was Pat McKinney alone with him for any period of time yesterday?"

Rose stopped typing and looked back at Battaglia's date book, as though trying to find a way to remind herself of the day's meetings.

"I know he called and asked if the boss would see him. They may have spoken for a minute or two, but Paul was tied up most of the afternoon with the accountants who've been working on that welfare fraud case. It couldn't have been much of a conversation."

I thanked her and walked back to my office. As much as McKinney may have wanted me off the Caxton case, I was still alive. I needed to sit down and go over what the rest of the week might produce for us, knowing that any kind of evidentiary break would help cement my position on the team.

I could hear Chapman serenading Laura as I went back to my office. What had probably started as a cross-examination of what she knew about my relationship with Jacob Tyler had segued into an impromptu version of Paul Simon's "Fifty Ways to

Leave Your Lover." As I turned the corner he grinned at me and continued singing. "Don't make a mistake, Jake. Just let yourself go."

"To what do I owe this unexpected pleasure?" I growled.

"People to talk to, places to go, subpoenas to get. Let's start with the latter. What happened to your manners? What about 'Good morning, Mr. Chapman. How are you today? Thank you for bringing me another cup of coffee,' huh? I'm even going out on a limb for a 'Don't *you* look lovely today, Miss Cooper. Could be you had a good night's rest at long last.'"

"Thanks. But I've already been told by Ellen Gunsher that even makeup can't help me in my current condition. Pat's trying to knock me off your investigation."

"What kind of suicide mission is *he* on?"

"There's a meeting at ten to assign one of the senior trial counsel to Mercer's shooting. And since I'm a witness to that, he wants to take me off the whole thing and set one of his pets up to handle it, before Rod Squires returns from vacation." My back was to the door as I reached across my desk to replace the case papers on top of the folder. "I'm trying to get a call into Battaglia before this morning's caucus on the subject."

"Speaking of carcass, what's up, McKinney?"

Mike warned me that Pat had appeared in the doorway, and I spun around.

"Now I'd like to talk to *you* alone, Alex. Why don't you wait down the hall, Mike?"

"Battaglia gave me strict orders that she's to have

police protection around the clock, Pat. No can do."
Mike sat behind the desk in my chair and lifted his feet
up on my desktop, one at a time, making the statement that he was not about to move. "We got some
breaking developments on Caxton you might want to
know about."

"Take a walk, Chapman. C'mon."

Mike checked with me before he slowly removed his
legs, then stood up and started for the exit. "Be sure to
give my best to your wife and kids, Pat."

The intercom buzzed and I could hear Laura calling
my name.

"Yes?"

"There's a gentleman downstairs who wants to talk
to you. His name is Frank Wrenley. Can he come up?"

I exchanged glances with Chapman, who had
stopped in the doorway, and he nodded at me in
response. "Keep him down there for ten minutes while
I make a few calls. Maybe he can clear up some of this
business about his relationship with Marina Sette. I'd
like to find out exactly where she is right now."

I told Laura to have security hold him there until
Mike could go to the lobby to escort him in. "This
isn't a very good time to talk, Pat. Might as well go
ahead with your ten o'clock meeting. I can't make it
anyway."

# 29

"I just woke up the housekeeper in Santa Fe. She doesn't expect Ms. Sette back there for another week. Laid on a heavy Spanish accent, says I must have misunderstood her when I called on Sunday. I'm telling you, Alex, I swear that woman told me Sette had just flown back home the other day. This is Mercer's life, for chrissakes. It's not anything I would have made a mistake about. Today when I press her about where I can get in touch with Sette, all I get is that the housekeeper doesn't know. '*La Señora*' is traveling." Mike was fuming.

"All right, relax. Let's just make a plan."

"You know why I like it better when I'm working on something where everybody's poor? 'Cause the friggin' perps can't go too far. One guy's maybe got a mother in Queens, next one chills out at his brother's place in the Bronx, another sleeps on the rooftop. None of this Airborne Express crap that the rich can pull. That mope I locked up for the triple homicide in the Polo Grounds projects two weeks ago? Gave me more trouble than any of 'em. His sister told me he lived in a mobile home. In New York City? No way— we don't have 'em here. Took me days to figure out she meant the A train. He just moved his plastic bag of worldly goods into the subway and rode from one end of the system to the other and then back, night after night. It should happen to these people. What if it actually *was* Marina Sette who left the message for you and Mercer to meet her?"

"Then she either has something to do with the killings or she's on the run because she's truly terrified of something or someone."

"When are you gonna get results on all the subpoenas for telephone records?" His impatience was palpable.

"I call every day, and every day they tell me that the volume is tremendous and I'll have what I need as soon as possible. The only ones back were in yesterday's mail. Omar Sheffield's phone calls made while he was in jail. I had Maxine and one of the other paralegals go through them to check for calls to Denise Caxton. Not a one."

"How can that be?"

"I checked with the warden. You'll love this one. There's a foolproof way for inmates to place untraceable calls now. They buy those prepaid telephone cards and then use the cards to make the calls from prison pay phones. All you're left with is a record of a call to the company that issued the card, but no link at all to the number actually dialed. Max says Omar's phone-privilege time slots—you know, the half hour each day he had access to the booth—show lots of activity in the period that would fit with the dates after Deni started to get letters from him, but all the outgoing ones he made just reflect the number of the calling card company in Brooklyn."

"Damn. And no word on when you'll have the incoming calls to the Caxton house or the galleries?"

"That takes longer. I'd guess we're at least a week away from that stuff."

"Let me go downstairs and get Wrenley. After he tells us why he's here, I'll move it to talk about Marina Sette, okay?"

I walked to my desk to find my file notes on the antiques dealer and review them. Laura stuck her head in the doorway and asked if she could borrow an emery board. I pointed to my handbag, which I had left on the leather armchair in front of the desk. "Just fish around in there. I know I've got a few on the bottom."

"Would you mind if I take the day off tomorrow?" she asked tentatively.

I guessed that was the real reason she had come into the room in the first place. "As long as you can get someone to cover the phones. They've been wild since this started. And help Mike with the subpoenas he needs you to type up this morning." We were short staffed because of the normal summer vacation schedule, but the pace of the investigation didn't correspond with the seasonal slowdown. "Any luck in finding Rod Squires?"

"Rose says he's on a sailboat off the coast of Maine. If he contacts Paul, she'll flip him over to you."

For the moment, Frank Wrenley's unexpected

appearance gave me a reprieve from McKinney's plan to boot me off the case.

Mike came back into my office with Wrenley and I rose to shake his hand across the desk. This time he was head-to-toe in slate gray, a slight contrast to his jet black hair and almost a match for the cloud-filled sky that hugged the city with its humidity.

"Why don't you have a seat and tell us what brings you down here?"

Wrenley turned to sit and I saw my bag in his way. "Just put it on the floor. Sorry."

He lifted it and sat it down next to the row of file cabinets. "Must have your whole arsenal in there, Miss Cooper."

Chapman laughed. "She would if we'd let her. Temper like hers, Mr. Wrenley, Cooper couldn't get a permit to carry a pointed pencil."

Wrenley looked directly at me. "I wasn't sure who to talk to about this, but perhaps you ought to know. And you might be able to help me, too."

It was getting harder and harder to find anyone to talk to us who didn't want something in return. "What is it?"

"Last evening I found out that Lowell Caxton is going to be closing his gallery."

He stopped speaking and both Mike and I waited for him to continue.

"I mean, this week. Abruptly. Doesn't that surprise you?"

"Elephants flying? Monkeys tap-dancing? Those things might surprise me. The people in this case, the pals you've been running with who've been scamming each other and the public for most of their adult lives? Very little they do could surprise me at this point."

Wrenley ignored Chapman and talked to me. "Caxton's had one of the most substantial businesses in this city for longer than I can remember. It would be one thing for him to announce a closing and wind down his affairs over the next few months. But to pull a few moving vans up to the front of the building and start loading them like a gypsy in the middle of the night, well, it's more than a bit odd."

"Last night?" I asked. "Who told you about it?"

"Bryan Daughtry called me. He still has a lot of contacts who work in the Fuller Building."

Wrenley's statement reminded me that before Daughtry went to jail on the tax case, his original gallery had been on Fifty-seventh Street, several floors below Caxton's suite.

"What else did he say?"

"One of the custodians, a fellow who runs the freight elevator, figured he could make a few dollars by passing the information to Daughtry. It worked. Bryan went right up there and gave the guy a hundred bucks. Saw what was going on himself. Paintings and sculptures being loaded onto a truck at eleven last night, complete with a cadre of security guards. But Caxton's employees wouldn't spill the beans. Not a word about where they were taking the stuff, or why. I'm sure he paid them well enough to ensure their loyalty."

"I guess I'm missing the reason why either you or Daughtry think any of this is your business," Chapman said.

"Understandable. That's why, as I said a few minutes ago, I wasn't sure what to do about it when Daughtry called me in the middle of the night. Both Bryan and I were involved in a number of art deals with Deni. She and I recently bought some paintings at auction together," he said, switching his attention to Mike. "You're the skeptic, Detective. Check with Christie's. Back in May we were partners on some minor Impressionist works that sold pretty reasonably."

"Lowell's in on this, too?"

"Oh, no. Not at all. But a lot of the things we bought—well, it just made more sense for Deni to keep them for us, to store them until we decided whether we were going to hang on to them or sell them to clients. I mean, Lowell had warehouses and guards and insurance. Even their apartment was a safer place to keep artworks than any temporary facility she and I could arrange. We were lovers, after all, Detective. I didn't have to get a signed pledge from Deni when I agreed to let her hold on to something we bought as partners. She wasn't trying to screw me out of anything, if you'll forgive the expression."

"So you think some of the art you own is being spirited away by Lowell?"

"Possibly. And I don't even mean intentionally. Lowell doesn't have any reason to know the details about Deni's latest acquisitions. I just think there should be some way for me to have a look at what he's got before he ships it out of town or abroad. I have papers and sales receipts for everything. I'm not asking you to get in the middle of deciding what's mine and what isn't. My lawyer will handle all that. He wanted me to, well, to exaggerate to you a bit."

"What do you mean?"

Wrenley was fidgeting now. "I called my lawyer to ask him to get involved this morning. The problem is, of course, that Lowell won't let me inside to look, neither at the gallery nor the apartment—still their home, certainly. It was my lawyer's idea to come to you, Miss Cooper. Look, I don't want to lie to you, but he suggested I swear to you that I know Lowell Caxton has got property in the gallery that belongs to Deni and to me. That perhaps then you could intercede and go in with a warrant to search for things." He tapped his fingers on the arm of the chair. "Frankly, I have no idea what Deni did with some of the paintings. I can't 'swear' where they are—that would simply be a logical guess, but not necessarily true. Bryan Daughtry's been very helpful. I'm going to go through his warehouse, too. Perhaps some of the things I'm looking for are stored with him."

"Can you give me an inventory, a list of the works you have a claim to?" I asked.

"I don't have one prepared right now, but I can have it drawn up within a day or two." Wrenley's hands were on his knees, and he looked down at the floor before he spoke again. "When you're in love with a woman as young and healthy as Deni, you just never think that she's going to walk out the door and . . . never, never come back. The business side of our partnership was the last thing it occurred to me to worry about during this past week. That afternoon, I just waited and waited for her to meet me for lunch—"

"The day she disappeared? She was on her way to meet you?" Chapman asked.

"Perhaps I have surprised you after all, Detective. I assumed you'd know that, from the housekeeper or someone you'd interviewed. Didn't you ask me that the first time we met? I was sure you had."

Chapman seemed embarrassed that he didn't know one of the fairly basic facts about Denise Caxton's last day. "The guys who work in her garage have her going out with the car early in the morning. No one else we talked to seemed to know much about her plans for the day. What did you do when she didn't show up for lunch?"

"I waited half an hour. Tried her at home, in the car, at the gallery. No luck. Check with the maître d' at Jean-Georges—I thought you would have done that by now. I must have tied up his phone for twenty minutes calling around to find Deni."

"Were you upset? Call the police to look for her?"

"No, I suppose the maître d' would also tell you I wasn't very upset, so there's no point pretending. Nothing from which a couple of martinis couldn't distract me. I'd half expected she might stand me up that day. We'd had a bit of a tiff the week before."

"Business?"

"Not business at all. And in retrospect, not exactly pleasure, either." Wrenley looked me in the eye. "I told you when I met you the first time that Deni and I dated other people. Well, I ran into someone in Paris, a woman who'd been recently widowed and was doing the grand tour to announce that her mourning period was officially over. We spent a weekend together, which there was no need for Deni to find out about. Unfortunate coincidence, she turned out to be a friend of Deni's."

"Marina Sette?" Chapman asked.

"*Bravo*, Detective! Forty-eight hours in a small hotel on the Left Bank, and *tout* New York seems to know all about it. I know Marina told Deni, and that's what had her so mad at me. Deni didn't mind what she didn't know about, but Marina really pushed her nose into it."

"Was it over between you and Deni?"

"Of course not. But it was cool, to say the least. She made a point of letting me know that she was spending a lot of time with Preston Mattox. But that was just to get back at me."

"You don't think she was in love with him?"

"Deni was an intensely physical creature, Ms. Cooper. She'd once made the mistake of telling me, when she was unusually giddy in the middle of a rather vigorous round of lovemaking, that there wasn't enough Viagra in all the laboratories in the country to get Preston through another month of his relationship with Deni."

Every time I was on the verge of liking her a bit more, I'd hear something that would cause me to take three mental giant steps in reverse. No point in exploring with Wrenley whether his rival had other redeeming features.

"When she didn't show up at the restaurant for lunch and I couldn't find out where she was, I thought that all she needed was some time to get over what I had done with Marina. She'd only graced me with the luncheon meeting because we had some business decisions to make and because she wouldn't accept an evening date with me. She already had dinner plans with Mattox." I didn't think I had displayed any expression, but Wrenley looked from me to Mike. "Surely you knew that, didn't you? Preston would have had more to worry about than I did when she didn't show up for that date.

"I guess my trip down here wasn't altogether useless," Wrenley said. "I do hope you'll give some thought to looking into why Lowell Caxton is in such a hurry to close his gallery."

I had no intention of telling Wrenley what we would do next. "I'd suggest you let your lawyer go ahead with whatever action he thinks will protect your business interests as well." I stood up to see him out. "Thanks for letting us know about it."

"Do you still have any contact with Marina Sette?" Mike asked.

"Nothing directly. But I hear about her from time to time."

"When's the last time you saw her?"

"Couple of months ago."

"She call you when she came to New York?"

"You mean yesterday?"

Chapman didn't hesitate for a moment. "Yeah, yesterday."

"No, but she called Bryan Daughtry. He told me that last night when he telephoned to let me know about Lowell Caxton. Bryan said that Marina had stopped by the new gallery on Twenty-second Street to see him. Probably to find out if he'd heard any rumors about whether Deni had left a will, or any instructions about who was to get which paintings."

I thought she had told us she detested Daughtry. "Why did she go to him?"

"She could hardly go to Lowell, considering their relationship, and she wasn't talking to me."

"What did Bryan tell her?"

"That the only will he knew of was the original one Lowell's lawyers had prepared for Deni when they first married. Like so many people her age, Deni thought she'd have all the time in the world to amend it. But Marina was still looking for her piece of the rock, what she thought was her 'entitlement.' She really believed, when their friendship was in full bloom, that she had convinced Deni to give her some of the Caxton heirlooms."

"So Lowell gets it all?"

"I suppose. I mean—except for the handful of things that Deni bought with either Bryan or me. Her fortune all started with Lowell, didn't it? In any event, Bryan just wanted me to know that Marina was bad-mouthing me, blaming me for her falling-out with Deni. And that she seemed frantic, out of control. Very hyper about something. That I should stay out of her way if she tried to see me."

"Will you let me know if Marina Sette calls you?" I asked.

"Certainly, Miss Cooper. Thanks for your time."

Chapman waited several seconds after Wrenley shook our hands and walked out the door. "Saddle up, blondie. Let's see why Caxton's heading for the hills."

# 30

___

Mike parked the unmarked car illegally and threw his
laminated police identification plate in the windshield.
The Fuller Building was on the northeast corner of the
intersection, with entrances on both Madison Avenue
and Fifty-seventh Street. An eighteen-wheeler was
parked in front of the side door in a large space protected by a red sign that announced NO STANDING
EXCEPT TRUCKS LOADING AND UNLOADING.

The lettering on the vehicle said *Long Island
Baking Potatoes, Bridgehampton, New York*. It was
definitely loading, and the cargo was not spuds.

There was a fine mist and I hurried to get inside the
lobby. In addition to the two men standing at the rear
of the truck, there was another person stationed inside
the double doors whom I assumed to be part of
Caxton's security team.

"Recognize any of them?" I asked Chapman, hoping to get lucky and discover that some retired cops
were on the payroll.

"Too ugly. Must've been Feds."

The building was familiar to me because I'd been coming to the hairdresser there for almost ten years. With the exception of the Stella salon on the second floor and a handful of dental and medical offices, the structure was almost entirely leased by gallery owners. I knew that the eastern bank of elevators I used once a month went up only eighteen stories, so I led Mike to the western bank and pressed 35 to get to the top floor and the Caxton Gallery.

We stepped off onto an empty hallway. The glass doors of the space were covered by some kind of makeshift screening, and a note that said the gallery was closed. There was a telephone number to call for people making inquiries about exhibits and purchases.

Mike tried the brass handles on the entrance behind the temporary partitions, but they didn't give. He knocked several times on the panels and the door was eventually opened by an unsmiling man in a dark suit.

"Lowell Caxton's expecting us," Mike said.

That brought a smile to one half of the man's mouth. "Mr. Caxton is not here."

"That's strange." Mike looked at me as though surprised and asked, "Didn't he say today, at eleven o'clock?"

The man didn't wait for me to answer. "He's been called out of town unexpectedly. You can leave a message for him at this number." He pointed to the paper that we had just seen.

"I'd like to leave a note for him. May I come in and—"

Mike had started to walk inside but was blocked by our somber gateman.

"Don't make it difficult for me, will ya?" He took the leather case from his pants pocket and held up the gold shield, expecting to be let through the doorway.

"Let's see your warrant, Detective."

"Very good, very good. So, you probably finished at the academy, huh? Must have worked your way right up to the top, ironing Mr. Hoover's dresses, to get yourself a plum job like this one when you left the Bureau. Can you at least call Caxton now and tell him that it's urgent we talk to him today?"

"I just told you how to leave him a message."

"Suppose I told you his life may be in danger. You realize there've been a series of killings since his wife was murdered, and we're the ones working on that case. It might behoove him to let us tell him what's been going on with—"

"Mr. Caxton is not in any danger. If he's interested in talking to you, he'll give you a call. He's a bit bored with being looked at as a suspect in Mrs. Caxton's death. He'll get back to you when he's ready."

"You know where he is right now?"

The man stared back at Mike without answering.

Mike took my arm and started to lead me away before turning back to his nemesis. "I'd rather have my balls cut off by a great white shark than end up doing bullshit security work for some billionaire dirtbag. Have a nice day."

On the way back down to the lobby, we talked about whether or not it was worthwhile to hang out there for a while to see who was coming and going from the thirty-fifth floor.

"Can't you get someone from your squad to sit on the place this afternoon and evening?" I asked.

"Let me call and find out who's around. Maybe the lieutenant can get the precinct to send some Anticrime guys over. We haven't got the manpower to do this stuff."

"Come up to my hairdresser. Elsa'll let us use the kitchen to make calls."

"Don't you have your cell phone with you?"

"Yes, but let's see what the girls know about what's happening in the gallery. When Daughtry had his business here, there wasn't much they hadn't heard about him. They had better sources than the Westchester District Attorney's Office. Sooner or later someone from the staff in just about every place in the Fuller Building uses Stella for color or cuts. Besides, wait till you see how adorable Elsa is."

We switched elevator banks and rode up to the second floor. Pat, the manager, was surprised to see me walk in without an appointment in the middle of the week. Her eyes went directly to my hairline, looking at the state of my roots.

"You're not due till Saturday morning, week after next, right?"

"That's some welcome. Just came by to gossip with Elsa and use the kitchen to make a few phone calls."

I introduced her to Mike and she led us past the reception desk into the rear of the busy salon. Elsa, my colorist, was wrapping foil around a client's hair strands while Mike watched in bewilderment. I signaled to her that we were going into the back room, and she mouthed to me that she'd join us as soon as she was finished.

Mike called to explain the situation, and the boss told him that he would try to arrange for coverage from the local precinct as soon as possible. Mike also asked that a car be sent to sit on Caxton's residence, check with the doormen, and monitor the movement of traffic in and out of that location, too. We helped ourselves to coffee and tried to figure out how we could find Caxton quickly and learn what had prompted this sudden move.

Elsa came into the kitchen, removed her rubber gloves, and washed her hands so that I could introduce her to Mike. I had spent so much time talking to each of them about the other over the years that it was hard to believe they had never met. Elsa had long been my friend, and in addition to restoring the blonde to my naturally light hair, as a devotee of the opera and ballet she alerted me to theater and art events that I had neglected to read about. I knew, also, that when there was a rare lull between clients, she explored the galleries throughout the building and collected catalogues of the shows.

"This is a nice surprise. Are you here to see Louis or Nana for a haircut," she said to me, then looking over at Mike, "or do you have a new customer for some streaks?"

"We were in the building trying to get into the Caxton Gallery, so I thought I'd come by and see if you had any scoops for us."

"About the move? Nobody knows what's going on. It's all so sudden."

"Didn't you have any connections there?"

"No, one of the other girls here did highlights for the receptionist, though. Her name was Genevieve. She called yesterday and canceled her appointment. Said she'd been laid off and wouldn't be working here anymore."

"Got a full name on her, and a home phone number?" Mike asked.

"Let me check with Pat. She's got a file on every client. I can get it for you before you leave."

"Have you ever spent time at Caxton's?"

"Browsing, sure. They always had fabulous things, stunning exhibits."

"D'you know either of them?"

"Not more than to say hello to. He knew I worked here—I usually walk around with my smock on during the day—so he didn't waste any time on me. He realized I wasn't a buyer. But Mrs. Caxton had a good sense of humor and was always very nice to me. She wasn't in the building all that much the last couple of years, but before that she'd often talk to me about what she'd picked up at auction or how much she'd sold something for. I didn't know her well, but I liked her."

Elsa was petite and thin, with short dark hair and creamy porcelain skin. She worked in a black painter's jacket, black slacks, and thick black clogs, exuding style and a quiet intensity. She took in everything that her surroundings—and her chatting customers—gave out. And as Joan Stafford always said, you could trust her like a grave to keep a confidence.

"What else have you heard?" I asked.

"Rumors. Nothing reliable."

"About her death?" I was incredulous, expecting that if she had heard anything, however unreliable, Elsa might have called me before our unplanned visit today.

"No, no, no. There was a commotion a couple of weeks ago, maybe a day or two before Mrs. Caxton disappeared. Genevieve's the one who told us about it. Sort of a row in the gallery."

"Between Denise and Lowell?"

"No, I don't think he was even in town, from what we were told."

That fit with what we knew of Lowell's movements.

"What was it?"

"Denise showed up in the gallery one afternoon carrying lots of bags, as though she had just been on a Madison Avenue shopping spree. Genevieve told me that most of the staff had remained loyal to her, but the guy who managed the place for Lowell wasn't a fan of hers. She did whatever business she had come in to do, and then left. The manager literally ran out of the gallery five minutes later, trying to stop Mrs. Caxton before she got into a cab. Genevieve says he accused her of making off with a painting—something small but valuable."

"Was there a scene on the street?" I asked.

"Actually, it was in the lobby. He reached the ground floor before she did. Stopped Mrs. Caxton in front of that clerk at the building's information booth and forced her to let him look through all her bags."

"Did she make a fuss?"

"Nope. Knowing her sense of humor as I did, I

expect she enjoyed the commotion. He pulled out all her purchases—lingerie, a peignoir set, a teddy—intimate items like that were flying out of his hands while everyone watched."

"And the painting?"

"No painting. Off she went. At least, that's the version we got down here."

Mike rested his elbow on the counter and looked at Elsa. "So, where did Mrs. Caxton stop on her way downstairs, so that he got to the lobby before she did, even though she had a good head start, huh?"

"Maybe she popped into one of the other galleries, to see a friend?"

"I'll follow up on that. See if I can get the date of the squabble from this Genevieve, when we find her." He paused. "But if Mrs. Caxton didn't pay a social call, and just supposing for the moment that she was trying to take a valuable item out of the building, can you think of any likely place to hide something between the thirty-fifth floor and the lobby?"

Elsa had worked in the salon for more than fifteen years. She had probably inspected every exhibit and office and nook of the Fuller Building during that time, shunning the elevators in favor of the back staircases, as she often told me, for exercise and to relieve the tedium of standing all day at a stationary place behind her work chair.

"I know where Denise used to go to sneak a cigarette," she said softly.

"Whaddaya mean?"

"Even before the city passed laws about smoking, Lowell never let anyone light a cigarette in the gallery.

He had all kinds of special air controls for the maintenance of the art, especially because he had so many old paintings. Most of the staff would go all the way down to the ground floor and stand out in front on the sidewalk to smoke. Denise wouldn't bother to go that far. She'd mooch a cigarette—I don't think she did it very often—and she found my secret hideout. That's where we ran into each other from time to time."

"You smoke?" Mike asked, like he was interviewing her as a prospect for a date.

"No. But I like to clear my head every now and then. The fumes of these hair dyes can get to you after a few hours. I just go up there for a breath of air, some peace and quiet, and a great view of the city."

"What is it, like a balcony?"

"Not even close. In fact," she said, giving Mike the once-over, "I'm not certain you'll fit. I'll show you if you'd like."

We left the salon and Elsa pressed the button to go to the eighteenth floor, which was the highest level we could reach from the eastern bank of elevators. She led us to the large gray fire door and pressed her weight against the long metal bar that opened it onto the staircase. Together we walked up to the nineteenth floor, which was basically a darkened hallway connecting the two sides of the building.

The only illumination came from the glare of the cherry red neon exit sign above the doorway we had just entered. My eyes tried to adjust to the gloomy corridor as I followed behind Elsa, with Mike bringing up the rear.

Two-thirds of the way to the far end, there was a

pocket in the wall on our right. Had Elsa not turned toward it, I doubt I would have noticed it at all. She moved surely in that direction and cautioned me to watch the two steps that she climbed, coming face-to-face with another, smaller fire door. As she turned the knob and pushed outward, the door gave way and a sliver of the gray midday sky appeared over her head.

Beyond where Elsa stood was a perch, no more than two feet wide and three feet long. It extended like a small lip, high above the street and out from the side of the building, completely open except for a small iron railing that stretched across it at chest height. My delicate friend stepped onto the ledge, held the bar, and leaned forward to look over the rooftops below.

Then she stepped back and suggested I do the same. "Vertigo," I said. "Not for me." I held on to her arm and tried to stand close to the rail with my eyes open, but I couldn't bear to stay out there. There didn't seem to be enough barriers between me and the sidewalk, nineteen stories down. I offered the post to Mike but he declined, crouching on the floor with his fingers outstretched, trying to measure the size of this exterior shelf.

"What are you doing?"

He stood up. "Great place to stash a painting, then come back to pick it up later on. Does the building stay open after the galleries close?"

"Sure. Our salon has much later appointments than the businesses do. Same for the dental offices. The only other office on this floor is the Malaysian Travel Bureau. It keeps regular hours but I've never seen much traffic there."

"Not that many people knocking each other down to get to Malaysia," Mike said.

Elsa smiled. "I guess not. Of course, lots of the dealers see people by private arrangements, anytime that's convenient. That's why there's always someone at the booth in the main lobby. Denise Caxton was well known to everyone here. She could walk in and out of this building whenever she wanted, without a problem. I just can't imagine her stealing a painting, or anything else for that matter. That's why I didn't think the story was anything serious. The way Genevieve told it, the manager was either simply trying to embarrass Mrs. Caxton or he was making a fool of himself."

"Suppose she wasn't 'stealing' anything," Mike suggested. "Maybe it was something that was hers, a painting Lowell didn't know about that she had warehoused at the gallery. Or that she had hidden up there in one of his storage areas."

Elsa didn't know anything about the Caxton business dealings, so now Mike was talking to me. "Maybe it was something that she felt she had every right to take, but Deni knew that Lowell's people wouldn't let her leave his place with anything. She goes in with lots of bags, makes her rounds, gets what she's after, and walks out before his manager can check what she's got. Then she stops by the little ledge and leaves this package—which I expect is wrapped in something protective. Am I safe in guessing this spot isn't very well trafficked?"

"I've never seen anyone here except Denise Caxton. I'd be willing to bet that ninety-nine percent of the people who work in this building don't even know it exists."

"She makes the drop and continues on to the lobby. Lowell's guy is waiting for her there. He either assumes, or she tells him, that she stopped off to see someone else in another gallery. Gives her a perfectly valid excuse for a short detour on her way downstairs.

"Then she comes back that same night or the next day to pick up her painting. Hell, she could even have circled the block in the cab and gone right back for it ten minutes later. Everyone says she was a risk taker."

Elsa looked concerned. "I hope this has nothing to do with her death. It was such a silly story—it didn't seem worth repeating when I heard about it. I never connected the two things."

"No reason for you to have thought anything about it," I assured her. Mike squinted to look at the number displayed on his beeper, which must have been vibrating on his waistband, while I went on talking. "At this point, we're just grasping at anything. It's good to know about this."

"Let's get back to the phone. The lieutenant's looking for me. This'll go over big when I tell him I'm at your hairdresser's."

We retraced our path back to the kitchen, where I had left my handbag. Mike called the squad while I asked Elsa to keep her eyes and ears open for information about the Caxton Gallery's closing and move.

Mike started singing the opening bars of Willie Nelson's "On the Road Again" as he hung up the phone. "Either make yourself comfortable and let Elsa lighten up your silken tresses, or I'll get you some escorts from Midtown North to take you back to work. I'm off to beautiful downtown Piscataway."

"What's there?"

"Man checked himself into the local hospital this morning. He's got an infected wound in his groin that's festering away. Told the E.R. staff that he had an accident on a construction site, but the X rays show there's a bullet inside. Right now the Jersey troopers are holding him. Could be that Mercer hit the bull's-eye after all. Patient matches the description of Anthony Bailor."

# 31

It pained me to admit that Pat McKinney might be right about anything, but there was no point in my asking Mike to go along with him on the ride to New Jersey. If Anthony Bailor was the person under guard in a hospital, then it was likely that he had been the gunman who had aimed at me, shot Mercer, and killed the young receptionist in Chelsea on Sunday. I had no business being anywhere near him.

"What's your plan?"

"To get my ass down there to Piscataway before that pair of clowns from Major Case find out about it."

Physicians were required by law to report gunshot wounds, and some clever detective in the town where Bailor sought treatment, recognizing that there were no open cases in his jurisdiction in which anyone had claimed to have injured an assailant, had the great sense to notify police in the tristate area about the suspect's appearance.

"It looks good?"

"Yeah, the guy's a transient, a walk-in. Used a common name but has no I.D. to back it up, and gave a phony address—a street that doesn't exist, in a neighboring town. Fits the physical scrip of Bailor. Elsa, she's all yours for the next fifteen minutes. Loo got a uniformed detail from the North to ferry you around and keep you safe till I come back this evening."

There was no point arguing. Mike wasn't going to undercut Battaglia's direction that someone escort me from place to place. "Should I keep working on trying to find Caxton?" I asked.

"Yeah, as long as you do it from behind your desk. If you get a lead on where he is, we can confront him tonight or tomorrow morning. What you could do, in the meanwhile, is let these cops take you to Denise's new gallery on your way downtown. See if you can charm Daughtry into telling you what he found out last night about Lowell Caxton's exodus from the city. You may do better with him if I'm over the border, Coop. Maybe you could coax him into letting you look around the storage area."

"Remind me what I'm looking for, exactly. The Vermeer? The Rembrandt?"

"Maybe I'll have a better idea of that after I talk to Bailor." He looked at his watch. "Give me an hour to get out to Piscataway, and another hour to talk to him, then I'll either beep you or call Caxton Due looking for you."

"Meet you at Mercer's room when you get back tonight?"

Mike was distracted. "Suppose you were Deni and you had something—a painting, in all likelihood—that someone else wanted. Where would you hide it?"

"Let's begin by recognizing that she had more options than most of us could even imagine. And who's she hiding it *from*? I mean, if it's Lowell, then I doubt she'd have it at home or anyplace they use together. If it's Daughtry, then she wouldn't hide it at their gallery. Depends, in part, on who she's avoiding, don't you think? It would help to know that first."

"Forget who it is. What *I'm* thinking is, if it's any kind of artwork, she could have hidden it in plain view, if you know what I mean. She could have had Marco Varelli undo any restoration. He could re-create the cover of a restored painting, or obscure a masterpiece. She could hide something like that in a warehouse, and if she treated it casually, maybe nobody would pay it any attention. You'd need *her* eye, *her* knowledge, *her* tutor. Maybe Deni could even carry it around in a shopping bag and nobody'd think twice of it. Maybe what's at the heart of this case is one giant optical illusion, Coop." Mike's idea wasn't altogether crazy.

"So I'll crank up the search for Lowell, stop in to schmooze with Brian Daughtry and scan the gallery's warehouse at the same time. Will I jinx things for you if I buy a bottle of champagne to open at Mercer's bedside when you come back from checking out Anthony Bailor?"

"Dom Pérignon. But you gotta promise that I can be the one to break the news to him. If you get over there before I do, don't even raise his hopes. I'd hate for this to be a false alarm. If it's the real deal, I want to tell Mercer myself."

Mike was ready to take off. "Great to meet you,

Elsa. Keep an eye on blondie till the precinct cops get here."

I called Laura to check my messages. There was a note from McKinney, who wanted to talk to me as soon as I got back to the office. I had a couple of hours to kill until I could expect to hear from Chapman about the identity of the man with the gunshot wound, and I had no intention of returning to Hogan Place until I knew whether this new development could turn the investigation around.

The more urgent message was from the sergeant at the Special Victims Squad, about a new case that had come in several hours ago. I phoned him immediately.

"What have you got?"

"Victim's at New York Hospital. Twenty-six-year-old businesswoman from Georgia, staying at a hotel in town. She's being treated for an inner ear disorder, comes to town to see a specialist. Woke up this morning but blacked out on her way out of the bathroom. She was able to call her husband back home, and he phoned the manager. Two hotel security guards got into the room and radioed for an ambulance. Then the older one told the second guy to go downstairs and wait for the EMS crew. He assumed the woman was unconscious, but she was just too weak to respond. In any event, he ripped her pajama top off and started to molest her. Finally she came around and was able to tell him to stop. Reported it to the ambulance driver as soon as she got inside and they closed the doors."

"What hotel?"

"Would you believe the Sussex House?"

"On Central Park South?"

"You got it. She paid six hundred fifty-three dollars for the privilege of being abused by a member of the staff."

"What do you need?"

"Her husband's flying up from Georgia this afternoon. Can you get her interviewed and set up the grand jury, so she can get back home when the doctor releases her?"

"Absolutely." I checked my watch. "I'll go over and talk to her now—I'm just ten blocks away from the hospital. I'll assign somebody senior to handle it. Need any help at the hotel? Are they being cooperative?"

"One of her girlfriends met us there to pack up her belongings. She's the one who found the two buttons on the floor—ripped off the shirt of the pajamas."

"Did you get the guy?"

"Yeah, but he's not talking. Ponied up with a lawyer right away. Just doing his job."

I called Catherine Dashfer to tell her about the case.

"I'm doing a hearing this afternoon in front of Judge Wetzel," she told me. "But I'm free the rest of the week. If she's released in the morning, just have her be in my office at ten, and I'll put it right in the jury. We can have her at the airport by this time tomorrow."

"Thanks a million. Would you do me another favor? Call McKinney for me and tell him I just got called out on a new case, and that I won't be back until late in the day, okay?"

Elsa had ordered two salads from the local deli, and

we were eating our lunch when a policewoman in uniform presented herself at the reception desk. I finished up before saying good-bye and heading off on my rounds.

Police Officers Brigid Brannigan and Harry Lazarro had been told that their assignment was to take me wherever I needed to go until they were relieved later this evening by another unit. On the short ride to New York Hospital I gave them a brief rundown on what had been happening in the Caxton case. The rest of the story they knew from newspaper accounts. One of *them* had been gravely wounded, and there was no more serious situation than that to a cop.

Brannigan got out of the car at the Sixty-eighth Street entrance to the large facility. "Want me to take you in?"

"I'm fine, thanks. This stop was just added to the itinerary, so I'm not expecting any trouble."

From the information booth I called the emergency room, but Callie Emerson had already been treated and had been admitted for observation and tests concerning her inner ear imbalance. She was on 6 North, and the volunteer worker directed me to that wing.

When I reached her room, Callie was sitting in an armchair dressed in a hospital gown and answering questions from a physician and a resident. I explained who I was and why I was there. My purpose was not to question her in depth about the assault—since Catherine would do that in the morning—but rather to explain the proceedings to her and engage her cooperation. Witnesses and their families were always surprised to learn how much gentler the process had become with a specialized unit like ours, and how comfortable we could make the person who had been victimized.

I stepped back outside the room and waited for the doctors to finish their examination. When they were through, I returned and sat with Callie, telling her what would happen the next day and answering all her questions about the system. She and her husband should go to Catherine's office, where the questioning would take place. The grand jury presentation would take less than ten minutes and the assailant would not be present for it, so she did not have to see him again or tell the story in front of him. After that, Catherine would be responsible for the motion practice in the case—presenting the court with information responding to defense requests for facts to which they were entitled. Three or four months thereafter, we would bring Callie back to New York for the trial, and with any luck Catherine would be working again in front of a jurist as sensitive and knowledgeable as Wetzel.

She seemed grateful for the overview and willing to participate.

"Were you examined in the emergency room?"

"Fortunately, I wasn't raped. So they didn't do an internal exam. They were more worried about my physical condition—that my blood pressure had dropped so dramatically and my vital signs were weak."

I knew from my conversation with the sergeant that the attacker had put his mouth on Callie's breast and sucked on it.

"Did anyone look at your chest?"

"I'm not sure. There was so much going on when we got here—I just don't know."

"Would you mind going into the bathroom and looking at yourself in the mirror?"

When she emerged, she was nodding her head. "There's a large discoloration on my skin, where his mouth was. And there are a few scratches on my breastbone, which might have happened when he was ripping at the buttons."

"I'm going to ask one of the nurses to come and look at you again, if you don't mind. I'd like her to note those marks on your medical chart. And Laura, who's one of our photographers, will take a few pictures of them tomorrow morning."

"They seem so minor."

"Even so, Callie, they corroborate exactly what you said this man did to you. It will be very useful for you at the trial."

We talked for a while longer before I thanked Callie, reassured her about what a good witness she would be, and left the hospital.

The patrol car was waiting for me in the parking circle off York Avenue.

"What's next, Miss Cooper?"

I checked my watch. It was almost an hour and a half since Mike had left for Jersey, and I was trying to control my curiosity about his encounter with the man who might be Bailor.

"Before we go to Chelsea, why don't you just swing by 890 Fifth Avenue? It's not too far out of the way. I want to check with the team that's watching an apartment there."

In ten minutes we were in front of Lowell Caxton's building. There was an unmarked detective car parked next to the awning. I got out to talk to the men sitting inside, both of whom were eating hot dogs and drinking root beer. They worked with Mike at the Homicide Squad and were annoyed at being stuck on such an uninteresting post.

"Nothin' happening here. Doorman says it's business as usual with Caxton. This guy only does days, so he don't know what time Lowell came home last night. But his chauffeur picked him up a little before eight this morning. I had him call up to the maid, too. She says Caxton's due home sometime after seven o'clock this evening. You and Chapman planning to come over then?"

"Yes, unless you see something else we should know about earlier. Have you got my beeper number?"

"No, but I got Mike's."

"He's not with me today, so why don't you write mine down, too?"

The surly fat one in the driver's seat took another bite from his tube steak and handed me the paper napkin that had been draped over his knee. I tore off the corner with the mustard stain on it and wrote down the number to hand back to him. He was as likely to call a D.A. with a hot lead as he was to run in the next marathon.

"Any other traffic in or out we should know about?"

"If you know a Mrs. Cadwalader on three, she's either turning tricks on the side or she's runnin' a halfway house for retired hockey players. She's got action comin' and goin' every twenty minutes, and most of her company's sportin' half their teeth and bowlegs. And there's a schnauzer on five with a very weak bladder, so he's out here peeing on my front tire once an hour, courtesy of his housekeeper, who's carrying a pooper scooper looks like it's made outta sterling silver. And she's got a great ass—the housekeeper, not the schnauzer. Now, are you gonna sit here and watch us watching them, or are you gonna find some way to make yourself useful to Mr. Battaglia?"

Brigid Brannigan was leaning against the patrol car and opened the door for me to get in the backseat. She looked crisp and cool in the police uniform, and her neat auburn ponytail set off her fine features handsomely. "I used to think *I* had a hard time, breaking in as a prosecutor with all these tough old dinosaurs in my department who thought handling homicides was only a man's prerogative. I bump into a guy like that one, and I bet you could tell me stories about what it was like for you to come onto this job that would make my experience seem like a cakewalk."

She got in the car laughing and started to talk about her rookie adventures with some of the hairbags—the stiff old-timers who never made it out of uniform—that she'd encountered in the four years she'd been on the force.

"Why don't you take the Sixty-sixth Street drive through the park and head down Ninth Avenue? I'm going to a gallery called Caxton Due, on Twenty-second Street, between Tenth and Eleventh."

Brigid continued to amuse me with her anecdotes while her partner weaved in and out of the midafternoon traffic on the approach to the Lincoln Tunnel. Once that cleared, Lazarro drove down to Twenty-first Street and came up Tenth Avenue, about to make the turn into the one-way westbound block on which the gallery entrance was located.

We could all see that it would be impossible to drive into the narrow street. In addition to the cars parked at meters on each side, there were three enormous trucks lined up in a row right in the middle of the pavement. Wooden stanchions were spread from the north corner of the curb to the south.

There didn't seem to be anyone directing this operation. Officer Lazarro gave off a few whelps, and two men in T-shirts and jeans poked their heads out of the cab of one of the trucks. Since they weren't moving, Brannigan got out of the car and walked over to them.

She came back and leaned in the window. "They've got a permit to block the street off for the afternoon. There's a place farther down the way called the Dia Center for the Arts. They're installing a major exhibition today, so this is legal while they're unloading sculpture for the new show. Want me to walk you into your gallery?"

"This might work even better. There's a rear door on Twenty-third Street, through the warehouse of the gallery. We saw the sign for it, like a service entrance, the first day we came here. Maybe Daughtry'll let me in that way. As Chapman said then, Daughtry might even prefer we use it." Again, I checked the time.

"Chapman should be calling soon. C'mon, let's go around the corner."

We drove up to Twenty-third and Lazarro signaled left, then made a U-turn to pull up to the curb in front of the spot I pointed out as the garage entrance to Deni's gallery. Brigid got out of the car when I did and walked with me over to the rusty-colored door frame, which had an intercom system with two buzzers next to a small enamel plate. One was marked CAXTON DUE—SERVICE, and the other said CAXTON DUE—GALLERY.

I pressed the second bell and waited a couple of minutes.

"Any idea how long we'll be here?" Brigid asked.

"With some luck, if he lets me poke around the warehouse, I might be an hour or more. If Chapman turns up anything important, be ready to fly out of here with me, okay?"

The gray haze seemed to be lifting, as the forecasters had promised, and the sun was beginning to filter through. I was hot and looked forward to being received in the cool of the air-conditioned art display space.

We both heard the sound of the intercom click.

"Yes?" Judging from the crackling quality of its sound, the system was as old as the building.

"Alexandra Cooper. From the District Attorney's Office," I identified myself to Daughtry.

"I'll buzz you in. Come on up—is not—but I'll—top—"

The entrance led directly up an old iron staircase, which bypassed the storage area to lead into the gallery itself. Before the door swung shut behind us, I heard Lazarro calling Brigid's name.

"Sergeant Danz wants to talk to you. Needs an idea of how long we're going be tied up here. Wanna take it?"

Brigid looked at me. "Do you mind?"

"Of course not. I do the same thing when my boss calls."

"Can you wait down here a few minutes while I report in? The sergeant's gonna have to get permission for us to work over the end of the shift at three thirty."

I pointed up. "You know right where I am. I'll be out as soon as Chapman calls."

As I climbed the steps, I could see scores of paintings arrayed in bins beneath, most of them covered in bubble wrap or kraft paper, and all labeled by the artist's name and some kind of numerical code. They varied in size from tiny objects, not larger than four by six inches, to giant canvases that were best suited for museum walls.

I rang at the door at the top of the stairs and the buzzer sounded to unlock the way into the small lift, which descended to this ground floor area to take me up to the top of the atrium, where Daughtry awaited my arrival. When the door slid back, I was again overwhelmed by the beauty of the open atrium space. Emerging from the elevator on the north side of the building, I was facing the glass wall of the southern exposure and its great view of the city sky.

As I stepped off into the room, I felt the relief of the cold surge of air that I had anticipated. It contrasted with the unexpected brightness of the afternoon sun at the end of a gloomy day, which lit up the gallery space and beamed down on the tracks of the deserted Hi-Line Railroad.

I took my sunglasses out of my jacket pocket for the first time that day.

"Over here," called a voice that was familiar to me, but it was not Daughtry's.

I looked around and saw Frank Wrenley sitting on one of the couches in the exhibition area one flight below me.

"Welcome, Ms. Cooper. I'm baby-sitting the art for Bryan. He should be back anytime now. May I offer you a cold drink?"

I remembered that this morning, in my office, Wrenley had told us that Daughtry was going to allow him to look through Denise's belongings to see whether any of his property was included there. He was holding a sheaf of papers in one hand and a tall glass in the other.

"Shall I come down?"

"Please."

I followed the catwalk around the bend until I arrived at the metal staircase that led to the level below. I walked down, shook Wrenley's hand, and accepted his offer to sit on the couch. I could see the documents he had laid out on the glass-topped table between us. He had a red pen and appeared to be going through lists that he was checking against his own.

"Will you join me in a Bloody Mary?"

"No thanks."

"Ah, the constable doesn't drink on duty, does she?"

"I'm so exhausted, Mr. Wrenley, that I'd probably curl up and take a nap if I so much as smelled a whiff of the vodka. Your inventory?"

"Bryan's off trying to solve the mystery of Lowell Caxton's hasty retreat. He's been good enough to let me attempt to reconcile some of my records with Deni's things before I return to Palm Beach." He waved his receipts in my direction as though to convince me that he had proof of title for anything he needed. "Where's your sidekick? I was beginning to think you and Detective Chapman were joined at the hip."

"He'll be along soon. We were—I was hoping to get Mr. Daughtry's permission to look around a bit at some of Denise's things."

"I thought that first day I met you here you'd gone all through this place with warrants and everything short of commando troops. Bryan was sure he was going back to prison."

I smiled at his exaggerated description. "That's one of the problems when you do a search before you know just what it is you're looking for."

"But now you *do* know?"

Not really. But I saw no reason to tell that to Wrenley. We'd try again with some of the information we had picked up after Varelli's murder and during our conversation with Don Cannon. "Do you have any idea when Mr. Daughtry is due to return?" I didn't know whether to try to wait it out or get down to my office and face the music with McKinney.

"Pretty soon, I should think. He's got to lock the place up for the night."

It was now going on three hours since Mike had left the city. I reached in my bag to get the cell phone to try to beep him. When I turned it on, the failure of the three green icons to light up reminded me that the battery must have run down. I kept the charger set up on my desk at home and plugged the phone into it every evening as a matter of habit, but since I had spent the last two nights at Jake's apartment, I had neglected to recharge it.

"Would you mind if I use the telephone for a moment?"

Wrenley pointed to the portable unit on the table next to his papers. "Help yourself."

I picked it up and dialed Chapman's beeper, punching in the number of the gallery as I read it off the plate on the receiver. Then I set it back down, knowing he would return the call to the unfamiliar number only when he was ready to take a break.

"I can't give you access to the storage area, but I don't imagine Bryan would mind if you look through the gallery and the office while you're waiting. After all, you've done that once already, haven't you?"

I was feeling even more foolish as I stood up and glanced around. There was nothing in the midst of this thoroughly modern exhibit that I could connect by my wildest stretch to the art treasures that I associated with Deni Caxton's troubles. I started to work my way about the place, reading the descriptions and trying to make sense of the works.

Within several minutes the phone rang and I hurried back to the area where Wrenley was sitting. He had answered it by saying, "Galleria Caxton Due," and passed it off to me when I approached the table.

Instinctively, I turned my back to him and started to walk a few steps off. I was aware that it was rude, but I also wanted whatever privacy might be necessary. "No, that was Wrenley. Frank Wrenley," I said, responding to Mike's question about whether the man who had spoken was Bryan Daughtry.

"Can you talk?"

"About what?"

"Never mind. You'll explain where Daughtry is later, I guess."

"Sure. No big deal. Is it our guy?" I whispered into the receiver.

"Order a magnum of the champagne, Coop. Anthony Bailor is about to have an incurable case of gangrenous balls. He's not talking, but he's the man."

"What do you mean he's not talking?"

"He still denies everything, including his name. But I've got his mug shots, and the Jersey police ran his prints this morning."

"Have you arrested him?"

"Why? You gonna give your pal Jake a scoop for the nightly news? No leaks on this one till we know who's behind it. Bailor took the fall for someone in that last theft he was involved in. There's got to be a link to somebody in this investigation."

"Don't be ridiculous. I just want to know what to do next. Should I go down to the office and draw up a complaint on Deni's homicide? You're going to have to lodge a warrant so we can start extradition proceedings from New Jersey."

"Take it easy. I haven't even told the lieutenant yet.

Let me see how the boss wants me to handle it and what the Jersey cops want to hold him on out here. You find out anything useful about Caxton?"

"Not a thing. Where do you want to meet?"

"I'll call you back as soon as I sort this out. I'll pick you up at Hogan Place and take you to Saint Vincent's."

I hung up and walked the phone back to Wrenley, who seemed absorbed in his checklist.

"Good news? You look a lot happier now than you did ten minutes ago."

"Please tell Mr. Daughtry I was here. Perhaps he could give me a call tomorrow, and I'll set up a time to see him."

"You've decided not to wait?" Wrenley stood up, looking at me and shielding his eyes with his right hand. He was facing directly into the sun, which had now saturated the atrium. "Must have some new developments on the case. Have you found Lowell Caxton?"

"No, it's another matter altogether. Nothing to do with the Caxtons. You'll probably hear it on the news tonight—an assault in a midtown hotel. I've got to get some things started on that one before morning." No point giving him any information on Anthony Bailor.

"Well, good luck with this. For Deni's sake I sure hope you get a break soon. I'll be back up from Florida next week, if you need me for anything." The late-August sun was like a ball of fire, coming over the tops of the low buildings across the street and sparkling through the wall of glass. I lifted my sunglasses off the top of my head and replaced them on my nose.

My heart was pounding as my mind pieced the clues together at precisely the wrong place and time. Like Anthony Bailor, Frank Wrenley had been raised in Florida. I picked up my bag to leave and did an involuntary double take at Wrenley, who was squinting back at me without benefit of sunglasses.

# 32

"You look as if you've seen an apparition, Ms. Cooper."

"Sorry, I'm just very tired. I don't feel well. I'll see myself out." I was backing away from the area around the two sofas, thinking of the sunglasses that had been vouchered at the scene of Marco Varelli's murder a week earlier. How many coincidences does it take to make a fact?

Wrenley was walking toward me. I quickened my pace, knowing that Brannigan and Lazarro were waiting for me right outside the warehouse door.

"I suppose Detective Chapman has managed to get his hands on Anthony Bailor. Is that what put you in such a good mood, Ms. Cooper?"

I was holding on to the railing now, two levels above the obsolete train tracks cutting through the center of the gallery, dizzy from the combination of vertigo and the question that Wrenley had just asked me.

He broke into a run before I did, and was upon me in a second, grabbing my free arm and spinning me around to face him. He was holding a small-caliber revolver in his right hand, the kind that was probably used to put a hole through the brain behind Marco Varelli's ear.

"Did Anthony's wound get worse? Is that how you found him? I couldn't come up with a physician anywhere to treat him. He's not exactly John Wilkes Booth. Just couldn't find a taker. And all I needed was another day or two to tie up loose ends so I could get myself out of town for good. I didn't want this to happen." His grip tightened on my wrist.

"So you, Ms. Cooper, will have to be the sacrificial lamb. You might take a terrible fall, say, from the level above us." He prodded me in the ribs with the gun.

"You can't get out of this building without me—alive and well." My voice must have been trembling as I tried to construct a reasonable bluff. "If you kill—" I stopped, unable to complete a sentence that held the implication of my own death. "If you try to hurt me, you won't be able to walk out the door. There are police officers stationed in the front and back of the building. They have orders not to let anyone in or out without my approval."

Wrenley stood still, not knowing whether to believe me or not. With the gun held against me, he lifted the glasses off my nose and placed them on himself. Now I blinked as I tried to avoid the direct glare. "Why should I think that's true? Have you seen the trucks unloading out front for the Dia exhibit? Not even a police car could get through that block."

"There are two men in plain clothes standing at the entrance of the gallery," I lied, "and a patrol car with two others out in back. You have yourself to thank for that. It all started after your efforts to kill me the first time, didn't it? There have been bodyguards taking me everywhere since your attempts on my life."

I remembered the day I had met Chapman and Wallace here to interview Bryan Daughtry. We had interrupted his meeting with Wrenley. My Jeep had been parked directly in front of the gallery, with my identification plate in the windshield. It was he who must have had me followed from Twenty-second Street to the garage at Lincoln Center. He'd had plenty of time to alert Bailor to try to run me down that night, after the ballet. Wrenley must have thought I'd known more than I did. Maybe he had relied on Mickey Diamond's made-up headline.

He was considering his options. "I can offer you a livelier proposition, then. You're going to be my passport out of town."

Anything that would get me away from this unlikely mausoleum. "What do you mean?"

"Take me downstairs with you and have them drive us wherever I decide to go."

My panic heightened at the thought of putting another police officer within range of a man with a loaded gun, of exposing Brannigan and Lazarro to this murderous thief. "That might not work," I said. "If they don't know you, they won't fall for that."

"It can't be your friend Chapman down there, can it? He just called you from somewhere else. So it must be some uniformed cops who pulled this duty. I'm sure they don't know you and all your colleagues, do they?"

I couldn't figure where he was going with this, so I

gave an honest answer instead of trying to outguess him. "They're precinct cops. They don't know me well."

"And tell me how well *you* know Charlie Rosenberg?"

My head was spinning. I couldn't follow him. The name sounded vaguely familiar but I couldn't think of who or what he meant. "Who?"

He reached into his left pants pocket and pulled out the gray security badge issued by my office, which dangled from a silver-colored metal chain. With one hand, Wrenley slipped it over his head and let it hang around his neck, like I wear mine at the office. Now it clicked. Charlie was a young assistant who worked in one of the trial bureaus. Like McKinney, he was a morning jogger.

"I picked this up at the front desk today when I came down to your office to see you. Tsk, tsk, tsk—they ought to be much more careful with those I.D. tags when you people leave them lying around. I actually had other plans for this, in case we needed to get past the doormen at your apartment building. But it will do fine for you to introduce me to your bodyguards. You can say I was here working on the case when you arrived. Charlie Rosenberg. Shit, some of my best friends are Jewish."

"But the photograph—"

"Can't even make it out with all the use the badge has had—dark hair, pleasant smile. I'll pass."

I thought of the morning two weeks ago, right after Deni's body had been found, when Mike and I came back from Compstat and McKinney's tag had been mislaid in the pile at the front desk. I was so pleased at the time that he had trouble getting back into the building that I hadn't raised a stink about the lax security.

Wrenley poked me again. "Where's your tag? Put it on."

"It's in my bag."

With his free hand he reached inside my oversized tote, never taking his eyes off me. It was hopeless that he'd find anything in it. He gave out a quick laugh. "I guess Chapman gave you away. Since he told me there's no gun in your bag, why don't you get the I.D. badge out yourself? And leave the sharp pencils inside there."

I set the bag on the floor and knelt down, riffling through it to feel for the chain and pull it out. It snagged on something and I grabbed at it. Now I could feel the plastic bag in which I had placed the toilet articles for Mercer. I pulled up the small plastic razor blade case and palmed it, bringing the chain and gray tag with my name on it out of the handbag. Still crouching, I hung the chain around my neck and pocketed the slim blade holder as I reached my hand to the floor to stand up again.

Wrenley jabbed at me to move toward the staircase. We were closer to it than to the lift in the far corner. There was no point making a dash to the elevator with a gun at my back. "Down the steps, Ms. Cooper. Let's try the back door, where you say the car is waiting."

I descended the stairs slowly, my hand shaking as I tried to grip the banister. We had gone from the fifth level to the fourth. I turned on the landing and went down to the third floor, where the old Hi-Line tracks ran through the length of the building.

"Hold it right there," he said sharply, drawing up by my side as I reached the bottom step. He rested a foot on top of the nearest railroad tie. "You've got to get this quivering under control, Alex. It's Alex, isn't it? These cops have to think we're partners, too, don't they?"

Wrenley didn't realize Battaglia was running the Children's Crusade. Most of my colleagues were kids right out of law school, staying in public service only as long as they could resist the lure of the high-paying private sector. Someone Wrenley's age would be an executive or supervisor, and not likely to be out in the field working cases or taking orders from me. Even if I could calm myself down, Brannigan was bright enough to know that something was wrong with this picture. I would put us all in grave danger.

He lowered his right arm, his gun to his side but still visible. "Never send a rapist to do a man's job."

"What?" I asked.

"Deni wasn't supposed to be murdered. Maybe I can make you more comfortable if you understand that I'm not a killer. Well, I didn't set out to be one. You just need to get me safe passage out of here, and then I'll simply disappear, leaving you unharmed. But we can't go anywhere until you settle down and stop shaking so badly."

I didn't believe him for a moment, but it was clear that he wasn't letting me move until he saw my tremors subside. "Tell me what you mean. If you want me to stop shivering, explain to me why Deni had to die."

"Two words: Anthony Bailor." Wrenley braced his back against the banister.

"You knew him in Florida?"

"Much to my father's regret. Wrong side of the tracks and all that. I met Anthony during my brief stay in a juvenile home, back when I was a delinquent. A quaint term you don't hear much of these days, do you, Alex?"

I was certain we had run a rap sheet on Wrenley and it had come up clean.

"You look puzzled. I was fifteen at the time. My father's lawyer was good. Had the case sealed because of my age. Knew enough to get the fingerprints and photos back. Most of them are too lazy to follow through on that, as you probably know. But then, it wasn't all bad. After I met Anthony I never had to do second-story work again.

"I've had an eye for nice things all my life. Couldn't always afford them. But I was able to get myself invited into the right homes for cocktails and dinner. Called Anthony a week or two later, gave him the layout and a schedule, arranged myself an alibi for the time of the burglary, and I built myself up a very nice little collection of antiques. The Keys were a bit confining for me, so we eventually set up shop further north. By the time Anthony got sent away big-time, I was flourishing in Palm Beach. The old ladies loved me."

"The Gardner heist. You—"

"Don't be stupid. I'd never have dared an operation like that one. Besides, Anthony was tucked away in prison ten years ago."

"But he did the theft from the museum at Amherst. That's what he went to jail for in New York."

"Exactly. One of the guys responsible for the Gardner masterminded the break-in at the Mead. Anthony took the weight for him when he got caught with some of the art."

"But never gave him up?"

"He's good at that. I'll bet your man Chapman is having a hard time."

"And Denise Caxton?"

"I'm sure you know by now that Anthony and Omar spent some time together in jail. Omar had that lamebrained scam of writing threatening letters to wealthy divorcées. He began to brag about it to Anthony. Told him about the Caxtons and their art connections. Bailor got in touch with me. I knew Deni and Lowell—everyone in the business knew them. We used Omar to stay close to Deni."

"Did she really hire him to kill Lowell?"

"She didn't want her husband dead. She just wanted him frightened a bit."

I'd say a bullet creasing his skull could do the trick. "Omar shot him?"

"No, he subcontracted that out to Anthony. Far more capable with a gun. You're doing much better, Alex. You're almost ready to go." He was watching my hands, which I had clasped together to keep from shaking as much.

"But the paintings from the Gardner, this all has to do with them, doesn't it?"

Wrenley paused.

"I know you showed one of them to Marco Varelli."

He looked me in the eye to see whether I was just testing him.

"Those paintings have been out of circulation for almost ten years, since the date of the theft. Everyone knows, Alex—well, everyone in *my circle*—that the thieves have had trouble unloading them. Some of the minor things have sold, of course—"

"But not the Rembrandt or the Vermeer."

"So Anthony was asked to get in touch with me long before he met Omar."

"By the thieves?"

"I prefer to call them the custodians. I have no idea who the Philistines were who actually broke into the building. Couldn't have been art lovers—I think they left the most valuable painting behind, in their ignorance."

Titian's *Rape of Europa,* wall-sized and worth even more than the Rembrandt and the Vermeer.

"I'd been trying to find a way to sell them, collect a broker's fee. I had heard about Lowell's fantastic private collection, and I knew Deni was supposed to be a bit of a wild card. They were still together at the time, of course. I thought I might interest her in buying one of the great pieces for their own collection. Discretion advised. It happens more often than you'd think with stolen art."

"And you called her shortly before she was supposed to travel to England with Lowell. That's why she didn't go on that trip with him, isn't it?" Sooner or later our subpoenaed phone records would show the incoming call to Deni from Frank Wrenley. If only those records had arrived before now.

"She was wild with excitement when I told her about the paintings. Funny thing is, she wanted to buy them for Lowell. It was to be the greatest coup of her life, to give him something he didn't have and couldn't have found anywhere else in the world. She sent him on ahead to England with the best intentions."

"And she took the Vermeer to Marco Varelli, to make sure it was the original?" I asked. I thought of our conversation with Don Cannon, who had witnessed the meeting.

"I never expected to become personally involved with Mrs. Caxton. That wasn't part of the grand design. But it was icing on the cake. She developed a serious case of cold feet once Varelli threw his tantrum, so she decided to catch up with Lowell in Bath. She'd been planning the surprise of a lifetime for him, and he's in bed with the young English girl. Drove Deni right back home, into my waiting arms."

"You convinced her to keep playing with the paintings, even though she knew they were stolen?"

"Let's say it was the free spirit in her. Once she and Lowell decided to split, she became more carnivorous, more worried about how she could maintain the lifestyle to which she'd become accustomed. Every now and then she'd get a little crazy on me. You know about the reward?"

"Five million dollars tax-free from the Feds, for the return of the art."

"Deni would occasionally try to convince me to turn in the paintings, in exchange for immunity from prosecution for possession of stolen property. Take the five million and run off with her—well, I can't tell you where, exactly. I'm still hoping to be there by tomorrow. Beyond your jurisdiction, Miss D.A. And no extradition policy, either."

"But the other man she was dating? Preston Mattox."

"Why is it women like you always enjoy a sad love story? I did have some competition. Deni wasn't quite ready to make a commitment after what happened with Lowell. Her self-confidence had skyrocketed after our first few months together."

The story was becoming clearer all the time. I stretched out the fingers of both hands, to see whether they trembled. Wrenley watched me. "Very good, Alex. Getting better."

I balled them into fists and looked back at Wrenley. "Then why was she killed? She had the paintings, didn't she? You were afraid you'd lose everything if she walked away from you?"

"Correction. One painting. We were going to be partners, so I let her hold on to the Vermeer. Less valuable than the Rembrandt, but she loved that domestic little scene. I favored the seascape.

"I called to tell her I thought she was right. That we ought to return the paintings to the museum and collect the reward. Her name wouldn't be connected to the scandal, and I'd give her half the proceeds. We had been doing other deals together, so it made perfect business sense. To prove my bona fides, I offered to take her to lunch so she could give me the painting—wrapped up, of course—at Jean-Georges. In public. Neat and clean. She could carry it to the table in a Bergdorf shopping bag and just pass it to me with a peck on the cheek. A check would eventually follow for two and a half million."

"But you must have concocted a way to get all five million?"

"Well, minus a slight commission for Anthony."

"Did you know where she kept the painting?"

"If I knew that I wouldn't have had to offer her a two-hundred-dollar lunch, would I? Anthony was to follow Deni from home. He had borrowed Omar's station wagon. He was to abduct Deni, drive her to a fairly remote spot, and steal her purse and whatever else was in the car. He knew he was after a painting, but the painting was supposed to look incidental to the usual money, jewelry, fancy-car theft."

I closed my eyes and my right hand covered my mouth, trying to keep the words inside. "But you knew he was a rapist. How could you let him near Deni?"

"I didn't know that Anthony had been convicted of rape. It's not a popular category of criminal acts among inmates. He always described himself as an armed robber. True, naturally. And a carjacker. True as well. He just neglected to tell me that he'd also raped his victims.

"All he was supposed to do was steal the Vermeer. Obviously, Deni wouldn't be able to report the crime to the police. That was the bottom line of my plan. She would have undermined her whole divorce settlement with Lowell if she had gone to the police. No judge would give her a nickel of Lowell's fortune, or any of his art, if she was caught with stolen paintings. A Vermeer that had been missing for a decade? How do you walk into a police station and tell them that you were just carrying it around when you went to meet a friend for lunch? Then, there'd be me to deal with. She'd feel badly about my loss, and I'd be sure to make her feel guilty, and there she'd be, owing me more than two and a half million dollars, just because she'd been careless and lost our painting."

"Plus, you'd still have the painting. Or both paintings?"

"*Voilà!*"

"Where did the plan go wrong?"

"Denise made Anthony angry." Wrenley's indifference was chilling. "First of all, he tells me that Denise didn't have the painting with her in the car. Lots of cash, enough jewelry to make a splash at our lunch— he was entitled to keep those things, under our agreement—but no Vermeer. Now, between you and me, Ms. Cooper, this is still a point of contention between me and my old pal Anthony. He's not beyond pulling a sting on me, either.

"So he was angry with her. And then—well—you know this better than I do. What makes a man decide to rape a woman? Anger? Lust? Control? Or the Willie Sutton theory of robbing banks—just because she's there?"

I had been doing this work for more than ten years and I had never seen or heard any satisfactory explanation of what motivates a human being to force another into an act of sexual intercourse, the most intimate contact two people can experience. The only factors that were the same in every case were the vulnerability of the victim at a particular moment in time and the opportunity that this presented to the assailant.

Wrenley stepped forward and moved closer to me, passing behind me and putting his left arm around my back, ready to lead me to the staircase going down to the street level.

"Bailor denied assaulting Deni at first. Made up a whole story about Omar being along for the ride, and blaming the rape on him. That's actually why he killed poor Omar—so that dumb con artist couldn't tell me otherwise. Worked fine with me until I read the news-paper story about the DNA eliminating Omar. Not so tense, Alex. C'mon. I'm telling you all this so that you don't waste the government's money trying to hunt me down. I don't have the damn paintings after all. I got screwed out of the Vermeer, and the Rembrandt was never actually in my control."

I pulled away from Wrenley and walked alongside him.

"So Anthony and I had another meeting. That's when he told me about getting mad at Deni for not having the painting. He knew I'd understand that, since I wanted it so badly. What he couldn't make me understand is why he made her get in the back of the station wagon and, well . . . He said he never meant to get rough with her. He just didn't expect her to resist, especially since he had a gun. Thought just the threat of it would make her tell him where the Vermeer was. But he couldn't scare it out of her. Said she fought like a tiger. Claimed he had to hit her in the back of the head with the gun to shut her up."

I was biting the inside of my cheek so hard that I

tore through the thin membrane and could taste blood in my mouth. I put my right hand in my jacket pocket and began to play with the case of Jake's razor blades, sliding one out the open end of the container and squeezing it between two fingers. I thought of Preston Mattox's description of Deni, so feminine looking but such a fighter, and his sorrowful certainty that she would have struggled against her attacker. For some women, resistance saves them from the completion of the assault, but for others it causes the attacker to use even more force to accomplish his goal.

"There's an object lesson in all this, Ms. Cooper." Wrenley held his revolver up for a moment for me to see, as a reminder. "I'm going to tuck this back in my waistband during my short freedom ride, but I know you're clever enough to understand that it's not smart to make me angry."

Frank Wrenley was standing at the top of the stairwell, lowering his arm from in front of my face as I took my fingers out of my pocket. With a single stroke, I sliced at his hand with one of the sharp cutting edges of the razor blade. The gun fell onto the steps beneath him and clattered to the floor below. Wrenley grabbed his wrist and howled in pain.

# 33

I ran as fast as I could go, in the direction of the double glass doors that surrounded the Hi-Line Railroad ties and opened out onto the antiquated structure leading downtown, several stories high above the streets of Chelsea. Wrenley had been at the top of the stairs, blocking my way to the patrol car in the rear of the building. I didn't waste time; he might have reached the gun before I did, which would have been deadly. I knew I had temporarily disarmed him, but I also guessed the wound had not disabled him completely.

The bolt affixed to the exit yielded easily to a twist of my hand. I yanked it back and was met by a blast of the hot August air as I escaped onto the tracks. For once—I prayed silently—don't let Chapman's stories be full of their usual exaggeration. I was trusting his brief oral history of the neighborhood to make my dash away from this callous killer, and I needed Chapman's facts to be right.

The rusted iron frame of the deserted railway rose

on thick beams over Twenty-second Street and stretched out ahead, cutting through the center of the buildings opposite me. The track bed was wider across than most small tenements in the city. Looking down at the littered ground, I chose a path directly between the parallel lines that were vestiges of old track, hoping to avoid tripping over pieces of wood and steel that were obscured by weeds and garbage of all sorts.

I screamed for help. I was headed south, and Brannigan and Lazarro were parked on the north side of Caxton Due. I knew they couldn't see or hear me as I ran, but I was sure I could attract the attention of someone who would call for assistance. "HELP! POLICE!" I yelled as I crossed to the far side of Twenty-second Street, looking down for signs of life amidst the vans that had congested the entire block since before I had arrived at the gallery. I gasped for breath, holding on to the edge of the building adjacent to the tracks, but could see no people on the pavement below. Wrenley was charging at me from the open glass doors of Caxton Due.

I started jogging again, slowing somewhat as I zigzagged around holes in the skeleton of the trail, afraid I would catch my foot and wedge myself in a crevice from which I'd be unable to retreat. There were shards of broken glass and dirty hypodermic needles, discarded sneakers and dead pigeons, and I danced around objects on the obstacle course, wanting none of them to bring me down in flight.

Racing through the valley of warehouses that rose above the tracks on either side of me, I emerged onto

Twenty-first Street, stopping to peer down and repeat my cries for help. Kids were playing ball at the far end of the block, near Eleventh Avenue, and they stopped to look as one of them heard and pointed up at me. "POLICE!" I shouted to them, not knowing if they could make out my words. I glanced back to see Wrenley gaining on me, so I ran again.

There was open iron grillwork on the side of the guardrail at the next intersection. I gave a fleeting thought to climbing over and trying to lower myself down from it. I was still too high off the street to jump, but perhaps I could cling to a ledge until police arrived. Then I saw the rolls of barbed-wire fencing directly below me, spitting their jagged edges upward, so I propelled myself on.

Wrenley was getting closer. His route was a more reckless one than mine, straightforward and relentless in pursuit. Taller buildings rose around me as I followed the next strip of tracks, the intense glare of the sun briefly lost to the shade of the brick walls.

I heard a grunt from behind me and ignored my own directive not to look back. Wrenley had tripped on something and fallen to the ground. Taking a deep breath, I surged ahead and ran on past the giant warehouses, onto a long open stretch of track. I must have been below Nineteenth Street by now. In the distance I could hear the faint wail of sirens. I had no idea how remote they were, or any hope that they would reach me in the maze of one-way streets.

Lowering my eyes to the pavement below in search of the blue-and-white patrol cars that might be on their way, I saw only the tall traffic signs on the nearest corner, their bright red flashers urging me on. DON'T WALK.

The length of the run had not been enough to slow me down, but the dense humidity and August heat were oppressive. I was gasping for air and felt like my body was running on fumes, trying to find oxygen in the stillness of the stale afternoon.

Wrenley was closing in again. I didn't have to turn my head to see him, but I could hear his labored panting over the noise coming from my own chest. We were somewhere below Seventeenth Street, and the entire structure of the railroad lay out before me, curving slowly around to the east, away from the surrounding buildings.

I felt the tug on the tail of my jacket a split second before Wrenley pushed me down from the rear, landing with me in a tangle of legs and arms. My knees slammed against the metal tracks as I tried hopelessly to break the fall. The palms of my hands stung as they landed on pieces of rusted metal, rocks, and debris I couldn't identify. I pushed up and kicked one leg out back behind me, smacking it against Wrenley's chin or chest—I couldn't see which—drawing a groan as his head snapped back.

As I raised myself up on my feet, I grabbed at one of the empty beer bottles scattered along the path and carried it in my hand as I resumed my gallop, heading to the section of the Hi-Line that crossed out over Tenth Avenue.

I was hugging the left side of the railing as the elevation passed over the piece of sidewalk edging the wide thoroughfare. I knew the danger that slowing down would bring Wrenley closer to me, but I also knew that this main artery running below me, four lanes wide, would be my most obvious chance to get help. I had no idea how much farther the tracks ran before they would corner me at the dead end of a brick wall on some abandoned tenement.

As I looked down I could see the mesh fencing and barbed wire that bordered a parking lot directly below me. Beyond that, for the first time since I began my run from the gallery, I was free of the prickly metal underpass that would have ripped my skin apart had I landed on it.

I was even with the curb of the sidewalk below me as I looked up the broad avenue. Moving against the sparse flow of uptown traffic were two patrol cars coming at us, lights spinning furiously atop them and sirens screaming their appearance.

I stopped at that point and stuck one foot in the iron gridwork of the side rail, lifting my other leg over the top, half dangling above the street, hoping to make it easier for the cops to see me as they approached, and harder for Wrenley to get to me. My right hand was still clutching the bottle, and with my left I tried to balance against the top of a billboard frame that was posted along the rail.

Wrenley was on me now, coming directly at me with his arms outstretched. His right hand looked like a road map, trickles of blood forming streets and highways. As he prepared to lunge at my neck, I shattered the bottle against the steel frame of the Hi-Line and screamed at him to keep back.

His right hand landed on my shoulder. I anchored

my foot in the open grille of the banister and pivoted out of his grip, my pants leg ripping as it twisted against the steel trim. He grasped again and caught a hunk of my hair, trying to pull me toward him, back onto the tracks. Gripping the billboard top to stay in place, I swung my right arm at Wrenley's head, slashing him with the fractured end of the broken brown bottle.

This time his screams were louder than mine, as I opened up a gaping hole between his ear and forehead, with blood erupting from the gash and spilling down into his eye.

He staggered back for a step or two, then vaulted at me like a wild animal that had been mortally wounded in a hunt. His hands still wanted my neck, and as he charged toward me I shifted my weight and swung my leg onto the track, flattening myself against the back of the billboard.

Blinded by the blood, Wrenley hurtled himself over the guardrail headfirst, onto the street below.

I bent over to see his body crumpled against the blacktop like a deer on a dark country road, with cars screeching to a halt to try to avoid him.

Within seconds the two police cars pulled up from the north, directly under the tracks. From above I watched Brigid Brannigan's ponytail swinging as she yelled to Lazarro to check the body, while she ran in my direction, looking up to see whether I was the woman slumped over the railing, staring down at the corpse of Frank Wrenley.

"Are you hurt?"

I shook my head from side to side, not daring to try

to speak. More sirens, and the large square shape of an ambulance lumbered into view. Too late to be of any use for Wrenley. What had Chapman called this street? I thought to myself. Death Avenue.

"Can you stay up there till I get the Fire Department here with a ladder?"

I nodded to her, then turned my back and sat down on the ground. I leaned against the railing, rubbing my calves with my scraped hands and trying to breathe at regular intervals.

Fifteen minutes later, after the body had been removed from the scene, I heard Brannigan calling my name again. I stood and looked down at the long red engine that had been summoned, watching as the ladder was hoisted into place. Two of the firemen climbed up it and over onto the Hi-Line tracks, introducing themselves and shaking my hand.

"Can you make it down?"

"I hate heights." I gave them as much of a smile as I could muster, not able to explain to them what it had taken for me to be poised on the edge of the railing when Wrenley had come at me just a little while ago.

"Nothing to it. I'll be one rung below you, guiding you down. Harry'll stay on top and load you on. Just close your eyes and trust me."

When I opened them again, I was on the street. The ad on the billboard plastered above my head was visible for the first time. It was a six-foot-tall vodka bottle in the shape of the fuselage of a jet airplane, with words beneath it in bold yellow paint: ABSOLUT ESCAPE.

The cluster of uniforms around me, all meaning to

be helpful, was stifling. Police and firemen were having a cordial turf battle over who would take me into their care—cops as first on the scene, or firemen as my rescuers.

I pulled Brigid Brannigan aside. "Tell them I'd like to ride with you."

"Will you go to Saint Vincent's so they can check you out?"

"Yes. I think I'd like a tetanus shot." I wasn't sure what my knees and hands had been raked against. "But I want to make a stop on the way there."

She explained to the others that I was going with her. I got in the front seat of the RMP. Someone handed me my bag, which I had dropped in the gallery. The beeper was going off, so I removed it and saw that it was my office number. Brannigan began driving up Tenth Avenue, about to turn east to loop around downtown to the hospital. "Would you just go straight a few blocks, to the corner of Twenty-first Street?"

I called Laura from Brannigan's cell phone. She sounded concerned. "Mike's been beeping you. He's probably through the tunnel now, back in Manhattan. Says he hasn't been able to find you. Are you okay?"

"I guess I didn't hear it. Would you call him back and tell him to meet me in Chelsea, the northwest corner of Twenty-first and Tenth, okay? I'll wait for him till he gets there." She'd know the rest of the details soon enough.

The car came to a stop just past the traffic light. "Here?"

"Yes."

Brannigan looked at the small graceful building

that I had noticed when we circled the block earlier today. "Want me to come in with you?"

"No thanks. I just want to wait there for Chapman. Think anyone would mind?"

She smiled back at me and simply said, "No."

I got out and walked up the four steps of the Church of the Guardian Angel. Its lovely Romanesque facade is bordered by two slim columns and a round stained-glass window. I pulled on the wooden door and walked inside, sitting down in the cool silence. I didn't know where the nearest synagogue was, but I needed to be in a place where I could be alone and pray. Somehow the name of this lovely church lent itself to the circumstances of the day.

Twenty minutes later I heard the door open and close, and the noise of a pair of footsteps walking toward me. I didn't turn my head.

Mike Chapman slipped into the pew beside me and looked at me, grimacing as he shook his head back and forth. He started to say something.

"Not right now."

He put his arm around my shoulder instead. I closed my eyes and rested my head against him until I was ready to leave.

# 34

Mike was singing background for Willie Nelson and Julio Iglesias—"To All the Girls I've Loved Before"—when Jake and I walked through the door at Rao's a week later. He got off the bar stool when he saw us come in. "They're playing my song. Best jukebox in the world."

Joey Palomino came out of the kitchen to greet us. "You got the first booth, Jake. Good to see you. Nice to have you back, Alex."

The tiny restaurant on the corner of 114th Street and Pleasant Avenue was like a private club. An unknown caller might hope for a reservation six months ahead, but the handful of tables were filled by regulars who came on a steady basis when Joey gave them their dates. Once in, since there is no second seating, you could sit for the night and feast on luscious Italian food and wine for hours, to the accompaniment of great music from the fifties and sixties. Mike and I had been guests there a couple of times over the years, but Jake had worked his way up to a weekly berth after he hit the national news desk. Mike had asked Jake to set up a dinner to get me out of my dismal mood and to mark Mercer's move from intensive care to a regular hospital room. It looked like he'd be released in another ten days.

We settled into the booth as Vic, the bartender, came over with the first round of drinks. He forgot names from time to time, but never faces or beverage favorites. "*Salute.*"

"To Mercer's recovery," Jake said, clicking glasses with us.

"So now you know why Caxton was packing up," Mike began.

"Let's not talk about the case tonight, please?" I looked from one to the other.

"You gotta face the music sooner or later, blondie."

I had avoided most discussions of the whole matter for the last week, immersing myself in the case folders that had been buried on my desktop since the evening I had learned of Denise Caxton's death. Jake hadn't pushed me, letting me ease back into my own apartment and assure family and friends that everything was fine.

Frankie Palomino, Joey's son, came to sit at the table and take our order. Mike was distracted for the moment. He'd obviously been thinking about what he'd eat from the moment I told him we'd be coming here for dinner.

"I gotta have the roasted peppers, clams *oreganate*, and the seafood salad to start. For pasta I want the fusilli with sausage and cabbage. Then some lemon chicken, veal parmigiana, and whatever else Coop wants. And a bottle of red wine. Tell Vic to make it a good one."

Mike had picked all the best things from the kitchen. Frankie laughed and asked if Jake and I wanted to add any choices of our own. The food was served family style, in portions large enough to feed half the guys back at the squad.

"Where was I? Oh, so you heard about Caxton?"

Jake looked at me and gave my hand a squeeze. "He's right. You've got to deal with this."

I played with the ice in my glass, drew in a breath, and answered Mike. "Kim McFadden called me at home this weekend, before the story broke in the papers on Monday." The U.S. Attorney's Office had brought down the first indictments in the auction bid–rigging case. Although Lowell Caxton was not among the defendants named, it had already been rumored that one of the dealers was cooperating and about to testify against others in the ring. Lowell had been moving his assets out of New York to some of his other properties, probably trying to get them out of the country before they could be seized by the government.

"Has Anthony Bailor talked?" Jake asked Mike.

"He's not exactly singing. The first time I saw him at the hospital, he wouldn't give up Wrenley for anything. Once he heard Frank was dead, he confirmed that's who he was working for. Still won't admit he did the hit on Deni, but we don't need his confession. We've got the DNA to make that case."

"Bailor was the guy in the garage after Alex?"

"Yeah. Seems Wrenley panicked at Mickey

Diamond's story in the paper that we were close to solving the case. He followed Alex to Lincoln Center, then called Bailor to run her down. Same for the attempt on Mercer and Alex. Wrenley was the one who hired the receptionist to freelance for him on Sunday morning. She called to leave the message, at his direction, pretending to be Marina Sette. He also paid her to let you into the gallery. Bailor was told to kill her on his way in, and then shoot both of you."

"What does Bailor say about the paintings?" I asked.

"Back to square one. Holds to his story that he doesn't know anything about the art. And now, with Wrenley dead, we'll never know if he really had the Rembrandt, too."

I knew that cops as well as F.B.I. agents had gone through Wrenley's apartments in New York and Florida in painstaking searches. The possibility that after a decade these priceless treasures would be restored to public view again had been dashed with the murder of Denise Caxton and the death of Frank Wrenley. Both paintings were still missing. Was I responsible for the fact that Wrenley's secret died with him in his fall from the railroad track?

"I know what you're thinking, Coop. He was a mutt who didn't deserve to live."

"But if he had some of the stolen paintings, and we could have found out . . ."

"Hey, the friggin' Feebies couldn't find the stuff for ten years. They're probably just sitting on the floor under somebody's bed, collecting dust. Or in some storage case left in a warehouse that won't get opened for another fifty years, and then they'll get discovered by accident. These thieves have been scamming off each other for so long now, the art could be anywhere. A lot of dead bodies left behind for this loot."

I thought of Marco Varelli and why the old man wasn't allowed to die a natural death, simply because he might connect Wrenley and Caxton to the stolen Vermeer.

"The Feds got nothin' better to do than look for counterfeit money and seize illegal Cuban cigars. This gives 'em a mission, Coop. It ain't all bad."

Mike was tucking his napkin into the collar of his shirt. "Hey, Jake, better stick that tie in your shirt. You get sauce on that thing it'll ruin the design completely. What's he got on this one, blondie? Gerbils? Wait'll I tell Mercer you got little rodents running around on your necktie."

Frankie came over to make sure everything was okay. "See the group at that table for six? It's the CEO of one of the big ad agencies, with a few of his models. One of the girls saw you on TV the other night and wants to meet you."

I turned to look around, assuming that Frankie was talking about Jake.

"Relax, it's not me for a change. It's Chapman."

The tall redhead was beaming at Mike. She must have seen him on the news, being interviewed about the close of the Caxton murder investigation.

"Tell her I'll be over as soon as I finish my dinner, will you, Frankie?" He wiped the empty pasta bowl with a piece of bread and winked at his admirer. "So, either of you guys hear the question tonight?"

We had been in the car on our way to the restaurant when *Jeopardy!* aired. "No."

"Easy one. Would have been a split."

"What was the category?"

"Religion."

"I never bet against you on that."

"Yeah, but since you spent some time in church last week, I thought you'd give it a shot. The answer was: Seventeenth-century cleric who created the most famous sparkling white wine."

I laughed. "That religious I am. Dom Pérignon, the monk who discovered champagne."

Mike got up from the booth and called over to the bar. "Hey, Vic, you got any champagne on ice? I'll be back over when they bring out the chicken. I'm gonna go introduce myself to my fans. You know how that is, Mr. Tyler, don't you?" He winked at me and put his napkin on his seat.

Jake turned to ask if I was all right. I smiled and nodded, reaching up to kiss him on the side of his neck. "Thanks for your patience. I'll be fine."

He held my face and pressed his mouth gently against mine. Then he sat back. "There's a follow-up question to the one about Dom Pérignon. I feel just like that lucky old monk. Know what he said when he took his first sip of champagne?"

"I have no idea."

" 'I'm tasting stars!' " Jake said, pulling me toward him and kissing me again.

I heard the sound of the cork popping out of the bottle and flying up against the ceiling. The Temptations were singing "My Girl," Mike had come back to the booth to await the next course, and Vic was pouring champagne for everyone. The events since the night I met Mike at Spuyten Duyvil would be less raw in a few weeks, we'd catch the West Side rapist soon, and new cases would draw me back into the work I loved.

We lifted our glasses to toast our missing partner once more, with Mike extracting a promise from us to bring Mercer to dinner here as soon as he was able. We would be a team again, in spite of the devil.

# Acknowledgments

For almost thirty-five years, Alexandra Denman has taught me everything there is to know about friendship. Her love, her loyalty, her humor, and her intelligence have enriched my life beyond measure. Ben Stein, Alex's husband, is right to call her "the goddess."

My fictional heroine draws her name as well from Alexander Cooper—artist, book lover, and devoted friend to Justin and me. This book owes much to Alex and Karen Cooper, who introduced me to the galleries of Chelsea, the brilliance of Richard Serra, and the existence of the Hi-Line Railroad. They advanced the plot over wonderful meals and lots of good wine.

Susan and Michael Goldberg give new meaning to the word "generosity." Along with the crew of the *Twilight*—Captain Cutter, Todd, Wes, Kelly, and Stephens—they have given us a paradise to which to retreat, calm seas for sailing, and a safe haven for dreaming. Their book parties make all the lonely hours at the keyboard worthwhile.

Although my beloved pal Jane Stanton Hitchcock

lives a shuttle flight away from me now, her fictional counterpart is ever present on the pages of this book. It was more reliable to research the art world capers with a phone call to Jane than through the texts.

I am deeply grateful to Vineyard friends, who help sustain and encourage me through long summer days, when writing novels seems to be the least likely way to pass the time. To Ann and Vernon Jordan, with enormous respect and boundless affection; and Louise and Henry Grunwald, with great admiration and eternal gratitude. Their morning phone calls boost my spirits and dinners together nourish my soul.

My prosecutorial patron saint remains Bob Morgenthau. I have been fortunate to have had the benefit of his guidance, his integrity, and his wisdom for a quarter of a century. The women and men of the Manhattan District Attorney's Office—and especially my devoted friends and colleagues in the Sex Crimes Prosecution Unit—are the best in the business. Along with our counterparts in the New York Police Department and the Office of the Chief Medical Examiner, they continue to work on the side of the angels. Survivors of violent crimes who come forward with courage and fortitude, and trust our ability to do justice for them, have my profound esteem.

Last year I lost two friends, each of great spirit and heart. Whenever Alex Cooper goes to the ballet—as she does here with Natalie Moody—she will be watching the dancers at American Ballet Theatre and honoring Howard Gilman, an extraordinary man whose spirit lives on in all of those—man and beast—whom he embraced.

And my young protégée, Maxine Pfeffer, who lost her valiant struggle with cancer, will always be Coop's paralegal, Max. Thinking of her will forever bring a smile to my face.

Some of my Vassar classmates asked me to create a character in memory of one of our dear friends, the actress Marilyn Swartz Seven, who also died too young. She is here as a woman of mystery—a role I hope she would have enjoyed performing.

The crews at Scribner and at Pocket Books have been a delight. I am especially grateful to Susan Moldow, for her support; John Fontana, for his stunning design; Giulia Melucci, for her relentless and enthusiastic efforts on my behalf; and Sunshine Lucas, for her patience and efficiency.

My thanks to all the booksellers and librarians who continue to put this series in the hands of readers, and to readers who wait for more.

The collaboration with Susanne Kirk, friend and editor, has been one of the blessings of this business. She has helped me make this a better book.

I have seen so many books dedicated to Esther Newberg in the last year that I have run out of superlatives for her. The best thing my husband ever did for me, other than ask me to marry him, was to introduce me to Esther—brilliant agent, brilliant friend.

My family remains my most precious gift. My only regret is that my father—the gentlest man I've ever known, who introduced me to this genre when I was a child—did not live long enough to see the joy this career has given me. But I thank my amazing mother, Alice, and all the Fairsteins—Guy, Marisa, Lisa, and

Marc—for their support, and the Feldmans and Zavislans—Diane, Jane, Jan, Matthew, and Alexander—for theirs as well.

Most of all, I am constantly inspired by the love of the most wonderful continuing character in this series—and in my life—Justin Feldman. He has made all my dreams come true.